D1560711

INTERIOR ARCHITECTURE

INTERIOR ARCHITECTURE

This publication is supported by a grant from
the Graham Foundation for
Advanced Studies in the Fine Arts.

JOHN KURTICH · GARRET EAKIN

 VAN NOSTRAND REINHOLD
New York

Library of Congress Catalog Card Number 91-44989
ISBN 0-442-24669-2

I(T)P   Van Nostrand Reinhold is a division of International Thomson Publishing.
         ITP logo is a trademark under license.

Printed in Mexico

Van Nostrand Reinhold
115 Fifth Avenue
New York, New York 10003

International Thomson Publishing
Berkshire House
168-173 High Holborn
London, WC1V 7AA, England

Thomas Nelson Australia
102 Dodds Street
South Melbourne 3205
Victoria, Australia

Nelson Canada
1120 Birchmount Road
Scarborough, Ontario MIK 5G4, Canada

16 15 14 13 12 11 10 9 8 7 6 5 4 3 2 1

Library of Congress Cataloging-in-Publication Data

Kurtich, John
     Interior architecture / John Kurtich, Garret Eakin.
        p.   cm.
        Includes index.
        ISBN 0-442-24669-2
        1. Interior architecture. 2. Interior decoration.
        1. Eakin, Garret. II. Title.
        NA2850.K85 1992
        729--dc20
                                                                91-44989
                                                                 CIP

CONTENTS

PREFACE

Interior Architecture is an exploration of the whole spectrum of architecture necessary for human accommodation, comfort, and delight. We felt that the separation of architecture, interior design, and fine arts during the Modernist period has limited the progress and development of truly humanistic architectonic space. Many outstanding designers practice Interior Architecture, yet the majority perpetuate the separation, causing the stagnation of the designed environment. Generations of architectural, interior design, and fine arts education have supported this separation by omitting concentration on each other's discipline. This division was encouraged by the specialization generated from the growth of complexity of information, technology, economics, politics, and social needs, the consequences of which are with us today.

A recent example of this separation is 333 Wacker Drive, Chicago. The highly praised building has been featured in a number of publications. The reviews focused on its beautiful relationship to the site and its engaging sculptural form. However, all the articles stopped short of reviewing the purpose of the building, which is to provide flexible office space for an unknown tenant. The floor plan, basically echoing the odd shape of the site, is far from flexible. This flexibility is further diminished with a curve, notches, and two acute angle corners. The resultant interior space presents formidable problems even to the best architect or space planner. What is the answer to this dilemma between interior use and exterior form?

The emergence of Interior Architecture as a new profession is an idea whose time has come. It is the link between art, architecture, and interior design. The professionals practicing in this area have created this term to express a humanistic approach toward the completion of interior spaces. This approach, shared by many design professionals, has begun to produce a definition that is distinct from current practice. Some of the ideas that characterize Interior Architecture are strong three-dimensional development, respect for the enclosing architecture, sensitivity to the human experience, primal significance of light, wealth and energy of color, and furnishings as an extension of the architecture.

This book explores such ideas, using architectural masterpieces from various historical periods, well-known modern examples, related contemporary design, and unbuilt projects to illustrate and underline them. Throughout the book, there has been a conscious attempt to unveil the essence of ideas that generate physical form and space. The exposition of the idea creates the structure and form of each chapter. For instance, chapter 2, Creativity: From Ideas to Reality, employs an in-depth case study of a single project to expose the principles of creativity. Chapter 5 is a chronological survey of the use of light to define space through a series of historic examples.

This is not a history book of interior design. The examples presented are not limited to interiors. By allowing the ideas to predominate, each chapter has its own structure with respect to the presentation of its material. For instance, it may appear that a Renaissance masterpiece is being equated with a late twentieth century shopping mall boutique, when actually two executions of the same idea are being presented. By posing these juxtapositions, readers may more easily relate the principle or idea to their own work.

The case study method allows an in-depth examination, which reveals the reasons behind the creation of the designs and the decision making that accompanied their execution. Some case study projects are used more than once as they represent the best example for each of several elemental ideas. This overlap is cross-referenced when it occurs so that the reader can skip from one part of the book to another if following a particular project. Wherever possible, quotations of artists, architects, and designers are included in order to reinforce the philosophy revealed by the case studies.

The book includes relevant information in related fields, such as physics, music, cinema, literature, and fine arts, to name a few. It is our belief that great Interior Architecture is created by the fusion of related disciplines. Extensive references are therefore included for those readers who wish to pursue particular subjects in greater depth.

ACKNOWLEDGMENTS

May Hawfield has been a provocative inspiration and example of dedication in bringing this work to reality. Her contribution, enthusiasm, and elegant point of view have been our perpetual internal stimulus. We can only hope that this experience will be a cornerstone of her bright future.

Susan Perry's devotion and persistent work have been indispensible in researching and acquiring the essential illustrations and elusive data. We greatly appreciate her skill and dedication to the literary process.

The Art Institute of Chicago has been very supportive in this endeavor. The School of the Art Institute has provided several grants, student assistants, and a rich, intellectual atmosphere in which to work. Roger Gilmore, former dean, Martin Prekop, dean, and Peter Brown, vice president of administration, have been strong advocates of the project. The John M. Flaxman Library within the School, directed by Nadine Byrne and assisted by Roland Hansen, provided us with research assistance. The extensive collection of The Museum of the Art Institute was a remarkable resource: American Art, Asian Art, European Decorative Arts and Sculpture, European Painting, Twentieth Century Painting and Sculpture, the Thorne Miniature Rooms, Adler and Sullivan's Trading Room, and the Ryerson/Burnham Libraries. Jack Brown, director, and Mary Woolever, architectural librarian, provided full access to the Libraries. We are indebted to this great institution's resources and professional staff.

The Graham Foundation for Advanced Study in the Fine Arts, Chicago, under the directorship of Carter Manny, has generously supported the completion of this book.

The additional museums and institutions have been most professional in sharing their fine collections: the Louis Kahn Collection, University of Pennsylvania, directed by Julia Moore Converse; the Museum of Modern Art, New York; the Metropolitan Museum of Art, New York; the American Museum of Natural History, New York; Fondation Le Corbusier, Paris; the Getty Center for the History of Art and the Humanities, Santa Monica; the Deutsches Architektur-Museum, Frankfort am Main; the Alvar Aalto Foundation, Helsinki; and the Dulwich Picture Gallery, London.

We appreciate the generous access extended by the following in Chicago: Crate and Barrel, Vivere of the Italian Village, North Pier, The Rookery, Cobbler Square, the Florian residence, Roosevelt University, the Glessner House, the Marriott residence, the Claridge Hotel, the Gretchen Bollinger Showroom, the ICF Showroom, the Palazetti Showroom, the Herman Miller Showroom, and the Knoll International

Showroom. Locations in New York: the Mallet residence, the Cohen residence, and the Rainbow Room of Rockefeller Center. Other locations include: the Douglas residence, Harbor Springs, Michigan; the Madonna Inn, San Luis Obispo, California; the Monterey Bay Aquarium, Monterey, California; the Farnsworth House, Plano, Illinois; and the Knoll International Showroom, Paris, France.

Without the energetic contribution of our research assistants, this publication would not have been possible. They include Jennifer Ehrenberg, Donna Falk, Kirsten Gladsky, JoAnn Stannard, and Glenn Traer.

Many caring individuals have graciously contributed their resources and expertise to this book. They include Paul Beitler, Mike DePoy, Michele Dremmer, Robert Fitzgerald, Joseph Gonzales, Elaine Harrington, Professor Kevin Harrington, Steven Holl, Professor Donald Kalec, Ronald Krueck, Celia Marriott, Anders Nereim, Jonathan Sherman, Allison Sky, Claudia Skylar, Christopher Wadsworth, Dieter Wagner, and James Zanzi.

We have special appreciation for the wonderful photographic collections of Hedric Blessing, Chicago; Art Resource and ARS, New York; and ESTO Photographics, New York; that remain extensive resources for Interior Architecture.

Cynthia Davidson-Powers, former editor of *Inland Architect,* published our first piece, "The Rise of Interior Architecture," January 1984, which was the outline for this book. We appreciate her support. After reading this article, Wendy Lochner, senior architecture editor of Van Nostrand Reinhold Company, had the vision to propose that we write a book on Interior Architecture. In addition, we wish to thank Frances Koblin and Anthony Calcara, production editors; Mimi Mikels, copy editor; Everett Smethurst, editor; John Pile, critic; and Lilly Kaufman, executive editor.

Finally, our families displayed great patience, generous encouragement, and a sense of humor during this project. In thanks, this book is dedicated to Lois Eakin, Amy, Elliot, and David Eakin, and to the loving memory of Elizabeth Kurtich.

THE ENTRANCE HALL, HILL HOUSE,
HELENSBURGH, DUNBARTONSHIRE,
SCOTLAND. CHARLES RENNIE
MACKINTOSH AND MARGARET
MacDONALD MACKINTOSH, 1902–
1904.

*Courtesy of The Art Institute of
Chicago.*

CHAPTER 1

INTERIOR ARCHITECTURE: THE PHILOSOPHY

What is Interior Architecture? Is it a visionary movement in response to a current need, or is it a name attached to a passing trend? Why do some designers use the term? Is there a need for a new humanistic force to respond to the demands generated by the intensity of the information age? Can this new spirit engender intellectual and emotional well-being? Why is there such a rift between interior designers and architects? Could the current polarized design professions ever accept Interior Architecture as this new vision?

Some progressive design firms began using the term *Interior Architecture* in the early 1970s. They felt at the time that no term properly described the unique quality of their work. They sensed a need to separate themselves from the current practice of architecture. They also did not feel any close allegiance to traditional interior design or decorating firms. Concurrently a few of the progressive design schools introduced the term to emphasize the allegiance with architectural thinking. Many interior design programs were part of home economics departments, which taught style and decoration as a complement to homemaking classes. This approach did not satisfy the needs of serious career-oriented students. A new professional emphasis was born out of the emerging demands under the banner "Interior Architecture."

After World War II, with the rise of the large corporate architectural firms, specialization became a matter of course, affecting the smaller firms and influencing the manner in which designers and architects were educated. Generations of architectural and interior design education supported this separation by omitting concentration in each other's discipline. There were few decent models of an architect who cared as much for interior space as for exterior shell. Designers dis-

dained the elitist architects for their compulsion for purity and maintenance of concept. Architects generally considered designers to be frivolous with no philosophical base of knowledge to guide their work. Architects did not understand the intimate qualities of carpet, fabrics, and wall covering. Many designers disregarded the qualities of the enclosure and simply made their own statement. The architects were merely technicians whose job stopped after "bricks and mortar." To fuel the fire, often clients gave more respect to the designers because they were making decisions that they could intimately understand. Sadly enough, all these accusations are true.

Interior Architecture is the holistic creation, development, and completion of space for human use. It follows the dicta of Vitruvius's classic definition of architecture—firmness, commodity, and delight. It focuses on humanistically conceived space, distinguishing Interior Architecture from the current practice of either architecture or interior design.

Interior Architecture is expressed in several ways. First, it can be the entire building designed as an external shell containing integrated and finished interiors. Second, Interior Architecture can be the completion of space within an existing architectural enclosure. Finally, it can be the preservation, renovation, or adaptive reuse of buildings, historic or otherwise, with a focus on the design of interior space.

The first aspect of Interior Architecture represents the usual practice of such masters of architecture as Frank Lloyd Wright, Le Corbusier, and Alvar Aalto. They designed their entire environments, from exterior enclosure to all aspects of the interior, including spatial arrangement; lighting, color, and texture; furniture; and all the details of human use. They were coordinators of all the arts and disciplines necessary to complete a piece of architecture. Their attitude toward architecture was not limited by boundaries of specialization that currently dominate architectural design.

The second aspect represents a new practice that is emerging from architectural and design firms that have recognized interior space to be as important as the exterior. This new movement is carrying on the tradition that the masters practiced, giving meaning and completion to the anonymous buildings that predominate the designed environment. These practitioners are sensitive to the architectural shell that they have to complete, and their design solutions are not limited by the confines of specialization.

The third aspect represents a practice that recognizes an increase in the need for preservation, restoration, renovation, and adaptive reuse of buildings, historic or otherwise, as the decline of new construction persists. Such projects require a perceptive understanding of history, careful research and thorough analysis of existing conditions, and a sensitive approach to how the interiors relate to the building as a whole.

These three aspects share one common theme —the completion of interior space. In order to complete interior space meaningfully, a thorough understanding of opportunities and constraints of the architectural enclosure is essential to the appropriate plan development. Interior Architecture not only accommodates functional and technical requirements but exploits the aesthetic potential inherent in the enclosing architecture and the design program.

Interior Architecture is comprised of the following elemental ideas that distinguish it as the link between architecture and interior design:

1. Inside/Outside. Interior Architecture respects the enclosing structure and consistently uses it as a point of departure.
2. The Third Dimension. Projects are thought of as three-dimensional spaces complete in themselves regardless of shape, size, or proportions.
3. The Fourth Dimension. The fourth dimension is generated as a conscious expansion of human experience in space and time.

4. Light. Light is recognized as the primary medium for defining interior space.
5. Color and Materials. Color and materials define the human character of Interior Architecture.
6. Furnishings. Furnishings are rendered as an extension of the architecture with custom-designed elements clearly a mark of the movement.

THE MASTERS OF ARCHITECTURE

FRANK LLOYD WRIGHT

The ideal practice of architecture has always been the design of the complete environment, from the site plan and exterior enclosure to all aspects and details of the interior. Throughout history only a few architects of talent and vision have been able to accomplish such all-encompassing design. In the twentieth century, three architects stand out as practitioners of complete design: Frank Lloyd Wright (1867–1959), Le Corbusier (1887–1965), and Alvar Aalto (1898–1976).

Frank Lloyd Wright believed in the concept of organic architecture—building with nature instead of against it.

In Organic Architecture, then, it is quite impossible to consider the building as one thing, its furnishings another and its setting and environment still another. The Spirit in which these buildings are conceived sees all these together at work as one thing. All are to be studiously foreseen and provided for in the nature of the structure. All these should become mere details of the character and completeness of the structure. Incorporated (or excluded) are lighting, heating and ventilation. The very chairs and tables, cabinets and even musical instruments, where practicable, are of the building itself, never fixtures upon it. No appliances or fixtures are admitted as such where circumstances permit the full development of the organic character of the building-scheme.[1]

Wright realized his philosophy with the development of the Prairie house. He designed a succession of such houses in the early years of the twentieth century, culminating in the Robie House, Chicago, Illinois, (1909). Wright made a commitment to the integration of inside and outside with his open-space planning and concern for natural light and ventilation. His Prairie houses

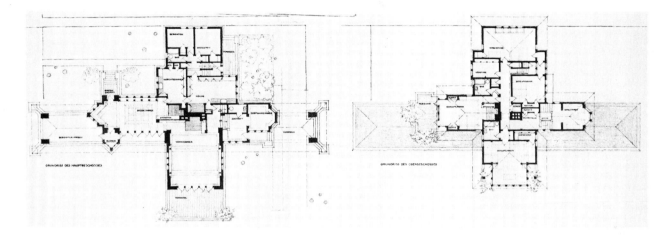

PLAN, WARD W. WILLETS RESIDENCE,
HIGHLAND PARK, ILLINOIS, FRANK
LLOYD WRIGHT, 1901.

*The windmill plan was the result of a
central space dominated by the hearth
with wings extended to the landscape.
Courtesy of The Art Institute of
Chicago.*

were expressions of the prairie landscape, a natural, organic response to nature.

Wright's houses centered on the hearth, and from this would radiate horizontal wings of interlocking space. By designing from the inside out, his exterior shell would be a direct expression of the space it contained. There was no separation of architectural parts. There was no compromise made with the interior space through irrelevant design of the shell. Interior space was not confined to the actual interior, for Wright would continue his interiors visually by extending terraces, trellises, and retaining walls beyond the glass lines of window openings (see Chapter 4 for a discussion of the four-dimensional features of Wright's interpenetration of inside and outside space).

Wright did not stop with the architectural shell and its development of interior space, but he took on the responsibility of completing the interior space with built-in or custom-designed furniture, built-in lighting fixtures, specially designed carpeting, patterned leaded glass windows, and extensive interior trim and molding, all of which were in direct response to and an extension of the overall architectural scheme.

The Robie House was a masterpiece of design. The living room and dining room were placed on either side of the central hearth of the house with not only spatial connections between the rooms occurring on either side of the fireplace but a large opening above the mantel that provided a two-way vista between the rooms. The

DINING ROOM, FREDERICK C. ROBIE RESIDENCE, CHICAGO, ILLINOIS. FRANK LLOYD WRIGHT, 1909.

The high-backed chairs create an intimate room within the dining room. Courtesy of The Domino's Center for Architecture and Design.

trim articulated and echoed the ribbon windows of the longitudinal walls, and this rhythm was further enhanced by the built-in lighting fixtures that crowned the overhanging lowered ceilings above these walls (see Chapter 5 for a further discussion of Wright's mastery of light).

Furniture included built-in pieces, such as the bench-and-storage unit at the living room fireplace, the dining room sideboard, and custom freestanding pieces, such as the dining room table complete with space-enclosing chairs and four corner light fixtures. Here, Wright designed a carpet that unified the floors of the two rooms with a repetitive geometric motif that responded directly to the patterns created by the colored glass in the leaded windows of the longitudinal walls.

LE CORBUSIER

Quite the opposite from Wright's architectural philosophy but equally complete in design conception and execution was the early domestic work of Le Corbusier. In defining architecture, Le Corbusier distinguished between aesthetic and functional considerations, aesthetic being clearly essential to the definition of a piece of architecture versus a building.

> *You employ stone, wood and concrete, and with these materials you build houses and palaces; that is construction. Ingenuity is at work.*
>
> *But suddenly you touch my heart, you do me good, I am happy and I say: "This is beautiful." That is Architecture. Art Enters in.*
>
> *My house is practical. I thank you, as I might thank Railway engineers or the Telephone service. You have not touched my heart.*
>
> *But suppose that walls rise towards heaven in such a way that I am moved. I perceive your intentions. Your mood has been gentle, brutal, charming or noble. The stones you have erected tell me so. You fix me to the place and my eyes regard it. They behold something which expresses a thought. A thought which reveals itself without word or sound, but solely by means of shapes which stand in a certain relationship to one another. These shapes are such that they are clearly revealed in light. The relationships between them have not necessarily any reference to what is practical or descriptive. They are a mathematical creation of your mind. They are the language of Architecture. But the use of inert materials and starting from conditions more or less utilitarian, you have established certain relationships which have aroused my emotions. This is Architecture.*[2]

In 1914 Le Corbusier developed an open plan theory based on the structural possibilities of reinforced concrete. He called his system *Dom-ino* and stated that the structural basis of the house should consist of a frame of six concrete columns supporting all concrete floor and roof slabs, linked together with cantilevered concrete stairs. These being the only fixed elements of the house, everything else—the walls, windows and doors, fireplaces, and so forth — could then be flexible since they were nonstructural.

Le Corbusier consciously separated his houses from the ground in order that the ground might be free of human-designed obstacles. He then would punch out space in his house structure in order to bring trees and vegetation into terraces and roof gardens, integrated with the house proper.

This architectural development was epitomized in the Villa Savoye, Poissy-sur-Seine, France (1929–1930). The villa is a cube of space quite set apart from the surrounding environment. The living quarters, located one floor above the ground level, are arranged about a garden court, which shares a band of ribbon windows (without glazing) with the living room. A ramp connects this court to yet another smaller roof garden above the living quarters.

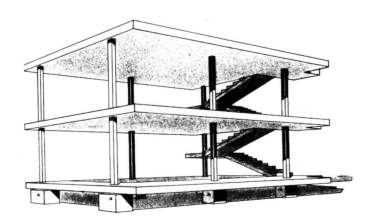

PERSPECTIVE DRAWING, DOM-INO HOUSE. LE CORBUSIER, 1914.

The columns are set back from the slab edge to allow for maximum freedom of fenestration. Droits de reproduction percus par la SPADEM Copyright 1991 ARS N.Y./SPADEM.

The ramp, a central spiral stair, the living room fireplace, and various columns and light fixtures serve as sculptural elements in the three-dimensional spatial grid of the villa. The interpenetration of outside to inside by holes of space cut into the volume create a fourth dimensional quality (see Chapter 4 for a discussion of the four-dimensional aspects of this villa).

ALVAR AALTO

The holism practiced by Alvar Aalto was guided by his humanistic concern for artistically solving functional problems.

Architecture should always offer a means whereby the organic connection between a building and nature (including man and human life as an element of greater importance than others) is provided for. This is also the most important thing in architectural standardisation. But this presupposes the development not only of building components but of a whole new architectural approach for this purpose.[3]

Aalto clearly saw architecture as a result of a physical understanding between humanity and nature. He felt that nature should be the inspiration, the guide, and the ultimate teacher of those designing building forms and habitats for humanity. He believed that nature was the softener through its vocabulary of colors, textures, and forms and that the architect should utilize this vocabulary as a major design resource. This notion was summarized in a lecture entitled "Between Humanism and Materialism," which he gave at the Central Union of Architects in Vienna, 1955: "It seems to me that there are too many situations in life in which the organisation is too brutal: *it is the task of the architect to give life a gentler structure.*"[4]

Aalto is as well known for his glassware, lighting fixtures, and furniture as for his architecture. His forms are rich with metaphorical references to his native Finland without sacrificing the intimate human needs. This combination of humanism and artistic exploration led Aalto to his greatest residential achievement, the Villa Mairea, Noormarkku, Finland, (1938–1939).

The L-shaped villa forms two sides of a courtyard, looking out to the forest beyond. The plan of the villa is an experimental manipulation of space. No formal or traditional concepts of space definition are employed, such as axial symmetry or formal sequence. Instead, there is a "forest space," the villa's single living room, which is open not only throughout its interior dimensions but also pulls the vertical proportions of the actual

LIVING ROOM, VILLA MAIREA, NOORMARKKU, FINLAND. ALVAR AALTO, 1937–1939.

The warmth of this room is created by the idea of bringing the forest inside. Photograph by Kevin Harrington.

forest beyond into the space. This is further enhanced by the use of natural wood for the ceiling, the columns, the staircase detailing, and the furniture. The effect is that of coming into a manicured forest resulting in a special sense of place. His work is clearly driven by his concerns of executing spaces of functional and human quality. Aalto's sensitivity to human needs were the basis of his creative designs.

Wright, Le Corbusier, and Aalto each had his own unique expression of Interior Architecture. Each was the master of his total environment. The best architects of the twentieth century have carried on this tradition of developing complete pieces of architecture, avoiding the limitations of their traditional educations.

THE MASTERS OF INTERIOR SPACE

The trend in today's commercial architecture is to build core and shell space that is to be completed by individual tenants. Quite unlike the architecture of the nineteenth and early twentieth centuries where buildings were designed for specific clients and uses, some of today's buildings are conceived to accommodate unidentified tenants. The architectural profession producing these buildings concentrate on the enclosure, leaving the contents to be completed by others.

Sensitive designers must meld the existing architecture with the needs of their clients in a cohesive composition. Their design solutions for completing the architectural space are not limited by the confines of designer specialization but exemplify a unified approach. Proven master designers and architects who can serve as models for the emerging profession of Interior Architecture are Charles Rennie Mackintosh, Sir John Soane, and Eileen Gray.

CHARLES RENNIE MACKINTOSH

Charles Rennie Mackintosh (1868–1928) is well known for his complete interior spaces. Miss Catherine Cranston, daughter of a wealthy Glasgow tea importer, chose Mackintosh to design her tea rooms such as the Buchanan Street Tea Rooms (1896) and the Willow Tea Rooms (1904). These facilities were designed as a response to a social problem plaguing Glasgow in the 1880s. The prosperity of heavy industry and shipbuilding attracted enough new workers to triple the population between 1830 and 1860. This phenomenon created many problems, one of which was daytime drunkenness of young workers. These workers had few places to go during lunchtime except to bars and public houses. To alleviate this situation, tea rooms sprang up and began to rival the public houses. Mackintosh designed the rooms, furniture, china, and murals of many of the establishments. The aesthetic quality of the rooms attracted people and they quickly became successful. Some of the rooms continue to be used today—a testimony to Miss Cranston's foresight and Mackintosh's brilliance.

In the Willow Tea Rooms, the Room de Luxe is a wonderfully intimate vaulted space conceived to symbolize a grove of willows. The white space contains an energy created by dialogue between the detailed architectural fenestration and the interpretive furnishings. The high-backed chairs literally represent a forest echoing a dado line established along the walls. Crowning the dado on three walls are rows of leaded mirror glass panels completed on the fourth wall by actual windows overlooking Sanchiehall Street (Scottish word meaning alley of willows). The surrounding frieze expands the room, creating a dazzling effect reflecting the activity within the tea room.

The Room de Luxe, being the most complete and the best known of Mackintosh's tea room interiors, is on the first floor overlooking the street. Its white walls, silver painted high-backed chairs, crisp white tablecloths and blue willow-pattern crockery, soft grey carpet, chairs and settees covered in a rich purple, leaded mirror glass, enamels in pastel pinks and mauves, and the famous leaded-glass doorway, combine to create a glittering elegance, widely celebrated.[5]

THE ROOM DELUXE, WILLOW TEA
ROOMS, GLASGOW, SCOTLAND.
CHARLES RENNIE MACKINTOSH,
1903–1094.

*No detail is left to chance as the architect
has extended the design to the furniture,
light fixtures, and tableware.
Photograph by Vincenza Frangella.*

SIR JOHN SOANE

Sir John Soane (1753–1837), like Mackintosh, was best known for his interior spaces. He used his own house as a model to develop spatial ideas that would later appear in his various commissions. Unlike Mackintosh's interest in decorative design, Soane exploited the possibilities of light and space manipulation. His surprising inventions to form new kinds of spatial relationships made him the greatest architect of his age.

Soane's house in London (begun in 1792, additions in 1812 and 1824) was a laboratory of spatial experimentation. He created an interior universe of immense complexity in a total volume that measures less than 90 feet wide, 90 feet deep, and 30 feet high. Soane favored a layered structuring wall system in the Library and Dining Room, which he considered as one room. The detached walls, articulated by nonstructural arches that create deep niches, vibrate with an optical tension from the Pompeiian red pigment bordered with complementary green trim. Such saturated colors for interior space went counter to the prevailing gold-and-white interiors of the period. Every available space on the walls of the two rooms is

LIBRARY, SIR JOHN SOANE RESIDENCE, LINCOLN'S INN FIELDS, LONDON, ENGLAND. SIR JOHN SOANE, 1812.

Detached walls form a shell rescaling the room while integrating book shelves and fenestration. Photograph by John Kurtich.

rich with pictures, sculptures, mirrored niches, urns, architectural models, and decorative objects, creating a variety of visual stimulation.

The Breakfast Parlour is an ingenious room created from leftover space hemmed in by a stairway on one side, the Monumental Court on another, and the Dome Room on the third side. Here Soane used a small pendentive dome, a type that had never been seen in England before, to create a space within a space. Instead of a dome rising on four pendentives common with Byzantine and Renaissance domes, it is itself a pendentive of one continuous spherical surface. The dome has an oculus ringed by eight convex mirrors and lit by an octagon-shaped lantern, the panels of which are painted with biblical scenes. A larger convex mirror is placed at each of the four bottom corners of the pendentive surface. "The complex subdivisions overhead, made magic by the mirrors, along with the illusion of

BREAKFAST ROOM, SIR JOHN SOANE RESIDENCE, LINCOLN'S INN FIELDS, LONDON, ENGLAND. SIR JOHN SOANE, 1812.

Spatial mystery is created by the unorthodox introduction of light which washes the walls beyond the dome. Photograph by John Kurtich.

depth in the tiny pictures, contribute to this room, seeming at once minuscule and cosmic. Soane's poignant exaltation of the almost trivial is peerless, beyond any hope of emulation."[6]

Soane layered his space both horizontally and vertically, employing many skylights to enhance the spatial expansion (see Chapter 5 for a discussion of Soane's use of natural light). In his Picture Room, Soane hinged multiple panels that would swing out from the wall to reveal more paintings mounted on the layers behind. The final panels swing to reveal a balconied window opening into a vertical space featuring the Monk's Parlour one story below and a skylight high above the window.

EILEEN GRAY

Eileen Gray (1878–1976) was originally trained at the Slade School of Art, London, around the beginning of the twentieth century and then acquired an apprenticeship to a Japanese lacquer craftsman. She eventually made Paris her permanent home and evolved from making lacquer objects to furniture, then complete interiors.

In the early years of the Modern Movement, interiors were largely neglected by even the best architects. Eileen Gray pioneered the notion that as much attention should be paid to the design of interiors as it had been to the exteriors. In 1924, Jean Badovici wrote of her in the Dutch magazine *Wendingen:* "We find in her compositions those marvelous abstract geometric elements which are the charm of modern furniture. Instead of presenting each piece separately, she makes them complement each other. Lines of individual pieces are no longer frontiers; they extend into the lines of a wall. It is a richly realized totality of space. . . ."[7]

In her first house, E-1027, built at Roquebrune on the French Riviera (1926–1929), she conceived the project as a total design problem, attending not only to a well-conceived plan of interior spaces but carefully choosing interior surface materials and arranging their colors, designing an entire range of furniture, and drafting and weaving custom rugs for all the rooms.

Eileen Gray referred to the open plan of the modernists as "le style camping." Her sensitivity to the practical uses of interior space allowed her designs to transcend the anonymity of modernist dictums. Although the house was small—a living room with an adjoining terrace and two small bedrooms—she achieved a feeling of spaciousness with her use of light partition walls as dividers and ingenious built-in furniture. The multiuse nature of the living room made it the central focus of the house. The generous interior (21 feet by 46 feet) provided space for repose, repast, recreation, and relaxation. Her completion of interior space included wonderful designs of intricate detail, wit, and thoughtfulness. Her concern for the control of natural light and ventilation was expressed in specially designed shutters that allowed a variety of sunlight and fresh air to permeate the interior conditional to the daily and seasonal changes of nature. For the bathrooms, she designed hinged mirrors that provided simultaneous multiple views for grooming. Special furniture, such as the "nonconformist chair," had only one elbow rest in order to give the human body more freedom of movement while seated. Her storage cabinets were inventive with pivoting drawers, sliding panels, and built-in electrical lighting. Her dictum of design was: "The interior plan should not be the incidental result of the facade; it should live a complete, harmonious, and logical life."[8] Her design of the kitchen reflected this philosophy by borrowing spatial arrangements "dictated by the habit of peasant women who prepare their meals outside in the summer, inside in the winter . . . [It] can be transformed into an open-air kitchen by a partition made of glass panels that fold flat. When . . . opened, the kitchen is nothing more than an alcove in the courtyard."[9]

Charles Rennie Mackintosh, Sir John Soane, and Eileen Gray are known primarily for their innovative and poetic interiors even though each produced buildings and architectural exteriors. All three cared about the fate of the human occupant in their architectural creations and thus articulated fresh, visionary plans made complete with custom designed furniture, imaginative lighting, exciting color, appropriate materials and textures, and provocative fabrics and rugs.

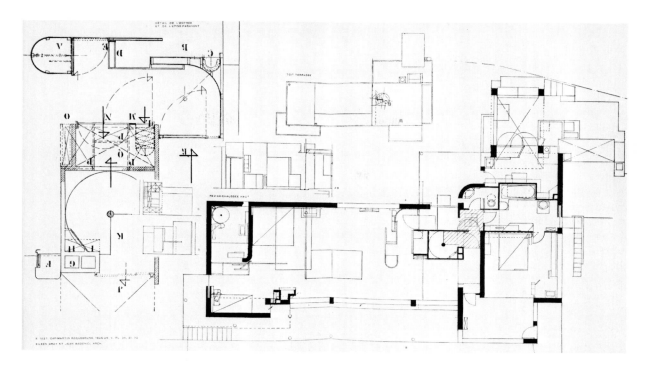

PLAN, HOUSE E-1027, CAP-MARTIN
ROQUEBRUNE, FRANCE. EILEEN
GRAY, 1926–1929.

*The inventive plan focused on a large
living room that was extended outside
via a terrace, taking advantage of the
French Riviera view and climate.
Courtesy of The Art Institute of
Chicago*

LIVING ROOM, HOUSE E–1027, CAP-
MARTIN ROQUEBRUNE, FRANCE.
EILEEN GRAY, 1926–1929.

*The planes of low walls, rugs, and art
emphasize the horizontal spatial quality
of the room. Courtesy of The Art
Institute of Chicago*

The completion of interior space, emphasizing its architectural character, is practiced by many enlightened architects and designers. This act of completion is the essential ingredient in the pursuit and creation of Interior Architecture. The architectural shell is more permanent than its interior configuration and space, yet the interior demands greater attention. The details of interior space that satisfy the requirements of human use are in fact the purpose of the building.

PRESERVATION, RESTORATION, RENOVATION, AND ADAPTIVE REUSE

The final aspect of Interior Architecture focuses on the older building and how it might best relate to the current needs of society. *Preservation* is the act of maintaining all or any part of a building in order to ensure its historic significance. *Restoration* is the act of returning the building in some manner to a condition deemed appropriate after it has been set aside to be "preserved." *Renovation* is the act of renewing and updating older buildings' original uses to satisfy contemporary needs. *Adaptive reuse* refers to the recycling of an older building by giving it a new use through renovation.

Most of the work on older buildings affects their interiors. Not only must designers or architects be competent with current code requirements, structural realities, mechanical and electrical services, and economic restrictions, but they must be knowledgeable of architectural and social history.

The preservation of a historical building to represent its original use is the purest of the four categories affecting an older structure. Preservation may include restoring the building on its original site or moving the building to preserve its past. The process of restoration is usually linked to preservation, in varying degrees depending upon the condition of any given building. Total reconstruction of a long-vanished building based on available research is the most extreme form of preservation.

During the nineteenth century there was a great interest in preserving past architectural monuments in both France and England. Each country approached the problem in its own way, France favoring a restorative approach to the point of adding features that were never originally built and England maintaining a preservationist approach that tried to minimize modern restoration.

PRESERVATION THEORIES OF VIOLLET-LE-DUC France took a great interest in her historic sites when Louis Philippe established an Inspector of Historic Monuments in 1830. The office that resulted from this appointment made an inventory of all the historic buildings and structures in the country. This inventory was the basis for protecting venerable structures, public or private, from alteration. The government also hired architects to restore certain old chateaux and churches. Viollet-le-Duc (1814–1879) was the most famous of these architects, and through his activity during the middle of the nineteenth century, he was able to establish and practice his theories of restoration. His definition of proper restoration was very specific. "To restore a building is not to preserve it, to repair, or rebuild it; it is to reinstate it in a condition of completeness which could never have existed at any given time." [10]

In describing Viollet-le-Duc's restoration of the cathedral of Notre-Dame, Paris, (1845–1864) Charles Wethered writes:

Standing in the midst of once the most picturesque and still the brightest of inland cities, Notre-Dame, "the old queen of French cathedrals," has been restored at the cost of a quarter of a million sterling, in the most conscientious and conservative manner throughout. Scrupulous care has been taken not to interfere with anything of real worth belonging to bygone ages. Here there has been no scraping of the surfaces of old stones: in all cases wherever unmutilated they have been left untouched . . . It is a typical instance of what the French understand by restoration—as complete a re-establishment as possible of everything known to have existed in the days of its fullest splendour. [11]

Viollet-le-Duc wanted to bring the cathedral up to its originally planned completion by finishing all of the uncompleted towers, including the twin towers of the west front. He produced drawings for this project, but it was never realized.

THE PRESERVATION THEORIES OF JOHN RUSKIN
In England during the nineteenth century, architectural preservationists were led by John Ruskin (1819–1900) and William Morris (1834–1896) rather than by the government. John Ruskin's attitude was that restoration was really destruction.

> *Neither by the public, nor by those who have the care of public monuments, is the true meaning of the word* restoration *understood. It means the most total destruction which a building can suffer: a destruction out of which no remnants can be gathered; a destruction accompanied with false description of the thing destroyed. Do not let us deceive ourselves in this important matter; it is* impossible, *as impossible as to raise the dead, to restore anything that has ever been great or beautiful in architecture . . . Do not let us talk then of restoration. The thing is a Lie from beginning to end . . . The principle of modern times (a principle which I believe, at least in France, to be* systematically *acted on by the masons,* in order to find themselves work, *as the abbey of St. Ouen was pulled down by the magistrates of the town by way of giving work to some vagrants,) is to neglect buildings first, and then restore them afterwards. Take proper care of your monuments, and you will not need to restore them.*[12]

Protection of ancient buildings, not restoration, was the philosophy preached. "The followers of Ruskin and Morris said that the only legitimate action open to contemporary workmen was to arrest the process of decay. No matter how venerable a building might have been, all later changes in it were to remain because they were just as valid as the original portions."[13]

WILLIAMSBURG, VIRGINIA

The major restoration project of the early twentieth century, which had great impact upon American taste and brought about a serious questioning of the limits of preservation, was the complete restoration of Williamsburg, Virginia, by John D. Rockefeller, Jr., in 1926. James Marston Fitch has pointed out the problems of the Williamsburg restoration:

> *The first is that time has been telescoped: buildings which never co-existed at precisely the same point in time and space have been restored to an artificial simultaneity. The resulting image is one of polished and manicured amenity which is not so much untruthful as incomplete. It is nonetheless misleading. The second problem is related to the first. Williamsburg in pre-Revolutionary times was a small provincial capital, technically backward and riddled with class divisions*

Entrance view, Governor's Mansion, Williamsburg, Virginia, 1706–1720 (restoration 1926 onwards).

The restoration epitomizes colonial idealism but is unfaithful to historical reality. Colonial Williamsburg Foundation.

including human slavery: It is difficult to "restore" this aspect of social reality. Slave pens and muddy streets, hunger and discomfort are difficult to display museologically: the natural tendency of any curatorial staff is to select, dramatize, hence prettify. Thus the result has been the creation of a stream of beguiling half-truths about the American past, all too easily vulgarized and fed into the bloodstream of popular taste.[14]

THE TEMPLE OF ARTEMIS, EPHESUS, TURKEY

Preservation and restoration of buildings in the ancient world was rare, but renovation was common, particularly when a revered temple or monument was damaged or destroyed. Generally such repair took place as reconstruction, with the adaptation of the latest architectural style prevailing. Such reconstruction was the ultimate renovation. The archaic temple of Artemis at Ephesus, Turkey, constructed ca. 550 B.C. on the site of yet an earlier temple, was famous throughout the ancient world for its size and rich sculptured reliefs. Its plan measured 413 feet by 214 feet with 127

sixty-five-foot-high columns supporting the entablature. This gigantic structure was torched and destroyed in 356 B.C. by a madman to ensure his immortality. The citizens of Ephesus spent the next 120 years rebuilding (i.e., renovating) the new temple of Artemis on the same site, following the same ground plan with identical length, breadth, and height. Differences occurred in the refinement of the Ionic order, the sculptural reliefs, and the fact that the temple was now built on a platform of thirteen steps, therefore making it stand 8 feet 10 inches higher than the old temple. This version became known as one of the Seven Wonders of the World.

THE PANTHEON, ROME, ITALY

The turning point for the renovation of the Pantheon, Rome, Italy, (A.D. 120–124), occurred during the era of early Christianity when it was dedicated in A.D. 608 by Pope Boniface IV to S. Maria ad Martyres. During the five centuries

RECONSTRUCTED PERSPECTIVE, TEMPLE OF ARTEMIS, EPHESUS, 356 B.C. DRAWN BY KRITZ KRISCHEN.

This wonder of the ancient world was meant to represent the sacred grove of the goddess with its sculpted forest of columns. Fritz Krischen, 1938.

ROTUNDA, PANTHEON, ROME, ITALY,
A.D. 120–124.

*The spatial power of the original temple
has been preserved by renovating the
pagan structure into a Christian church.
Photograph by John Kurtich.*

between its construction and its consecration as a church, the area around the building became dilapidated. The interior changed from a pagan temple to a Christian church. Various "renovations" continued, such as its gilded bronze roof tiles being robbed by Constans II in A.D. 663, a new lead roof covering in the eighth century, a bell tower over the center of the facade in the late thirteenth century, twin bell towers at the ends of the intermediate block in the early seventeenth century (dismantled in the 1880s), and a new stucco decor to the interior attic zone in the mid-eighteenth century.

THE CAPITOLINE HILL, ROME, ITALY

In the sixteenth century Michelangelo (1475–1564) transformed the Capitoline Hill into the sec-

ular heart of Rome. He had to retain the existing Palazzo del Senatore and the Palazzo dei Conservatori, medieval buildings that existed in a formless, unplanned relationship. Through Michelangelo's renovation of the facades of the two existing buildings and the addition of a third as a flanking counterpoint to the Palazzo dei Conservatori, he created a united urban interior space. The boundaries of the space were unified by a powerful columnar order of primary and secondary members, which clearly articulated the facades of the Palazzo dei Conservatori and the Palazzo Nuovo. The expanding oval pavement pattern created a dynamic tension with the enclosing trapezoid of the three building facades. The simultaneous contraction and expansion of this space makes it one of the great interior places of the human-built environment.

PLAN, CAPITOLINE HILL, ROME, ITALY, PRIOR TO 1546.

The original space was crudely defined by three buildings, having no visual relationship or harmony. Drawing by Garret Eakin, after John Andrew Gallery.

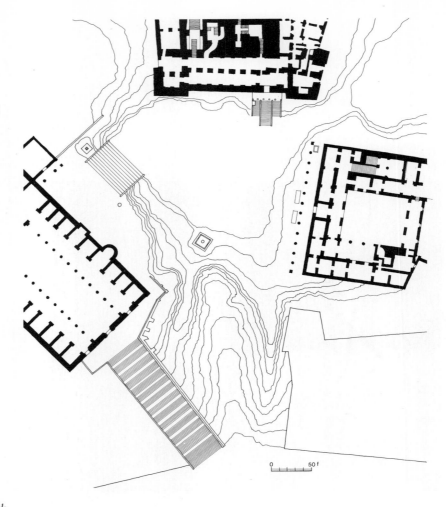

CAPITOLINE HILL, ROME, ITALY, BEGUN 1546.

Michelangelo's renovation brought back a secular focus to Rome by unifying the articulation of the buildings and plaza. Photograph by John Kurtich.

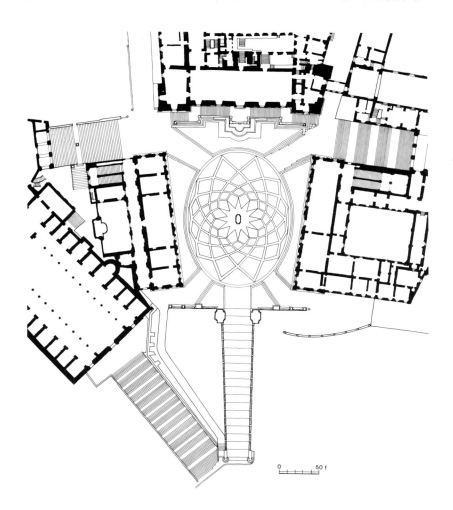

PLAN, CAPITOLINE HILL, ROME, ITALY, MICHELANGELO'S RENOVATION, BEGUN 1546.

The new scheme contained a clear geometric order with a formalized entrance and focal point. Drawing by Garret Eakin, after the Accademia Nazionale di San Luca, Rome.

ENTRANCE VIEW, OSTERLEY PARK HOUSE, MIDDLESEX, ENGLAND. ROBERT ADAM, 1761–1780.

Adam's renovation of the original Elizabethan house is an unhappy marriage of eighteenth century classicism with stoic medieval massing. Courtesy of The Art Institute of Chicago.

OSTERLEY PARK HOUSE, MIDDLESEX

In 1761 Robert Adam (1728–1792) was commissioned to renovate and decorate Osterley Park House, Middlesex. A country Tudor house built approximately 1575, Osterley Park still retained its original corner towers and some Tudor masonry, particularly on the west wing. Adam redesigned almost all the interiors and part of the exterior. An innovative feature of the renovation was the addition of a classical portico to the medieval structure, which now would link the inner courtyard with the gardens and relate the redecorated interiors to the exterior. Pevsner describes the new portico as follows: "The effect with the slim unfluted Ionic columns is as delicate and celestial and as chastely theatrical as any opera Gluck might have composed in these very same years." [15]

THE ROOKERY, CHICAGO, ILLINOIS

The Rookery, Chicago, Illinois (1886), designed by Burnham & Root, derived its name from its predecessor, a jerry-built, crowded city building that attracted roosting birds. The new eleven-story brick and terra cotta building was built as a massive block with an interior light court. The original court was covered with a metal-framed vault, featuring an intricate geometric pattern of transluscent glass and black iron tracery. Frank Lloyd Wright (1867–1959) was commissioned in 1905 to modernize the building's central court and entrance lobbies. Wright's renovation covered much of the original iron columns and spandrels with white marble incised with gold patterning. Later remodelings and repairs destroyed much of the beauty of Burnham & Root's and Wright's designs. The stairs and mezzanines of the two entrance lobbies were eliminated, along with Wright's marble cladding. Due to persistant leakage in the light court, the skylight was covered with an opaque roofing membrane, eliminating all natural light from this space. In 1992, a complete restoration and renovation of the Rookery's public spaces have been completed, returning nat-

COURT LOBBY, THE ROOKERY, CHICAGO, ILLINOIS. BURNHAM AND ROOT, 1886; LOBBY REMODELED BY FRANK LLOYD WRIGHT, 1905. RESTORED AND RENOVATED BY THOMAS M. HARBOE OF McCLIER, 1991–1992.

The meticulous restoration of The Rookery's public spaces has revealed the remarkable spatial sequence of Burnham & Root's original scheme, climaxing in the newly uncovered skylit central court lobby. Photograph by John Kurtich.

ural light to the central court and a reinstatement of the entrance lobbies to Wright's original renovation (for further discussion of the restoration and renovation of the Rookery, see Chapter 9).

THE ALEXANDER THE GREAT MONUMENT, MT. ATHOS, GREECE

Adaptive reuse of buildings has been relatively common throughout history, although many designs remained as unbuilt projects. One of the most outrageous examples of adaptive reuse was a project proposed by the architect Dinocrates to Alexander the Great. Dinocrates said: "I have made a design for the shaping of Mount Athos into the statue of a man, in whose left hand I have represented a very spacious fortified city, and in his right a bowl to receive the water of all the streams which are in that mountain, so that it may pour from the bowl into the sea."[16] Alexander was naturally flattered by his design but found the plan impractical as there was no way to furnish the city with its own food supplies. He said to Dinocrates, "Therefore, while thinking that your design is commendable, I consider the site as not commendable; but I would have you stay with me, because I mean to make use of your services."[17]

THE THEATER OF MARCELLUS, ROME, ITALY

Many houses of medieval Rome were built into the abundant ruins of the ancient city, making adaptive reuse a major means of habitation. The ancient buildings were actually exploited wherever possible for housing. The Theater of Marcellus, Rome, Italy, (23–13 B.C.), was apparently in a state of ruin by the end of the fourth century A.D. as it furnished building material for the reconstruction of the Pons Cesstius. Several hundred years later the theater ruins were rea-

ALEXANDER THE GREAT SCULPTED INTO MT. ATHOS, GREECE. DRAWING BY FISCHER VON ERLACH, 1721.

This visionary drawing depicts the glorification of ego, one of the driving forces of creativity. In this case, the execution of renovating Mt. Athos was beyond the capabilities and resources of the ancient world. Courtesy of The Art Institute of Chicago.

THEATRE OF MARCELLUS, ROME, ITALY, 21–13 B.C.

Until the 1920s, the exterior surviving arches and vaults of the theatre were filled with merchant-squatters. Today, these arches and vaults have been emptied and returned to their original function as an arcade without altering the medieval residential additions. Photograph by John Kurtich.

dapted as a residence and fortress for the Roman families of Pierleoni, Savelli, and Orsini, respectively. When the Savelli family held the theater, they leased the vaults on the ground floor to butchers and craftsmen. A new building was actually constructed on the top floor of the theater when the Orsini family occupied the site.

THE COLOSSEUM, ROME, ITALY

During the eleventh century A.D., almost all of the surviving vaulted spaces of the Colosseum (A.D. 70–82) were occupied. A deed from the period describes such property:

a crypt in its entirety, all vaulted, with half of the Traverine piers on either side, in the Amphitheatre which is called the Colosseum, bordering on one side on the crypt and lot of Guido de Berta, on the other the crypt of Doda, on the third the crypt and lot of Singiorectus and on the fourth the public road.[18]

Pope Sixtus V (1585–1590) had a project to transform the Colosseum into a factory for wool spinning. In 1590, he commissioned Domenico Fontana (1543–1607) to draw up plans that would readapt the amphitheater into a colony of workshops for wool spinners, where they could have their living quarters in the upper stories and working areas on the ground floor. The pope died before the project could be realized.

THE CLUNY BATHS, PARIS, FRANCE

The ancient Roman thermae, known either as the Cluny Baths or the "Hôtel de Cluny," Paris, France (ca. A.D. 215), went through several major adaptive reuse transformations during its long history. After the fall of the Roman empire, the massive remains of the original Roman baths lost their practical use and were eventually acquired by the monks of Cluny in 1340. On the site, Peter of Chalus, twenty-first abbot of the order, built an abbatial mansion called the "Maison des Thermes." During the next century, somewhere between 1485 to 1498, another dwelling was built into the structure known as the "Hôtel de Cluny." This then served as a temporary residence for the abbots of the order and their guests. During the eighteenth century the building was no longer occupied by the monks of Cluny, although it was still owned by them. During the French Revolution the building became national property but was resold to private owners. The

PLAN, COLOSSEUM, ROME, ITALY, REMODELED AS A FACTORY FOR WOOL SPINNING WHICH WOULD INCLUDE WORKSHOPS AND LIVING QUARTERS BY DOMENICO FONTANA, 1590.

This adaptive reuse project, in maintaining the formal integrity of the original building, predates similar Post-Modern projects of the late twentieth century, such as Les Espaces d'Abraxas, Marne-la-Vallée, by Ricardo Bofill. From the Resource Collections of the Getty Center for the History of Art and the Humanities.

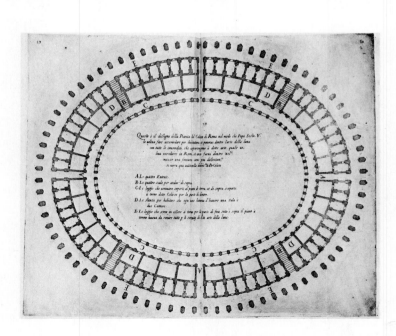

abbot's chapel was converted into a dissecting room. In other parts of the building complex appeared a bookseller, a laundress, and a cooper. The top of the tower became an observatory, used by the astronomer Messier for half a century. Finally in 1843, the state bought back the Hôtel de Cluny, acquiring the Palais des Thermes shortly thereafter. The building complex was then converted into a museum devoted to French history, which it remains today.

THE CASTELVECCHIO, VERONA, ITALY

The Castelvecchio, Verona, Italy (1353), was radically transformed into the city's premier archaeological and art museum in 1957–1964 by Carlo

Scarpa (1906–1978). Scarpa achieved three things in this adaptive reuse project. First he accepted and presented parts of the building complex as historically preexisting, therefore maintaining their original integrity. Second, he laid bare through conceptual surgery all the genuine survivals of the Castelvecchio. Finally, he added new parts, which would bind together the entire complex and fill in the gaps without destroying the patina or even the mishaps and wounds of time.

At the Castelvecchio, tall towers, walls, canals, reflecting pools, hedges, and alleyways are all interrelated, pushed back to the boundaries of the spacious lawn, and each element enhances all the others. They are set around a space which is not a garden but an ancient agora. A drawing of this project reveals the way Scarpa related the space in front of the gallery to the whole network of structural divisions within the rooms . . . Scarpa not only reveals the essential coordinates of the complex but also the materials that constitute its corporeal essence. This is the story of what happened at Castelvecchio, both directly, in the excavation and rediscovery of old stonework, marble, and brickwork, and also in Scarpa's familiarity with the city, enabling him to absorb the local color of its walls, streets, pavements, and stone cladding. In this way, not the form but the corporal essence of medieval Verona comes to life in the restoration, utterly creative and yet consistent with Scarpa's own genuinely modern training.[19]

THE SALINE ROYALE, ARC–ET–SENANS, FRANCE

A recent adaptive reuse has been made of the Saline Royale, Arc-et-Senans, France, (1775–1779), originally designed by Claude-Nicolas Ledoux (1736–1806). The city was planned as a large ellipse, with the director's mansion occupying the central position. Radiating from this center were symmetrically placed buildings at the circumference which housed the saltworks and lodging for the employees. Only half of the ellipse was constructed, including the director's mansion, and a monumental gate to the complex, on axis with the mansion. In planning such a complex,

Ledoux did not want civic art to be strictly utilitarian, he did not want the city to be simply an agglomer-

MAIN GATE, SALINE ROYALE, ARC-ET-SENANS, FRANCE. CLAUDE-NICOLAS LEDOUX, 1775–1779.

The monumentality of the gate is more successful today as a portal to a convention and research center than it was as the entry to a factory town for the production of salt. Photograph by John Kurtich.

ation of houses; he wanted it to be the crown of all architectural endeavors: . . . j'ai place tous les genres d'edifices que reclame l'ordre social, on verra des usines importantes . . . donner naissance a des reunions populeuses. Une ville s'elevera pour les enceindre et les couronner.[20]

The remains of this city were taken over by the French government in 1927 and went through a long process of restoration and adaptive reuse, which has now turned the complex into a convention center, with one of the saltworks converted into a theatre, others into hotels, the director's mansion into convention meeting rooms, and another perimeter building into the headquarters of the Fondation Claude-Nicolas Ledoux, an organization researching a variety of future perspectives.

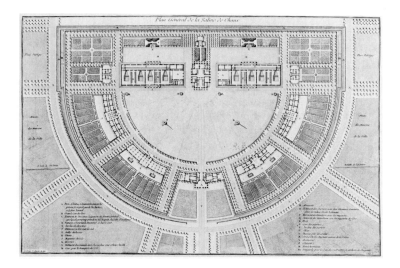

PLAN, SALINE ROYALE, ARC-ET-SENANS, FRANCE. CLAUDE-NICOLAS LEDOUX, 1775–1779.

The realized portion of the plan created a powerful and elegant assembly of buildings and space. Courtesy of The Art Institute of Chicago.

AERIAL PERSPECTIVE, SALINE ROYALE, ARC-ET-SENANS, FRANCE. CLAUDE-NICOLAS LEDOUX, 1775–1779.

The idealized vision included a complete ellipse in plan with radiating axes, focused on the centralized director's mansion, symbolized the autocratic society of the times. Courtesy of The Art Institute of Chicago.

PRESERVATION IN THE UNITED STATES

Until very recently in the United States, preservation, restoration, renovation, and adaptive reuse were considered unpopular forms of work that architects and designers would do. Following the oil embargo of the 1970s a reevaluation of older buildings has brought a significant change in this attitude. No longer does the U.S. economy support the construction of new buildings to the same degree as the boom years following World

War II. The importance of older buildings, structurally, aesthetically, and economically have brought about a new interest in preservation tactics. The rethinking of the Modern Movement also contributed to this attitude.

When the Modern Movement was at its height most architects and designers would not have considered preservation projects as desirable or serious work. Led by Mies Van der Rohe in this country after the late 1940s, the Modernists followed a hard line of purity.

When the Modern Movement was finally challenged by a so-called Post-Modern transition, the spell of purity was finally broken. However, a return to classical details, color, and eclectic ornamentation revealed a surprising amount of shallowness in the resulting work. Few contemporary architects and designers have been trained in the classical tradition, undermining Post-Modern ideals, yet this did lead to a rediscovery of the history of architecture and design.

The realization of the architectural heritage of the many older, non-Modernist buildings has brought about a serious reevaluation of these structures. Preservation tactics have created a new life for many of these buildings which, in turn, have revitalized the urban environment of many cities. The best of today's architects and designers are now practicing preservation, restoration, renovation, and adaptive reuse with enthusiasm equal or greater than that attached to new work.

One of the shortcomings of this current trend is that the education of architects and designers has not kept pace with reality. Architectural education still stresses form making. Design education does not emphasize relationships of interiors to their architectural shells. A complete approach to building design is sadly lacking in most academic settings. Schools need to balance their new construction emphasis with an appreciation for the preservation of older structures.

Summary

Interior Architecture can achieve this holism through the linking of architecture with interior design. It requires a fresh look at the real objectives of architecture in its broadest sense and the education necessary to bring this about. The following chapters focus on the importance of creativity, the elements of Interior Architecture that provide the link between the existing practices of architecture and interior design, and the future of Interior Architecture based on the realities of the present.

NOTES

1. Edgar Kaufmann and Ben Raeburn, *Frank Lloyd Wright: Writings and Buildings* (New York: Meridian Books, 1960), p. 102.

2. Le Corbusier, *Towards a New Architecture* (New York: Dover Publications, 1986), p. 203.

3. Malcolm Quantrill, *Alvar Aalto* (New York: Schocken Books, 1983), p. 6.

4. Ibid. p. 7.

5. Jackie Cooper, ed., *Mackintosh: Architecture* (New York: St. Martin's Press, 1978), p. 70.

6. Charles Moore, Gerald Allen, and Donlyn Lyndon, *The Place of Houses* (New York: Holt, Rinehart and Winston, 1974), p. 233.

7. Peter Adams, *Eileen Gray: Architect/Designer* (New York: Harry N. Abrams, Inc., 1987), p. 166.

8. Ibid. p. 198.

9. Ibid. p. 214.

10. Eugene Emmanuel Viollet-le-Duc, *On Restoration, and a Notice in Connection with Historical Monuments of France* (London: Sampson, Low, Marston, Low, and Searle, 1875), p. 9.

11. Ibid. p. 79–81.

12. John Ruskin, *The Seven Lamps of Architecture* (New York: The Noonday Press, 1961), p. 184–186.

13. Charles B. Hosmer, Jr., *Presence of the Past* (New York: G. P. Putnam's Sons, 1965), p. 24.

14. James Marston Fitch, *American Building: The Historical Forces That Shaped It* (Boston: Houghton Mifflin Company, 1966), p. 252.

15. Nikolaus Pevsner, *The Buildings of England: Middlesex* (Harmondsworth: Penguin Books, 1951), p. 128.

16. Vitruvius, *The Ten Books on Architecture,* trans. by Morris Hicky Morgan (New York: Dover Publications, 1960), p. 35.

17. Ibid., p. 36.

18. Richard Krautheimer, *Rome: Profile of a City, 312–1308* (Princeton: Princeton University Press, 1980), p. 300.

19. Francesco Dal Co and Giuseppe Mazzariol, *Carlo Scarpa: The Complete Works* (New York: Rizzoli, 1985), p. 159.

20. Emil Kaufmann, "Three revolutionary architects, Boullee, Ledoux, and Lequeu," *Transactions of the American Philosophical Society,* Vol. 42, part 3, 1952, p. 512.

CHAPTER 2

CREATIVITY: FROM IDEAS TO REALITY

CREATIVITY AND THE CRAFTING OF INTERIOR ARCHITECTURE

What is creativity? Is it a mysterious gift available only to a chosen few? Must one wait for the profound moment of inspiration? Are certain conditions necessary for creativity to flourish?

Creativity is the struggle to find and release what is within. The struggle is a process of clarifying the essence of the opportunity—paring down the extraneous notions to reveal the inherent relationships. Creativity is the ability to invent rather than imitate.

Creativity is not a mysterious subject: It can be understood and developed like any other tool of the architect or designer. Furthermore, creativity is not an isolated euphoric moment in the design process but must be integral and continuous to the work. Creativity is a process of recognizing the problem, understanding the situation, finding relationships, visualizing the solution, and testing the consequences. Dr. Edwards, in her book, *Drawing on the Artist Within,* sums this process up as follows: "1. First Insight 2. Saturation 3. Incubation 4. Illumination 5. Verification."[1]

The two ingredients required to bring creativity into existence are process and setting. The process in pure artistic expression is generally internal and thus uniquely and independently developed by the artist. Conversely, the process in design usually involves the dynamic interaction of the designer with clients, consultants, and associates. This process is therefore dependent on the ability of the designer to relate to and control the obstacles and opportunities formed by the various participants in the process.

CREATIVITY: EXTERNAL INFLUENCES

A creative setting is most influenced by external forces such as society and individual patrons. There are certain periods in history, such as fifth century B.C. Athens during the age of Pericles, sixteenth century Renaissance Italy, and late nineteenth century Chicago after the 1871 fire, in which an unusual abundance of creative work was produced. These periods were characterized by political stability, expanding economy, and superior building construction. Fortunately these situations produced many patrons, which in turn produced a setting in which creativity could flourish. These essential ingredients of creativity are important to consider in any historical period affected by accelerated changes in technology and society.

During the mid-fifth century B.C., Pericles rose to power in the *demokratia* (people's rule) of Athens, Greece. The Greeks finally had rid themselves of the Persian threat, although Athens had been sacked by the Persians. During a fourteen year period of peace, Athens quickly recovered and rebuilt itself as a major power; with "protection" money from weaker city-states, Pericles decided to rebuild the destroyed temples of the Acropolis, particularly the one dedicated to the patron goddess of the city, Athena, as the greatest architectural achievement of his age. He felt that "the brilliance of the present is the glory of the future stored up for ever in the memory of man."[2]

Athena's temple, known as the Parthenon, was built under the artistic guidance of the master

THE ACROPOLIS, ATHENS, GREECE,
FIFTH CENTURY B.C. FOR THE
REMAINS OF THE CURRENT BUILDINGS.

*The Acropolis is symbolic of the
stability and rich creativity manifest
during the rule of Pericles. Photograph
by John Kurtich.*

sculptor, Phidias, who also constructed its huge cult statue of Athena in gold and ivory. The temple was truly a culmination of the Doric order, built with more refined and complex proportions than any of its predecessors (the front had eight columns instead of the usual six). The richness of the exterior sculpture was a departure from the usual Doric simplicity: the pediments were filled with sculpture in the round; the metopes were high relief sculpture; a continuous frieze on the exterior cella walls brought integrated Doric with Ionic features that would affect future Greek temple architecture.

Michelangelo (1475–1564), bridging the turbulent period between Italian renaissance and baroque, was one of the greatest creative forces in the history of art. He was a master of sculpture, painting, and architecture, all of which he viewed as one art. With this renaissance view he was able to produce work with great creativity, harmony,

and balance. Through one of his unfinished works, the Atlas figure for the tomb of Julius II, one can speculate on his process. The unfinished figure appears to be bursting to life out of the marble block, yet the rough hewn stone is a metaphor for the enslaved figure. Michelangelo saw the block as a container the form was inhabiting, perhaps waiting for the artist to reveal its presence. In 1505 Michelangelo went to Carrara with two workmen for eight months to select the stone to be quarried and used for the tomb. He had an ability to visualize his sculptures in the raw material, and he took great care in selecting the blocks and quarries from which they were cut. This creative setting could only be realized in a period of prosperity and stability.

Louis Sullivan (1856–1924), who had been working for Frank Furness (1839–1912) in Philadelphia, was drawn to Chicago after the Great Fire of 1871. Chicago's catastrophe created a great

"ATLAS" (ALSO KNOWN AS THE
"ATLAS BOBOLI SLAVE" OR "A
PRISONER"), SCULPTURE BY
MICHELANGELO, CA. 1516–1534,
MUSEO ACCADEMIA, FLORENCE,
ITALY.

*The figure perhaps has more emotional
power being unfinished—a frozen image
of Michelangelo's working method.
Alinari/Art Resource, N.Y.*

demand for architects and their building skills. When Sullivan arrived in Chicago, he walked the streets, looking at the new architecture. He was impressed by the Portland Block, designed by William LeBaron Jenney (1832–1907). He, in turn, secured a position with Jenney's firm. Even though he stayed with Jenney for only one year, he knew that Chicago would be the setting for his future work.

Sullivan believed that nature was the source and inspiration of true art through poetic expression. He said in his essay, "Ornament in Architecture" (1892):

"But for this we must turn again to Nature, and hearkening to her melodious voice, learn, as children learn, the accent of its rhythmic cadences. We must view the sunrise with ambition, the twilight wistfully; then, when our eyes have learned to see, we shall know how great is the simplicity of nature, that it brings forth in serenity such endless variation. We shall learn from this to consider man and his ways, to the end that we behold the unfolding of the soul in all its beauty, and know that the fragrance of a living art shall float again in the garden of our world."[3]

He contrasted massive male forms in his buildings with lyrical, feminine ornament based on nature. In essence he created a balance between the animus and anima of a building, understanding in the architectural sense the harmony Carl Jung would develop about human psychology thirty years in the future. He did not believe that architecture should be restricted by intellectual dogma but should be democratic in form and spirit.

This belief was the basis for the design of the Auditorium Theater, Chicago (1887–1889), designed by Adler and Sullivan. The desire to create an acoustically appropriate space for music generated the volume. This volume was articulated to equitably distribute the seating. By eliminating

the boxes of nobility, they were making a radical departure in theater design. This bold step established Sullivan's democratic principles toward architecture. The structural ribbing spanning the volume was balanced by the intricate ornament and lighting to make an elegant but powerful statement reflecting the optimism of the time.

CREATIVITY: INTERNAL METHODOLOGY

An ideal setting creates an atmosphere in which artists can flourish, although their method of working is not always obvious. This process is based on a deep understanding of the nature of the problem or materials with which the artists are working.

Like Michelangelo and Sullivan, Louis I. Kahn (1902–1974) had a deep understanding and respect for the materials he used. Upon considering the nature of brick, he said:

If you think of brick, and you're consulting the Orders, you consider the nature of brick. You say to brick, "What do you want, brick?" Brick says to you, "I like an arch." . . . You can have the same conversation with concrete, with paper of papier-mâché, or with plastic, or marble, or any material. The beauty of what you create comes if you honor the material for what it really is.[4]

Kahn felt that the beauty of materials is clearest when used honorably and appropriately. The Salk Institute of Biological Studies, La Jolla, California, 1962–1966, is a beautiful example of the process Kahn used to select and use materials. The palette of materials was chosen to withstand the climate at the ocean's edge. The unique combination of concrete, teak, glass, and slate is clearly a solution to the understanding of the nature of materials appropriate to the situation. Kahn's affinity for materials was paramount to his philosophy of design.

COURTYARD, SALK INSTITUTE, LA JOLLA, CALIFORNIA. LOUIS I. KAHN, 1959–1965.

The beautiful architectural complex seems to become more at one with the site as the years of sun and ocean sprays create patina on the teak, concrete and slate. Photograph by John Kurtich.

Working intuitively, Jackson Pollock (1912–1956) developed a process of painting that allowed him to be spontaneous. Concerning his process, he said,

> On the floor I am more at ease. I feel nearer, more a part of the painting, since this way I can walk around it, work from the four sides and literally be in the painting. When I am in my painting, I'm not aware of what I am doing. It is only after a sort of "get acquainted" period that I see what I have been about. I have no fears about making changes, destroying the image, etc., because the painting has a life of its own. I try to let it come through.[5]

Pollock's ability to become lost in his work is central to his creative process. His loss of self-consciousness or ego allows him to become a part of the work and intensely concentrate on the process. "Lost in the present"[6] is described by Abraham H. Maslow as an essential component for creativeness of any kind. Maslow says of this creative process, "The best way to view a present problem is to give it all you've got, to study it and its nature, to perceive within it the intrinsic interrelationships, to discover (rather than to invent) the answer to the problem within the problem itself."[7] It is the understanding of the essence of process that frees the artist of dogma and -isms to truly create.

THE PAINTED APARTMENT

The story of the process of completing The Painted Apartment is characterized by a patron who had an idea and an architecture firm's intense commitment to that idea. This modest project was raised to the level of fine art by the patron's and the architect's interest in creating something special. The story contains an inspiring example of a rich creative process within an idealized setting.

The painted apartment, Chicago (1983), by Krueck and Olsen, is located in a Mies van der Rohe aluminum and glass tower facing Lake Michigan. The building contains his formula lobby of glass, marble, and Barcelona chairs. The core elevators, accessing anonymous hallways, complete the sequence of Miesian experiences leading to the Painted Apartment. The entry door is the last connection with the familiar. Upon crossing the threshold, one is met by a transformed world. This new world is abstract, curvilinear, translucent, soft, precise, sensuous, diaphanous, shiny, sexy, elegant. Light is the source of this magic. Curving perforated metal screens sift; abundant high-gloss lacquer reflects; undulating glass block glows; chrome and glass sparkle; window louvers filter; velvet shimmers. The cyclic continuum of light seems to be at one

JACKSON POLLOCK PRETENDING TO WORK ON PAINTING ENTITLED "NUMBER 32," CA. 1950.

Huge canvasses worked on the floor allowed Pollock freedom to be spontaneous and directly relate his method to the language of expression. Photograph by Rudolph Burckhardt. Jackson Pollock Papers. Archives of American Art. Smithsonian Institution.

with the sculpture of the space. The space is ever-changing in its focus, reflectivity, apparent size, color, transparency, and energy. The study and control of this energy is the essence of the creative act resulting in the Painted Apartment.

THE CLIENT   Celia Marriott is the Associate Director of Media Programs at The Art Institute of Chicago. Her main responsibility is to communicate to mass audiences the significance of the museum's art exhibitions. This daily immersion in works of art keeps Marriott sensitive to the value of creativity. The artists she exposes to the public took risks in creating their art. By accepting these risks, the artists confronted the prospects of self-doubt, failure, and embarrassment. She appreciates their courage and extends that spirit into her work and personal life. This was demonstrated by her desire to create a new level of experience in her own lifestyle.

Upon asking Marriott how such a remarkable piece of interior architecture was accomplished, she said, "Find a creative person and say yes!" This seemingly simplistic answer becomes complex when considering underlying implications of the parts of the statement.

First, to find in this case means much more than thumbing through the pages of eleven hundred architectural and design firms in Chicago and calling to arrange interviews. To intelligently select among architects, one must have a well-developed sense of personal taste. Since Marriott has a remarkable exposure to art and architecture, she was well prepared to find an appropriate architect. "It was a good match," says Marriott of the resultant relationship between her and her architect. This positive relationship is crucial to the success of any creative project.

Second, identifying a creative person assumes that creativity is understood and accepted as an essential component of the professional. Without this basic belief grounded in the client it is difficult for even a highly creative professional to achieve progressive work. It is necessary for the client to understand the importance of working with the professional to achieve a common goal. Creative work by its very nature is about exploring and pursuing new ideas. This process is not linear and can become uncomfortable for the most savvy client and professional. Therefore, establishing and maintaining a relationship of trust becomes crucial when discovering and resolving the multitude of obstacles of creative work.

Third, to say "Find a creative person and say yes!" means "Yes, I trust you." For a client to trust a young architect with one of the largest investments of her lifetime is daring. Of course Marriott made this statement after the apartment

LOBBY, 2400 LAKE VIEW AVENUE BUILDING, CHICAGO, ILLINOIS. LUDWIG MIES VAN DER ROHE, 1963.

Mies van der Rohe's elegant, orthogonal lobby sets the stage for the Painted Apartment's wild juxtaposition. Photograph by John Kurtich.

was completed and was fully recognized as a success. Yet the importance of a client's brave acceptance of new ideas in the creative process cannot be overemphasized. This is not to say that a client should not question the judgments and functional decisions of the architect. But to overly police and challenge each decision becomes a constant inhibition to free creative work. Much of the success of any original project is owed to the enlightened client or patron.

Celia Marriott would certainly be considered a modern day patron. Her project, a small apartment renovation, was not the kind of work generally sought after by creative designers. Yet Marriott established the atmosphere in which creativity could flourish. It is precisely this nourishing setting that allows good designers to achieve their most innovative work.

Marriott lives in a highrise apartment building designed by Mies van der Rohe in 1963. In the same year Mies said it was his duty to use "the scientific and technological driving and sustaining forces of our time."[8] Further he said, "I work so hard to find out what I have to do, not what I like to do."[9] Mies was not interested in building for a single person or site but solving general "problems of build-

ing." Therefore, his work in some cases became anonymous and impersonal, reinforced with his desire to abstract elements to the essential.

When Mies's building was completed, a model apartment was constructed to give personality to the interior and suggest to potential residents how the spaces could be finished. The furnishing and decoration of this apartment was a reaction to its anonymous quality, a denial of the inherent potential of the spaces. The designers seemed intent on transforming the spaces into something they were not. A high contrast color scheme was employed. Light-colored furniture filled the room of dark walls and floors. Drama was created at the expense of exploiting the spectacular views of Lake Michigan and sunlight. An eclectic collection of furniture included Barcelona chairs, white sheepskin rugs, pseudo bamboo chairs, chrome, steel, and glass-topped tables, traditional shaded lamps, an ill-suited chandelier, and pinch-pleated drapes. The overall combination suggests an artificial world, unrelated to its location. This kind of mindless interior decoration is a prime example of why there has been a wide separation between architects and interior designers. Interior Architects explore the architec-

MODEL APARTMENT, 2400 LAKE VIEW AVENUE BUILDING, CHICAGO, ILLINOIS, 1963.

The model apartment's design and decoration had nothing to do with the architecture. This is an example of what Interior Architecture is not. Communications Center, Inc., Chicago, Illinois.

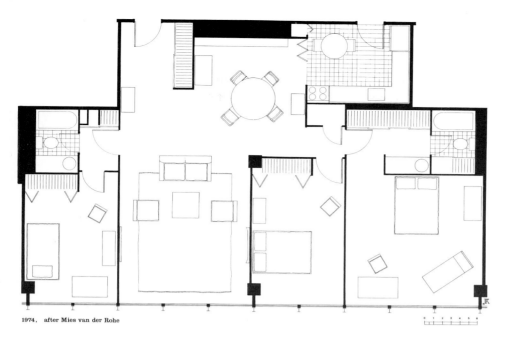

1974, after Mies van der Rohe

PLAN, "PAINTED APARTMENT,"
BEFORE REMODELING, 2400 LAKE
VIEW AVENUE BUILDING, CHICAGO,
ILLINOIS, 1974.

*The original utilitarian plan was
designed to accommodate a variety of
lifestyles. The plan failed to take
advantage of the continuous curtain
wall. Drawing by John Kurtich.*

REMODELED PLAN, "PAINTED
APARTMENT," 2400 LAKE VIEW
AVENUE BUILDING, CHICAGO,
ILLINOIS. KRUECK AND OLSEN, 1983.

*The new plan freed the expansive view
and contrasted the rectangular enclosure
with energized curves. Drawing by John
Kurtich.*

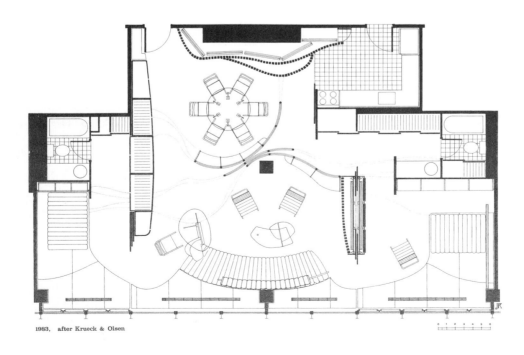

1983, after Krueck & Olsen

ture and the larger environment as a point of departure for their concepts. Such concepts are central to developing appropriate and meaningful interiors.

Marriott's three-bedroom apartment enjoys a spectacular view of Lincoln Park and Lake Michigan, yet the interior is an anonymous composition of rectangular volumes and minimal details. The original plan was functional. The interior was previously furnished in the spare Miesian tradition with contemporary art on the white walls and free standing furniture placed on an oriental rug. The basic appearance of the apartment had been unchanged for ten years until a particular event occurred.

As her children reached college age and began considering where to go to school, Marriott started to realize the freedom she might have with this change in the family. With two extra bedrooms there was an opportunity to open up the space to make it function more appropriately for her changing lifestyle. She always felt the living room seemed like a shoebox and did not take advantage of the view. Also, enlarging the living room would accommodate her desire to entertain —from dinner parties for six to cocktail parties for seventy guests.

THE ARCHITECT   Celia Marriott commissioned Ronald Krueck (1946–), of Krueck and Olsen Architects, to design her residence. He studied architecture at the Illinois Institute of Technology (IIT), Chicago. IIT's School of Architecture is well known for its rigorous training established by the former head, Mies van der Rohe.[10] The institution has also produced its own share of influential twentieth century architects, such as Myron Goldsmith (1918–), John Vinci (1937–), and Helmut Jahn (1940–).

Mies strongly believed in creating buildings that were characterized by the "spirit of the times." He thought of his work not as single buildings but as prototype solutions to particular problems, for example mass housing (860–880 Lake Shore Drive Apartment Towers). Mies, the abstractionist, reduced his buildings to the essential parts, replacing the embellishment of orna-

EAST FACADES, 860–880 LAKE SHORE DRIVE APARTMENT TOWERS, CHICAGO, ILLINOIS. LUDWIG MIES VAN DER ROHE WITH ASSOCIATE ARCHITECTS P A C E AND HOLSMAN, HOLSMAN, KLEKAMP AND TAYLOR, 1952.

The abstract facades emphasized the changing quality of light—reflections, shadows, and highlights—to perpetuate visual interest. Photograph by John Kurtich.

ment with reveals and the play of reflections on glass. Because his ideas had such sureness and clarity embodied in the work, he evolved into one of the masters of modern architecture.

Ronald Krueck and Keith Olsen both graduated from Mies's famous school. Krueck also taught there for seven years and learned well the master's discipline and methodology of working. While teaching, Krueck also studied painting for three years at The School of the Art Institute of Chicago where he learned to appreciate color and light. Krueck as painter learned how Lichtenstein applied color as distinct dots, forcing the eye of the perceiver to mix the dots and read the resultant color. Lichtenstein is interested in the potential of paint and how this medium can transform the meaning of the image. For example, his profane copy of a Picasso still life (Still Life, 1964) is executed with pure glossy paint on plastic—a cheap, artificial industrial product. Lichtenstein has thereby transformed or recreated the Picasso into an image of consumerism with all of its coarsened edges. This transformation of a carefully chosen subject forces one to consider what has happened to our society in the industrial world. His use of benday dots to replace brush strokes not only becomes a metaphor of mechanization but marks his work as individual.

Krueck is interested in transformation of three-dimensional space into a four-dimensional experience. He also becomes interested in the process of painting benday dot patterns and its application to architectural surfaces. The dots are applied through a screen with the imposition of one color upon the other. This causes the optical pattern to be read.

Krueck's interest in color was extended by the study of light as an art form. Dan Flavin's light sculpture taught him how light could destroy space, imply edges or planes, and paint surfaces with light. The artful use of color and light as an extension of what Krueck learned from IIT becomes central to his work.

THE MEETING Celia Marriott and Ronald Krueck had been friends for ten years prior to the commissioning for the design of her apartment.

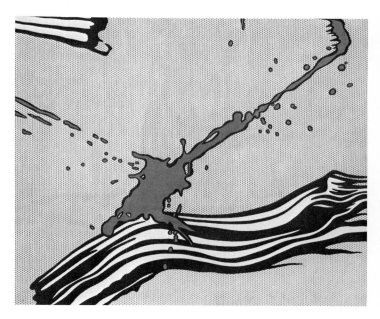

ROY LICHTENSTEIN, AMERICAN, B.1923, "BRUSHSTROKE WITH SPATTER," OIL AND MAGNA ON CANVAS, 1966, 172.7 x 203.2 CM, BARBARA NEFF AND SOLOMON BYRON SMITH PURCHASE FUND, 1966.3.

The painting's half-tone qualities displayed a method to express light in a graphic medium. © 1990 The Art Institute of Chicago, All Rights Reserved.

To Marriott the firm's work conveyed an image of high quality and sophistication. Projects such as the Steel and Glass House and the Victorian Town House Extended were perceived by Marriott as too large and expensive for her own means. Yet when she saw the Thonet showroom installation in the Chicago Merchandise mart, she started to consider Krueck and Olsen as potential architects for her apartment.

DAN FLAVIN: "INSTALLATIONS AT THE
GREEN GALLERY, NYC. 1965," NEW
YORK, NEW YORK.

*The unadorned application of fluorescent
lights to architecture is potent in
transforming space. Copyright 1992
DAN FLAVIN/ARS, NYC.*

The Thonet installation brought a lot of public attention to Krueck and Olsen because it was the first time that the young firm was compared to more established and famous architects. Five architects were commissioned for the installation, including Stanley Tigerman (1930–), Helmut Jahn (1940–), Kenneth Schroeder (1943–), Thomas Beeby (1941–), and Ronald Krueck (1946–).

The association proved to be a potent image builder for the young firm. The important element to Marriott was not this prestigious association but the image that the architects created for a very modest $5,000 budget. Thonet's assignment was simple: In a given space within the Chicago showroom, build a temporary environment to display the manufacturer's well-known furniture.

While viewing the exhibition Marriott said to herself, "I could live in a space like this." Therefore, the image of Krueck and Olsen as being expensive architects was dissolved. This was the first step toward the commissioning and the idea of the apartment.

When talking with Krueck about a particular project their firm has designed, he insists upon

looking at the continuum or progression of work that led to that particular project. He views his firm's work going in a specific direction, right or wrong, but in one direction. The reasoning is clear. If the firm continues in one direction, it will either come to a dead end after exhausting all the possibilities in that area or find new and unexplored possibilities. So far, there is no dead end in sight, and the possibilities have been transformed into a distinctive architectural expression. Leading architects and designers have always developed a personal style that identifies and elevates them in the professional world. As in any business, product identity is critical to the relative success in a highly competitive profession.

The Thonet installation had great identity when compared to the rooms or vignettes by the other four architects. The Krueck and Olsen was neither a room nor a vignette but an installation that implied space through the use of light and two-dimensional painted surfaces. The free standing space was defined by employing eight foot lengths of fluorescent lights as a series from floor to ceiling. The floor and ceiling were painted a glossy finish to create horizontal edges and reflect and extend the bright light sources. A stack of bentwood chairs were carefully placed in the composition as the only real element in this rather cold and surreal space. The whole effect seemed very unfamiliar and artistic as opposed to architectural. The implied definition of the edge was so clear that when one approached the space, the impulse was to reach out and make sure there was not glass defining the volume. The Thonet chairs were placed symbolically in a "museum case" of light with the intent of eliciting an emotional response. The architects were experimenting with the fourth dimension as metaphor for this piece of interior architecture.

To most people, it would be difficult to translate the idea of the Thonet installation into an image of home. Marriott's imagination was stimulated by this rather austere space and saw it as more of a three-dimensional painting with light. It reminded her of work by the sculptor, Dan Flavin. The fantastic idea of living in a work of art became an exciting possibility.

The concept was further reinforced when Marriott realized she would never be able to buy the art she had grown to appreciate through her work at the museum. After seeing the $120,000 price tag on a painting that she liked by Cy Twombly, the price of redoing her apartment seemed less extravagant. The implications of this thinking would transform her lifestyle. The thinking led quickly to a commission for Krueck to design her apartment.

THE DESIGN   Ronald Krueck measures the relative successes of his firm's projects by how complete the transformation from reality to a new reality has been made. This actuality of architecture as experience is very fragile. He is aware that the slightest imperfection can diminish or spoil the aesthetic experience. In striving for this impossible perfection, the firm spends endless hours studying, experimenting, modeling, researching, and rethinking each concept, material, and detail. They feel it is only through the intimate understanding of problems that solutions can surface and become integrated into the whole. This is the basis for what we call creativity.

When the Krueck and Olsen team talk about their work, they often use terms such as *force, power, it wants to, tension between,* and *movement.* They work very hard to uncover these underlying qualities of design problems so that the truth or most appropriate solution may be seen. The major objective of their search is to find new ways to transform reality. They are trying to see a new reality inherent in the problem through disciplined study. Most creative architects and designers believe that each problem that they work on is unique and contains a special solution. Yet few exercise a discipline in design that reveals such fresh solutions as this team.

For anyone to discover fresh or new ideas requires a certain freedom from the pressures of dogmas or ideologies. To gain that freedom, one must become "at one" with a problem. Being "at one" or totally immersed in a problem allows the designer to see the appropriate solution without external influences. To create a situation that allows the designer to spend the time to uncover

Thonet Showroom, Merchandise Mart, Chicago, Illinois. Krueck and Olsen, 1982.

The abstract illusion of space created by perforated screens, fluorescent light, and reflective surfaces contrasts the bentwood chairs to form a surrealistic display.

the best solution is difficult today. It is, in fact, contrary to this place in time, which has placed such emphasis on speed. "Time is money" has never had such meaning as now, and it is certain to continue into the future.

Like Mies van der Rohe, Krueck and Olsen have strategies to make time to develop their architecture. First, as Mies did, the architects use one project to finance another. This setting of priorities is a conscious decision to make more available time for projects of high design potential. This strategy is fairly common in the better design firms. The qualities that contribute to this high prioritization may be a good budget, an interesting client, timing, quality of the site, or program potential. This is not to say the architects are at all irresponsible concerning the projects that do not receive a high priority, but that the priority

Aerial view of Lake Shore Drive, in 1970, looking north, Chicago, Illinois.

The contrast of geometric human-made structures against the lake shore edge forms a dynamic view from the apartment. Photograph by John Kurtich.

ranking allows them to concentrate on work of greater potential.

Another strategy to make more time for design is to position themselves in the public's eye as high quality professionals. Therefore, it is logical that the fees should be higher for the work. The reasoning is that Krueck and Olsen typically provide much more service. This kind of thinking certainly decreases the number and type of clients that are attracted to the firm. Such a commitment allows the young firm to have more creative control of its architecture.

The Painted Apartment in Mies van der Rohe's Lincoln Park apartment building has its roots in its predecessor, the famous 860–880 Lakeshore Drive apartment towers. His original proposal for the apartment plans kept the core elements (kitchen and bathrooms) located along the interior corridor wall and left the remaining space free of permanent walls. This plan allowed the exterior curtain wall to be free and unbroken, emphasizing the spectacular views. Mies' original proposal was rejected by the developer as impractical and unmarketable. The Lincoln Park building followed suit and was executed with traditional apartment plans. This compartmentalization was what Marriott disliked. With this situation in mind, the architects studied the apartment to find what could be altered to correct this problem.

The view during the day is spectacular, unobstructed across Lincoln Park and Lakeshore Drive to Lake Michigan. With an eastern orientation, the light quality changed radically from morning to evening. At night that view dissolved into blackness, becoming a mirror image of the interior rather than a visual extension of the space. The only life in the curtain wall at night was the reflection of lights and forms off the glass. These observations led to the thought that the architectural concept must relate to the daily changing qualities of light that transform the apartment.

The predecessor to this project was the Steel and Glass House, completed in 1981. In this project, the architects experimented with textures of glass, ranges of materials from industrial to sensual, and qualities of light during the day and at night. They were fascinated by being able to reverse the perception of solids and voids through manipulation of light. Their choice of colors would vary from cool tones during the day to golden at night. The spaces they created could best be described as parallel and perpendicular stratifications. This layering was further reinforced through contrasting one material against another, creating a "tension between flatness and dimensionality."[11]

In contrast to the rectangular solution to the Steel and Glass House, the Painted Apartment employs free-form curvilinear lines, planes, and forms. These organic shapes are in direct contrast to the rectangular enclosure, breaking the boxlike feeling of the original plan, satisfying the owner's interest, and resulting in only a relationship with the curvilinear forms of the park and shoreline far below. Such forms dramatized natural light, emphasizing the ever-changing quality of the interior. The idea of destroying the rigidity of the rectangular plan was literally achieved by demolishing all of the bedroom walls and shifting the in-board corridor to the curtain wall. Early in the design process it was decided not to alter the kitchen and two bathrooms. This decision was easy as Marriott explains she was not interested in kitchens and bathrooms and was convinced by the architects that the budget would not allow for remodeling these areas. Keeping the rooms with plumbing intact created fixed volumes with existing access points. It became obvious to the architects that these rooms would be accessed via adjacent spaces as opposed to through a typical hallway. This relationship was not traditional, yet it seemed natural to enter the kitchen via the dining room and access the baths through the bedrooms.

With the objective of expanding the views and "breaking the box," the architects discovered the seemingly illogical placement of circulation along the window wall worked well in several ways. First, the width of the public view was greatly expanded by borrowing window space from the adjacent private bedrooms. This act also increased the apparent size of the apartment by eliminating the original, dark internal corridor.

LIVING AND DINING AREAS, PAINTED APARTMENT, 2400 LAKE VIEW AVENUE BUILDING, CHICAGO, ILLINOIS. KRUECK AND OLSEN, 1983.

The organic shapes formed in steel and glass are illuminated by back lit glass block walls which are extended visually in the reflective floors and ceiling. Photograph by John Kurtich.

LIVING ROOM AND STAIRCASE, STEEL AND GLASS HOUSE, CHICAGO, ILLINOIS. KRUECK AND OLSEN, 1982.

The asymmetrical composition, materials, and importance of light become a basis for the design of the apartment. Hedrich-Blessing © All Rights Reserved.

LIVING AREA, PAINTED APARTMENT, 2400 LAKE VIEW AVENUE BUILDING, CHICAGO, ILLINOIS. KRUECK AND OLSEN, 1983.

The window wall was freed of any wall interruptions and accentuated by the long, luxurious banquette. Photograph by John Kurtich.

People are naturally drawn to the view upon entering the apartment, so why not pull the walls away from the glass and let that be the passageway. The only problem was how to make the bedrooms private without doors. The general idea was discussed with Marriott. She liked the idea and felt that if there was visual privacy in her bedroom and some sort of enclosure for the guest room, it would work. To provide that enclosure and keep the window wall free and unbroken as

Mies had originally intended would require some creative analysis.

In studying the window wall condition, several questions arose. How to provide a door without interrupting the continuity of the curtain wall? How to treat the bedroom windows to ensure privacy and sun control? What to do aesthetically with the continuous baseboard heater? First, the architects devised special telescoping sliding pocket doors enclosed in storage units, which sep-

Detail of sliding doors, Painted Apartment, 2400 Lake View Avenue Building, Chicago, Illinois. Krueck and Olsen, 1983.

The lacquered, telescoping doors, with their rounded ends and routed finger pulls, became a beautiful, functional detail to discover. Photograph by John Kurtich.

arated the living room from the bedrooms. These sectional doors glided on three tracks recessed in the ceiling and floor. This solution was the least obtrusive and provided a generous opening for circulation. Not only did the doors ensure the continuity of the curtain wall but became a beautiful design detail. The ends were rounded, and simple recessed finger pulls were routed into the faces. The doors are generally left protruding from their storage positions as though they were anxious to be pulled out ready to expose their metallic lacquered finish. It is no accident that the architect felt compelled to express movement in the design of these doors because it was his goal to transform functional reality into dynamic actuality. What could have become a standard solution became a beautiful detail, driven by the architect's disciplined search for creative expression.

Housing one set of the doors, a subtly curving storage wall was employed as an unorthodox solution to establish a dynamic separation between the living area and the guest bedroom. This long unit was treated as a piece of furniture with reveals at the floor and ceiling, implying a continuation of the horizontal surfaces. The soft curve formed by floor-to-ceiling flush doors, absent of any hardware, was finished in metallic, high-gloss lacquer. Curving this wall and omitting any trace of hardware transformed the functional volume

into an abstract component of the overall composition.

Glossy reflective surfaces throughout the apartment were brilliantly employed to dematerialize and blur the edges of the space. Twenty different shades and colors of equal value were applied to the surfaces to exploit the opportunity for color to reflect on color, creating a richly everchanging surface. The floors and ceilings were painted with five shades of gray in graduated bands, dramatizing the decreasing brightness of natural light from the window wall. Overlaying this background were patterns of ribbons and benday dots, delineating lines of force and resultant shadows from the perforated metal screens dividing the living and dining areas. This subtle concretization of abstract forces within the space became a sensual score of the architect's creative vision.

The dividing screens were made up of three layers, which merged and split to define specific areas of lounging and eating. A decision was made on site to echo the distant landscape in the vertical shapes of the screening material while studying the relative transparencies of different perforations. Such a design opportunity could only be revealed if the architect were open to spontaneous alterations during construction. On-site creative decisions are often very important to the success of a project, even though the construction

SCREEN DETAIL, PAINTED
APARTMENT, 2400 LAKE VIEW
AVENUE BUILDING, CHICAGO,
ILLINOIS. KRUECK AND OLSEN, 1983.

*The sensuous perforated screens imply
divisions of space without forming
rooms. Photograph by John Kurtich.*

FLOOR AND SCREEN DETAILS, PAINTED
APARTMENT, 2400 LAKE VIEW
AVENUE BUILDING, CHICAGO,
ILLINOIS. KRUECK AND OLSEN, 1983.

*The painted floor details visually extend
the energetic moves established by the
metal screens. Photograph by John
Kurtich.*

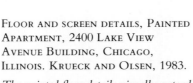

and budget processes do not encourage change. Therefore the designer must be decisive and persuasive to capitalize upon creative opportunities.

The construction of the screens were articulated as though they were a sophisticated curtain wall consisting of curved, perforated sheetmetal sandwiched between painted steel angles bolted together. The meticulous spacing of the polished acorn bolts displays the architect's desire to express the clarity of the construction. Simultaneously, the bolts act as jewelry.

The overlapping layers of perforated sheets of aluminum were carefully selected to create vibrant moiré effects. This is the dominant force in the apartment. These perforated sheets filter light. They imply space. They create energy. They invite movement. One is captivated by the ever-changing patterns of sifted light while the curvilinear forms recall the landscape far below. The layering of patterns is a consistent theme throughout the space. The overlap of translucent screens on curved glass block panels mixed with the opaque jalousy shades produces a complex kinetic texture. All of the surfaces contribute to the complexity or dramatize the patterning, charging the space with energy.

This energy depends on the ever-changing quality of light. Illumination comes exclusively from the window wall and two glass block walls, which are back lit by fluorescent tubes. In the morning, direct sunlight floods the interior. The bright rays of light are screened, colored, reflected, and distorted by the complex surfaces. Afternoon brings reflected light. The softer illumination heightens the view of the lake. A feeling of serenity and expansiveness pervades. Dramatic changes occur at night. The window wall becomes a black face mirroring the collage of forms and light. The glass block walls become the dominant light source. The curved wall is illuminated only from the floor by cool white fluorescent tubes. The flat wall is lit along its perimeter by warm fluorescent tubes. This illumination balances the color composition of the interior light.

DESK, PAINTED APARTMENT, 2400 LAKE VIEW AVENUE BUILDING, CHICAGO, ILLINOIS. KRUECK AND OLSEN, 1983.

The tiered desk terminates the end of the sofa, positioned for good reading light and view. Photograph by John Kurtich.

DINING AREA, PAINTED APARTMENT, 2400 LAKE VIEW AVENUE BUILDING, CHICAGO, ILLINOIS. KRUECK AND OLSEN, 1983.

The steel and glass dining table was an extension of the language of the screens, establishing a dialogue between the two elements. Photograph by John Kurtich.

The curved glass block wall not only masks the space beyond but is split horizontally by a sideboard for the dining area. Spanning floor to ceiling, the glowing walls are extended into the horizontal surfaces of the floor and ceiling, through reflection blurring the edges. The architect's commitment to integrate walls, lighting, and furniture are accomplished in an unprecedented way. This creative approach is a direct result of the rigorous study of these functional elements with the intent to discover fresh solutions to common problems.

The design of the furniture is viewed by the architect as one of structure. Each piece must be studied in three dimensions with careful consideration of the adjacent forms. These miniature structural forms, with their elaborate details, are rendered as focal points. Clear glass tops are supported by plate steel bolted to the floor. The simple construction of the bases consist of double vertical plates sandwiching horizontal support members. The shapes of the members are curvilinear and express the transfer of weight. Select pieces of the supports are painted primary red to dramatize their focal intent. The pure red color is also intended to be the base color that all other colors in the apartment are judged against. Red acts as a constant that dramatizes the chameleon-

Coffee table, Painted Apartment, 2400 Lake View Avenue Building, Chicago, Illinois. Krueck and Olsen, 1983.

The coffee table structure is stabilized by bolting steel sections to the floor while a tenuous steel tube becomes a tenuous counterpoint. Photograph by John Kurtich.

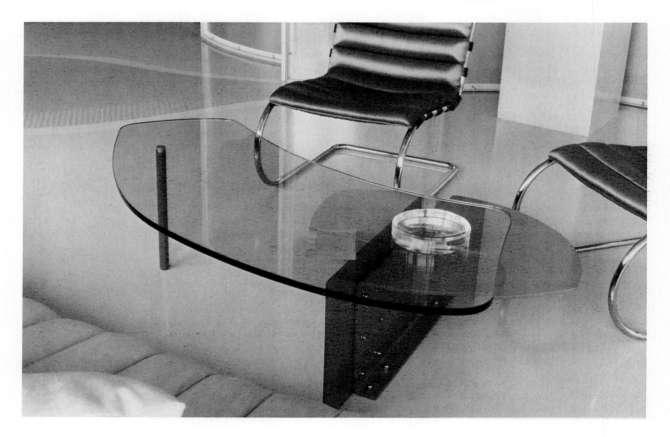

like quality of the muted surface colors. The reveals in the furniture as well as the screen wall are also painted red. This idea originated from a design drawing of the Steel and Glass House. While designing the facade, the architect could not see the reveal detail due to the small scale of the drawing. To emphasize this detail, he used a red line. He liked it. This idea was carried over to the Painted Apartment as a progression of his creative search.

LIVING AREA, PAINTED APARTMENT, 2400 LAKE VIEW AVENUE BUILDING, CHICAGO, ILLINOIS. KRUECK AND OLSEN, 1983.

The color and materials of the apartment were selected for the affinity to light. The colors were mixed and tinted gray to dramatize the chameleon quality of the surfaces. Photograph by John Kurtich.

Three free-standing glass-top tables were designed and installed. The dining room table is round, supported by six symmetrical supports, which are like petals of an opening flower. The individual supports, with bolted, knuckle connections, act like arms with hands, which solve the need for leveling the table top. The dimensions and placement of the supports were determined by the width of Mies van der Rohe's MR Chair. The creative aspect of the design was driven by the expression of the functional needs of dining. The coffee table is an asymmetrical composition, responding to its edge conditions, which is generated by the living room's furniture arrangement. The table is an exploitation of the sandwiched construction or language of the perforated screens. Red plate and tubular steel support the glass top, providing the vivid accent. Gray bent plates slip away from the red support, extending beyond the glass top, offering a secondary surface oriented to the movable chairs opposing the built-in sofa. Again, the form of the table is responding to the functional needs, or, as the architect refers to it, the powers and forces of the space. The third table, acting both as an end table and a tiered desk, becomes a sculptural counterpoint to the long, curving sofa. The desk is oriented to allow Marriott a commanding view of the apartment as well as the lake. Similar in construction to the coffee table, the desk repeats the red accent color in its three support members. The adjacent sofa is upholstered in pale gray-lavender velvet with a rolled bolster as a backrest, sustained by red tubular supports. Multicolored satin pillows punctuate the sofa, which provides the major softening element of the apartment. All of the furniture is in dialogue with the enclosing architectural elements and finishes. The furniture pieces are beautiful details in themselves, yet always subservient to the whole.

SUMMARY

The struggle to create this apartment had its roots in studying, digesting, and expressing the inherent and unique relationships within the project. Clarifying these relationships, without extraneous content, gives the Interior Architecture an enduring presence. Because the ideas expressed are poignant, without historic precedent, there is a timeless quality that transcends fashion or trend. The architect has exposed the essence of design in a very creative expression. Truly creative people must have the courage to be willing to break the rules when necessary to achieve the unexpected. The struggle requires inexhaustible perseverance and discipline to elevate design to a work of art. The crossover of knowledge in the arts dissolves the traditional boundaries of design and must be acknowledged as a critical, creative source. The setting for creativity requires an enlightened client or patron who fosters an atmosphere where imaginative ideas can flourish. An intense and passionate creative desire must exist within the designer to exploit the opportunity.

The major creative tool necessary to achieve Interior Architecture is the development of the third dimension. Chapter 3 explores this subject through the use of case studies.

NOTES

1. Betty Edwards, *Drawing on the Artist Within* (New York: Simon & Schuster, 1986), p. 4.
2. Rex Warner, *Men of Athens* (New York: Viking Press, 1972), p. 86.
3. Robert Twombly, *Louis Sullivan, The Public Papers* (Chicago: University of Chicago Press, 1988), p. 89ff.
4. John Lobell, *Between Silence and Light* (Boulder, CO: Shambhala, 1979), p. 40.
5. *Possibilities* (Winter 1947), p. 79.

6. Abraham H. Maslow, *The Farther Reaches of Human Nature* (London: Penguin, 1971), p. 60.

7. Ibid. p. 61.

8. Muriel Emanuel, ed., *Contemporary Architects* (New York: St. Martin's Press, 1980), p. 548.

9. Ibid.

10. At IIT, spending weeks reproducing in ink on mylar a Mies brick wall is a traditional problem aimed at disciplining the eye and hand of the student. One of the original visual training exercises taught by Mies is a five-week line composition problem. In this period the students are to work with two elements only: a twenty-by-thirty-inch white Strathmore board and two lines of black casin paper, which must be less than one-quarter inch thick. The problem is to develop a composition using the entire board divided into four rectangles with the black lines. This composition must be in perfect balance between opposing rectangles, lines, and overall composition. Craftsmanship is of equal importance in this minimalist exercise. At first one wonders how a student could spend five weeks completing such a primary problem. Yet soon into the process of solving or discovering the problem, the logistics of the exercise become evident and pose a series of mechanical problems.

First, how does one cut a line out of a thin sheet of paper thirty inches long? Usually after various attempts with knives, scissors, and straight edges, the student discovers the difficulty of achieving any precision without devising a more sophisticated method using special tools. The cutting tool needs two blades to make parallel cuts and must be adjustable to produce variable width. Most of the students end up spending a day in the model shop building their own version of the needed cutting tool. Once this obstacle is conquered, the next logistical problem surfaces. After cutting the lines, how does the student apply the long delicate material to the pure white board? What happens if the line is too thick or thin or placed in the wrong location? What if the adhesive oozes out from under the casin paper? These problems lead to an investigation of adhesives, spray-on glues, and double-stick tapes to find out what works best. With these logistic problems discovered and resolved, the student can now begin to work on the compositional portion of the exercise without spending a small fortune on Strathmore boards.

Trial and error becomes the main process of developing the composition. A composition is developed, and it is critiqued again and again until the student starts to see the visual relationship between line weight, planar shapes, and plate composition and how they balance. This process starts the student not only to understand composition but reveals the discovery process of creative work. The student finds that the apparent problem may be underscored by various logistical problems that must be discovered and resolved before actually working on the *real problem*. The development of this discipline is inherent in the institution. This seemingly tiresome and dogmatic educational method has produced its share of well-trained modernists working in steel and glass searching for God in the details.

11. Nory Miller, "Mies in Wonderland," *Progressive Architecture,* December 1981, p. 67.

CHAPTER 3

THE THIRD DIMENSION: NAVIGATION OF SPACE

Human beings and the higher animals are highly dependent upon accurate depth and distance perception for successful navigation through the physical world. This means having the ability to perceive a three-dimensional world. In the human-designed environment, architectural space is physically three dimensional. However all spaces are not equal in terms of three-dimensional development. As one of its aspects, Interior Architecture exploits the three-dimensional world it creates, ensuring every spatial entity as complete in itself regardless of shape, size, or proportions.

Very often in today's complex and temporary world, designers are faced with composing space that is only a portion of a whole. These spaces, often in anonymous high-rise buildings, beg for completion as a whole as opposed to parts of a larger body. The spaces require flexibility and expandability in three dimensions. Understanding the dimensional qualities of space and their interrelations is key to the aesthetic and functional success.

The human being uses a complex arrangement of physiological, kinetic, and pictorial cues in order to form a three-dimensional picture of the world. The physiological and kinetic cues are directly linked to the activity of the observer and thus constitute primary cues for depth perception. The pictorial cues are more secondary in nature as they are the devices that artists, particularly in western civilization, have been using for centuries to create three-dimensional impressions. These cues can produce dramatic effects, such as the visual expansion of existing space or the creation of an architectural space when it actually does not exist.

Chief among the physiological cues is *stereopsis,* an amazing and elegant faculty of the central nervous system. Normally, within the central

nervous system, any given point on the retina of one eye is parried with a corresponding point on the retina in the opposite eye. Rays of light reflected from the object on which one's attention is focused are always brought to bear on corresponding points of the two retinas in the central areas of highest resolution. Because of the slight spatial separation (about ten centimeters) of the eyes, their respective views of the world are ever so slightly different. Consequently, images of objects closer or further from the viewer than the object of regard will fall on slightly noncorresponding points on the two retinas. The brain utilizes the degree of location disparity of the images of an object to judge the distance of that object from the observer. Constant, unconscious

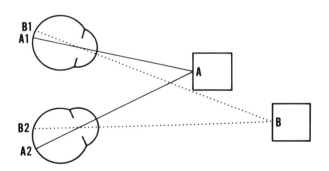

DIAGRAM OF STEREOPSIS.

Stereopsis records the disparity of depth perception between an individual's right and left eye. Drawing by Jennifer Ehrenberg.

assessments of the relative image disparities of all objects in view are integrated by the brain into a richly three-dimensional perception of one's surroundings. Witness how the world "collapses" when one eye is covered by the palm of the hand.

And yet not *all* sense of depth is abolished by this maneuver. Other useful cues still exist. The human being is in constant motion. Rarely is one's head stationary for very long: Every movement changes the position of one's eyes in space, continually shifting the images on the retina. These shifts provide important kinetic cues to three-dimensional perception. When one is observing the world while moving about, generally those objects close to the viewer appear to move at a greater speed than the more distant ones. Objects nearer one's point of fixation also appear to move in the opposite direction to the observer while those beyond the point of fixation seem to move with the observer. This apparent motion of objects, the direction of which is governed by distance from the observer, is called motion parallax.[1] For motion parallax to work effectively as a cue to depth perception, one's perceptual system must first organize the overall pattern of objects in the field of view before motion is introduced.

The pictorial cues are those which the artist must master in order to achieve realistic representations of the world. These include perspective, size, shadow, and interposition. Perspective is the

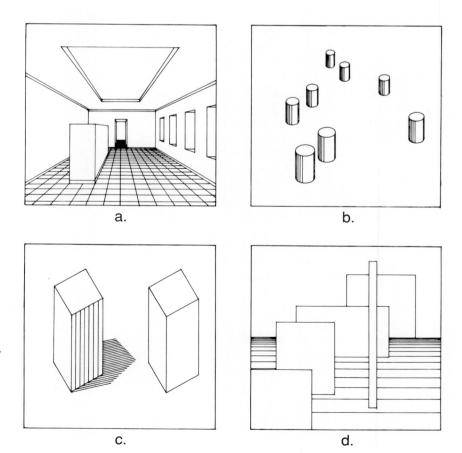

DIAGRAMS OF PICTORIAL CUES.

Pictorial cues demonstrate how depth perception affects a human being's sense of movement.
a. Linear perspective b. Size constancy c. Shade and shadow d. Interposition
Drawing by Garret Eakin.

a.

b.

c.

d.

most familiar cue. Perspective includes linear perspective (parallel lines that regress into the depth of the real world appear to the eye as converging lines), texture gradient[2] (texture density increases with distance), aerial perspective (the effect from the scattering and filtering of light, producing a bluish tint and increasingly less distinct detail as distance increases), and foreshortening (the distortion of an object because it is no longer being viewed in the frontal plane).

The cue of size depends upon the viewer's familiarity with an object's characteristic size. Size constancy comes into action here; the image of an object doubles in size whenever its distance is cut in half, a fact of geometric optics. However the brain "knows" that two identical objects are the same size in physical reality and infers from the disparity of the image sizes of the two objects that they lie at different distances from the observer.

Shadow and shading is an important cue because normally objects are illuminated with a nonuniform distribution of light. The nonuniformity occurs because the object is three dimensional and produces patterns of light and shadow on its surface. There are two kinds of shadow, attached and cast. Attached shadow seems to produce a greater image of depth. Shading on a surface is similar for either a depression in the surface or an elevation, providing some ambiguity unless the viewer knows the direction of the light source.

Interposition is the partial blocking of one object by another. The object being blocked is perceived as being farther away. Artists have used this cue for hundreds of years, and it proves to be a very strong depth cue.

The development of the third dimension is one of the major elements of Interior Architecture. This aspect works at multiple scales, involving not only the spatial arrangement of the overall architectural complex but the very surface treatment of furniture pieces. The excitement of moving through articulated three-dimensional space stimulates the participant's perception of and subsequent navigation through the space by means of an interaction of the physiological, kinetic, and pictorial cues.

UNITY CHURCH, OAK PARK, ILLINOIS

A preeminent example of such three-dimensional experience is the spatial sequence of Unity Church, Oak Park, Illinois, designed in 1904 by Frank Lloyd Wright (1847–1959). The binuclear plan is composed of an entry loggia connecting a large cubic sanctuary (Unity Temple) with a rectangular parish house (Unity House). The dominant temple form is massive in scale and austere in finish. The monolithic concrete structure is relieved only by vertical slits of leaded glass and abstractly detailed column capitals. One enters along the sides of the temple to stairs flanked by monumental planters. This leads to a raised terrace, revealing a light screen of glazed doors where the monolithic forms open and welcome the visitor.

Entering the loggia, one is compressed by the low, long-span ceiling. This is the pausing space, which allows one to enter either the open, glass-walled Unity House or the opaque, cloistered Unity Temple. Moving into the dark cloister, one is further compacted through smaller passages, which leak views into the temple. One realizes that its main floor level is above the loggia and cloister. Various passages along the way lead to the floor of the main space. Stairs in the four corners allow one to continue up to the six discrete balconies of terrace seating. From the dark cloister, one experiences a highly controlled three-dimensional journey weaving up through compressive forms to the explosive main space filled with natural light. To continue up to the balconies, one turns to the corner stairs with their series of intimate volumes punctuated by glimpses to the outside through vertical slits of leaded glass. Visitors enter from behind a wall of raised seating, turning and penetrating into the main space. From the parapet of the balcony, one again arrives at the main space to experience its volume from another vantage point.

Several elements accentuate the three-dimensional development of the temple. First, the deep, coffered ceiling with geometric stained glass, framed by medium-toned oak trim, crowns the volume with golden light. The ceiling rests upon

EXTERIOR VIEW OF UNITY CHURCH, OAK PARK, ILLINOIS. FRANK LLOYD WRIGHT, 1904.

The monolithic fortress-like structure masks an internal spatial complexity of warmth and intimacy. Photograph by John Kurtich.

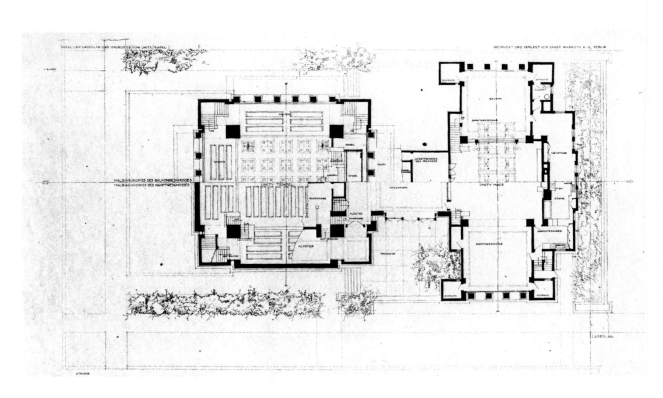

PLAN OF UNITY CHURCH, OAK PARK, ILLINOIS. FRANK LLOYD WRIGHT, 1904.

The evolution of a dual plan was in response to differing ecclesiastical activities. Courtesy of The Art Institute of Chicago.

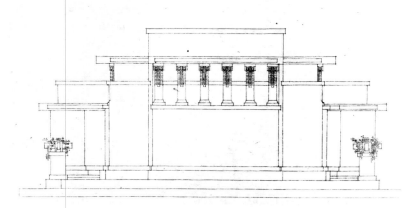

ELEVATION OF UNITY CHURCH, OAK PARK, ILLINOIS. FRANK LLOYD WRIGHT, 1904.

The planters and steps flanking the front facade introduce Wright's circuitous entry sequence into Unity Church. Courtesy of The Art Institute of Chicago.

ENTRANCE LOBBY, UNITY CHURCH, OAK PARK, ILLINOIS. FRANK LLOYD WRIGHT, 1904.

The low-ceilinged horizontal entry loggia provides a dynamic spatial counterpoint to the adjacent vertical spaces. Photograph by John Kurtich.

SECTION OF UNITY CHURCH, OAK
PARK, ILLINOIS. FRANK LLOYD
WRIGHT, 1904.

*The tiered seating of Unity Temple
reinforces the verticality of the main
sanctuary. Courtesy of The Art
Institute of Chicago.*

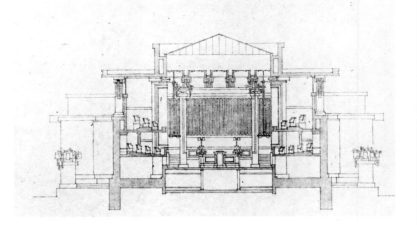

SANCTUARY, UNITY TEMPLE, UNITY
CHURCH, OAK PARK, ILLINOIS.
FRANK LLOYD WRIGHT, 1904.

*Wright's use of clerestory windows and
skylights as a vertical connection to the
heavens, heightens the mystical
atmosphere of the sanctuary. Photograph
by John Kurtich.*

transparent clerestory windows that alternate with the massive column capitals, providing relief to the enclosure. Suspended from the four corners of the coffered ceiling, clusters of stained-glass light fixtures interpose the volume, accentuating the vertical lines of the corner stairs. The interplay of mass and volume produced by the vertical stairs and the horizontal balconies is made distinct by strong light and shadow. Medium-toned wood banding is used to complicate the simple forms while knitting together the composition as a whole. These bands create a plastic effect, separating the three colors: gray, yellow, and green. The trim bands and colors create constant visual movement while interacting with the three-dimensional forms.

MANIFESTATIONS OF THE THIRD DIMENSION

Unity Church illustrates a number of ways in which the three dimensionality of space can be expressed and developed. Identification of the various manifestations to achieve powerful three-dimensional expression is essential for the understanding of Interior Architecture. Following this listing of the vocabulary of the third dimension is a series of examples.

1. Sequence of Spaces
2. Extension of Space beyond the Enclosure
3. Interlocking Form and Space
4. Spatial Interposition
5. Dynamic Tension through Compression and Expansion
6. Perspective
7. Aedicular Development
8. Vertical Development of Horizontal Planes
9. Exploitation of Scale
10. Animation through Furnishings
11. Reaction to Context
12. Excavated Interior Architecture
13. Constructed Interior Architecture

SEQUENCE OF SPACES

BATHS OF CARACALLA, ROME

A series of spaces in an ordered sequence is a classic way to establish the three-dimensional development of a building complex. When axially planned, the ability to look into the unentered

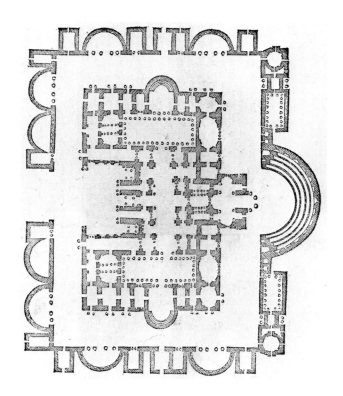

PLAN OF A ROMAN BATH DRAWN BY LEON BATTISTA ALBERTI FROM THE ITALIAN EDITION OF "L'ARCHITETTURA DIE LEONBATISTA ALBERTI," 1565.

The axial spatial sequence found in the planning of Roman baths provided ever unfolding three dimensional vistas.
Courtesy of The Art Institute of Chicago.

portion of the sequence further reinforces the sense of the third dimension. The ancient Romans were masters at exploiting the third dimension through elaborate, axial *sequence of spaces*. They used this as the organizational device for their thermae or public baths; the baths reached their zenith with those of Caracalla (A.D. 211–217) and Diocletian (A.D. 302), Rome.

The layout of spaces for the baths, such as Caracalla, positioned a large, circular space, known as the *calidarium* (hot bath) at the head of the central axis in a southwest orientation to maximize the greatest amount of natural heat and light from the afternoon sun. Moving into the next space on the central axis with the calidarium was a small *tepidarium* (warm bath), which opened on a large *frigidarium* (cold bath). The *frigidarium* established a cross-axis, which connected a symmetrical series of antechambers leading to colonnaded palaestrae[3] as the termination. The main axis through the *frigidarium* connected it to a large *natatio* (swimming pool) as a termination. The bath chambers were enclosed with cross vaulting resting on huge columns, which formed a succession of canopies, further enhancing the third dimension. The spatial sequences were most strongly developed in the two horizontal directions of the main axis and its cross-axis, and the

participant could always view the spaces beyond, richly articulated with the vaulting, colonnades, mosaic surfaces, and shimmering pools of water.

IL REDENTORE, VENICE

Andrea Palladio (1508–1580) studied the remains of the baths of Rome, particularly the Baths of Caracalla; from these studies he drew reconstructions of the baths, which would influence him in his design of Il Redentore (1577–1592), Venice. At the time Palladio designed this church, there was much vacillation between the centrally planned churches that Renaissance architects favored and the more traditional longitudinally planned churches from the medieval period preferred by the clergy. Palladio combined the two plan types because this particular church had to accommodate three activities that were somewhat independent of each other: a choir space for monastic functions, a central space (called the *tribune*) for votive activities, and the nave and adjoining chapels for congregational functions. The central altar, located in the tribune, had to be visible from all parts of the space. A spatial separation between the tribune and nave/chapels was achieved by narrowing the nave with piers as it connected to the

THE NATATIO (SWIMMING POOL) OF THE BATHS OF CARACALLA, ROME, ITALY, A.D. 211–217.

Open to the sky, the natatio *formed a refreshing haven from the sultry climate. Photograph by John Kurtich.*

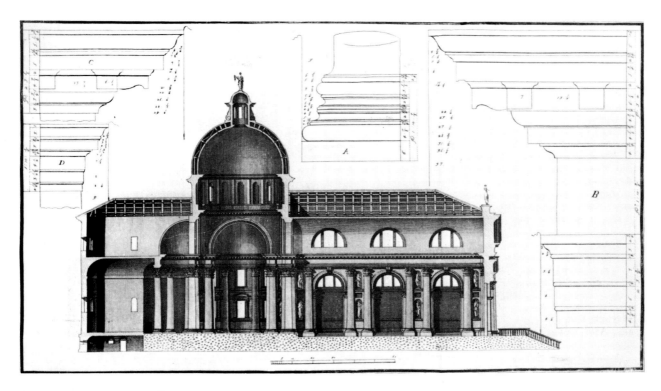

LONGITUDINAL SECTION OF IL
REDENTORE, VENICE, ITALY. ANDREA
PALLADIO, 1577–1592.

*Light entering along the nave chapels, at
the ceiling vault and around the central
dome, extended the three dimensional
spatial experience vertically. Courtesy
of The Art Institute of Chicago.*

PLAN OF IL REDENTORE, VENICE,
ITALY. ANDREA PALLADIO, 1577–
1592.

*This plan illustrates three distinct
spaces: a longitudinal nave with adjacent
chapels, the domed tribune containing
the altar, and the choir space. Courtesy
of The Art Institute of Chicago.*

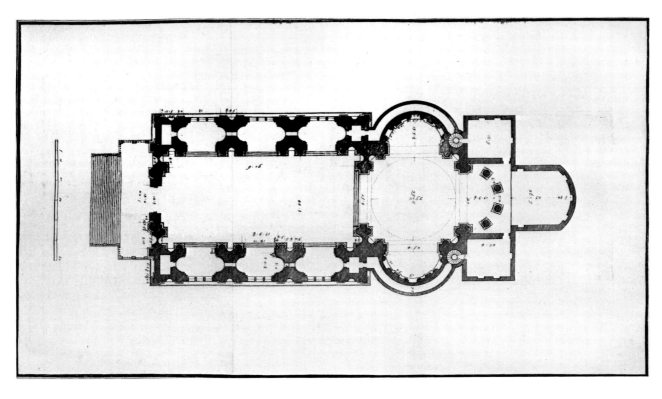

THE NAVE, IL REDENTORE, VENICE,
ITALY. ANDREA PALLADIO, 1577–
1592.

*Palladio adapted the basilican form for
the church's nave to accommodate the
processional needs of the worshippers.
Photograph by John Kurtich.*

tribune. The boundary of the choir, located behind the altar, was defined by a hemicycle of columns, which created a screen transparent to light
and sound but provided the monks with some
visual privacy.

Palladio solved the spatial requirements by
joining independent shapes together as an axial
sequence of spaces not unlike the ancient Roman
baths. The rectangular nave was similar to the
frigidarium, the centralized tribune was like the *tepidarium,* and the choir akin to the *calidarium.* The
spatial boundaries of each (the piers between the
nave and tribune and the columnar screen between the tribune and choir) contributed a strong
sense of the third dimension as one could view the
entire spatial sequence anywhere along the route
and see the spaces beyond through their boundaries. Palladio used Roman vaulting techniques,
which further emphasized a three-dimensional development of plastic wall masses penetrated by
arched niches for light.

EXTENSION OF SPACE BEYOND
THE ENCLOSURE

A greater sense of three-dimensional space can be
achieved by *extension of space beyond the enclosure.*
By extending elements, implying enclosure, and
forming focal points, grand three dimensional
vistas can be formed.

VILLA ALMERICO–VALMARANA
(LA ROTONDA), VICENZA

Andrea Palladio (1508–1580) exploited this idea in
several of his villas for wealthy landowners. His
famous Villa Almerico-Valmarana (La Rotonda)
(1565–1566, 1569) was sited at the crest of a hill
overlooking the owner's land. The symmetrical
plan was organized around a central dome with
two identical axes radiating from this center.
These axes are physically expressed as halls lead-

The Villa Almerico-Valmarana (La Rotonda), Vicenza, Italy. Andrea Palladio, 1565/1566–1569.

Responding to magnificent views for the hilltop site, Palladio designed a symmetrical villa with four identical porticoes to celebrate the vistas. Photograph by John Kurtich.

View from one of the porches of the Villa Almerico-Valmarana (La Rotonda), Vicenza, Italy. Andrea Palladio, 1565/1566–1569.

This view frames the main access to the villa from the city. Photograph by John Kurtich.

ing to four porticoes facing north, south, east, and west. Colonnades on these porches framed the view, thereby establishing a grand foreground to the expansive vista defined by land forms, walls, sculpture, buildings, and landscape.

THE BRICK COUNTRY HOUSE

Ludwig Mies van der Rohe (1886–1969) designed a project in 1924, the main feature of which was the extension of space beyond the formal enclo-

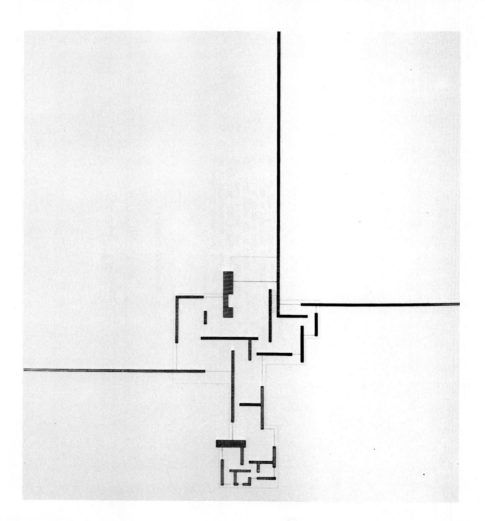

GROUND FLOOR PLAN OF BRICK COUNTRY HOUSE BY LUDWIG MIES VAN DER ROHE, 1924.

The plan illustrates how the use and placement of three long walls visually borrowed outside space, blurring the normal constraints of inside to outside. Collection, The Museum of Modern Art, New York. Gift of the architect.

sure—the Brick Country House. This project was never executed, but it represented Mies's exploration into spatial definition, which was both linear and plastic. The nucleus of the house was made up of a series of spaces, defined by orthogonal brick walls, but partially open to each other to allow a continuous flow of movement. His spaces, instead of being definite "rooms," actually melted one into the other. The viewer, moving through this spatial continuum, could experience three-dimensional dissolves as no movie film could emulate. The flow of space extended outward into the landscape, guided by three long walls that dynamically claimed the exterior vistas as part of the three-dimensional composition.

GERMAN PAVILION, BARCELONA, SPAIN

Mies's German Pavilion, Barcelona, Spain, (1929), achieved in reality what he theorized in his Brick Country House project. Built as the German government's contribution to the Barcelona International Exposition, it represented a new culmination of open space planning. Constructed in the rich and noble materials of Roman travertine, green Tinian marble, Moroccan onyx dorée, gray tinted glass, and chromium-plated steel columns, the pavilion realized the vibrant and dynamic three-dimensional extension from enclosure to beyond. Mies transcended the influences of Theo van Doesburg's de Stijl paintings (such as "Rhythm of a Russian Dance," 1918) and Frank Lloyd Wright's Prairie house open plans (such as the Robie House, Chicago, 1909).

Visitors had to move through the pavilion to appreciate the concept of spatial continuum from outside to inside to outside. The journey through the building required participants to change direction a number of times, exposing them to shifting vistas that reinforced the three-dimensional spatial extensions. The flowing space was further emphasized by reflections from the polished marble planes, the glass surfaces, the shiny columns, the luxuriant colors, and the rippling water of the black-glass-lined pool. Since the structure was actually supported by the steel columns, the wall planes were totally free to define space as gliding and floating geometric planes, partially enclosing, partially revealing surprises as one moved through the eloquent complex.

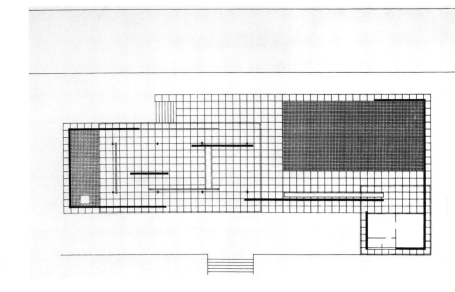

FLOOR PLAN OF THE GERMAN PAVILION, BARCELONA, SPAIN. LUDWIG MIES VAN DER ROHE, 1928–1929.

Positioned on a raised travertine plinth, topped by a flat roof, the asymmetrical freestanding walls appear to glide past each other, creating fluid space. Collection, The Museum of Modern Art, New York. Gift of the architect.

INTERIOR VIEW OF THE GERMAN
PAVILION, BARCELONA, SPAIN.
LUDWIG MIES VAN DER ROHE, 1928–
1929. RESTORED BY CRISTIAN CIRICI,
FERNANDO RAMOS, AND IGNASI DE
SOLA-MORALES, 1986.

*Using the same sumptuous materials on
the interior and exterior adds to the
sensation of free-flowing space.
Photograph by Don Kalec.*

KNOLL INTERNATIONAL SHOWROOM,
PARIS, FRANCE. CHARLES PFISTER,
1989.

*The mirrored steps invite the visitor to
experience the sensation of being
fragmented in space. Photograph by
John Kurtich.*

KNOLL INTERNATIONAL SHOWROOM, PARIS, FRANCE

The Knoll International Showroom (1989) in Paris, France, designed by Charles Pfister (1939–1990) is an exciting use of reflective materials to exaggerate the perception of interior space. Mirrors provide not only the illusion of more space than actually exists but also the visual fabrication of interlocking space that continually confronts and surprises the visitor. This amounts to the virtual extension of space beyond the enclosure. Knoll is located in a narrow building on the Boulevard Saint Germain. Pfister decided to manipulate reflection to not only perceptibly widen and deepen the existing space but to develop a strong three-dimensional sense of space as one penetrates the showroom. The main entrance envelops the visitor within the oversized window display, defined by floor-to-ceiling glass on the street wall, forming a corner, and floor-to-ceiling mirrors on the wall to the left of the display space, doubling its apparent size. Molded chair torsos are suspended at random heights in the window display, appearing as giant, curved color chips, which immediately announce Knoll's available color spectrum. One is able to walk through and about this room-size window display for closer inspection of any sample.

The receptionist's station divides the initial entry space from the main body of the showroom, where various groupings of Knoll's furniture are exhibited. The main space is molded into subareas by wall partitions that appear as two-dimensional cutouts of evenly stepped panels. These dividers create stunning spatial apparitions through a combination of their geometry and their highly reflective surface treatment. A mixture of mirrors and reflective black surfaces clad the partitions. Some of these partitions join to form inside corners of multiple reflections, which fool the eye, confusing the actual boundaries.

Concealed behind one of the stepped walls is the stairway to the second floor. The cutout "steps" of the partition match the measurements of the risers and treads of the stairs, establishing

geometric unity. Pfister has carpeted the treads, but mirrored the risers, so that people ascending are faced with horizontal strips of their reflected body images, each slice presenting an increasingly smaller body reflection. There is no way to avoid seeing this spatial distortion of oneself while ascending, short of a blindfold. The experience, however, is a fascinating lesson in mirror optics, which greatly enhances the three-dimensional potential of the common stair.

In a very small basement space, Knoll's fabric sample room and "vault," is fully exploited by mirrors. By cladding almost every surface with mirrors except the floor, the "barbershop effect" comes into full force, creating horizontal spatial infinity as one both traverses the stair and occupies the samples room.

INTERLOCKING FORM AND SPACE

ROBIE HOUSE, CHICAGO, ILLINOIS

Frank Lloyd Wright (1867–1959) was the master of *interlocking form and space*. He developed through his Prairie houses a spatial freedom that continuously interlocked with the form needed to define it. Generally the Prairie house radiated outward from a powerful, central masonry hearth, which anchored the plan. By establishing a vertical element of strength and solidity in the form of a hearth, the rest of the house could be freely opened to extend into the landscape. His interiors became a series of interlocking spaces, without doors, separated by skillfully contrived vistas through the use of freestanding walls, built-in furniture, variations in ceiling heights, changes in floor levels, unexpected light sources, controlled glimpses of outdoor landscape, and dramatic use of building materials. The flow of space in terms of its ability to interlock throughout was the most intriguing feature.

Wright generally used a larger space as a centralizing element, usually a two-story living room that also highlighted the verticality and strength of the central masonry hearth. From this space, various wings of the house extended in all directions. One was not only aware of the way in which the interior flowed through these wings, but also how the space flowed beyond them to the outside, interlocking with the landscape through cantilevered, horizontal roof planes; extensive, multileveled terraces; and linear parapets that both linked and subdivided the exterior space to intermingle brilliantly with the house itself.

Wright's Robie House, Chicago, Illinois (1909), represents the epitome of his Prairie houses. The exterior south facade, along Fifty-Eighth Street, is a composition of ribbon windows, floating roofs, horizontal masonry masses anchored to short upright masonry posts, and the vertical accent of the centralized hearth. A highly three-dimensional quality dominates the facade by the resulting solids and voids created by the linear balconies, cantilevered roofs, ribbon windows, and vertical accents.

Wright employed visual refinements to emphasize the horizontal nature of the house. The living and dining room balcony running most of the length of the south facade is actually supported by metal beams cantilevered at prescribed intervals from the interior floor. By capping the brick parapet above and below with stone, he created the effect of a giant brick bridge spanning between the two end vertical brick posts. The balcony's overhang puts the ground floor below into shadow, as do the horizontal roof overhangs casting strong shadows on the ribbon windows above.

The living and dining portion of the house is located one flight of stairs above the entry ground level, recalling the traditional Italian *piano nobile*. The rooms of the ground floor have low ceilings and are relatively dark, encouraging those entering the house to immediately ascend a staircase; this vertical shaft of interlocking circulation space uses the contrast of light differential to dramatize movement from darkness to light. The spatial complex of the *piano nobile* was made unconventional by the way Wright bonded the living room to the dining room, separated by a central hearth, which was punctuated to allow the two spaces to interlock and flow together. The boundaries of both rooms, made up primarily of windows, glazed doors, and thin screens, create a sense of

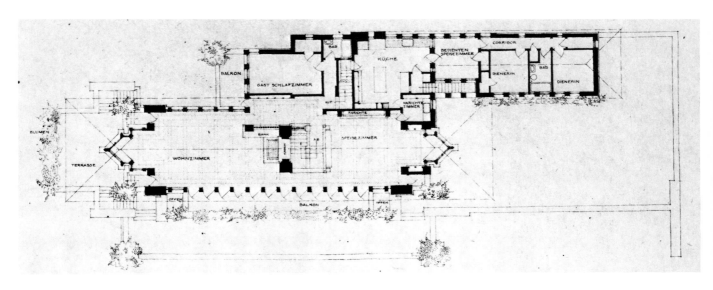

First floor plan, Robie House,
Chicago, Illinois. Frank Lloyd
Wright, 1909.

*The plan shows that the only spatial
interruption between the dining and
living space is provided by a stair from
the ground floor, and a fireplace.
Courtesy of The Art Institute of
Chicago.*

South facade of the Robie House,
Chicago, Illinois. Frank Lloyd
Wright, 1909.

*The emphasis of this facade promotes
horizontality, from the strong
cantilevered roof forms to the long,
continuous lines of capping on the brick
masonry to the highlighting of the
horizontal mortared joints of the brick.
Photograph by John Kurtich.*

lightness and openness. Built-in furniture further underlines the three-dimensional interlocking of space and form. The dining room sideboard, built into the north wall, is a kind of miniature reflection of the south elevation of the house itself. Cantilevered elements combine with the post-and-beam bridge effect of the exterior facade. The free-standing dining room table with its corner light fixtures and high-backed chairs complete the extraordinary three-dimensional composition (see Chapter 7 for further discussion of the Robie House dining room furniture).

SCHRÖDER HOUSE, UTRECHT, NETHERLANDS

The Dutch movement known as *De Stijl* (The Style) (1917–1931) had a significant impact on the concept of interlocking space. (See Chapter 7 for

SOUTHEAST FACADE OF THE SCHROEDER HOUSE, UTRECHT, THE NETHERLANDS. GERRIT RIETVELD, 1923. RESTORED BY BERTUS MULDER, 1974–1987.

The intersecting planes which create this house produce a very flexible system of interlocking spaces within the interior. Photograph by Don Kalec.

discussion of this movement and the furniture it produced.) Gerrit Rietveld (1888–1964) used the linear, planar, and color theories of De Stijl to produce a variable, interlocking spatial continuum for the interior of his masterpiece, the Schröder House, Utrecht, Netherlands (1924). The first floor was designed with only two fixed spaces: the bathroom and the stairs. The interior that remained could be turned into smaller spatial units by sliding panels. These flexible panels allowed for numerous spatial arrangements, actually overlapping or interlocking one space with another.

This integration of variable space was further amplified by built-in furniture that did not respect rigid boundaries. The floating quality of the lines and planes were enhanced by design devices that visually reduced any rigid spatial definitions of corners. Primary-colored planes were meant to provide a continuous experience of color in space, and as these planes defined spaces within, the resulting composition was not restricted by the basic shell of the house but actually penetrated the exterior skin and extended the notion of interlocking space to the exterior world.

SPATIAL INTERPOSITION

SOANE HOUSE, LONDON, ENGLAND

When an interior complex is made up of a series or sequence of spaces that overlap in such a way that one space partially blocks the view into the

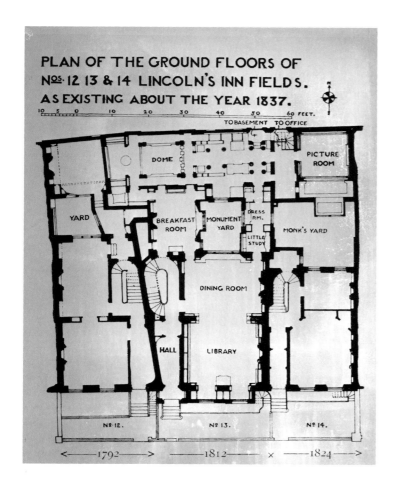

GROUND FLOOR PLAN, SIR JOHN SOANE RESIDENCE, LINCOLN'S INN FIELDS, LONDON, ENGLAND. SIR JOHN SOANE, 1837.

Through the device of interposition, Soane made his rather small interiors seem much bigger than they actually were. Courtesy of The Art Institute of Chicago.

next, *spatial interposition* exists. A very strong three-dimensional situation can be established through this arrangement, particularly if the spaces extend both horizontally and vertically. The master of spatial interposition was Sir John Soane (1753–1837), as used in his London house (begun in 1792, additions in 1812 and 1824; see Chapter 1 for additional material on Soane's house).

The spaces that Soane achieved are intriguing three-dimensional sequences that lead one through his house on a seemingly never-ending path of self-discovery. Spaces beyond full view produce an air of mystery and drama. Soane manipulated the scale of such interpositioned spaces so that some might be entered but others might be a source of light only. Many of his interiors were variations of spatial interposition, such as the Breakfast Parlour (see discussion later in this chapter), the Picture Room (see Chapter 1), and the Dome or Plaister Room and its adjacent spaces.

The dome actually is not a true dome but a construction rising three stories made of pendentives changing a square space to a circle at the top, which is covered by a conical skylight. Soane pursued the *lumière mystérieuse* by partially illuminating the space by daylight from above and partly from a hidden lamp behind a cornice fragment.

DOME ROOM, SIR JOHN SOANE RESIDENCE, LINCOLN'S INN FIELDS, LONDON, ENGLAND. SIR JOHN SOANE, 1812.

This part of Soane's house was the respository for most of his plaster casts, architectural fragments, and actual antiquities. The orchestration of the space and the way it is illuminated exaggerates the third dimension. Photograph by John Kurtich.

Entering the dome space on the ground floor level from the eastern part of the house, one traverses a colonnaded space on axis with the Dome Room, the floor and ceiling of which both disappear dramatically. Besides the spaces beyond in the vertical, various spaces are interposed in the horizontal behind columns and the mammoth collection of plaster casts of statues, architectural fragments, urns, and medallions. The spatial intrigue is further enhanced by various degrees of lighting that additionally emphasize the three-dimensional quality of the object-loaded walls and piers. One can always look through to space beyond many individual objects, both horizontally and vertically. In unexpected places, corridorlike subsidiary spaces will soar vertically and disappear horizontally above the viewer's sight. Lighting, again, through hidden skylights and lamps, accents these spatial deviations.

NEUE STAATSGALERIE, STUTTGART, GERMANY

Soane's house is a fascinating example of interposition of space at an intimate residential scale. In large public complexes, this same three-dimensional tool can be magnified to produce similar intriguing spatial sequences. The Neue Staatsgalerie, Stuttgart, Germany, (1984) by James Sterling (1929–) is just such a collage of grand spaces, punctuated with metaphorical references. The museum is organized around a heart space reminiscent of the ancient Colosseum, Rome. The round, three-story open-air volume is defined by stone-patterned walls. The public space is accessed by three distinct approaches: a centrifugal ramp linking two parallel city streets, an axial staircase connecting a gallery terrace, and a sunken temple portal joining the lobby below. By placing the temple in an "excavated" position, Sterling has made a unique interposition of a historic symbol with the ground plane. The temple, surrounded by the great space, becomes a direct metaphor, referencing ancient Rome.

Various openings in the "colosseum" wall frame views of spaces beyond, interposed by frag-

DETAIL OF CIRCULAR COURT WALL,
NEUE STAATSGALARIE, STUTTGART,
GERMANY. JAMES STIRLING, 1984.

*One of the windows in the circular court
wall promises intriguing spatial
experiences beyond its formal
boundaries. Photograph by John
Kurtich.*

CIRCULAR COURT, NEUE
STAATSGALARIE, STUTTGART,
GERMANY. JAMES STIRLING, 1984.

*The bold circular court, referencing
imperial Rome, has unexpected punched
out windows which allow glimpses into
spaces beyond, using the device of
interposition to enhance the three
dimensional experience. Photograph by
John Kurtich.*

ments of unrelated forms. The contrasting geometry of these forms is successfully conveyed as components of the museum complex due to the unity of color and materials. This effective use of spatial interposition encourages the visitor to explore, creates mystery, heightens experience through metaphor, and establishes a dialogue with the various three-dimensional components of this fascinating architectural achievement.

DYNAMIC TENSION THROUGH COMPRESSION AND EXPANSION

The placement of objects, patterns, or forms in opposition or contrast to each other creates a *dynamic tension* within Interior Architecture. Elements with a directional quality placed in contrast to a static enclosure can infuse energy and drama. The implied energy can be manipulated to excite or surprise the perceiver while giving directional cues or emphasis to elements in space. Directional cues can clarify circulation, making navigation through space more comprehensible. Strong emphasis on elements in space can be achieved through contrasting the static with the dynamic. Michelangelo (1475–1564) was a master of the use of dynamic tension.

CAPITOLINE HILL, ROME, ITALY

On the Capitoline Hill, Rome (1538–1546), Michelangelo (1475–1564) planned a trio of buildings to form a piazza intended to be the heart of the city. The space is entered by ascending a monumental set of steep stairs to the summit of a hill overlooking Rome. The perceiver is received in a trapezoidal piazza defined by three palaces symmetrically placed. The main building, Palazzo del Senatore (completed 1600) terminates the axis approach. Palazzo dei Conservatori (1564–1568) and Palazzo Nuovo (1644–1655) flank the axis and

PIAZZA DEL CAMPIDOGLIO,
CAPITOLINE HILL, ROME, ITALY.
MICHELANGELO, 1538 ONWARD.

Raw energy exudes from Michelangelo's ingenious resolution to a difficult coordination of divergent building fragments and leftover space. Photograph by John Kurtich.

frame the main building by widening toward the dominant facade forming a wedge-shaped space. The nonparallel buildings compress the piazza and emphasize the main building.

The wedge-shaped piazza is contrasted by an oval mound with a Roman equestrian statue of Marcus Aurelius at its center. The expansive oval form is further accentuated by a star-shaped radial pattern in granite cobbles and travertine pavers. The juxtaposition of converging buildings surrounding an expanding oval piazza causes a dynamic tension in the space. This subtle tension forms the special character of Michelangelo's composition for the heart of Rome.

LAURENTIAN LIBRARY, FLORENCE

In Florence, at the Laurentian Library (1523–1559) located in the cloister of San Lorenzo, Michelangelo (1475–1564) shows more evidence of his control of dynamic tension to define three-dimensional spaces. The library was originally planned to be three distinct parts: a dramatic vestibule, a tranquil reading room, and a vaultlike rare books room (unexecuted). The three rooms were to contrast sharply in shape and articulation to reinforce their purposes. The vestibule is square in plan, the reading room rectangular, and the rare books room was planned to be triangular.

The tall square vestibule contains a large monumental stair that leads to the reading room. The stair spills from the entrance of the reading room with a robust exaggeration of forms splitting into three stairs at the landing. The stair fills the room, creating a strong directional quality in contrast to the nondirectional square room. Michelangelo accentuated the tension between the enclosure and stair by positioning the entrance to the room at ninety degrees to the directional thrust, thereby avoiding the obvious entry point on axis with the energetic stair design. Further tension is introduced in the room by the treatment of the elaborate walls. Paired columns supported by rather weak volute brackets are recessed between the plaster walls, giving the impression of great compression in contrast to the expansive stair. The overall scheme is unorthodox, forming uneasy spatial relationships that create a space one wants to move through quickly. The purpose of this transition space is to establish a prelude experience of tension and compression in contrast to the restful and sedate reading room.

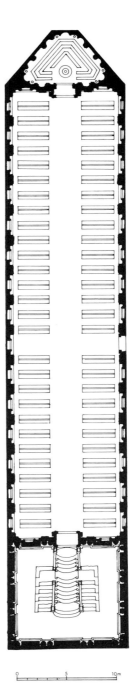

PLAN OF LAURENTIAN LIBRARY, WITH UNBUILT PROJECT FOR RARE-BOOK STUDY, FLORENCE, ITALY. MICHELANGELO, 1523–1559.

This is a hypothetical reconstruction of Michelangelo's original scheme for the library: a square vestibule with dominating stairs, a long, rectilinear, quiet reading room, and a triangular rare books room. Drawing by Garret Eakin.

VESTIBULE AND STAIRWAY, LAURENTIAN LIBRARY, FLORENCE, ITALY. MICHELANGELO, 1524–1533.

The stairs dominate a space which seems too small to contain them. The structural elements on the walls seem to reverse their normal roles—wall panels and niche frames which should be passive crowd and compress the columns and brackets which should be dominant in their structural roles. Alinari/Art Resource, New York.

PERSPECTIVE

TROMPE L'OEIL PAINTING A *perspective* drawing gives the illusion of depth and distance. This pictorial phenomenon provides the viewer with a strong sense of three-dimensional space. Evidence, such as fresco paintings found in the House of the Vetti, Pompeii (first century A.D.), indicates that the ancient world understood the principle of linear perspective. During the Italian Renaissance, perspective held a special fascination for artists because it allowed them to explore the possibilities of portraying three-dimensional space realistically in their art. Two prominent Florentine architects, Filippo Brunelleschi (1377–1446) and Leon Battista Alberti (1404–1472) had a profound impact on the development of linear perspective in the early fifteenth century. Brunelleschi's unique public perspective demonstration, "Peepshows," and Alberti's book, *Della Pitura,*

ARCHITECTURAL FRESCOES, HOUSE OF VETTII, POMPEII, ITALY, A.D. FIRST CENTURY.

A number of architectural vistas have been discovered in wall frescoes from Pompeii which illustrate the Romans' knowledge of linear perspective. Photograph by John Kurtich.

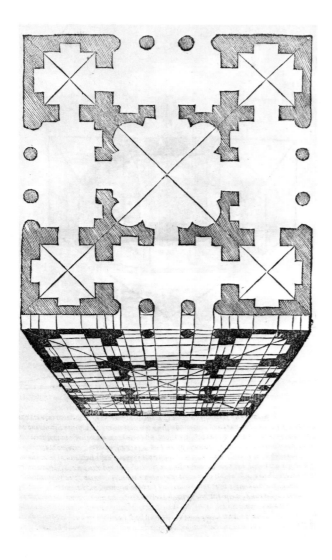

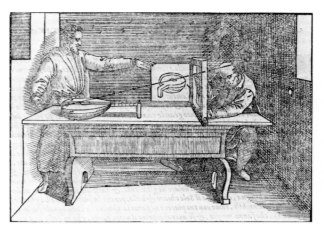

PERSPECTIVE DRAWING BY DANIELLO BARBARO FROM *LA PRATICA DELLA PERSPETTIVA DI MONSIGNOR DANIEL BARBARO*, ITALIAN EDITION, 1568.

Various mechanical devices were invented during the Renaissance and years following to simplify and make more accurate drawings with linear perspective. Courtesy of The Art Institute of Chicago.

PERSPECTIVE DRAWING BY SEBASTIANO SERLIO FROM *LIBRO PRIMO*, ITALIAN EDITION, 1566.

The Italian Renaissance marked the rediscovery of linear perspective, encouraging many books and treatises, such as Serlio's, to expound and explain the wonders of this method of expression. Courtesy of The Art Institute of Chicago.

written in 1435, detailing the principles of perspective, provided rich stimuli that encouraged artists to experiment with this scientific technique. Such exploration sent artists in new directions, with many designers focusing on the creation of illusionary space, not only in painting but also in architecture.

Also as a result of this experimentation, several devices were developed to aid the artist in the quest for pictorial accuracy. The mirror is one of the most basic optical instruments. Flemish artists were known to have used mirrors to illustrate interiors.[4] Another drawing machine used a single pane of glass, taking Alberti's definition of the picture plane as a window literally.[5] A more sophisticated device used a pane of glass with vertical and horizontal lines, forming a grid.[6] The most complicated drawing apparatus was the camera obscura, which became a popular drawing machine by the mid-sixteenth century.[7]

Trompe l'oeil painting reached a high level of sophistication during the Renaissance, where it became a crucial factor in creating successful illusionary space. Taking full advantage of the symbiotic relationship between perspective and trompe l'oeil, artists were able to extend beyond the traditional enclosure of architecture, literally exploding the shell illusionistically. (See Chapter 4 for further discussion of trompe l'oeil as an element of the fourth dimension.)

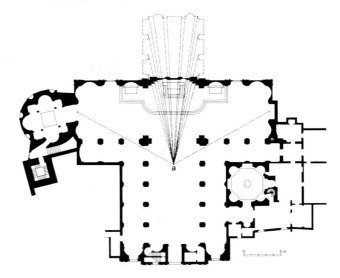

VIEW OF ALTAR AND FALSE CHOIR,
S. MARIA PRESSO S. SATIRO, MILAN,
ITALY. DONATO BRAMANTE, 1482–
1494.

*Bramante employed the Renaissance
painter's new knowledge of the laws of
linear perspective and translated them
into three dimensional architectural
solutions. Photograph by Thomas Lehn.*

PLAN OF S. MARIA PRESSO S. SATIRO,
MILAN, ITALY. DONATO BRAMANTE,
1482–1494.

*The plan shows Bramante's genius in
translating the laws of perspective into
an architectural solution which could
overcome the limitations of the site. The
dotted choir on the plan represents the
illusionistic depth through trompe l'oeil
if the observer stands at point "a."
Drawing by Garret Eakin, after Rilievo
E. Strada, 1884.*

S. MARIA PRESSO S. SATIRO, MILAN, ITALY

The Renaissance architect and painter, Donato
Bramante (1444–1514), was highly influenced by
perspective and its illusionistic qualities. He applied his extensive knowledge of perspective to
the expansion of the church of S. Maria presso S.
Satiro, Milan, Italy (1482–1492). Challenged by a
site condition that would not allow enough space
to accommodate a cruciform plan, Bramante
completed the shape of his structure through illu-

sion. The cruciform plan was changed to a T shape, giving up the choir beyond the altar. The viewer does not detect the plan substitution until very close to the altar, because from a distance the choir is perceived as having useable depth. In fact, the choir is approximately six feet deep. The illusion of the choir is created by steeply raking down the entablature and capitals, rendering the surfaces in three-dimensional trompe l'oeil. By manipulating architectural details and painting technique to achieve illusionary space, Bramante brilliantly turned the church's limitation into a positive architectural feature.

TEATRO OLIMPICO, VICENZA, ITALY

In the Teatro Olimpico, Vicenza, Italy, (1580), by Andre Palladio (1508–1580), accelerated perspective was used to create unexpected three-dimensional effects. The exterior of the building does not offer any clues to its dramatic interior. Palladio patterned his design in the Greco-Roman tradition. The semicircular auditorium encompasses thirteen tiers of seats that have unimpeded views of the stage. Though the proscenium is richly festooned with carved statuary, the audience's attention is immediately directed to the five

ELEVATION OF THE SCENAE FRONS, TEATRO OLIMPICO, VICENZA, ITALY. ANDREA PALLADIO, 1580. DRAWN BY OCTAVE BERTOTTI SCAMOZZI FROM THE ITALIAN (ROSSI) EDITION, 1796.

The elevation reveals the differences between the flat facade and the one-point perspectives of the "streets." Courtesy of The Art Institute of Chicago.

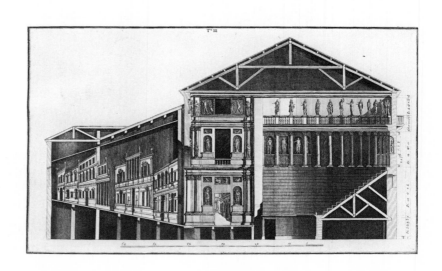

TRANSVERSE SECTION, TEATRO OLIMPICO, VICENZA, ITALY. ANDREA PALLADIO, 1580. DRAWN BY OCTAVE BERTOTTI SCAMOZZI FROM THE ITALIAN (ROSSI) EDITION, 1796.

The transverse section reveals the amount of physical compression necessary to achieve the forced perspective within the given backstage space. Courtesy of The Art Institute of Chicago.

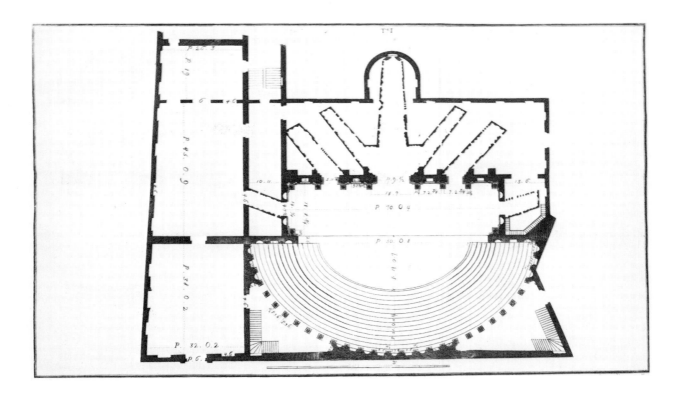

PLAN, TEATRO OLIMPICO, VICENZA,
ITALY. ANDREA PALLADIO, 1580.
DRAWN BY OCTAVE BERTOTTI
SCAMOZZI FROM THE ITALIAN (ROSSI)
EDITION, 1796.

*The plan reveals the "street" angles and
backstage space required to achieve the
desired forced perspective. Courtesy of
The Art Institute of Chicago.*

SCENAE FRONS, TEATRO OLIMPICO,
VICENZA, ITALY. ANDREA PALLADIO,
1580.

*The stage of this theatre is very three
dimensional not only in its perspective
city "streets," but also in its richly
carved facade. Photograph by John
Kurtich.*

openings that lead to the background street perspectives of "The Ideal City." Vincenzo Scamozzi (1552–1616) is usually credited for designing the extraordinary backstage, which creates the illusion of a three-dimensional cityscape. Buildings and streets were constructed of wood and carefully painted in *faux marbre* with stucco decoration adorning the facades to capture a quality of realism. To evoke a strong sense of depth, the streets and facades are raked or inclined, accelerating the perspective view with proportionally diminishing architectural details toward the rear of the stage.

Scamozzi used color and light to further enhance the three-dimensional impact of his permanent set design.

PALAZZO SPADA GARDEN, ROME, ITALY

The garden colonnade in the Palazzo Spada, Rome, Italy, (ca. 1635) by Francesco Borromini (1599–1667), has the magical quality of a stage set. While renovating Cardinal Spada's palace, Borromini managed to transform an ordinary corridor into a passage that appears to be about

GARDEN PERSPECTIVE COLONNADE, PALAZZO SPADA, ROME, ITALY. FRANCESCO BORROMINI, 1635.

A woman stands at the entry to Borromini's garden colonnade, showing her height as compared to the much higher barrel vault above. Photograph by John Kurtich.

GARDEN PERSPECTIVE COLONNADE, PALAZZO SPADA, ROME, ITALY. FRANCESCO BORROMINI, 1635.

The same woman stands at the rear of the garden colonnade. Now she is much taller and bigger when compared to the enclosing barrel vault. Photograph by John Kurtich.

four times longer than it is. Using accelerated perspective, he developed false cues by continually reducing the scale of his architectural elements as they retreat from the entry in concert with the raking floor and diminishing width. Though visually exciting, this kind of three-dimensional enhancement has its limitations; it requires that one view the corridor from a particular fixed position in order to align the distorted architectural elements to appear normal.

UNITED AIRLINES TERMINAL, O'HARE AIRPORT, CHICAGO, ILLINOIS

At the United Airlines Terminal, O'Hare International Airport, Chicago, Illinois, (1987), Helmut Jahn (1940–) was challenged with connecting two major aboveground flight concourses. To allow for the maximum passenger gateways, an underground corridor was the obvious solution. At its narrowest, the tunnel be-

CONCOURSE TUNNEL, UNITED AIRLINES TERMINAL, O'HARE INTERNATIONAL AIRPORT, CHICAGO, ILLINOIS. HELMUT JAHN, 1983–1988. NEON SCULPTURE BY MICHAEL HAYDEN.

The combination of kinesthetic movement with exaggerated neon perspective was felt necessary to relieve an otherwise boring trip through a long tunnel from one concourse to another. Photograph by John Kurtich.

tween concourses B and C is 52 feet wide, and its length, including escalators, is 860 feet. By using backlit, multicolored, serpentine walls, the designer effectively altered the user's spatial perception. The undulating walls along the perimeter foreshorten the corridor's perspective, making the space appear shorter than it actually is.

At the mirrored ceiling, the kinetic neon sculpture by Michael Hayden (1943–   ) adds to the illusion by radiating colors up and down the tunnel. The color mix, using warm and cool color combinations, also contributes to the depth distortion. The horizontal people movers accelerate the shortened effect. The only way to accurately gauge the depth of the passage is to walk through it. The combined effect of the curved walls, the energized ceiling, and the people movers creates a mechanized trompe l'oeil—a three-dimensional trompe l'oeil for the twenty-first century.

AEDICULAR DEVELOPMENT

TEMPLE OF BACCHUS, BAALBEK, LEBANON

Aedicular development creates very strong three-dimensional space. *Aedicula* is the Latin word for a little building. In the classical era, such a little

building was used for symbolic and ceremonial functions.

It was applied to a shrine placed at the far end, from the entrance, of a temple to receive the statue of a deity—a sort of architectural canopy in the form of a rudimentary temple, complete with gable—or, to use the classical word, pediment. It was also used for the shrines—again miniature temples—in which the lares of titular deities of a house or street were preserved.[8]

An example of a little temple within a large temple is the so-called Temple of Bacchus, Baalbek, Lebanon. This richly decorated Roman temple (second century A.D.) had at the altar end of its interior a broad staircase leading up to a smaller temple structure that housed the statue of the deity. The little temple was an elaborate canopy supported by engaged columns that alternated with shrine-niches for additional statues. From the preserved ruins, one can appreciate the powerful three-dimensional effect this interior complex commanded.

MOORE HOUSE, ORINDA, CALIFORNIA

Charles Moore (1925–   ) used the aedicula as the spatial organizer of his own house in Orinda, California (1962). This 720-square foot single room

WEST END OF INTERIOR OF THE TEMPLE OF BACCHUS, BAALBEK, LEBANON, A.D. SECOND CENTURY.

A smaller temple, as the holy of holies, used to exist on the platform defined by the wide staircase. Photograph by John Kurtich.

structure, reminiscent of both a barn and a Japanese pavilion on the exterior, contains two square, unequally-sized, templelike structures that define two specific places within the larger interior. The spatial integrity of each of these interior pavilions comes from their similar structural pattern of four round wooden columns supporting a roof canopy that ultimately connects and supports the overall roof structure of the entire house. Each canopy lets in filtered natural light from above. The larger pavilion houses a living/sitting area while the smaller contains a sunken tub with a large, freestanding shower head. These two aediculae successfully create a three-dimensional organization, with strong development in all three directions (length, width, and height) in the bathtub pavilion, where the floor surface drops down as a depressed vessel and the overhead within the canopy is bright with natural light from above.

MOORE HOUSE, NEW HAVEN, CONNECTICUT

When Moore became the chairman of the Department of Architecture at Yale University (1965), he renovated a small nineteenth century frame house in New Haven, Connecticut, (1966) for himself by totally transforming its interior with three vertical tubes or interior towers. These towers became an abstracted refinement of his aedicular approach to the organization of interior space. The first tower, called "Howard,"[9] connected the first floor near the main entrance with Moore's studio and office below in the basement. Its interior surface was metallic gold and could be viewed through huge circular cutouts. The second tower, "Berengaria,"[10] was silver on its interior and rose from the living room floor to the top of the house. A stair wrapping around its exterior perimeter allowed one to peer into some of

Shower aedicula, Charles Moore House, Orinda, California. Charles Moore, 1962.

Instead of separate rooms, Moore designed his house as a series of open aediculae. Photograph by Morley Baer.

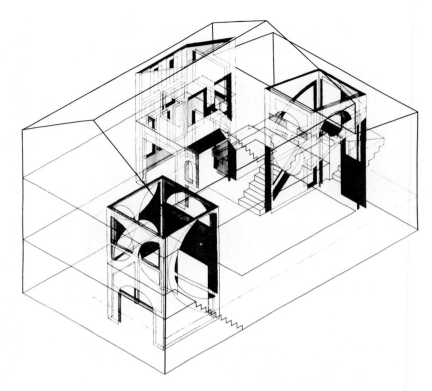

ISOMETRIC DIAGRAM, CHARLES
MOORE HOUSE, NEW HAVEN,
CONNECTICUT. CHARLES MOORE,
1966.

*Moore's development of interior space
became more three dimensional as he
extended the aedicula concept to include
more than one floor at a time. Drawing
by William Turnbull, Jr., FAIA.*

"BERENGARIA," CHARLES MOORE
HOUSE, NEW HAVEN, CONNECTICUT.
CHARLES MOORE, 1966.

*This aedicular tower was the tallest and
most formal of Moore's spatial
organization as it represented the most
complete opportunity for vertical
circulation and overview of the interior.
Photograph by John Kurtich.*

MAMA MIA! PASTA, CHICAGO,
ILLINOIS. BANKS/EAKIN, 1984.

*The ceiling became an opportunity to
exploit the location of this restaurant and
put it more in context with its
surroundings. Photograph by Orlando
Cabanban.*

its fifteen openings (some glazed, some open, and
one infilled with leaded stained glass). It was
topped with a skylight. The final tower,
"Ethel,"[11] started in the basement where a kitchen
and breakfast area were placed, and rose up along-
side the rear of the house, which was generously
glazed for views into the garden and was topped
with a small skylight. These three vertical tubes
were not only spaces within the larger space of
the overall house, but spatial connectors, vertically to floors above and below, and horizontally
to rooms in all directions on each floor.

VERTICAL DEVELOPMENT OF HORIZONTAL PLANES

MAMA MIA! PASTA, CHICAGO, ILLINOIS

The ceiling is often forgotten as a three-dimensional design element. The complexity of contemporary technologies tends to restrict freedom
of manipulation of this most important spatial
plane. Functional requirements such as sprinkler
systems, air distribution, smoke detectors, speak-

ers, exit signs, acoustical needs, accessibility, and lighting all contribute to the difficulty of creatively designing three-dimensional ceilings. Ceiling height dictates the relative degree of relief that a designer may exploit. Interest or subtle relief can be achieved through surface patterns, color variations, applied textures, or multiple ceiling layers that become activated by light. More three dimensionality can be achieved where ceiling heights permit. Vaulting, ribbing, and coffering are traditional ways of expressing the ceiling structure. This technique creates scale and rhythm. Nonstructural rhythmic expression can achieve the same effects. For example, the ceiling of Mama Mia! Pasta, Chicago (Banks/Eakin, architects, 1984), undulates to relieve and articulate the long, low dining room. The ceiling design echoes the adjacent Chicago River as a three-dimensional metaphor. Organizing and confining the mechanical, electrical, and plumbing systems on the perimeter of the ceiling allowed a pure surface without access panels, sprinkler heads, or diffusers.

GRAND HOTEL, WASHINGTON, D.C.

In the Grand Hotel, Washington, D.C. (1987), Charles Pfister (1939–1990) had the opportunity to ensure a lofty ceiling height. Pfister needed such height to satisfy the client's desire to model the design after the Plaza Athénée in Paris. The client realized that he could not duplicate the Beaux Arts architecture but wanted to capture the same sense of grandness and elegance. Pfister designed an impressive, round, colonnaded lobby, rich with fine materials and graceful details. The most striking feature is the ceiling. The multiple tiered rings of plaster rise to form a dome crowned by a gold leaf oculus. The oculus is emphasized by integrating lighting within its coffer. The rings create a highly sophisticated three-dimensional effect when various lights cast shadows across their edges. The classical translation becomes a stylized and impressive volume.

The lobby is connected on axis via a marble staircase to a long promenade defined by paired mahogany columns and a vaulted cove lit ceiling.

ALLÉE, GRAND HOTEL, WASHINGTON, D.C. CHARLES PFISTER, 1987.

The allée ties together the circular entrance lobby with the courtyard, punctuating the axis with added depth by utilizing paired columns to define the promenade. Photograph by John Kurtich.

LOBBY, GRAND HOTEL,
WASHINGTON, D.C. CHARLES
PFISTER, 1987.

*The mirroring of the ceiling design to
the floor is a conceptual continuation of
Robert Adam interiors. Photograph by
John Kurtich.*

Adjacent to the allée[12] is the oval-shaped Garden Room restaurant. This room is also topped by a stepped rotunda. In this case, the steps are wrapped generously with gathered fabric, which softens the space, producing a senuous effect. By changing ceiling heights and their finish treatment, Pfister has been able to transform his hotel into an exhilarating three-dimensional space.

TRADING ROOM, STOCK EXCHANGE, CHICAGO, ILLINOIS

The Trading Room of the Chicago Stock Exchange, Chicago, Illinois (1893, reconstructed in the Art Institute in 1976) by Adler and Sullivan, is another powerful example of three-dimensional development. In fact, the designers made the ceil-

ing the most dominant focal point of the space. The walls of the enclosure are comprised of either doors, windows, or chalk boards encased by mahogany wainscoting. While the lower portion of the room has a very businesslike atmosphere, the upper third of the walls and ceilings are riotous with light. color, and pattern. The simple rectangular shape of the space and its ceiling is relieved by the unique ceiling treatment. The ceiling is a highly elegant composition of alternating coffers and beams supported by four gigantic columns. Art glass panels illuminate the perimeter of the ceiling. All the solid surfaces are embellished with intricately stenciled patterns. The delicacy of the patterns and the warmth of the colors are also carried into the design of the art glass as well as the ventilating grilles. By applying this vibrant

TRADING ROOM, CHICAGO STOCK
EXCHANGE, CHICAGO, ILLINOIS.
ADLER AND SULLIVAN, 1894.
RECONSTRUCTED AT THE ART
INSTITUTE OF CHICAGO, 1977.

*The perimeter skylight separates the
central ceiling from the traditional walls,
making a subtle central space defined
individually from the larger overall
shell. Photograph by John Kurtich.*

surface treatment to the entire ceiling, a strong and cohesive three-dimensional effect was achieved within the simplest of architectural frameworks. Sullivan's inspired approach to this project transported a place of day-to-day business into the realm of art.

STATE OF ILLINOIS CENTER, CHICAGO, ILLINOIS

The floor is probably the most neglected surface for interior three-dimensional development. Since the floor is usually the main means of circulation, it is impractical to create a sculptural composition full of three-dimensional obstacles. However, this does not mean that the floor should be ignored as a spatial opportunity. Helmut Jahn (1940–) did not exclude the floor in his vertical expansion of interior space of the State of Illinois Center, Chicago, Illinois, (1979). The floor at the street level is actually a large mezzanine, with a centralized sublevel restaurant and shop area. A gigantic cutout is centrally located, revealing a spiralling geometric design reminiscent of the floors of the enigmatic tholoi of ancient Greece, such as those found in Epidaurus or Delphi.

Seen from the top of the building, the pattern of the floor is projected on both levels. Smaller cutouts accent the edges, accommodating vertical circulation via escalators and elevators. Jahn em-

ploys a cascading waterfall between the entry escalators to dramatize the descent to the lower level. The various cutouts allow visitors to survey two floor levels simultaneously as they move through the interior, enriching the three-dimensional experience.

GUGGENHEIM MUSEUM, NEW YORK, NEW YORK

A continuous three-dimensional floor can occur with the use of the ramp and the stair. The corkscrew ramp of the Solomon R. Guggenheim Museum, New York, New York (1956–1960), designed by Frank Lloyd Wright (1867–1959), is the ultimate spatial statement of ramp-becoming-floor. No longer is the ramp merely the means to move from one level to another but is the determiner of any given level for the entire display area of the museum.

Wright had several reasons to justify the great spiral space. First, visitors were meant to take an elevator to the top of the museum and slowly work their way down the continuous ramp, looking at the art with a minimum of fatigue. Second, the solid walls of the ramp which formed the exterior shell of the building, would slant outward, creating what Wright argued was similar to the surface of a continuous painting easel, providing a more accurate presentation of paintings. Finally, Wright rationalized his non-

VIEW FROM THE SIXTEENTH LEVEL,
LOOKING DOWN, THE STATE OF
ILLINOIS CENTER, CHICAGO, ILLINOIS.
HELMUT JAHN, 1980.

*Jahn's use of a spiralling floor pattern at
the subterranean level visually extends
the vertical space. Photograph by John
Kurtich.*

VIEW FROM THE TOP RAMP, LOOKING
DOWN, SOLOMON R. GUGGENHEIM
MUSEUM, NEW YORK, NEW YORK.
FRANK LLOYD WRIGHT, 1956.

*The spiraling ramp generates human
movement, establishing a kinetic
counterpoint to the fixed inanimate art.
Photograph by John Kurtich.*

rectilinear spatial design by taking a "cue from founder Guggenheim's notion that the rectilinear frame of reference in a painting had more to do with the frame than with the painting . . . The result, as Wright promised, is 'a great repose, like the atmosphere of an unbroken wave.' "[13]

No photograph can substitute for the experience one has of walking the grand ramp. Wright capitalized on the force of gravity to help propel the visitor through his museum, adding unexpected kinesthetic excitement. Standard paintings take on a secondary importance when displayed in this giant helix, for they have to compete with the ever-changing views of the central space and the exciting way people themselves are displayed. The three-dimensional result of this spiral incline has created one of the most dynamic plastic interiors of the twentieth century with its uncompromising vertical continuity.

EXPLOITATION OF SCALE

A conscious understanding and the deliberate *exploitation of scale* is one of the most important elements to define three-dimensional interior architecture. Scale is the relationship of elements or parts to their combined whole, to one another, and to the human body. Altering the size and its proportion can drastically affect the scale and therefore deliver a message to the perceiver about what a person's relationship is to the defined space. During the Gothic period, the cathedrals' soaring interiors were intended to intimidate their human users by reducing mortal importance in comparison to the omnipotent church. Historically, most public architecture has employed grand scale to create a sense of drama while emphasizing the period's significant political or social ideologies.

Scale can also be thought of in terms of experience: primary, secondary, and tertiary. Primary scale is perceived upon the initial entry into a room or space. It is the larger space-defining elements that one comprehends. These architectural elements generally set the stage for secondary scaling features, such as wall and ceiling fenestration, which further break the scale into smaller components. The tertiary elements, such as texture, pattern, and decorative embellishments enriches the reading of the space at the intimate scale.

TRADING ROOM, STOCK EXCHANGE, CHICAGO, ILLINOIS

A clear example of these three levels of scale working simultaneously to create a strong three-dimensional space is the Trading Room of the Chicago Stock Exchange, Chicago, Illinois (1893), by Adler and Sullivan. The primary scale here is created by four gigantic columns supporting massive ceiling beams. The secondary scaling is achieved through the articulation of the four walls by a series of windows, doors, and paneled walls. Finely detailed rhythmically stenciled ceiling patterns constitute the tertiary scale, which extends the observer's interest in the space while balancing the larger scalar elements. This three-level scale principle can be found in all successful three-dimensional spaces.

MUSEUM TOWER APARTMENT, NEW YORK, NEW YORK

Steven Holl (1947–   ), architect, is interested in developing a rich dialogue of three-dimensional expression. Not only does he employ the principle of three-level scale in his work, but he infuses his designs with a mixture of ideas often generated by literature, site conditions, and construction technology, as well as craftsmanship. Through observation and study of site conditions and how they affect scale, certain opportunities or situations arise that can lead to unique three-dimensional concepts. In the Museum of Modern Art Tower Apartment, New York, New York, (1987), Holl observed an optical illusion that was created by the fact that the tower was built on the lot line. To Holl, the apartment seemed to be cantilevered over the grid of the city. This observation led to the choice of the Cartesian coordinate system as his theme in his manipulation of urban scale. When designing three dimensionally, Holl establishes his basic concepts and employs the

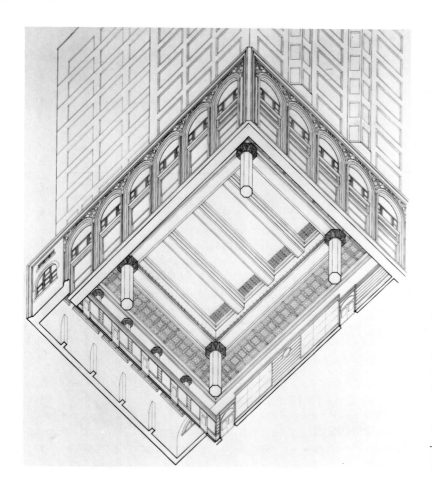

AXONOMETRIC DRAWING OF
RECONSTRUCTION OF THE TRADING
ROOM, CHICAGO STOCK EXCHANGE,
CHICAGO, ILLINOIS. ADLER AND
SULLIVAN, 1894. RECONSTRUCTED BY
JOHN VINCI AT THE ART INSTITUTE
OF CHICAGO, 1977.

*The plan oblique view of the ceiling
illustrates Sullivan's finesse in
manipulating scaling elements from the
large and robust columns down to the
delicate and intimate ceiling patterning.
Drawing by Lawrence C. Kenny, ink
and pencil on Mylar, 1977. Gift of
John Vinci and Lawrence C. Kenny,
1982.754. © 1990 The Art Institute of
Chicago, All Rights Reserved.*

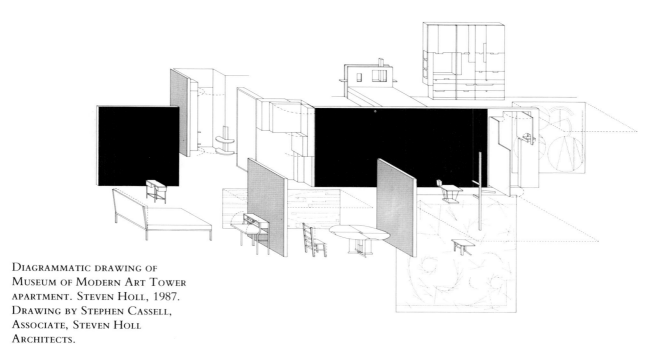

DIAGRAMMATIC DRAWING OF
MUSEUM OF MODERN ART TOWER
APARTMENT. STEVEN HOLL, 1987.
DRAWING BY STEPHEN CASSELL,
ASSOCIATE, STEVEN HOLL
ARCHITECTS.

*The juxtaposition of large planes
representing urban scale to small,
delicate furniture responding to human
scale results in a taut environment.
Drawing by Steven Holl.*

"golden section" to lend rigor and substance to all his visual proportions.[14]

The plan of the apartment is organized by a series of coded planes. The planes are perpendicular to each other with charcoal gray walls representing midtown avenues running north-south while butter yellow walls imply east-west streets. These large-scale planes contrast sharply with his delicately scaled furniture. Shakerlike ladderback chairs stained black surround an oval table, which continues the thematic content at a secondary scale. The light wood top is divided into four quadrants by a black pinwheel pattern which expresses the supporting member's composition while providing the tertiary scale. The cabinetry and vertical furniture elements are used as a counterpoint to the space-defining elements while alluding to the skyline of Manhattan. Holl's articulation of cabinetry further scales the space while transforming their function into visual pleasure. The unconventional cabinets look as good open as they do closed because the shapes are so three dimensional, creating a sense of excitement in their use. Establishing a rigorous design methodology, softened by intuitive interpretations, Holl has created a very powerful but intimately scaled space.

NOTRE DAME DU HAUT, RONCHAMP, FRANCE

Another example of using levels of scale to produce dramatic juxtaposition between monumentality and intimacy is the Chapel of Notre Dame du Haut, Ronchamp, France (1951–1953), by Le Corbusier (1887–1965). This hilltop chapel initially demonstrated how massive scale and heavy materials can be formed to define visually exciting three-dimensional space. The south wall is made of recycled stone from the preexisting church and encased in concrete. It tapers from 3.7 meters at the base to 1.4–1.5 meters at the top of the wall. Acting as a visual point of terminus to the pilgrimage route, the south wall is concave to control the entrance sequence. The wall becomes a symbolic barrier—a mass to be penetrated to access the sacred interior. The scale of the battered

wall metaphorically recalls castellated walls of the medieval period, complete with splayed openings, symbols of strength and permanence. The weight of the material expressed by the thickness of the walls was contrasted by the unorthodox insertion of *vitrages*.[15] From the outside, these small scaled openings provide contrast to the massive tapered wall, distorting the apparent size of the wall. The walls are huge and somber whereas the glass is delicate and colorful. Le Corbusier's chapel successfully contrasts monumental space balanced by intimately scaled details.

THE OFFICE LANDSCAPE   Intimate scale is driven by the human body and ergonomic or physiological requirements and can relate directly to both the work and home environments. A current example by Knoll International is the ergonomically derived office landscape. This system is designed to increase an individual's productivity while encouraging communication among employees by providing compact and efficient work environments scaled to the user's needs. Living spaces can be scaled to create a strong sense of intimacy. The most inviting and successful living spaces are scaled to encourage conversation and comfort. The best way to learn about scale is through observation and personal experience. If elements appear to be at the correct scale, they also appear to be in proportion, which is the harmonious relationship between the parts to the whole. Throughout history, humanity has been interested in achieving pleasing proportional relationships in both interior and exterior architecture.

KNOLL INTERNATIONAL OFFICE FURNITURE GROUP, "REFF SYSTEM 6," KNOLL INTERNATIONAL, NEW YORK, NEW YORK, 1991.

Efficient and conducive work environments are responsive to ergonomic needs that are based on the human body. Photograph by John Kurtich.

INTERIOR SOUTH WALL, CHAPEL OF
NOTRE-DAME-DU-HAUT,
RONCHAMP, FRANCE. LE CORBUSIER,
1954.

*Le Corbusier enhanced the chapel's
ethereal quality by "floating" the
massive ceiling on steel piers above the
sanctuary. Photograph by John Kurtich.*

Animation Through Furnishings

The purpose of space is usually defined by the furnishings. The animation of such space can be achieved either through the harmonious or the contrasting placement of the furnishings in relation to the enclosure. Creating a dialogue between the structural shell and the contents is a major goal of the interior architect. Establishing a direction for that exchange to occur, whether it be traditionally defined rooms with symmetrical organization or contemporary fluid space with asymmetrical arrangements, is critical to the cohesion of the interior.

Furnishings create the personality of the space by setting the tone. Such moods as mysterious, playful, architectural, eclectic, historical, minimal, comfortable, or formal are established by the furniture's expressive quality. The designer must consider all furnishings at the onset of the planning stages to ensure a strong three-dimensional design. Internal forces generated by the client's needs must be expressed in harmony with external forces that are predicated by spatial conditions.

White Bedroom, Hill House, Helensburgh, Scotland

Charles Rennie Mackintosh (1868–1928) (see Chapter 1 for a discussion of Mackintosh's ability to design complete interiors) was interested in designing his interiors as a complete environment with all furniture and minor elements relating to this vision. This cohesive, holistic design approach allowed total control over the three-dimensional development of the space. His wife, Margaret MacDonald Mackintosh (1865–1933), collaborated with him on his best interiors. One of the most successful designs was the White Bedroom of Hill House, Helensburgh, Scotland (1902–1903). The modestly sized bedroom was planned to function dually as a bedroom and morning room. To distinguish the sleeping area's separate identity from the sitting room, the bed was placed in one part of the L-shaped plan. The bed alcove was spatially enhanced by a vaulted ceiling and a matching curved bay window with curved shutters. Mackintosh's original idea for a curtained glass and wooden screen between the sleeping and sitting area never materialized. The sitting room portion had additional windows with curtains designed and embroidered by his wife.

Mr. Blackie, the client, placed his designers on a very restricted furnishings budget. Responding creatively to both this constraint and to the architect's own design aesthetic, built-in furniture was used as often as possible. Mackintosh designed all the furniture, including such pieces as the wardrobes and full length freestanding mirror, bed, and chairs. Most of the room's freestanding and all of its fitted furniture was painted white to match the walls, giving the bedroom a bright and spacious quality. The delineation of much of the room's furniture, whether massive or delicate, has a strong verticality, making the interior appear much grander, three dimensionally. Even the applied decorative motifs found in paint stenciling, fabric design, lighting fixtures, and furniture detailing reinforce the design direction. By introducing two high-backed "ladder" chairs, painted black, Mackintosh introduced visual geometric punctuation to the interior, completing the powerful three-dimensional composition.

White Bedroom, Hill House, Helensburgh, Scotland. Charles Rennie Mackintosh and Margaret MacDonald Mackintosh, 1902–1903.

Placement of both built-in and moveable furniture at the perimeter walls gives the day room a spacious atmosphere. Photograph by May Hawfield.

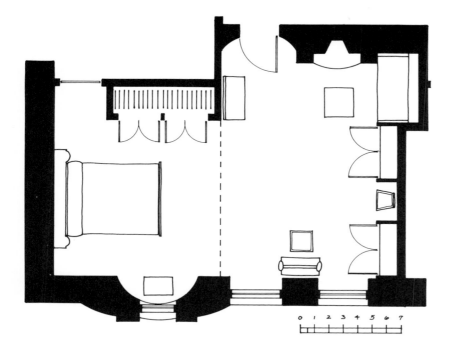

PLAN, WHITE BEDROOM, HILL
HOUSE, HELENSBURGH, SCOTLAND.
CHARLES RENNIE MACKINTOSH AND
MARGARET MACDONALD
MACKINTOSH, 1902–1903.

*The "L" shaped master bedroom plan
comprises two distinct spaces: a large
sitting and dressing area opening onto an
intimate sleeping alcove. Drawing by
May Hawfield.*

COHEN APARTMENT, NEW YORK, NEW YORK

The design approach of Steven Holl (1947–   ) for the Cohen Apartment, New York, New York, (1984), was based on the exploitation of skeletal, planar, and volumetric elements to define the three primary living areas. He relied heavily on furnishings to create the three-dimensional energy of the space. The furniture expands the elemental language by exercising the contents of color, texture, light, and shadow. By incorporating only custom design furnishings, Holl was able to reiterate the conceptual ideas at an intimate scale. The apartment is a collage of parts, to be viewed either as a whole entity or as smaller vignettes created by the furniture and carpet design. Though separate and unique, these parts have a cohesiveness

DINING ROOM, COHEN APARTMENT, NEW YORK, NEW YORK. STEVEN HOLL, 1984.

The furnishings in the dining space reinforce the linear language Holl was exploring in the architecture. Photograph by John Kurtich.

because of the uniformity of color and finish employed on all surfaces. Walls are grey-blue over white plaster, and the furnishings are a contrasting foil, utilizing such colors as red, black, and yellow. In the dining area, the red ladderback chairs are in concert with the skeletal table base and energetic design of the yellow, black, and gray custom carpet.

To arrive at the designer's very personalized three-dimensional composition, traditional furniture detailing was rejected. Such items as cabinet pulls became abstracted to the point of being simply a series of rectilinear cutouts that expose black interiors beyond. Varying in size from tiny squares to long thin openings, the highly inventive pulls are placed in unorthodox locations. The apartment and its furnishings capitalize on the unexpected. Delivering a powerful message, the interior celebrates the unconventional, demanding the viewer to participate in the three-dimensional quality of the design.

REACTION TO CONTEXT

The architectural enclosure is the most immediate contextual influence. Whether the building is historic or contemporary, low- or high-rise, brick or glass, or any distinctive architectural style, responding to the structure's unique characteristics can be a major theme in any design scheme. The form, language, materials, or details can be used as a point of departure for generating ideas through *reaction to context*.

In some instances, the architectural character, history, or activities of the district can be a rich source to draw upon, lending validity to design ideas. Light and views, or the lack of, can be exploited to form relationships to these ever-changing external elements. Furthermore, the client's personality, taste, or idiosyncratic ideas can provide another rich source for creativity.

Strong three-dimensional concepts can evolve by analyzing the context of a specific interior project. Taking a broader view can stimulate ideas beyond the immediate enclosure as well as the obvious design solution. Careful considera-

tion of the architectural enclosure, district, character, adjacent views, quality of light, or the client's personality as a whole or singularly should be incorporated in the final design direction. Contextual exploration can elevate a design aesthetically, freeing the designer from the mundane solutions often generated by a client's functional requirements.

VILLA MAIREA, NOORMARKKU, FINLAND

In the Villa Mairea, Noormarkku, Finland, (1937), by Alvar Aalto (1898–1976), reaction to context was a strong design influence. The building was sited within a spectacular natural forest. The L-shaped residence with adjacent swimming pool and sauna was carefully nestled into a clearing. Instead of ignoring the surrounding landscape, Aalto used the forest as the metaphorical theme for his architectural forms and interiors.

A progression starting from the forest clearing through the porte cochère and into the house reveals Aalto's interest in contextualism. The porte cochère contrasts boldly with the planar geometry of the exterior facade, revealing a clue to the dynamic interior beyond. The organic form of the structure extends the entrance, creating an inviting portal, one side screened by curvaceous saplings contrasted by an open side supported by two columns of clustered tree trunks. This original design, employing natural trees, establishes an exciting transition from the natural forest to the human-designed interior. The ceiling is rendered in natural rough wooden decking.

Upon entering the house's warm interior, the forest metaphor is refined. Wood continues on the ceiling, but becomes smooth. A forest rhythm is created by Aalto's sensitive placement of structural columns and decorative elements. Adding further to the forest illusion, interior plantings in strategic locations continue to soften the hard edges of the metaphoric interior "trees" while reinforcing the organic theme. By incorporating one of his most impressive three-dimensional design elements, the screen, Aalto transformed the stair balustrade from the merely functional to an

FOREST SURROUNDING VILLA MAIREA, NOORMARKKU, FINLAND. ALVAR AALTO, 1938.

Aalto often translated contextual conditions into a metaphorical language that enriched his architecture language. A forest could become wall screens filtering light, or a tree could become a column supporting a roof. Photograph by Kevin Harrington.

PORTE-COCHÈRE, VILLA MAIREA, NOORMARKKU, FINLAND. ALVAR AALTO, 1938.

By using natural trees as an integral part of the porte-cochère design, Aalto has made the transition from nature into human made space less abrupt. Photograph by Kevin Harrington.

STAIRWAY SCREEN, VILLA MAIREA, NOORMARKKU, FINLAND. ALVAR AALTO, 1938.

Aalto's staircase is transformed into an interior forest, with the balustrade "trees" shifting and filtering light. Photograph by Kevin Harrington.

inspired interior forest. The wooden vertical elements are irregularly placed, filtering the light in the same way one experiences the contrasts of light and shadow while walking through the woods. By cladding the living room ceiling in strips of pine, which conceal the air-conditioning vents, the edges between the indoors and outdoors are further blurred.

To provide privacy without totally compromising the visual connectedness of the living room and study, Aalto used another ingenious screening device. Much smaller in scale and located at the ceiling above solid straight walls, a serpentine screen provides an exciting three-dimensional juncture between the spaces. The curving screen is composed of clerestory windows and wooden slats in an alternating composition, allowing vertical slices of light to illuminate the adjacent rooms. Depending on the time of day, a high contrast quality of light occurs, resulting in beams of light radiating across the wooden ceiling, a lighting effect highly reminiscent of the early morning or late afternoon sun in the forest.

The Villa Mairea is one of Aalto's finest works. Much of its success is due to Aalto's imaginative use of contextualism. A rich design language freed Aalto from rigid formalistic architectural vocabulary, resulting in a highly three-dimensional interior.

DRIEHAUS RESEARCH ASSOCIATES, CHICAGO, ILLINOIS

The design for Driehaus Research Associates by the Landahl Group, Chicago, Illinois, (1982), takes its cue from the saw-toothed high rise in which it resides. Three First National Plaza by Skidmore, Owings & Merrill is shaped by an orthogonal series of bay windows that exploit the views to Lake Michigan. The architectural character of the building is mimicked in various ways in the eighteen-hundred-square-foot brokerage firm. Custom wood desks, corner top detailing on desks and conference table, brass strips in terrazzo flooring, stepped detail of portals, and the bases of bronze computer covers demonstrate the zigzag motif at varying scales. Using the building

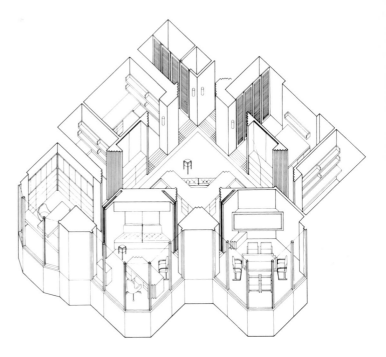

AXONOMETRIC DRAWING, DRIEHAUS RESEARCH ASSOCIATES OFFICE COMPLEX, THREE FIRST NATIONAL PLAZA BUILDING, CHICAGO, ILLINOIS. THE LANDAHL GROUP, INC., 1982.

The contextual zig-zag detailing at differing scales throughout the office complex gives the interior a cohesive design language. Drawing by Jamie Snavley.

module of 5'0" as another point of departure, Greg Landahl (1947–) divided that number in half (60", 30", 15", 7½", 3¾" . . .) arriving at different scaling multiples that generated both the vertical and horizontal interior dimensions. An example of this are the highly three-dimensional office entrances, using stepped portals derived from the 3¾" scaling multiple.

Luxurious materials were incorporated to achieve an elegant and inviting interior while softening the strong geometric design language. By

EAST FACADE OF THE THREE FIRST
NATIONAL PLAZA BUILDING,
CHICAGO, ILLINOIS. SKIDMORE,
OWINGS, AND MERRILL, 1981.

Photograph by John Kurtich.

DETAIL OF DOOR FRAME AND
TERRAZZO FLOOR, DRIEHAUS
RESEARCH ASSOCIATES, THREE FIRST
NATIONAL PLAZA BUILDING,
CHICAGO, ILLINOIS. THE LANDAHL
GROUP, INC., 1982.

Photograph by Jim Norris.

*In a direct response to the building shape
of Three First National Plaza, the
Landahl Group incorporated a saw-tooth
or zig-zag motif as a prominent
contextual design detail.*

using a rich mixture of redwood burl veneers, dark green leather, lush wool carpet, velvets, and silks, the designer was able to further convey the client's successful image to the business community. The predominant color palette of green, the client's favorite, ranging from light to dark shades, was inspired by the coloration of a dollar bill. Even the bronze and brass metals recall precious gold bullion. Other neutral colors serve as an appropriate backdrop for the client's art collection.

The Landahl Group drew upon contextualism as a rich source, giving both direction and validity to the design work. Carefully avoiding the sense of being heavy handed in relating to context, they were able to create a dynamic design with the enduring quality found in all great interiors.

MALLET HOUSE, NEW YORK, NEW YORK

SITE's project, the Mallet House, New York, New York, (1986), is a compelling study of a reaction to context.[16] By employing images that have been fabricated as historic artifacts, the designers have been able to create a mystical experience. The 160-year-old Greenwich Village row house was originally owned by a French immigrant. The designers imagined the long hidden history that the house must have contained previous to the current owner. Laurie Mallet was drawn to the house because of its age and apparent charm. Instead of gutting the decaying interior, the thought was to accentuate the inherent patina and sense of the past. The preservation of the past was achieved by careful manipulation of the functional elements while retaining original materials and details. The designers were very successful in combining new elements with the existing, blurring the distinction between the past and the present. SITE's Alison Sky (1946–) felt strongly that the current accepted practice of gutting and rebuilding was not appropriate for this project. A more selective and sensitive approach was needed to successfully insert the new owner's requirements without losing the intimacy of the past. All too often the charm of history is destroyed by the desire to be efficient and modern.

Elements of a fabricated history that may or may not have occurred were inserted into a preserved shell. These elements were derived from the designers' imagination based on the knowledge of the past occupants, combined with the personal interests of the client. Architectural elements and furniture symbolizing the past emerge in three dimensions skewed from the plane of the plaster walls. These elements are rendered as a plastic projection of the past, caught midstream in a time warp. It is as though the objects are frozen in the middle of a cinematic dissolve. In the foyer an eighteenth century rococo table projects askew from the wall with a riding hat, gloves, and whip as a sculptural composition. This is part of a larger vignette that includes an ornately framed mirror, a heavy coat, and a pair of high-top riding boots, complete with spurs, all integral to and projected from the wall in monochrome. This scene depicts

FRONT FACADE, LAURIE MALLET HOUSE, NEW YORK, NEW YORK. SITE, 1985.

The row house facade does not give any clue to the rich contextualism SITE explores within the interior. Photograph by John Kurtich.

the new owner's interest in the hunt, adding another layer of history.

The owner's history merges with a fabricated past based on the original occupant. In the living room, a Louis XV chair edges out of the wall,

ENTRANCE HALL, LAURIE MALLET
HOUSE, NEW YORK, NEW YORK.
SITE, 1985.

*The entry hall introduces the visitor to
evocative images from the past in ghosted
array. Photograph by John Kurtich.*

FIREPLACE MANTEL, DINING ROOM,
LAURIE MALLET HOUSE, NEW YORK,
NEW YORK. SITE, 1985.

*SITE's "haunting of the house" places
all "real" objects in jeopardy of being
absorbed by the ghostly world at any
moment. Photograph by John Kurtich.*

unusable in its partially buried state but asserting itself with confident authority. In the dining room, the same design technique is employed. Here, a fireplace mantel holding a candelabra and Houdin bust of a child, all partially buried in the plaster wall, evoke the lost past of French aristocracy.

The final layer of history has been supplied by Laurie Mallet's furniture and possessions. A decidedly undesigned approach, a collection of contemporary avant garde furniture and art mixed with fifties period "antiques" completes the interiors. The colorful and robust furnishings unfortunately draw too much attention to themselves, overpowering the elegantly projected architectural elements. SITE has discovered in this project an imaginative source of exploiting the third dimension, rendering meaning and mystery.

EXCAVATED INTERIOR ARCHITECTURE

Excavated Interior Architecture results when space is either carved from solid mass or built with such massive components that it seems carved, creating a distinct positive-negative relationship. A sculptor uses this traditional method when working blocks of solid material. The sculptor concentrates on the limited palette of the homogeneous

material and its resulting forms, producing light and shadow. The power of this primary relationship is an essential ingredient to the three-dimensional interior.

THE CAVE   One of humanity's earliest dwellings, the cave, provided such a primal interior, which thus began the fascination with carved space. Once the essential needs for survival were satisfied, new technologies, which freed humanity to live in more desirable locations, were developed. New forms of enclosure were created that tried to retain the essential ingredients of the earlier excavations: permanence, strength, security, and protection.

CAVE COMPLEXES: KARLI AND ELEPHANTA, INDIA

Religious architecture following the Maurya period in India (after the end of the first century B.C. to the third century A.D.) included a considerable number of interior spaces literally carved out of living rock. A spatial form known as the *chaitya* became prescribed. In plan, the *chaitya* was characterized by a navelike hall with a semicircular apse and false side aisles too narrow for actual use. Architectural features such as columns seemingly supporting arched vaulting above were all carved as a continuum from living rock. The complex at

ENTRANCE TO ELEPHANTA CAVE, INDIA, A.D. EIGHTH CENTURY.

The exterior temple front announces the carved temple complex waiting within the living rock. Photograph by Pradumna Tana.

Karli (from A.D. 120) is a particularly rich example of a carved interior made very three-dimensional with elaborately carved colonnades topped with figurative groupings as "capitals," all to lead the eye to the climax of the space, the holy *stupa* at the apsidal end of the nave.

A more complicated cave complex is the Elephanta cave-temple, dating from after the Gupta period of India (A.D. 320 to 600). Located on Elephanta Island, near Bombay, this temple was carved from living rock to embody two symbols: the sea and the island. To ancient worshippers, the sea represented unlimited life energy, which was both nourisher and destroyer. The island was relief from the raw chaos of the sea, a peaceful haven and spiritual center. The temple was dedicated to the god, Shiva, the lord of the universal energies of change, transformation, alteration, and re-creation. The temple interior is a more complicated spatial composition than the nave at Karli; Elephanta had three entrances, creating a cruciform in plan. The main shrine within is on axis with the east entrance and is detached (such a sanctuary was normally attached to the back wall of the temple, opposite the east entrance) to allow worshippers to circumambulate, characterizing the symbolism of the shrine radiating its spiritual power in all directions. The columns appear to be architectural supports but serve no purpose structurally. No two columns are alike, and this lack of symmetry is probably caused by the very difficult task of carving each column out of solid rock.

INTERIORS OF MASSIVE COMPONENTS: SIMULATED CARVED SPACE

HYPOSTYLE HALL, KARNAK, EGYPT

Ancient civilizations, such as the Egyptians, utilized column and beam construction out of stone, creating strong three-dimensional spaces of long-lasting quality. The limited spanning properties of stone required closely spaced columns, effecting dark, secure, permanent interiors. The close-

HYPOSTYLE HALL, TEMPLE OF AMMON, KARNAK, EGYPT, 1530–330 B.C.

The impressive Hypostyle Hall appears to be chisled out of a solid block of stone. Photograph by John Kurtich.

ness of the massive columns to each other created the impression that this forestlike space could have been carved from one huge mass of solid stone. The Hypostyle Hall of the Temple of

Rotunda, the Pantheon, Rome,
Italy, A.D. 120–124.

*Coffering along the dome accentuates the
impression that the central space is
carved and not constructed. Photograph
by John Kurtich.*

Ammon at Karnak, Egypt (ca. 1312–1301 B.C.), used this construction system to create awe-inspiring interiors of seemingly unlimited extent. Like the cave, the perimeter was dark, contrasting with the clerestory-lit central passageway. This fading of light toward the exterior gave the space an illusion of limitless boundaries.

PANTHEON, ROME

The ancient Romans revolutionized interior space with their ability to span great distances through the use of the arch and vault, made out of brick and concrete. The mass required to support these great vaults and subsequent domes continued the feeling of great permanence and strength. Their greatest surviving interior space is the Pantheon, Rome (A.D. 120–124), a sphere of a space defined by the heavy massing of masonry needed to support the extraordinary dome (diameter: 142 feet, 6 inches).

POST–ROMAN CARVED SPACE   The Roman mastery of space was refined during the Italian Renaissance. During this period, architectural drawings became common. Wall sections of the building plans were rendered by means of *poché*, which was the technique of blacking those areas which were meant to be solid. Due to the thickness of masonry walls, the rendered appearance of buildings resembled a series of spaces carved out of solid material. Architectural design was worked out through drawing compositions which contrasted mass and void. The technique of *poché* reinforced this mode of design. The appearance of carved or excavated space was further enhanced by richly embellished interiors of intricate moldings, attached columns and pilasters,

deep frames and pediments, and multi-layered panels.

Until the advent of the Industrial Revolution, at the end of the eighteenth century, the tradition of contrasting mass and void persisted. The Industrial Revolution dramatically changed both building technology and materials available. When glass and iron became abundantly available, buildings became planar and skeletal in character. The first "glass boxes" altered the public's sense of traditional security. Containing interior space without solidity, these "modern" buildings took the human race further away from its original cave than ever before.

GOVERNMENT BUILDINGS,
CHANDIGARH, INDIA

During the Brutalist Movement of the mid-twentieth century, a return to the primordial characteristics of raw and massive building materials occurred. Le Corbusier (1887–1965), reacting to the apparent deterioration of his prized Villa Sa-

voye after World War II, turned his attention toward building with permanence. Le Corbusier's exploitation of the new technology led to his fascination with sculpted spaces executed in rough, unfinished reinforced concrete, as exemplified by his designs for the government buildings at Chandigarh, India (1951–1961).

The High Court (1951–1955) was the first building to be completed. It is essentially a monumental shaded concrete box frame filled with mammoth piers and complex *brises-soleil,* Le Corbusier's inventive sunbreakers. It recalls ancient Roman architecture, particularly the Basilica of Constantine, Rome, which the architect had sketched fifty years earlier. The High Court was a new building which looked like it had existed for hundreds of years, a building built to last. The sculptural quality and composition recall the pre-Industrial Revolution concerns of contrasting mass and void, using super-scaled spaces and volumes.

GEORGE'S RESTAURANT AND CABARET, CHICAGO, ILLINOIS

Spatial approaches are often a product of the building materials being used. Thin materials like drywall, metal sheets, or glass will generate a planar or constructed interior, while poured concrete or masonry will usually deal with "excavated" or solid-and-void massing. Neither

PALACE OF JUSTICE (HIGH COURT), CHANDIGARH, INDIA. LE CORBUSIER, 1951–1955.

Implying permanence and strength, the High Court has an added architectural presence as a result of the massive building material used in its construction. Droits de reproduction percus par la SPADEM. Copyright 1991 ARS N.Y./SPADEM.

method is more correct or appropriate than the other. In an age in which current technology affords the designer so many options, it is important to realize that such an ancient and basic design idea of sculpting space through mass and void is still a valid and viable approach in creating strong three-dimensional space.

George's Restaurant and Cabaret, Chicago (1979) by Banks/Eakin Architects is an exercise in the manipulation of mass and void. The original 4,000 square foot space was divided by a row of timber columns cutting the space virtually in half. Various existing stairs, elevator, and shafts posed further planning obstacles. As a result of the building's irregularities, and the restaurant and cabaret each having different requirements, a binary plan became an obvious direction to explore.

The program called for a 160-seat restaurant with all seats having a clear view to a small stage. In addition a bar accommodating forty seats, a coat room, bus stations, and an open kitchen were also to be included.

The solution emphasized the divided space by placing the bar and kitchen on one side of the column line opposed by the dining room and cabaret. The volumetric treatment of the adjacent spaces was in direct opposition. The bar, bus stations, and elevator were contained in a single curvilinear mass, floating in space. The serpentine glass block bar created a dynamic horizontal element. The bar's rhythmic undulation with the columns was intended to encourage movement while metaphorically alluding to the musical character of the nightclub.

When one passes through the colonnade into the dining area, a complete spatial reversal from charged negative space to static positive space happens. Although long and narrow, the room is open and spacious, with tiered seating levels overlooking a round marble stage. The room appears to be carved out of the solid mass into a simple lozenge shape. The shape is emphasized by a continuous cove light and semicircular backlit glass block walls that act as a terminus to the room while implying space beyond. The detailing of the room accentuates the plastic quality of drywall and plaster construction. Thickness and weight

BAR AND DINING ROOM, GEORGE'S
RESTAURANT, CHICAGO, ILLINOIS.
BANKS/EAKIN, 1979.

*The carved solid and void effect of the
restaurant belies the materials used to
construct it. Photograph by Jaime
Ardiles-Arce.*

MODEL, GEORGE'S RESTAURANT,
CHICAGO, ILLINOIS. BANKS/EAKIN,
1979.

*The massing model of the restaurant
clearly shows the "carved" concept of
the scheme. Photograph by Garret
Eakin.*

reinforces the massive three-dimensional character of the dining room. Nowhere does one see thinness or planar elements usually associated with drywall construction.

By studying the nature of the space, what appeared as three-dimensional limitations actually formed the basis for the final design concept. The skillful balancing of solid and void created an exciting sense of place.

SINGLE FAMILY HOUSE, MASSAGNO, SWITZERLAND

The architecture of Mario Botta (1943–   ) has been described as pure geometric masses that have been excavated to form habitable interior space.

The three-dimensional expression of his architecture has been influenced by site specific conditions, vernacular architecture, and Louis I. Kahn (1901–1974). His bold forms of brick and concrete are intended to create a place between earth and sky. Many of his residences, built on the southern slopes of the Alps, possess a strong graphic identity when viewed from afar.

Botta's single family house at Massagno, Switzerland (1979–1981), establishes such a striking presence on the landscape. The structure, built parallel to the slope, is a simple rectangular form with one main facade facing south. Alternating bands of red and gray concrete brick animate the facade. At a distance, the main elevation appears symmetrical with a large circular opening at the

SINGLE-FAMILY HOUSE, MASSAGNO,
SWITZERLAND. MARIO BOTTA, 1979–
1981.

*Through the contrast of mass and void,
the cave-like entry reveals deep shadows,
enhancing its three dimensional reality.
Photograph by Alo Zanetta.*

building's center. Upon closer inspection, various architectural details start to relate the formal idea to the site conditions and internal spatial organization. One corner is carved out, announcing the point of entry. The detail is balanced by two vertical rows of square voids that articulate the intersection of diagonal walls of glass with the masonry enclosure. The massive elevation is relieved by the incision of a large circular opening that exposes the carved interior beyond. This subtraction of mass creates a deep void, producing a cavelike opening, establishing a dialogue with its hillside location. By contrasting mass and void, deep shadows are produced on a grand scale, giving the facade a strong three-dimensional quality. The massive opening reveals the more delicate carved interior. The solidity of the exterior contrasts dramatically with the airy spaces. The plan is organized axially around the wide portal. Diagonal glass walls overlook an open air interior terrace space connecting all the rooms. Large glazed sliding doors concealed in a brick cavity can be closed during inclement weather to form a winter garden. The carved portal shades the southern exposure, allowing a comfortable amount of light to flood the interior space. From the interior, one feels very protected by the cavelike manipulation of space, which is reinforced by deeply recessing all window glazing from the edge of the masonry shell.

Not only did Botta carve space horizontally, he took full advantage of creating three-dimensional vertical space. By using strategically placed skylights over the staircase and above a light well, he opened his "box" to the sky. The light spills down the voids, accentuating the climb up through space to the primary living areas on the second and third floors. By "carving out" his interior, Botta was able to transform a modest size interior into spacious and expansive spaces.

CONSTRUCTED INTERIOR ARCHITECTURE

Another approach in creating strong three-dimensional space is the *constructed interior*. The opposite of carved or excavated interior space, con-structed interiors occur with the addition of architectural formats to establish the volume. This additive process is aimed at creating interlocking spaces. Exploiting such ideas as revealing construction method, using raw or natural materials, using transparency, and creating rhythm can infuse these spaces with high levels of energy. This manipulation of interiors can cover a broad spectrum from very formalistic architectural concepts to a free form of collaged parts.

The constructed interior expresses and celebrates the pieces that create the whole composition. Historically, architects have been fascinated by the bare frame or bones of the building being exposed. Even today, when finished solid walls encase the structural framework, a sense of disappointment occurs. The feeling of excitement generated by the skeleton is lost. It is often hard, if not impossible, to recapture that energy. That power is generated by the use of transparency, seeing through screened space, revealing the spatial dynamics of light and shadow, solid and void, and movement.

By showing the structure, a reduced palette of building materials can evolve. No longer are such traditional architectural embellishments as crown molding or classical capitals necessary or relevant. The exposed structure becomes the interior detailing. By using this honest, nonapplied approach, a spirited interior can be achieved.

FLORIAN APARTMENT, CHICAGO, ILLINOIS

Paul Florian (1950–   ) attributes his inspiration for his Chicago residence to the Russian Constructivists. A movement dating back to the 1920s, the Constructivists were concerned with creating an art form based on the scientific investigation of the abstract ideas of picture surface, color, line, and construction. The 600-square-foot second floor residential renovation of a two-flat building presented the challenge of getting the most out of a small space, both functionally and architecturally. The simplistic rectangular plan is knit together with exciting neo-Constructivist elements. The space focuses on the sculptural

APARTMENT, CHICAGO, ILLINOIS.
PAUL FLORIAN, 1986.

*The orchestration of linear parts,
through their particular forms and colors,
produces a strong three dimensional
continuity. Photograph by John
Kurtich.*

quality of space through the expression of the architectural components. A suspended horizontal red plane slices through spaces, a green rhythmic wall defines an edge, yellow volumes protrude and punctuate. These additive elements directly contrast the white rectilinear shell. The functional requirements such as stairs, toilets, shower, and closets were buried along the perimeter of one wall. The mass does not engage the ceiling and is painted green to separate it from the enclosing shell. The long, thin, straight stair hall is transformed into an engaging composition by a few skillful moves. By freeing the wood stair on one side, the designer creates a trough, loosening it from the wall, making the stair a more three-dimensional component. A strong focal point drawing the eye upward is created at the top of the stair by the juxtaposition of a yellow column

with a fragment of the red plane abutting it. The components are expressed as a fractional composition. This simple move exposes a part of the dynamic three-dimensional story beyond. Though open and seemingly obvious, the interior space cannot be read as a whole entity. By not knowing exactly where the architectural components end and begin, the observer is visually trying to find the points of origin. Florian's enigmatic compositional treatment, plus his skillful use of color, creates an intense three-dimensional experience.

SPILLER HOUSE, VENICE, CALIFORNIA

In the Spiller House, Venice, California (1980), Frank Gehry (1929–   ) was confronted with the complexity of locating two houses on a tiny urban

LIVING ROOM, SPILLER HOUSE, VENICE, CALIFORNIA. FRANK GEHRY, 1980.

Interlocking volumes of partially finished walls emphasize a constructivist approach to three dimensional space. Photograph by Tim Street-Porter/Esto.

site. The limitations of that lot led the designer to develop a strong vertical scheme. The building is composed of a two-story guest house with the main domicile rising four stories at the rear of the lot. In Gehry's typical playful design approach, this project has incorporated the collagelike appearance of the immediate urban setting. Both the exterior and interior of the complex are consistent in the use of exposed wood studs, unfinished plywood, corrugated sheet metal, all inexpensive and honest materials. The simplicity of the materials is contrasted by the complexity of the interior three-dimensional composition.

Having four floors allowed Gehry to assemble a series of dynamic interlocking spaces. Spaces, often flooded with natural light were rendered complex by the deliberate expression of wood construction. The combination of stud walls and glass create a high contrast when laced with light and shadow. By exposing the transparent and skeletal characteristics of the building materials, Gehry has revealed an energized three-dimensional constructed environment.

Summary

Space is not perceived in plan, elevation, or section but as a total three-dimensional experience. These drawing conventions, reinforced by the complexity of contemporary project programs, tend to limit concentration on the full development of three-dimensional Interior Architecture. Yet the power and excitement produced from a dynamic relationship between mass and void is undeniable. The contrast formed by compressive masses and expansive volumes can create memorable interior space. It is to this end the chapter's projects exemplify how strong three-dimensional exploitation can elevate one's experience, opening the door to the fourth dimension.

NOTES

1. J. J. Gibson, in his studies of visual perception, "has made the interesting suggestion that motion parallax is part of a more general source of motion-produced distance information which he terms motion perspective. Gibson points out that when an observer is in motion, the retinal projections of objects undergo continuous transformations that are regular and lawful in character. Wherever the observer looks, the scene flows past in a continuous stream. The flow decreases at the top of the visual field and vanishes at the horizon. If we consider the terrain of the environment to be projected as a plane in front of the eye, the rate at which any element flows is inversely related to its physical distance from the observer. There is, in Gibson's terms, a gradient of velocity from a maximum at the bottom of the visual field—the ground over which we travel—to the horizon." From William N. Dember and Joel S. Warm, *Psychology of Perception* (New York: Holt, Rinehart and Winston, 1979), p. 291.

2. This is actually a special case of size perspective, "which refers to the fact that objects of equal size at varying distances project images whose visual angles are inversely proportional to their distance." From Irvin Rock, *Perception* (New York: Scientific American Books, 1984), p. 76.

3. A *palaestra* was a public place for exercise in wrestling and athletics in ancient Greece and Rome.

4. In order to use this method, a mirror must be in a stationary position with the artist looking through a fixed viewfinder while painting the outlines of the subject on the mirror. This procedure was difficult, since the artist's own reflection tended to get in the way.

5. Such a contrivance would require a large pane of clear glass in a fixed vertical position on a flat surface and a device for holding the artist's head in a rigid position while covering one eye. The artist would then paint the contours of his subject on the pane of glass.

6. The artist would place a piece of gridded paper on the horizontal surface in front of the vertical gridded glass. Looking through this window, the artist would record the subject's contours on the paper. This method assisted the artist in proportionally enlarging or reducing a drawing.

7. The camera obscura was an enclosure that produced projected images through the positioning of a mirror and a double convex lens. If projected on a piece of paper, the contours of the image could be traced by the artist.

8. John Summerson, *Heavenly Mansions* (New York: W. W. Norton & Co., 1963), p. 3.

9. Moore named the tower after a dog he once knew in

New Orleans. From David Littlejohn, Architect: *The Life & Work of Charles W. Moore* (New York: Holt, Rinehart & Winston, 1984), p. 78.

10. The second tower was named after the wife of King Richard the Lionhearted. Ibid, p. 78.

11. The source of the name is unknown. Ibid, p. 79.

12. *Allee* is a French word for a walk or passage, usually in a garden or park, bordered by rows of trees or bushes. Here it is used to denote a bordered way within the interior, which forms a strong axis in the French sense.

13. "The Guggenheim Museum," *Architectural Forum,* June 1959, p. 127.

14. The *golden section* is an elaborate proportional system dating back to ancient Greece and the Pythagorean concept of "all is number." A rectangle becomes "golden" when its width is to the length as the length is to the sum of the width and length (a:b = b:a + b).

15. *Vitrage* is a French word for glass windows or glazing but does not mean stained glass windows.

16. SITE is a design organization, the name of which originally meant "Sculpture in the Environment." The spelled out version of the name was eventually abbreviated to SITE when the group felt that their projects were more architectural than sculptural.

CHAPTER 4

THE FOURTH DIMENSION: SPACE-TIME

THE CONCEPT OF SPACE-TIME

Remarkable architectural space possesses the ability to engage human participants and open their senses fully to new experience. The sensation of feeling and comprehending the space through a temporal heightening of one's perceptions—visual, aural, olfactory, tactile, thermal, kinesthetic—adds another dimension by which such architectural space can be measured. This additional dimension is temporal and is made manifest by human interaction with the architecture—a differentiated and special experience through the passage of time. When the dimension of time is combined with the three dimensions of spatial measurement, a new, collective concept of space-time must be recognized.

Conventional, Newtonian three-dimensional space, measured by width, height, and depth, is made up of locations or places. Space-time is composed of occurrences or events, which are those things happening to someone at a given place and a given time. Each sense imprint of one's perception is such an event. These events occur continuously as the process of living cannot avoid the interaction between person and environment. When a series of events provides a rich or unique environmental experience for the participant, the resultant space-time becomes an important criterion for measuring the quality of the architecture. Space-time is an essential component of Interior Architecture. This space-time concept is also central to relativistic physics, stream-of-consciousness literature, and cubist painting. Space-time is a new idea for the West, and only since the early twentieth century has it affected and transformed Western science, humanities, and the arts. The East, however, has always understood the interrelation of space and time and the unity of all things. Eastern philosophy is guided by the quest for the experience of the ultimate reality.

THE UNITY OF ALL THINGS: HINDUISM, BUDDHISM, THE TAO, MA

Hinduism communicates its philosophy through myths, great epics that involve a vast number of gods and goddesses in countless events. These mythical images, however, are the many faces of reality. "Myth embodies the nearest approach to absolute truth that can be stated in words."[1] The ultimate reality is where time and space merge as a continuum, and the individual is part of the whole.

Eastern mystics of Buddhism, particularly the Avatamsaka school of Mahayana Buddhism, attain states of consciousness that actually transcend the ordinary three-dimensional world. Their enlightened awareness is experienced as a kind of space-time of the ultimate reality.

The significance of the Avatamsaka and its philosophy is unintelligible unless we once experience . . . a state of complete dissolution where there is no more distinction between mind and body, subject and object . . . We look around and perceive that . . . every object is related to every other object . . . not only spatially, but temporally . . . As a fact of pure experience, there is no space without time, no time without space; they are interpenetrating.[2]

The Chinese belief in the ultimate reality is the *Tao*. All of the seemingly separate things that humans observe are unified through this philosophy. "There are the three terms—'complete,' 'all-embracing,' 'the whole.' These names are differ-

HINDU SCULPTURE. INDIAN, SHIVA
NATARAJA, LORD OF THE DANCE,
BRONZE, CHOLA DYNASTY, 10TH–
11TH CENTURY A.D., HT.: 71.1 CM,
KATE S. BUCKINGHAM FUND,
1967.1130

*The duality of creation and destruction is
the ultimate continuum of the god,
Shiva, a metaphor for the continuum of
space and time.* © 1990 The Art
Institute of Chicago, All Rights
Reserved.

BUDDHA SCULPTURE. SOUTH INDIAN,
NAGAPATTINAM, SEATED BUDDHA,
STONE, 11TH CENTURY, 134.6 CM,
MR. AND MRS. ROBERT ANDREW
BROWN RESTRICTED GIFT, 1964.556.

*Enlightenment is the means for
understanding the merging of space and
time in Buddhism. This ultimate truth is
found through focused meditation as
personified by the seated Buddha.* ©
1990 The Art Institute of Chicago, All
Rights Reserved.

ent, but the reality sought in them is the same: referring to the One thing."[3] Tao is the essence of the universe. Its actuality is the undefinable reality, a process characterized by endless, constant, cyclical change. The duality of opposites, the *yin* and the *yang,* represent the limits of this cyclical flow and form a unity of opposites, which are really aspects of the same whole. "The 'this' is also 'that.' The 'that' is also 'this.' . . . That the 'that' and the 'this' cease to be opposites is the very essence of Tao. Only this essence, an axis as it were, is the center of the circle responding to the endless changes."[4]

The Japanese have a concept of the unity of space and time, known as *MA*. To them, space was never perceived independently from time. Furthermore, time was not abstracted as a flow but was an element relative to movements or spaces. Their space-time, MA, is defined by Iwanami's *Dictionary of Ancient Terms* as "the natural distance between two or more things existing in a continuity" or "the space delineated by posts and screens (rooms)" or "the natural pause or interval between two or more phenomena occurring continuously."[5]

JAPANESE, ILLUSTRATED LEGENDS OF THE YUZU NEMBUTSU SECT (YUZU MEMBUTSU ENGI), HANDSCROLL, INK, COLOR AND GOLD ON PAPER, KAMAKURA PERIOD, 14TH CENTURY, 30.5 x 1018 CM, KATE S. BUCKINGHAM COLLECTION, 1956.1256. VIEW 6 LEFT TO RIGHT.

MA is the foundation of most aspects of Japanese life. The equating of time and space underlie Japanese artistic expression, particularly architecture, fine arts, music, and drama. © 1990 The Art Institute of Chicago, All Rights Reserved.

CHINESE SCROLL PAINTING. HSU-PEN, CHINESE, ACTIVE 1370–1380, LANDSCAPE, HANGING SCROLL, INK ON PAPER, ADA TURNBULL HERTLE FUND, 1967.377.

Tao *represents the cosmic geometry of the world and the dynamics which stimulate it. The underlying order of nature is central to the cyclical duality of yin and yang.* © 1990 The Art Institute of Chicago, All Rights Reserved.

THE BIRTH OF WESTERN SPACE-TIME

The discovery or realization of space-time in the West in science, humanities, and the arts resulted, in part, from the growing pains of the Industrial Revolution. Challenging the basic foundations of the old order, the Industrial Revolution fostered political and social unrest in Europe. Russia was on the verge of a major revolution. Germany was a newly created nation filled with nationalistic pride. The Austro-Hungarian Empire, weakened by the diversity of ethnic and religious differences of its subjects, was about to split into a number of smaller, independent nations. England's hold over a worldwide empire was weakening as Queen Victoria (1819–1901), the longest reigning English monarch, died. France was struggling with a third attempt at democracy and would experience fifty governments by the beginning of the First World War. Barbara Tuchman (1912–1989) sums up the West's conflicts and restlessness of this age in *The Proud Tower.*

Industrialization, imperialism, the growth of cities, the decline of the countryside, the power of money and the power of machines, the clenched fist of the working class, the red flag of Socialism, the wane of the aristocracy, all these forces and factors were churning like the bowels of a volcano about to erupt.[6]

During this period scientists developed a theory of space-time as they were struggling with conflicts and inconsistencies in Newtonian physics. Newtonian physics maintained that time was absolute and space was absolute.[7] This meant that two observers would agree on a time assigned to any given event, no matter how far apart the observers were or in what condition their relative motion was to each other. Albert Einstein (1879–1955) revolutionized classical physics in 1905 with his special theory of relativity in which he calculated how time in one reference system moving away at a constant velocity appears to slow down when viewed from another system at rest relative to it. He concluded that "every reference body has its own particular time."[8] In his general theory of relativity of 1916, he explained: "We entirely shun the vague word *space,* of which, we must honestly acknowledge, we cannot form the slightest conception and we must replace it by *motion relative to a practically rigid body of reference.*"[9] In other words, "space has no objective reality except as an order or arrangement of the objects we perceive in it, and time has no independent existence apart from the order of events by which we measure it."[10]

In 1908, Hermann Minkowski (1864–1909), a former Zürich professor of Einstein, drew upon Einstein's special theory of relativity to speculate on the fate of space and time as separate dimensions of experience. He presented to an assembly of German natural scientists and physicians an address that began

The views of space and time which I wish to lay before you have sprung from the soil of experimental physics, and therein lies their strength. They are radical. Henceforth space by itself, and time by itself, are doomed to fade away into mere shadows, and only a kind of union of the two will preserve an independent reality.[11]

THE X-RAY: SPACE-TIME OF INSIDE/OUTSIDE

Another contribution to the new consciousness of space-time was the discovery of the X-ray. In 1895, Wilhelm Konrad Roentgen (1845–1923) accidentally observed that a screen coated with a fluorescent salt, such as potassium platinocyanide, became luminous every time he switched on a nearby cathode-ray tube. What caused this? Roentgen knew that cathode rays themselves could not escape from the glass tube, but some kind of invisible radiation was contacting the screen. He placed a thick piece of metal between the tube and a surface covered with the phosphorescent salt and found that a distinct shadow of the metal was cast on this surface. Opaque materials such as wood or thinner metal would create only partial shadows. He deduced that the greater the density of the material, the stronger the shadow or opacity. By passing these rays through human flesh, he could obtain a precise photographic record of the bones beneath the flesh. He labeled these mysterious radiations X-rays, "X" representing the algebraic symbol for an unknown. With the invention of the fluoroscope in 1896 by Thomas Edison (1847–1931), the inside of a living human body could be viewed and inspected. "The opening up of the interior anatomical terrain of the human body by X-ray was part of a general reappraisal of what is properly inside and what is outside the body, the mind, physical objects, and nations."[12] The ability to transcend the opaque wall with this new vision altered the sense of time. Thomas Mann (1875–1955) described this profound experience of temporal alteration in *The Magic Mountain*.

He was so kind as to permit the patient, at his request, to look at his own hand through the screen. And Hans Castorp saw, precisely what he had never thought it would be vouchsafed him to see: he looked into his own grave. The process of decay was forestalled by the powers of the light-ray, the flesh in which he walked disintegrated, annihilated, dissolved in vacant mist, and there within it was the finely turned skeleton of his own hand, the seal ring he had inherited from his grandfather hanging loose and black on the joint of his ring-finger—a hard, material object, with which man adorns the body that is fated to melt away beneath it, when it passes on to another flesh that can wear it for yet a little while.[13]

THE CINEMA: MANIPULATION OF SPACE AND TIME

The invention of the cinema altered time directly. Not only could it portray *real* time, but it could speed up time, stop time, or reverse time. Through the development of intercutting, simultaneity of time and space was achieved. Intercutting began with *The Ex-Convict* (1905), by Edwin S. Porter (1869–1941) the same year as Einstein's special theory of relativity. In 1908, D. W. Griffith (1874–1948) started producing films that revolutionized filmmaking techniques. He "introduced the fade-in, the fade-out, the long shot, the full shot, the close-up, the moving camera shot, the flashback, crosscutting and MON-TAGE,"[14] establishing cinematic space-time.

Movement presented in cinema appears to be continuous, but it is actually discontinuous because it is created by a series of still images projected at a high speed. Thus the dimensions of space and time can be altered or distorted by manipulation, giving the observer new dimensions of experience. Cinema corresponded to the scientific theories of Einstein with the assimilation of space and time into a space-time continuum. Einstein argued that space and time were combined to form the framework of the universe. The framework upon which cinema existed likewise combined space and time. One could move about in time as much as in space, and space had the flowing quality of time. Cinema became the synthesis of space and time.

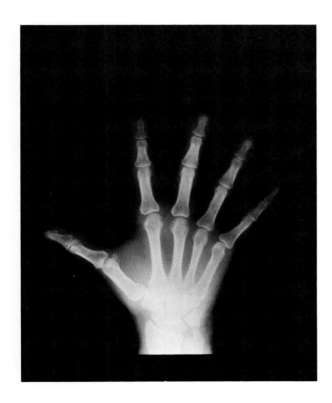

X-RAY OF A HAND, 1991.

The X-ray altered the sense of time and space, allowing the viewer to experience the space-time of the living human body. Photograph by John Kurtich.

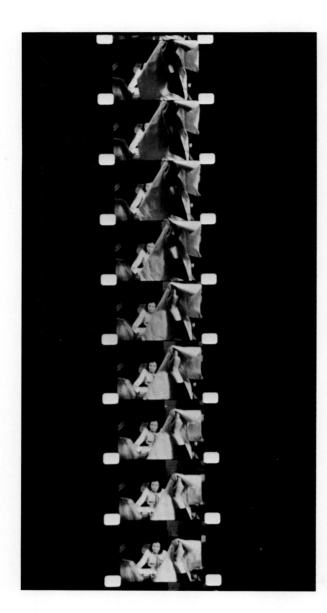

16MM FILM CLIP FROM *FASHION '72*, A
FILM BY JOHN KURTICH, 1972, ABOUT
DESIGNING AND FABRICATING HIGH
FASHION CLOTHES.

*The discontinuity of film image is
possible to view in an actual strip of
movie film. Altering time and space for
the viewer occurs through high speed
projection of these still images, creating
the space-time continuum. Photograph
by John Kurtich.*

STREAM-OF-CONSCIOUSNESS LITERATURE: NARRATIVE SPACE-TIME

Space-time in literature became manifest in the writings of Virginia Woolf (1882–1941) and James Joyce (1882–1941). Woolf transformed the English novel with time shifts and stream-of-consciousness. She declared that "life is not a series of gig lamps symmetrically arranged; but a luminous halo, a semi-transparent envelope surrounding us from the beginning of consciousness to the end." [15]

Stream-of-consciousness techniques share much with those of the cinema, that is, similar methods to show composite or diverse views of a subject, flow of events, and interrelation or association of ideas. There is a freedom of shifting back and forth in time, of mixing or intermingling past, present, and future. Two methods predominate:

One is that in which the subject can remain fixed in space and his consciousness can move in time—the result is time-montage or the superimposition of images or ideas from one time on those of another; the other possibility, of course, is for time to remain fixed and for the spatial element to change, which results in space-montage. [16]

James Joyce uses this latter technique with brilliance in his revolutionary *Ulysses*.

Mr. Bloom, alone, looked at the titles.
Fair Tyrants *by James Lovebirch. Know the kind that is. Had it! Yes.*
He opened it. Thought so.
A woman's voice behind the dingy curtain.
Listen: *The man.*
No: she wouldn't like that much. Got her it once.
He read the other title: Sweets of Sin. *More in her line. Let us see.*
He read where his finger opened.
—All the dollarbills her husband gave her were spent in the stores on wondrous gowns and costliest frillies. For him! For Raoul!
Yes. This. Here. Try.
—Her mouth glued on his in a luscious voluptuous kiss while his hands felt for the opulent curves inside her déshabillé.
Yes. Take this. The end. [17]

LE SACRE DU PRINTEMPS: MUSIC IN SPACE-TIME

Igor Stravinsky (1882–1971), by understanding the space-time consciousness, revolutionized the sound of music with *Le Sacre du Printemps,* which was presented as a Diaghilev ballet at the Théâtre du Champs-Élysées, Paris, on May 29, 1913. The premiere produced a riot of protest as the audience was confronted with unfamiliar sounds and rhythms. Musically it had reverted to the primitive sources of performance art—tribal drums, the worship of nature, human sacrifice.

. . . No one had ever heard music like it before; it seemed to violate all the most hallowed concepts of beauty, harmony, tone, and expression. Never had an audience heard music so brutal, savage, aggressive, and apparently chaotic; it hit the public like a hurricane, like some uncontrolled primeval force. The Rite of Spring is the very antithesis of all those saccharine "Springs" one had come to expect from every musician, painter, and writer under the sun. Hẹ *̣pring seen from within, from the very bowels of*̣ *̣e pregnant earth, which writhes in the pangs of labour and gives birth to dark tellurian forces. "What I was trying to convey," says Stravinsky, "was the surge of spring, the magnificent upsurge of nature reborn."*[18]

Stravinsky accomplished this by altering familiar time patterns of existing music and creating a new space-time continuum where the rhythm of the music was released from any regularly repetitive pulse. Time signatures constantly change —$2/8$, $3/16$, $2/16$, $3/16$, $2/8$, $2/16$, $3/16$—measure by measure. He simultaneously combined chords to produce new sound so that

the effect of juxtaposing two heterogeneous harmonic poles in this way is like the effect of short circuiting or combustion, melting the musical fabric and welding it into a solid plastic mass. The forces of harmonic, melodic and tonal propulsion are canceled out, and the opaque, inert material thus created serves merely to give body to the rhythm. The incredible dynamic intensity of the rhythm swallows up every other element of the musical discourse.[19]

The release of energy presented by this work marked the birth of contemporary music and had a profound effect upon the sense of time and space

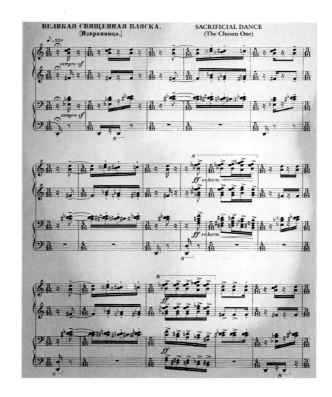

A PAGE FROM THE PIANO REDUCTION SCORE OF LE SACRE DU PRINTEMPS, "SACRIFICIAL DANCE (THE CHOSEN ONE)," 1911–1913.

The constant shifting and changing of Stravinsky's musical patterns and time values altered the consciousness of the traditional concert audience, propelling them into the aural equivalent of space-time. Courtesy: Dover Publications, Inc., New York, New York.

in subsequent music. Stravinsky was the first composer to tackle the "tyranny of the bar line," a kind of absolute time against which composers had long protested. Here was a composer who shared a similar attitude toward time and space with Einstein. Stravinsky was actually creating music in space-time. His technique with *The Rite of Spring* was to use displaced accent and dissonance balanced by the device of melodic fragmentation through which he achieved a structural continuity. The complex rhythm did not exist independently for its own sake but was cohesively combined with melody and harmony. This unity of new time and space overwhelmed the listener with its shattering, elemental power. "Stravinsky's music . . . seem(ed) to transform . . . the barbaric cries of modern life; and to transform these despairing noises into music."[20]

"LES DEMOISELLES D'AVIGNON" BY PABLO PICASSO. PARIS (BEGUN MAY, REWORKED JULY 1907). OIL ON CANVAS, 8' x 7'8". COLLECTION, THE MUSEUM OF MODERN ART, NEW YORK. ACQUIRED THROUGH THE LILLIE P. BLISS BEQUEST.

Hailed by some scholars as the first twentieth century painting, "Les Demoiselles d'Avignon" broke completely away from the tradition of European classical painting, particularly with the depiction of the human figure and the presentation of three-dimensional space. Collection. The Museum of Modern Art, New York.

CUBISM: SPACE-TIME OF MULTIPLE PERSPECTIVE

As Stravinsky scandalized the music world with his new sound, Pablo Picasso (1881–1973) stunned the art world with his new vision of painting. His *Les Demoiselles d'Avignon* (1907) is widely recognized as the beginning of cubism. It was a shocking picture for its time, with nudes and seminudes affronting the Renaissance canons of female beauty. It expressed the development of irrational forms equivalent only to psychic responses, multiple viewpoints of the space the nudes were occupying, and simultaneous visions of the human body. The two figures in a frontal pose have their noses in sharp profile. The seated figure on the lower right has her back to the viewer, but her head is seen from the front. Cubism grew up in Paris between 1907 and 1914, with Picasso and Georges Braque (1882–1963) the two principal pioneers. Linear perspective was abandoned for multiple perspectives with X-ray views of their interiors. Roger Allard (1885–1961) wrote of cubist painting in 1910 as "elements of a synthesis situated in time."[21] In 1913, Guillaume Apollinaire (1880–1918) remarked that cubists have followed scientists beyond the third dimension and "have been led quite naturally . . . to preoccupy themselves with new possibilities of spatial measurement which, in the language of the modern studies, are designated by the term: the fourth dimension."[22] In Picasso's *Wineglass* (1911), advancing and retreating planes of information represented sometimes fragments of identifiable objects, sometimes objects presented so that the interior and exterior could be seen simultaneously, and irrational forms evoking psychic responses.

LE CORBUSIER: THE CONTINUUM OF SPACE AND TIME

Cubism had an important influence on architecture, particularly with Le Corbusier (1887–1965). As Picasso and Braque were exhibiting interiors and exteriors of objects simultaneously in their paintings, Le Corbusier developed in both paint-

ing and architecture the interpenetration of inner and outer space. He used painting and architecture as two different disciplines to achieve the same result. His *Nature Morte de l'Esprit Nouveau* (1924) is a painting that expresses planes of transparency, boundaries and outlines between the different objects, and interpenetrations of inner and outer space. His architecture of the same period similarly treated inner and outer space. He issued a manifesto, the "five points of a new architecture."[23] This proclamation was based on a structural argument that suggested that the new architecture was the passive result of a proper and effective use of the concrete frame. By designing houses under this manifesto, Le Corbusier produced constructions in space-time. His houses could not be comprehended from a single point of view. They had to be viewed from above and

"WINEGLASS" BY PABLO PICASSO, SPANISH, 1881–1973, OIL ON CANVAS, 1911/12, 33x17.8 CM, GIFT OF CLAIRE ZEISLER IN MEMORY OF A. JAMES SPEYER, 1986.1410.

"Wineglass" is a classic example of an object broken down into its component parts and reconstituted into a kaleidoscopic presentation of decomposed form. © 1990 The Art Institute of Chicago, All Rights Reserved.

"NATURE MORTE DE L'ESPRIT NOUVEAU" BY LE CORBUSIER, 1924.

Le Corbusier treated painting as a means to inform architecture in terms of the interpenetrations of inner and outer space. Droits de reproduction perçus par la SPADEM. Copyright 1991 ARS N.Y./SPADEM.

below as well as all the way around. The continuity of inside-to-outside space was total from any viewpoint.

ARCHITECTURE AND SPACE-TIME

Architecture conceived in space-time is four dimensional. Space-time is a concept that depends upon the idea of the unity of all things, the whole. When applied to architecture, this notion of wholeness requires the interdependent and inseparable nature of the inside from the outside, a basic element defining Interior Architecture. The Roman god of doors, Janus, might well be invoked as the patron god of Interior Architecture, because this two-faced deity could see inside and outside of a building simultaneously.

The fact that space-time is composed of events continuously occurring to humans interacting with their environment, perceptual experiences through the passage of time become an important criterion for judging the four-dimensional quality of a building or space. This is part of the conscious design of Interior Architecture, whether the participant is static or in motion. ". . . man *moving about within the building,* studying it from successive points of views, himself creates, so to speak, the fourth dimension, giving space an integrated reality . . ."[24]

For humans to experience space-time, a supportive architectural attitude had to be developed. The ancient Greeks thought that geometry was inherent in nature. Euclid developed the science of geometry, which controlled the West for the next two thousand years. Sir Isaac Newton (1642–1727) based his classical laws of physics on an absolute three-dimensional world, obeying the laws of Euclidean geometry, and a separate, independent, absolute dimension of time. Newtonian physics dominated Western science until Einstein's theory of relativity profoundly altered this viewpoint in the early twentieth century. The Industrial Revolution of the nineteenth century made an unexpected impact on architectural attitudes through structural technology. By midcentury, the countries that had achieved major transformations through the Industrial Revolu-

tion were literally drunk with the potential and possibilities of all kinds of technology. England and France, in particular, competed with each other for dominance in technical and industrial achievements, presenting these through universal expositions, housed in structural engineering wonders of their time. Throughout the rest of the century, London and Paris tried to outdo each other with successive world's fairs, not only presenting new inventions and industrial processes but also showcasing them in innovative structures.

The Industrial Revolution brought about the means to use iron and glass as building materials. In England the Crystal Palace of 1851, covering almost 800,000 square feet, stunned the world. The French, not to be outdone, in 1889 constructed two astounding structures for their Exposition Universelle: the Galerie des Machines, the arches of which had the greatest unsupported span in the world (115 meters or 377 feet) and the Eiffel Tower, then the tallest structure in the world at 300 meters (984 feet).

SIMULTANEITY OF INSIDE AND OUTSIDE

THE EIFFEL TOWER

The Eiffel Tower (1887–1889) by Gustave Eiffel (1832–1923), presented for the first time in a public structure the unique experience of the simultaneity of being inside and outside. This can be readily experienced by anyone who ascends the tower via the stairs. As one climbs the stairs, one's focus of ascent continually changes in three major ways: a confined, enclosing structure about the stairs; an expansive, unimpeded view of the city; a larger internal structural umbrella of the entire tower. From inside small scale to outside large scale to inside large scale, back and forth and in-between, with the sensation of being inside and outside changing so rapidly that one cannot necessarily pinpoint what is truly enclosed or what is actually exterior space. Yet space is defined. There is a true sense of being inside, which changes the instant one turns the corner on the

stairs and literally hangs out over Paris. There is
nothing monotonous about this experience, because as one ascends, the structure of the tower
comes together, getting tighter at the same time
one climbs higher and higher above the city. Robert Delaunay's (1885–1941) painting, *The Red
Tower* (1911), captures this simultaneity of inside-
outside space. Space-time is portrayed by a spinning movement of vistas of sky, fragments of
houses, and multiple views of all parts of the tower.

"CHAMP DE MARS (THE RED
TOWER)" BY ROBERT DELAUNAY,
FRENCH, 1885–1941, OIL ON CANVAS,
1911, 162.6x130.8 CM, THE JOSEPH
WINTERBOTHAM COLLECTION,
1959.1.

*Delaunay captured the space-time
experience of the Eiffel Tower and its
perceptual impact on the surround
cityscape. © 1990 The Art Institute of
Chicago, All Rights Reserved.*

EIFFEL TOWER, PARIS, FRANCE.
GUSTAVE EIFFEL, 1887–1889.

*The experience of moving up and
through the Eiffel Tower paved the way
for the revolutionary depiction of
simultaneity of inside and outside space
in early twentieth century art and
architecture. Photograph by John
Kurtich.*

SOUTHWEST ELEVATION, VILLA
SAVOYE, POISSY-SUR-SEINE, FRANCE.
LE CORBUSIER, 1929–1930.

*The Villa Savoye cannot be
comprehended from a single viewpoint;
instead its spaces penetrate each other,
inside to outside and back again, from
any view—looking up, looking down,
looking out in every direction.
Photograph by John Kurtich.*

The simultaneity of inside and outside is a very strong four-dimensional architectural phenomenon. The Eiffel Tower is an extreme example because the experience occurs while one is physically moving in the three spatial dimensions at the same time. The resulting combination of these actions and perceptions results in a unique space-time phenomenon for the participant.

SPACE-TIME HOUSE

VILLA SAVOYE, POISSY

Le Corbusier (1887–1965) achieved the space-time house with his Villa Savoye at Poissy-sur-Seine, France, (1928–1930). This villa was designed to face all directions and represented the

culmination of ideas expressed in Le Corbusier's five points of a new architecture. The house is a rectangular box, elevated above the landscape on round, concrete pillars. It is situated in the middle of a meadow originally overlooking an orchard. The box is segmented by elongated, rectilinear windows, some glazed, some unglazed, providing a continuity of form between enclosed inside spaces and enclosed garden spaces. The ground level of the house is primarily a continuation of the meadow and space for moving vehicles. The radius of the entry lobby's semicircular plan results from the minimum space required by a turning car.

The important feature of the villa is how one moves through it from the ground level to the roof. The villa has two principal means of vertical circulation, a spiral staircase and a ramp system, existing side by side. The staircase was intended for servants to quickly ascend or descend as priority demanded. The ramp was to be used by the villa's owners and their guests.

Le Corbusier achieved with his ramp the dynamic inside-outside space-time of the Eiffel Tower. The ramp system effectively defies the conventional boundaries of inside and outside space. One first approaches the ramp head-on after entering the main door on the ground floor. Light from above encourages the visitor to ascend the ramp. This ramp runs directly south-north through the heart of the villa, zigzagging its way past all the principal features of the dwelling, connecting the most enclosed ground floor to the open deck on the upper roof.

The openness of the Villa Savoye to light and air not only from all sides but also the top, with its terrace garden and solarium penetrating the very center of the house and its bottom raised up from the ground plane with both a ramp and a spiral staircase penetrating vertically through its core, provides an architectural expression with multiple viewpoints. Le Corbusier achieved in the actual four dimensions of space-time what the cubist painters were exploring and expressing in their paintings before World War I. As Picasso provided us with the possibility of seeing inside-outside simultaneously and multiple perspective of objects, Le Corbusier did the same to architecture.

SPACE-TIME OF INSIDE OUTSIDE

BEST PRODUCTS COMPANY, MILWAUKEE, WISCONSIN

The Inside-Outside Building of Best Products Company, Inc., in Milwaukee, Wisconsin, exemplifies not only the interpenetration of inside and outside space in a commercial application, but presents materials and construction techniques exposed in the process of "unbuilding." Designed by SITE (1985), this showroom is a 1000-foot-long piece of public sculpture in a typical suburban shopping center.

The building features an ambiguous interior recess between the jagged and broken exterior brick shell and a second interior shell of thermal glass (which actually encloses the store proper). Merchandise on display is seen simultaneously inside and out, the thermal glass screen being the boundary between actual objects for sale and neutral gray-colored reproductions of the same objects in the recess space. The duality of inside/outside is reinforced by sample wares physically bisected by the glass screen, existing in full color on one side and dull gray on the other.

The "unbuilding" presentation of the outer shell is a remarkable cutaway of how a typical suburban shopping mall store is constructed. Gaping holes in the exterior wall reveal the various building components frozen in space and time. The sculptural result tells a detailed story of architectural fabrication. James Wines (1932–   ), principal of SITE, says:

We've been working with narrative architecture a long time, using construction as a sort of biography of a building. Other narrative artists take a subject from life and abstract it through a graphic process to such an extent that the source is lost. Our idea is that the story is already there in the building.[25]

SPACE-TIME INTERACTION WITH THE CYCLES OF NATURE

MONTEREY BAY AQUARIUM, MONTEREY, CALIFORNIA

The interpenetration of inside and outside space cannot avoid the interaction of the cycles of na-

INSIDE/OUTSIDE BUILDING,
CATALOGUE SHOWROOM, BEST
PRODUCTS CO., INC., MILWAUKEE,
WISCONSIN. SITE, 1984.

*This building not only shows its insides
outside, but displays its sale merchandise
through space-time. Photograph by John
Kurtich.*

ture. When a building consciously interacts with nature, the results can be dramatic. The Monterey Bay Aquarium, designed by Esherick, Homsey, Dodge and Davis in 1985, is a building complex on the edge of Monterey Bay, so situated that the Pacific Ocean literally penetrates the building cyclicly with the tides. This creates "natural" tanks that house the various species of sea life found in Monterey Bay inside the aquarium, providing human access to and experience of this alien world.

The aquarium is built on the site of the former Hovden Cannery, adapting a renovated warehouse in its complex of new construction. (See Chapter 8 for a discussion of the adapted reuse of the cannery into an aquarium.) It is ironic that this cannery was once committed to the destruction of marine life but is now dedicated to its preservation. The building complex wraps around a large tidal pool, partially natural and partially constructed, which is the main focal point of the aquarium and clearly exemplifies the relationship of the architecture to nature.

Human experience is enriched by the Kelp Forest Tank (66 feet long by 28 feet high, open to the sky), the 90-foot-long Monterey Bay Tank (housing bat rays, large sharks, and numerous

ocean fish), and the Sea Otter Tank, all of which can be viewed as a scuba diver would see them. Other experiences include the Touch Pool in which visitors are encouraged to actually handle various forms of sea life, and the Sandy Shore, a two-story cage containing an actual sandy beach interacting with the ocean. This sustains various forms of coastal plant life and a typical seabird population contained within the aquarium proper. Wavelets periodically wash over the sandy beach, bringing ocean nutrients to birds. The cyclic nature of these waves reminds the viewer that this human-made environment responds directly to the ocean's rhythm, which constantly changes the contours of the beach as it brings in fresh food.

SPACE-TIME OF THE DAILY SOLAR CYCLE

PANTHEON, ROME, ITALY

Direct architectural response to the cycles of nature can create unique space-time. The ancient Pantheon of Rome (ca. A.D. 120–126) is a primary example of a building that responds directly to the

KELP FOREST TANK, MONTEREY BAY AQUARIUM, MONTEREY, CALIFORNIA. ESHERICK, HOMSEY, DODGE AND DAVIS, 1985.

The Kelp Forest Tank is directly linked to the tides and natural light of the Monterey Bay, physically demonstrating an architectural interaction with physical cycles of the ocean. Photograph by John Kurtich.

PORCH FACADE, PANTHEON, ROME, ITALY. A.D. 120–124.

This view of the Pantheon emphasizes the traditional Roman temple form, hiding the unique rotunda and dome which, in reality, dominates the building complex both inside and out. Photograph by John Kurtich.

PORCH, PANTHEON, ROME, ITALY. A.D. 120–124.

The standard Roman longitudinal axis of the porch terminates at the giant bronze doors, the boundary between the world of the third dimension and that of the fourth. Photograph by John Kurtich.

daily cyclic changes of the sun. The human experience that results from this building is created by a combination of strong geometric volumes and axial patterns, which are coordinated with the sun's apparent movement across the sky.

The geometry of the Pantheon was bold and original for its time. Basically it is a traditional Roman rectangular temple porch attached to a larger cylinder topped with a dome. The temple porch is octastyle, that is, it has eight Corinthian columns supporting its pedimental roof. The porch is three columns deep, providing enough volume and depth to give the effect of a substantial temple. Although the cylindrical part of the building is evident when viewing the front, it is the ornate porch that first captures the viewer's attention. In ancient times this porch would have been even more dominant because the level of the surrounding city was much lower (the original porch had five steep steps).

The porch provides a strong longitudinal axial path for the viewer to enter the building.

This axis appears to continue through into the interior of the entire complex because it is grounded in the stability of the classical temple form. The viewer is led through the central passage of the porch to monumental bronze-plated double doors. In ancient times the ceiling of the porch had bronze barrel vaults running in the direction of the path of entry, reinforcing this axis. The porch is relatively dark because of its depth.

Passing through the double doors, one literally steps into the fourth dimension. The space is a domed cylinder, so vast and powerful yet simple

MOVEMENT OF SUN (3), ROTUNDA, PANTHEON, ROME, ITALY. A.D. 120–124.

The "eye of Zeus" moves about the interior space, first spotlighting the coffers, reaching into the lower regions of the rotunda, and finally illuminating the humans within the space. Photographs by John Kurtich.

MOVEMENT OF SUN (1), ROTUNDA, PANTHEON, ROME, ITALY. A.D. 120–124.

MOVEMENT OF SUN (2), ROTUNDA, PANTHEON, ROME, ITALY. A.D. 120–124.

in its geometric purity. There is a dramatic change in the quality of light, from the dark porch to the focused sunlight, illuminating the rotunda. The dominant longitudinal axis vanishes; in its place is a vertical axis running through the center of the dome, through a 30-foot oculus. One's eyes are immediately drawn to this oculus because the coffers of the lacunar[26] optically emphasize it.

The human viewer is both dwarfed by the space and yet in command of the space by its strong centralizing organization. A rich articulation of columns, niches, and aediculae grace the lower level of the cylindrical wall, giving a human scale the viewer can better relate to. The upper level of the wall has a series of blind windows that continue this scalar relationship. The first rank of the optically manipulated coffers marks the beginning of the dome, and the resulting optical vortex created by the coffered design emphasizes the viewer's attention on the oculus. There are twenty-eight radiating coffers in each of five ranks. Each coffer is articulated with a descending order of three steps so constructed that its steps are shallower on its lower edge and steeper on its higher, making the rotunda seem wider than it actually is and leading the eye of the viewer directly to the oculus.

The most dramatic feature of the interior is the way in which the light of the sun is projected through the oculus. This projected circle of hot light moves about the space with the apparent movement of the sun across the sky. The sense of this movement is possible even in a short visit to the monument. When the sun is high overhead during the middle of a summer day, the floor is spotlighted. As the day progresses, the circle of light climbs back up the wall, first illuminating the ornate level of columns, niches, and aediculae, then the second level of ornamental windows, then finally ascends into the coffers of the dome itself before it is swallowed up by the oculus as the sun begins to set. Every day is a new experience with the circle of light as the position of the sun is constantly changing.

The conscious attention of the building to the changing aspects of sunlight is a potent expression of the fourth dimension. The oculus focuses the light and forces the viewer to be aware of the nature of this light and how it can move about in the space. Although the Pantheon was originally intended to be a temple to all the gods and goddesses, clearly the "eye of Zeus" dominates the interior by means of the sun projecting through the oculus.

SPACE-TIME OF DYNAMIC LIGHT

THE PAINTED APARTMENT, CHICAGO, ILLINOIS

When a designer consciously uses the changing quality of natural light, the space produced can be a magical experience for the observer. The Painted Apartment (1983) by Krueck and Olsen (see Chapter 2 for a complete case study of this project) represents a sensitivity to not only the ever-changing natural light but also a juxtaposition to outside natural conditions. The apartment, located on an upper floor of the 2400 Lakeview Avenue Building designed by Mies Van der Rohe (1886–1969), overlooking Chicago's Lincoln Park and Lake Michigan, responds directly to the spectacular view and the natural shapes of the shoreline and landscape. The exterior window wall establishes the link with nature; all interior partitions stop short of this wall, allowing the panoramic view to dominate the interior. The use of overlapping, curved, and perforated metal screens as a space divider reflects the natural shapes of the outside landscape and filters daily and seasonal light qualities. It is as though the outside atmosphere has been brought indoors because these screens become transparent, translucent, or opaque as the light in the space dictates.

The floor, walls, and ceiling are painted in high gloss to reflect light and extend the space in all directions as a response to the infinite space beyond the window wall. Painted patterns on the floor and ceiling, such as dots and curving ribbon-lines, extend the diaphanous metal screens. Curved, back-lit, glass-block walls terminate the real space with an illusion of infinite space beyond. The space dramatizes the natural and continuous change of light from morning to night.

Living room area, "Painted
Apartment," 2400 Lake View
Avenue Building, Chicago,
Illinois. Krueck and Olsen, 1983.

*Interior space is linked directly with the
exterior through the continuum of
changing light. Photograph by John
Kurtich.*

Space-Time of Architectural Dematerialization

THE FARNSWORTH HOUSE, PLANO, ILLINOIS

Architecture juxtaposed with nature can either de-materialize itself so that nature is dominant or it can create a cooperative symbiosis with nature on an equal basis. An example of the former is the Farnsworth House (1946–1951) by Ludwig Mies van der Rohe (1886–1969). This house was de-signed to be a country retreat on the banks of the Fox River near Plano, Illinois, about 50 miles west of Chicago. It is a single, rectangular box with four transparent walls of glass and a flat floor and ceiling. The entire mass is raised five feet off the ground on the same columns that form the basic structure of the box itself, a functional concession to the fact that the river occasionally floods. Asymmetrical to the house is another raised platform halfway up from the ground level, serving as an outdoor patio and transition surface.

This travertine terrace exists in vivid contrast to its surrounding soft and colorful landscape. In order to reach the house, one must walk across a meadow without the definition of paving or path. The sense of isolation of this pristine, machinelike object is assured by the absence of a defined con-nection to the approach road. The visitor experi-ences a dramatic change underfoot of texture and sound when crossing the meadow to the traver-tine stair. The sense of arrival is vivid and com-plete.

The combination of the floor-to-ceiling glass walls and the raised condition of the entire house dematerializes the interior architecture. The ex-perience one has inside is that of being part of the infinite expansion of nature. In the spring and summer, a rich green turf extends through the site, which includes magnificent trees with thick green foliage. One is living in the middle of a green forest on the banks of a river. In the au-tumn, the leaves of the trees produce a riot of color that totally changes the atmospheric quality of the house. In the winter, a blanket of snow dominates the landscape, and the occupant of the house is aware of the cold expanse in every direc-tion as well as the sensation of floating above it.

SOUTH ELEVATION, FARNSWORTH
HOUSE, FOX RIVER VALLEY, SOUTH
OF PLANO, ILLINOIS. LUDWIG MIES
VAN DER ROHE, 1945–1951.

*The house is a sculptural object in the
landscape, defining various levels of
dematerialized interior spaces through
orchestrated planes of transparency,
translucency, and opacity. Photograph
by John Kurtich.*

SPACE-TIME OF ARCHITECTURAL SYMBIOSIS WITH NATURE

FALLING WATER, BEAR RUN, PENNSYLVANIA

A house that forms a cooperative symbiosis with
nature is the Kaufmann residence, known as Falling Water, at Bear Run, Pennsylvania (1935–

1937). Frank Lloyd Wright (1867–1959) took advantage of a wooded Pennsylvania stream with a
rocky waterfall and created a four-dimensional.
statement about the relationship between a house
and its natural site. The building he designed par-
ticipates fully with its surroundings, from the dramatic cantilevered projection of the house over
the waterfall to the blurred edges between the
house boundary and forest. "There in a beautiful
forest was a solid, high rock ledge rising beside a

WATERFALL VIEW, EDGAR J.
KAUFMANN, SR., RESIDENCE
("FALLINGWATER"), OHIOPYLE,
PENNSYLVANIA. FRANK LLOYD
WRIGHT, 1935.

*"Fallingwater" becomes one with nature
as it grows out of the rocky canyon and
embraces the waterfall. Photograph by
John Kurtich.*

waterfall, and the natural thing seemed to be to
cantilever the house from that rock bank over the
falling water . . ."[27] said Wright, describing the
house he had designed.

When one first approaches Falling Water, the
impression is that of a series of pale yellow-col-
ored horizontal planes hovering above ground at
varying heights within a forest, defying gravity,
yet nestled within the protective confines of the
forest. The actual supports for these planes are
massive vertical elements built from the natural

stone of the area. The color of the stone blends
into the landscape so well that the horizontal
planes seem miraculous in their apparent suspen-
sion of natural laws.

The climax of the viewer's experience comes
when the house is viewed from below the waterfall, which is reached by passing by the entire
south elevation of the house, following the directional flow of the stream. This journey slowly
reveals the drama of the cantilevered planes until
suddenly the stream drops twenty feet, and the

house is suspended, jutting out over the falls. The relationship of the house to its natural site is total. There are no compromises. The integrity of the human-made structure is maintained by the pure, smooth rectangular forms of the horizontal planes. The integrity of nature is represented by the completely natural waterfall and rocky streambed. The fusion of the two occurs with the natural rock vertical supports for the house, rising out of the bedrock and locking into the variously poised horizontal planes.

The interior of the house is a continued statement about the house's relationship with nature. Natural stone walls and flag stone floors create an impression that the interiors were almost carved out of the bedrock of the stream banks. As in the Farnsworth House, glass walls are used to extend the interior spaces to the stream below, the forest beyond, and the sky above. House boundaries are blurred by cantilevered trellises, forming a glazed trellis roofing on the interior and unglazed open trellis on the exterior. A transparent glass wall separates the actual inside from the outside, but the effect is that the house seems to extend directly into nature, with no normal boundaries of enclosure.

Details of glazing enhance this effect. Glass walls are designed to fit directly into the vertical stone piers and towers, without bulky frames to betray the boundary. Mullions are minimal and slender. In critical places such as corners, the edge of the glass is mitered forty-five degrees and cemented together so that no opaque mullion or structural member obstructs the view.

A suspended staircase leads one down from a terrace off the living room to an outdoor landing below it at the stream level. This is a pure gesture of communion with nature. One is at the stream just before it plunges into the waterfall. The moving water, the sound of the out-of-sight waterfall, the reflection of the water on the natural stone support wall, and the bottom of the cantilevered platform above all contribute to the closeness to nature one experiences.

The maintenance of the integrity of nature is all-important with this design. Although the house has imposed its presence on the site, it does

WINDOW DETAIL, EDGAR J. KAUFMANN, SR., RESIDENCE ("FALLINGWATER"), OHIOPYLE, PENNSYLVANIA. FRANK LLOYD WRIGHT, 1935.

The disappearing corner in the window reinforces the symbiotic relationship between the house and its natural setting. Photograph by John Kurtich.

so with such complete sensitivity to the natural surroundings that symbiosis is complete. The normally dissimilar elements of nature and human structure live together in close association and cooperation. Over the driveway on the north side of the house, Wright designed a trellis covering, which joined the house to a rock cliff north of it. In order not to disturb an existing large tree near the house, one trellis beam was curved around the trunk of the tree in order to accommodate it without interrupting the spacing rhythm of the trellis. Falling Water is a four-dimensional house, from its bold siting on the banks of Bear Run to its details of mitered glass corner windows. Frank Lloyd Wright was totally involved in relating every aspect of the house to its natural setting. One experiences a meaningful and profound communication with nature. Wright achieved a noble equilibrium between nature outside and living quarters inside, between an infinity of outward spatial flow and inward refuge.

Integration of Space-Time Trompe l'Oeil

Villa Barbaro, Maser, Italy

Architectural space can be transformed through illusion with nature by trompe l'oeil painting. An excellent example of this concept is found in the Villa Barbaro at Maser, Italy, which combines trompe l'oeil landscape paintings framed by trompe l'oeil windows adjacent to actual windows revealing the genuine Italian landscape. This villa was designed by Andrea Palladio (1508–1580) about 1560 for Daniele Barbaro, patriarch of Aquileja, and his brother Marcantonio Barbaro, ambassador of the Republic of Venice. The pictorial decoration and trompe l'oeil painting

SOUTH ELEVATION, VILLA BARBARO-LULING BUSCHETTI, MASER, ITALY. ANDREA PALLADIO, 1549/1551–1558.

The villa is built into a hill in such a way that the front of the building is a full two stories, but the rear is only the upper story which opens out into a hillside garden at the same level. Photograph by John Kurtich.

CRUCIFORM HALL, VILLA BARBARO-LULING BUSCHETTI, MASER, ITALY. ANDREA PALLADIO, 1549/1551–1558. FRESCO PAINTING BY PAOLO VERONESE, 1560–1562.

Trompe l'oeil *architectural details and moldings blur painting with reality in this highly stylized interior. Copyright 1991, G. Paolo Marton.*

was by Paolo Veronese (1528–1588) and his assistants. The villa was built as the principal building for its owners, on the edge of the farm fields it commands.

The villa is a symmetrical arrangement built into a hillside with arcaded side wings projecting forward onto the landscape. This central portion is of a modified classical temple form with four Ionic columns engaged in its facade supporting an elaborate pediment complete with sculpture. The *piano nobile* or upper level is the principal living quarters, and the hillside permits this level to terminate at its rear with an enclosed court featuring an antiquarian's nymphaeum filled with the deities of Olympus.

Every room of the *piano nobile* was frescoed by Paolo Veronese. The principal device employed by the artist was trompe l'oeil painting portraying mythological scenes, allegorical statements, portraits of the family, and contemporary landscape scenes. Painted architectural frames enclose these scenes, blurring the edges between them and the actual architecture.

The most four-dimensional space in the villa is the Cruciform Hall, the central organizing space of the *piano nobile*. The frescoes of this room successfully achieve their own architectural structure, almost independent of Palladio's architecture. The cross-shaped room is light, appearing to be open to the sky. Painted landscapes imitating ancient perspectives allow one to see through the actual walls. The views are seen through painted arches with balustrades, framed by painted Corinthian columns that seem to support a heavy entablature just under the ceiling plane. Genuine doors to adjoining spaces are confused with equal-size painted doors that feature life-size members of the family and staff entering the real space of the hall. At the front of the longitudinal portion of the room, a large, authentic window commands a spectacular view of the villa's farmlands and surrounding countryside. At the opposite end of this axis is a large set of genuine double doors opening out to the hillside courtyard that features the elaborate nymphaeum.

One experiences a space that is greatly expanded beyond the actual architecture. There are glimpses into false rooms, which are in turn confirmed by real doors leading into genuine rooms adjoining the hall. The perspective vistas realistically framed by painted architecture are verified by the central window of the front of the facade commanding the major view of the landscaped extension of the villa and the distant countryside.

In spite of the dominance of the wall fresco employed as a decorative device, there is no feeling of tension or instability. The illusionistic expansiveness of the hall is in perfect harmony with the architecture and surrounding landscape. The idealism expressed in Palladio's villa design is reinforced with Veronese's ideal views of antique and contemporary scenes. A mastery of light and color is evident in both the architecture and the frescoes. The elusive, effervescent light of northern Italy is perfectly captured by Veronese's painting technique.

TROMPE L'OEIL SPACE-TIME WARP

THE PALAZZO DEL TE, MANTUA, ITALY

The exclusive use of trompe l'oeil painting to distort and alter the geometry of space can create a significant four-dimensional experience, a space-time warp. Such experience is found in the Palazzo del Te in Mantua, Italy, the masterpiece of Guilio Romano (1499–1546). The palazzo was built between 1526 and 1534 as a summer palace or *villa suburbana* for the Gonzaga family, the dominating family of Mantua at the time. The palazzo is essentially a square building with a large interior square courtyard attached to a larger garden on the east side with outbuildings and walls maintaining a strong axial symmetry with the square building. The eastern end of the garden enclosure terminates with large-scale, hemicycle arches.

The palazzo represents an outstanding example of *mannerism*, the transitional period between High Renaissance and Baroque in Italian art and architecture. Mannerist architecture expressed themes and motifs in opposition to their

Courtyard, Palazzo del Te, Mantua, Italy. Guilio Romano, 1525–1535.

The central courtyard expresses through classical architectural vocabulary a new language of Italian Mannerism. Photograph by John Kurtich.

original meanings or context. Romano violated the rules of classical architecture by using classical motifs in original ways. Keystones of arches were greatly exaggerated in size and rusticated to contrast with the surrounding wall treatment. A rhythm of slipped triglyphs in the Doric entablature of the courtyard disturbs the viewer who is used to the serenity and stability of the normal classical order.

Inside, there is a series of chambers, each ornately and elaborately decorated with wall and ceiling frescoes and stucco work. The most notable of the rooms are the *Camera dei Cavalli* with life-size portraits of Gonzaga's horses perched on fireplace mantels and the tops of door frames; the *Camera di Psiche,* depicting the story of Psyche from Apuleius; the *Camera di Fetonte,* illustrating the fall of Phaeton; and the *Sala dei Giganti,* depicting the battle between the gods and the titans for supremacy over the world.

It is in the *Sala dei Giganti* that painting dominates the space. The room is a nearly square rectangle. All four walls and ceiling are covered with a continuous fresco depicting a tremendous battle to the death. The intersections between the walls and ceilings are blurred and rounded with plaster so that there is no discernable distinction between planes as the fresco continues. Windows and doors, necessary for light and circulation, are simply cut through the fresco with no frame or treatment to identify them as such. The geometry of

the room has been distorted beyond perception, a space-time warp, as one becomes engrossed in the story. An excerpt from Edgar Allan Poe's *The Pit and the Pendulum* aptly describes what a viewer might experience in this space.

I had observed that, although the outlines of the figures upon the walls were sufficiently distinct, yet the colors seemed blurred and indefinite. These colors had now assumed, and were momentarily assuming, a startling and most intense brilliancy, that gave to the spectral and fiendish portraitures an aspect that might have thrilled even firmer nerves than my own. Demon eyes, of a wild and ghastly vivacity, glared upon me in a thousand directions where none had been visible before, and gleamed with the lurid lustre of a fire that I could not force my imagination to regard as unreal.

Unreal! . . . A deeper glow settled each moment in the eyes that glared at my agonies! A richer tint of crimson diffused itself over the pictured horrors of blood. I panted! I gasped for breath! . . . —Oh! for a voice to speak!—oh! horror!—oh! any horror but this! With a shriek, I rushed from the margin, and buried my face in my hands—weeping bitterly.

. . . The room had been square . . . In an instant the apartment had shifted its form into that of a lozenge . . . And now, flatter and flatter, grew the lozenge, with a rapidity that left me no time for contemplation . . . I shrank back—but the closing walls pressed me resistlessly onward.[28]

The expressions on both the gods and the titans are sinister. The battle is very intense, with

SALA DEI GIGANTI, PALAZZO DEL TE, MANTUA, ITALY. GUILIO ROMANO, 1525–1535.

The destruction of the painted architecture and agony of the defeated giants reinforce the apparent instability of the actual room. Photograph by John Kurtich.

Zeus near the center of the ceiling hurling light-
ning bolts upon the enemy. The titans are losing
the battle. They are collapsing as the architecture
around them is collapsing. The entire fresco is a
whirl of activity, destruction, instability. The
viewer cannot avoid getting totally involved in
the pictorial story.

The scale of the room and its frescoes is appropriate to the effect. The titans are painted
much larger than human scale, and these are the
creatures that the viewer sees at eye level. The
gods are mainly in the ceiling, which includes a
trompe l'oeil dome and thunderclouds supporting

the Olympian entourage. The floor is a circular,
inlaid colored stone design that corresponds to the
dome and circle of gods above, adding to the
frenzy of color and activity. Originally, the entire
room was a singular painting, with the walls and
floor blending into the continuum as the walls and
ceiling currently do. Before the eighteenth century severe damage that destroyed the transitional
floor/wall paintings up to about seven feet occurred in the room. The wall paintings were subsequently restored without this important
transition, abruptly ending the illusion at the intersection of the wall and floor.

The room also had a fireplace located between the two windows in its original version. The painted illusion of the battle would be dramatically enhanced by the light of a flickering fire. The acoustical quality of the space completed the four-dimensional experience. Because of the hard surfaces of floor, walls, and ceiling, the room echoes and reverberates with any acoustical activity. The addition of the human observer moving about in the space creates the sound effects, which reinforce the visual drama.

Trompe l'Oeil Space-Time Expansion

AUDIOKRAFTERS, FAIRFAX, VIRGINIA

A contemporary example of the use of trompe l'oeil to enhance and expand space into the fourth dimension is a small high fidelity components shop, AudioKrafters, Fairfax, Virginia (1987), created by Chicago designer Jonathan Sherman (1958–) in collaboration with Chicago artist Charles Nitti (1952–). The basic space for the shop was carved out of a 1960s movie theater that had been converted into eight shops for a new shopping mall. Basically a narrow rectangle, the resulting plan had an angled cross-wall that could not be removed near the entry. This wall became the rationale for a series of other angled cross-walls, all with cutouts, allowing the customer to see through a series of varying framed spaces, much like a complicated stage set.

The public area of the shop was divided into four trapezoids in plan. The concept was that each zone would contain audio equipment that became progressively better in quality and higher in price as one proceeded through the store. The walls of zone 1 were painted in faux stone, which included remnants of classical architectural entablature, molding, and columns. The wall dividing this zone from the next had large, irregular cutouts that were determined in part by the architectural elements painted on them. Zone 2 featured faux marble walls appearing to be constructed of heavy marble blocks. The dividing wall of this zone to

the next had an irregular proscenium cutout that exposed zone 3, a space dominated by heavenly clouds over all the visible wall surfaces. Its back wall featured one cutout, an abstracted **A** outlined within the frame with a continuous teal blue neon light coloring the entire frame with a vibrant blue. This **A** cutout was the entry into the final space, which spotlighted a state-of-the-art video theater. This space was relatively dark and without trompe l'oeil treatment so that total focus would be on projection video demonstrations with high-fidelity surround sound.

The progression of spaces from stone through marble to clouds was a four-dimensional journey where space-time merges with sound. Participants were literally transported out of their ordinary environment into one of dreams and fantasy by means of trompe l'oeil painting and high tech audio. These intensifying zones prepare them for the electronic nirvana through the vibrant blue A-frame door.

Trompe l'Oeil Space-Time Dynamism

THE FOUNTAIN OF ROME, VILLA D'ESTE, TIVOLI, ITALY

When the elements of trompe l'oeil are combined with any sort of elements of motion, a dynamic four-dimensional space-time is the result. The gardens of the Villa d'Este of Tivoli, Italy, have the remains of such an example. The Villa d'Este was the sumptuous hillside residence of the governor of Tivoli, Ippolito II d'Este, the cardinal of Ferrara. In 1550, he commissioned Pirro Ligorio (1520–1580) to transform what was originally a Benedictine convent into a richly decorated and appointed residence with elaborate gardens covering two steep slopes adjoining the building structure.

The architecture of the villa is not particularly significant, but the experience of the gardens is a four-dimensional extravaganza. The gardens cover two adjacent slopes that converge to a flat terrace at the bottom. A primary axis centers on

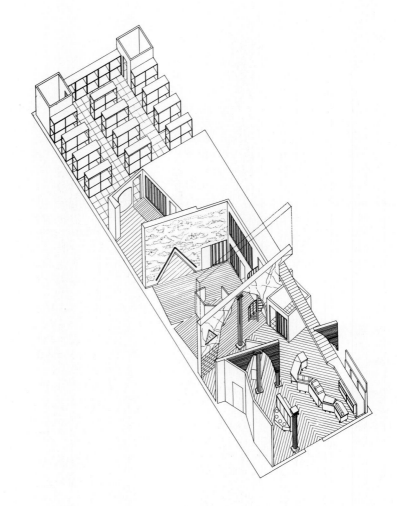

PLAN OBLIQUE, AUDIOKRAFTERS, FAIRFAX, VIRGINIA. JONATHAN SHERMAN, 1987.

The designer took advantage of a non-removeable angled wall in the existing space to create a series of spatial and perceptual experiences in this specialty showroom. Drawing by Jonathan Sherman.

SHOWROOM, AUDIOKRAFTERS, FAIRFAX, VIRGINIA. JONATHAN SHERMAN, 1987. TROMPE L'OEIL PAINTING BY CHARLES NITTI.

The showroom is a series of spaces defined by faux architectural fragments and trompe l'oeil painting. Photograph by Jonathan Sherman.

ALLÉE OF ONE HUNDRED FOUNTAINS, VILLA D'ESTE, TIVOLI, ITALY. PIRRO LIGORIO, 1569.

A major cross-axis of the garden is the Allée of One Hundred Fountains, unified by a long chain of water jets spurting from the retaining wall, and seasoned with the occasional fantasy creature such as the full-breasted sphinx announcing a diverse path from the allée. Photograph by John Kurtich.

FOUNTAIN OF ROMA, VILLA D'ESTE, TIVOLI, ITALY. CURZIO MACCARONE, 1568.

The Fountain of Roma was perhaps the most ambitious fountain in the garden as it portrayed a three-dimensional city in forced perspective with two "rivers" flowing with fountain water to symbolically link Tivoli with Rome. Photograph by John Kurtich.

the villa and several cross-axes at right angles. Although the primary axis creates a sense of visual unity, the viewer is constantly diverted by cross-axes, which lead to the most interesting fountains of the gardens.

One such fountain is the Fountain of Rome, a three-dimensional theatrical set in miniature, using fore-shortened, exaggerated perspective to portray the buildings of ancient Rome. This amounts to a three-dimensional trompe l'oeil, producing the illusion of greater depth than the space actually provides. If that were not enough,

water cascades out of miniature cliffs to the left of the fountain, representing the river Anio at Tivoli; this water then flows to join a representation of the Tiber River, which forms a flat water foreground to the miniature city. In the center of this Tiber is a small stone boat with an obelisk as its mast, depicting the actual island of San Bartolomeo at Rome.

The Fountain of Rome has the appearance of a background for theatrical presentations, but the way water was employed did not particularly suggest a theater. The original seats from which to admire the fountain were designed with secret holes so that the visitor would get his rear end soaking wet. "The stairs to the little flat green below the cascade were made with a surprise jet of water which 'bathes from the navel down' whoever steps there."[29]

SPACE-TIME OF MOTION

THE VILLA D'ESTE GARDENS, TIVOLI, ITALY

Moving water is a very powerful medium for creating four-dimensional space-time. The gardens at Villa d'Este are rich with working fountains and water complexes. However the viewer can never experience the gardens from a fixed place but must experience a subjective adventure of exploration, deviation, and surprise. The sound of moving water, varying from gurgles to splashes, drips to torrents, is a unifying force.

The many fountains of the gardens provide rich sight, sound, and tactile sensations. There is always a background sound of water in its many manifestations. The fountains provide visual distractions to lead one astray from an intended path.

A variety of fountains play with mythological, geographical, and abstract themes. Finally the moving water itself defines enclosed space in diverse and interesting ways.

A significant experience of the gardens during the sixteenth century was the Water Organ, an architectural fountain developed by Claude Venard. "A sudden rush of water also by its flow activated the mechanical controls which opened and closed the different pipes, producing a harmony of music introduced by two trumpet calls."[30] Water organs were known in antiquity, as Vitruvius describes in his *Book X,* Chapter 8, and Hero of Alexandria also had descriptions. But in antiquity, such a water organ was played by an organist upon keys. The Water Organ of the Villa d'Este was operated by water only.

Another fountain with unusual sounds was the Fountain of the Owl. In the sixteenth century the central portion of this fountain was composed of a large niche in which three stucco youths were standing above a large vase, holding a wineskin that poured water into the vase and beyond into a basin. An artificial rock was the niche background and support for the vase; upon this were delicate bronze tree branches supporting bronze birds that chirped by means of the same principle as the

OVAL FOUNTAIN, VILLA D'ESTE, TIVOLI, ITALY. CURZIO MACCARONE, 1565–1570.

The Oval Fountain is designed to enter and walk through, the visitor being literally inside the water flow, looking out at the gardens through a shimmering curtain. Photograph by John Kurtich.

Water Organ. Their song would stop only when an owl, again powered by a water device, would suddenly appear and hoot.

In addition to aural surprises by these special water devices, there were tactile surprises as well. Designed within the pavement here and there were trick water jets that would spurt suddenly and surprise visitors.

SPACE-TIME OF MOTION AND SCULPTURE

WILLIAMS SQUARE, IRVING, TEXAS

Water moving about bronze sculptures of mustangs combine to create the space-time of the plaza at Williams Square, Irving, Texas (1985). Robert Glen sculpted and cast the mustangs, the SWA Group of Houston, Texas, created the splashing effects of the fountain and the surrounding plaza. The plaza itself is like a prairie—300 square feet of flat, granite paving. Its boundaries are enclosed on three sides by office buildings, a pair of opposing fourteen-story towers flanking a twenty-six-story central tower. Without the focal element of the water and sculpture, the space would be a deadly expanse of flatness, uninviting to any human participant. The water and sculpture transform the space into a dynamic experience, a space-time event that makes the entire office complex and plaza work as a unit.

The water fountain is a visual representation of a Texas stream cutting through the abstraction of the flat, arid Texas prairie. The stream is located diagonally in the square, with its widest portion approximately in the center. Depressions and texturing of the granite paving at the water's edge abstract the geological reality of water wearing away layers of earth. This geologic simulation is further enhanced by the use of different textures and colors of granite paving, recalling the subtle variety found in the actual prairie.

The bronze mustangs are running and splashing through the stream. They have been sculpted 1.5 times life size, muscles taut, manes flying, the epitome of raw energy. When first viewing this sculptural fountain from afar, the horses look small in the vast plaza, but the viewer experiences

MUSTANG FOUNTAIN, WILLIAMS
SQUARE, IRVING, TEXAS. SCULPTURE
BY ROB GLEN; FOUNTAIN BY SWA
GROUP OF HOUSTON, TEXAS; 1985.

*The interaction of the mustangs and the
water realistically portray the energy of
wild horses galloping through a flowing
river. Photograph by Tennyson
Stannard.*

a dramatic change of scale upon closer inspection.
The realization of their true proportions provides
one of the events of the experience.

SPACE-TIME THROUGH
SCULPTURE

THE PARTHENON, ATHENS, GREECE

The complete infusion of sculpture with architecture can produce a powerful four-dimensional experience, especially when the boundaries between

the two are indistinct. The building that epitomizes this combination is the Parthenon of ancient
Athens, Greece, constructed between 447 and 432
B.C. Pericles (495–429 B.C.) had political control
of Athens at the time, and in the wake of defeating
the Persians for the last time, he wanted to honor
Athens's victory at Salamis over the Persians with
the greatest, most lavish temple in the Greek
world. The temple would be dedicated to Athena,
patron goddess of Athens, as well as the multiple
personifications of virginity, wisdom, weaving,
and martial protection. Major sculptures were incorporated into the architecture to highlight the
patriotic achievements of the Athenians as well as

WEST ELEVATION, PARTHENON,
ATHENS, GREECE. PHIDIAS, ICTINUS,
AND CALLICRATES, 447–432 B.C.

*The Parthenon was built as a monument
rather than as a "working" temple; it
epitomized the refinement of the Doric
order. Photograph by John Kurtich.*

to display the triumph of civilization over barbarism.

Phidias (500–430 B.C.), the renowned sculptor, was chosen not only to create the temple's new cult statue but to supervise the overall design and construction of the temple and its other sculptural elements. The architects Callicrates (mid-fifth century B.C.) and Iktinus (mid-fifth century B.C.) worked under Phidias. The temple that this team designed was basically Doric, but it departed from the usual formula. Because of the need for a larger cella than normal, the temple dimensions were altered by adding two columns to the usual six in its front facade, thereby maintaining the proportional ratio of a normal temple but achieving a larger one at the same time.

The principal sculptures included ninety-two high relief metopes, an Ionic frieze on the exterior cella walls measuring 524 linear feet, three-dimensional sculptural events in each of the pediments, and the giant cult statue of Athena in the sanctuary. The utilization of sophisticated optical adjustments in the construction of the building blurred the distinction between traditional decorative sculpture and the overall sculptural tendencies of the temple structure itself.

The Parthenon was the culmination of a building that departed from traditional geometric

DETAIL OF OPTICAL CORRECTION OF
STYLOBATE, PARTHENON, ATHENS,
GREECE. PHIDIAS, ICTINUS, AND
CALLICRATES, 447–432 B.C.

*The stylobate and steps curve very
noticeably in this view of east side of the
Parthenon. Photograph by John
Kurtich.*

THE MEASURED HORIZONTAL
CURVATURE OF THE LINES IN THE
UPPER STEP AND ARCHITRAVE OF THE
PARTHENON, DRAWN BY JOHN
PENNETHORNE, 1878.

*This nineteenth century drawing shows,
in exaggerated format, the curvatures of
the stylobate and architrave. Courtesy of
The Art Institute of Chicago.*

shapes. One type of intentional distortion was entasis, the outward curvature of the column shaft. This distortion was to correct the optical illusion observed in a column with perfectly straight sides if seen against a background of light; such a column seems to be thinner at its midpoint than at its top or bottom. The Parthenon's entasis is thought by some scholars to be a "circular arc, with a maximum increment of about $^{11}/_{16}$ inch, so that the radius would have been nearly half a mile."[31]

The columns were tapered as well, originating from such natural tapering found in tree trunks, which were the first columns. Visually, tapering upward increased the apparent height of the column, which also reduced the feeling of strain that a perpendicular shaft might induce. Then the columns themselves were given an inward slant, which gave the end (front and rear) elevations of the temple something of a pyramid's silhouette, the feeling of power, stability, and repose.

The entire temple was constructed so that the horizontal lines of the stylobate and entablature curved upward at the centers. This optically compensated for the visual effect of sagging from a long row of columns that bear down on the stylobate.

The treads of the steps and the platform rise from each corner to the middle of the frontage; on the ends of the temple the gradient of the curve is 1 in 450, on the sides 1 in 170—a matter of 4 inches. But there is also an inward slant, and so the whole floor is very slightly domed, with its highest point at the centre of the building and lowest points at the corners of the platform . . .[32]

Visiting the Parthenon, even today when it is largely in ruins, with most of the figurative sculptural elements either destroyed or in European museums, is inspiring and uplifting. The perceptual senses are brought together with intellectual and spiritual ones to give the viewer a four-dimensional presentation of art that is totally inseparable from architecture. The Greek idea of the sculptural human-made temple in the natural landscape, standing out in contrast to but obviously derived from nature, is epitomized in the Parthenon.

METAPHORIC SPACE–TIME THROUGH NARRATIVE ART

NOTRE DAME, CHARTRES, FRANCE

The artistic epitome of the Gothic era, the Cathedral of Notre Dame at Chartres, France, (1194–1260) infused art in its entire structure as an iconographic encyclopedia of the teachings of the Bible. The exterior skin of the church is literally covered with sculpture depicting the teachings of Christ, the lives of the saints, the wages of sin, and the glories of heaven. Intense sculptural iconography surrounds the main entries at the west and south facades.

The interior of the cathedral was consciously built to be a metaphor for the celestial city of Jerusalem, a medieval depiction of heaven on earth. One of the most penetrating ways to experience this four-dimensional metaphor is to be blindfolded outside the west front and be guided into the cathedral by a friend. The transformation from outside to inside is unexpectedly dramatic without the sense of sight. Humans depend so much on their eyes for information about the environment that other sensual data become overwhelmed or absorbed into the visual.

Several subtle environmental phenomena can be experienced more easily when one is deprived of sight. First, there is an almost instantaneous change of air temperature, pressure, and humidity immediately felt by the body's largest organ, the skin. Entering the cathedral on a warm summer day emphasizes this change dramatically. Coolness honed with humidity envelopes the skin and stimulates the pores.

Accompanying the feel of the air is the smell. Most humans have a very keen sense of smell although it is not often exploited critically in the environment. Again, the visual dominates, so that unless the smell is quite strong, it will be ignored. At Chartres, the atmosphere of the interior is rich with smells of incense, beeswax, cool earthy stone, and oiled wood, the combination of which dramatizes the difference between the outside secular world and the inside sacred one.

CATHEDRAL OF NOTRE DAME, IN THE
CONTEXT OF THE CITY OF CHARTRES,
FRANCE, 1194–1260.

*The Cathedral of Notre Dame still
dominates the city of Chartres, as all
Gothic cathedrals did throughout France
when they were first built. Photograph
by John Kurtich.*

AMBULATORY, CATHEDRAL OF NOTRE
DAME, CHARTRES, FRANCE, 1194–
1260.

*The ambulatory of the cathedral is
particularly rich with light, shadow,
spatial diversity and intrigue, and
material richness. Photograph by John
Kurtich.*

Finally, but not least important, is the change in acoustics. This is usually always noticed, even when not blindfolded. But the deprivation of sight focuses attention on the directionality of sound as one is moving through space. Humans with two functioning ears can determine direction and depth of sound, which becomes a primary means of navigation if blinded. The human ear can also focus on particular sounds at will, in spite of general chaotic background noise.[33] In addition to particular directional sounds, there is the environmental ambience created by the combination of all the sounds. Chartres's long reverberation time is due to the geometry and hard-surfaced nature of the building material of its interior. The space exaggerates and distorts the sounds by prolonging, overlapping, and deepening them. The acoustical environment is not that of the everyday world, whether it be the thirteenth century or the twentieth.

The climax of the four-dimensional experi-ence occurs when the participant is led down the central aisle of the nave, just short of the crossing, and turned around to face the west before removing the blindfold. At last, all of the senses work together with the dazzling beauty of the predominantly blue rose window. The visual effect during the thirteenth century was even more pronounced, as Chartres was famous throughout the medieval world for its other-world stained glass which featured this remarkable blue. These windows continued the education of the worshipper through multicolored fragments arranged to form sophisticated pictures, lessons, and stories from the Bible. The powerful experience of the sacred environment, combined with the arts of sculpture and stained glass, directly affected the physical senses of the illiterate medieval worshippers, assisting them in transcending their physical limitations to achieve a higher spiritual existence. This crowning achievement of the Gothic cathedral created a new space-time through metaphor.

OFFICE COMPLEX, PANNELL KERR
FORSTER, CHICAGO, ILLINOIS. THE
LANDAHL GROUP, INC., 1985.

*A view of the entrance lobby shows the
teak "deck," which abuts against a
series of "sailboats" on the left, the
ingenious sunshades to control the bright
east light from Lake Michigan.
Photograph by Karant and Associates.*

SPACE-TIME OF SUBSTITUTIVE METAPHOR

PANNELL KERR FORSTER, CHICAGO, ILLINOIS

Metaphor is a powerful device for achieving a four-dimensional space in the present-day business world. The accounting firm of Pannell Kerr Forster, Chicago, Illinois, designed by the Landahl Group in 1985, achieves a space-time of the Chicago lakefront the moment one enters the office complex. The substitution of a sailboat marina for an office complex is further dramatized by its location: the truncated thirty-seventh and thirty-eighth floors of The Associates Center at 150 North Michigan Avenue.

One's attention is immediately drawn to Chicago's actual lakefront through the sloping glass upon entering the office. In order to control the bright east light from the lake, Landahl designed and installed triangular-shaped silk sails to line the conference rooms, complementing the view of Lake Michigan on a summer day with its many sailboats skimming the surface of the water. To complete the metaphor, Landahl used a bleached teak floor for the lobby to suggest a ship's deck or pier and teal blue carpeting throughout the offices and work stations to allude to the lake.

Light entering the sloping glass "roof" of the office complex passes through trellises, deflecting the harsh morning light. Projected shadows and changing light patterns add to the dynamism of the space throughout the morning, making the metaphor of sailing on the lake direct and immediate.

SPACE-TIME OF SEXUAL METAPHOR

THE ROYALTON HOTEL, NEW YORK, NEW YORK

A subtler metaphor is central to the interior architectural renovation of the Royalton Hotel, New York, New York, (1988), by Philippe Starck (1949–   ). Starck uses every aspect of the interior to create unfamiliar surroundings replete with symbols of horns, snakes, spermatozoa, caves, wombs, waterfalls. Sex is heavy in the air. Visitors are both disconcerted and excited, encouraged to alter their behavior to match the unorthodox furniture, lighting, railings, carpeting, fabric, surface finishes, and plumbing fixtures. Starck believes, "People are fascinated by danger." [34]

Upon entering the hotel, one is confronted with a long, linear lobby, bounded on the west by a gradually curved colonnade wall featuring a series of large, identical, horizontally protruding upturned horn lights, mounted near the ceiling. The east side of the lobby is a long seating area on two levels, filled with an array of Starck's furniture of various sizes and shapes. Some support shiny chrome horned backrests. Some are double

couches with a curving chrome snake dividing the two seating areas. A deep blue carpet runner, designed by Brigitte Laurent (Starck's wife), separates the east from the west and displays a lively, off-center, linear white band of cavorting snakes and spermatozoa.

The double-level lobby divides circulation from seating. The lower seating level is accessed by a long, continuous band of steps with multiple polished snake-shaped handrails. The furniture is arranged in vignettes, each different, yet related through detailing. By creating choices in seating, people are encouraged to participate with the theatrical surroundings. One can sit by the symbolic hearth or around a large library table covered with picture books related to the arts or at one of four gaming tables. This group of tables is anchored to the east wall with a large tilted mirror directly opposite the main elevators. This setting emphasizes the competitive nature of today's world. The four game tables have polished goat legs of a satyr, while skirted seats, embraced by taunt double-horned backrests, are supported by stiletto heels. To complete the vignette, each game is illuminated with a single candle mounted on a curved armature attached to the table. No lighting is more potent for creating mystery, allure, and seduction than candlelight. The metaphors implying sensual beastiality in the furniture promote the fascination with danger.

A small round room off the lobby features floor-to-ceiling upholstered walls in pale blue. It is the womb of the hotel, intimate but a source of power. A radial checkerboard floor sharply defines the geometry of the room and contrasts to the soft-edged, velvety walls. Small, free-standing tables with double-horned chairs complete the furnishings. It is a sacred cave of a Minoan snake goddess. The disorienting and unusual aspects of the space reinforce the sexual and dream metaphors that actuate four dimensional adventure. Starck describes his lobby: ". . . It is part of dreams. It is not the future or the past. When you arrive, you cannot know what time it is." [35]

Starck thought of the bedroom as a haven, but not without its dark, dangerous side. The bed is the room's centerpiece, creating a sensuously soft receptacle. Each bed is covered with a Swed-

LOBBY, THE ROYALTON HOTEL, NEW YORK, NEW YORK. PHILIPPE STARCK, 1988.

The "spermatozoa" path of the lobby rug and the illuminated horns lead guests from the main entrance of the hotel to the check-in desk. Photograph by Tom Vack.

BEDROOM, THE ROYALTON HOTEL, NEW YORK, NEW YORK. PHILIPPE STARCK, 1988.

A voluptuous bed is the centerpiece of the guest room, expressing a tenuous edge between safe comfort and dangerous adventure. Photograph by John Kurtich.

ish goose down comforter and features four overstuffed down pillows propped against a draped, padded headboard. Lacquered mahogany walls frame the recessed bed, providing a hard-edged, dark contrast. The bed becomes a soft, white, inviting tongue extending from a geometric orifice threatening to swallow the occupant alive.

The fantasy of the Royalton is completed with the plumbing. The men's room off the lobby is dominated by a wide, tall stainless steel urinal, which is the backdrop for a waterfall. The individual bathrooms feature deep, circular cones of shiny stainless steel, set in a triangle of thick clear glass spanning the interior corner of the slate-tiled walls. Beveled mirrors above the basin create four basins radiating around the corner joint and can give a right-reversed image of the user. The larger suites have circular bathtubs with phalliclike flexible shower hoses. Horns are used for coat hooks and cabinet pulls. Down to the smallest detail, Starck has consistently designed his interiors to achieve the dream metaphor. This particular space-time encourages its participants to act out their fantasies.

SPACE-TIME OF PROCESS

THE CRESCENDO PROJECT, CHICAGO, ILLINOIS

The most dynamic kind of four-dimensional architecture is that of a building or space that is not only usable but is also in the process of completion. Such a project has been proposed for a site in Lake Michigan just opposite Chicago's downtown Loop area. This proposal was conceptualized by a German-born painter/sculptor, Dieter Wagner (1944–), who describes it as " 'the monument in memory of the future,' a living legacy for present and future generations." The monument is called *Crescendo* and is a freestanding transparent bridge made up of seven arches, the middle arch still in the process of construction. The scale is mammoth; the complex is 600 feet high, 1200 feet long, and 150 feet wide.

Crescendo is meant to symbolize the culmination of our civilization, particularly in merging the arts/humanities with science/technology. The structure itself, predominantly glass with an airy steel construction supporting the bridge, seems

MODEL, CRESCENDO PROJECT, CHICAGO, ILLINOIS. DIETER WAGNER, 1987.

Originally designed as a possible theme for the 1992 Chicago Columbian Exposition which was subsequently cancelled, Crescendo would have been the ultimate architectural space-time statement of a building in process, a paradox of transitory limitations and impossible perfection. Photograph by John Kurtich.

beyond current building technology, but it is really at the cutting edge. The fact that it would be built as a process, in other words not completed until humanity reached a new level of consciousness, puts this monument directly into the realm of the fourth dimension, a dynamic, non-static building that uses the dimension of time as part of its properties of definition. Crescendo would portray the idea that limitations are transitory, that the very idea of incompleteness and lack of possible perfection in the building could nevertheless symbolize the fruition of the greatest in human achievement for our civilization.

Wagner's detracters claim that Crescendo is an impossible scheme, one that would take great sums of money to realize, draining the resources of more immediate and useful projects. One then thinks of the billions of dollars that were being poured into national defense Star Wars efforts in the 1980s and wonders if our current civilization has its priorities confused.

The last great culture that did something idealistic through a four-dimensional monument was Periclean Athens when the city-state dedicated its resources and talents to rebuilding the Acropolis complex and the final version of the Parthenon (discussed earlier in this chapter) after defeating the Persians in 479 B.C. The Parthenon was to be the finest temple ever constructed, using the noblest of materials, state-of-the-art optical refinements, and infusion of sculpture from the greatest artists of the day. Pericles was sharply criticized for the amount of money being spent on the project, but he defended his actions by stating that Athens was entitled to beautify the city and provide full employment for her citizens. The result of this program was the golden age of classical Greece. The Parthenon became the symbol of confidence that encouraged the Greeks to develop and excel in other fields. The Parthenon was the standard of beauty and perfection in western architecture and the symbol of the highest culture of western civilization. This symbol is as valid today, over two thousand years later.

SUMMARY

The realization of space-time in architecture is indispensable to the comprehensive human experience. This experiential element when synthesized with the fusion of space and time is the fourth dimension, the most profound component of Interior Architecture. At this juncture the basic oneness of Interior Architecture can become the most evident. There can be no disunity of "inside" from "outside," no conceptual division between enclosure and contents, no philosophical segregation of function and aesthetic, no discord between space and time. Metaphorically, Interior Architecture parallels itself with the notion of the basic oneness of the cosmos. This concept is central to Eastern mystical philosophies and the current view of unity of all things, which constitutes the foundation of modern subatomic physics. The fundamental feature of reality as vindicated by both the mystic and the physicist is the "oneness of the totality of all things, the great all-including whole."[36]

The remarkable four-dimensional architecture of the past is a rich and vibrant resource for the awareness and comprehension of space-time. The cognition of the fourth dimension raises the consciousness of human participants, making them interconnected, interrelated, and integrated with their environment. This potent concept is generally considered as an intangible element, one manipulated only by the most creative minds. The power of emotion is exploited as though it were a natural part of the design palette. Designers who are sensitive to this palette can create interactive environments charged with emotional experience that goes beyond the ordinary to create the extraordinary.

NOTES

1. A. K. Coomaraswamy, *Hinduism and Buddhism* (Westport, CT: Greenwood Press, Inc., 1971), p. 33.
2. D. T. Suzuki, Preface to B. L. Suzuki, *Mahayana Buddhism* (New York: Macmillan, 1969), p. 33.

3. J. Needham, *Science and Civilization in China,* vol. II (New York: Cambridge University Press, 1962), p. 35.

4. Fung Yu-Lan, *A Short History of Chinese Philosophy* (New York: Free Press, 1966), p. 112.

5. Arata Isozaki, "Space-time in Japan—MA," in *Ma: Space-Time in Japan* (New York: Cooper-Hewitt Museum, 1979), p. 12.

6. Barbara Tuchman, *The Proud Tower* (New York: Bantam Books, 1966), p. 209.

7. Newton firmly believed in the concept of absolute time and space. He argued that absolute time would flow without relation to anything external. Similarly, absolute space would remain immutable and immovable.

8. Albert Einstein, *Relativity: The Special and General Theory* (New York: Crown Publishers, 1961), p. 26.

9. Ibid., p. 9.

10. Lincoln Barnett, *The Universe and Dr. Einstein* (New York: Bantam Books, 1968), p. 19.

11. A. Einstein, H. A. Lorentz, H. Minkowski, and H. Weyl, *The Principle of Relativity: A Collection of Original Memoirs* (New York: Dover Publications, 1923), p. 75.

12. Stephen Kern, *The Culture of Time and Space, 1880–1918* (Cambridge, MA: Harvard University Press, 1983), p. 7.

13. Thomas Mann, *The Magic Mountain* (New York: Vintage Books, 1969), p. 218.

14. "Griffith, D. W." in *The New Columbia Encyclopedia,* ed. by William H. Harris and Judith S. Levey (New York: Columbia University Press, 1975), p. 1147.

15. Richard Freedman, *The Novel* (New York: Newsweek Books, 1975), p. 118.

16. David Daiches, *Virginia Woolf* (Norfolk, CT: New Directions, 1942), p. 66 ff.

17. James Joyce, *Ulysses* (New York: Random House, 1961), p. 235.

18. Roman Vlad, *Stravinsky* (New York: Oxford University Press, 1967), p. 29.

19. Ibid., p. 30.

20. T. S. Eliot, "London Letter," (New York: Dial, 1921).

21. Roger Allard, "At the Paris Salon d'Automne," (1910) in *Cubism,* ed. Edward Fry, (New York: Oxford University Press, 1966), p. 62.

22. Guillaume Apollinaire, *Cubist Painters* (New York: George Wittenborn, Inc., 1962), p. 13.

23. The five points were

1. *The Pilotis.* The Pilotis or Pillar released the house from the ground.
2. *The Roof Garden.* The roof garden was made feasible by the flat cement roof and drainage occurring in the center of the building rather than down the exterior walls.
3. *The Free Plan.* The free plan suggested complete independence of structural support and architectural "infill."
4. *The Elongated Window.* The facade-long window was now totally independent of the structure.
5. *The Free Facade.* The free facade came about as a result of skeleton construction.

24. Bruno Zevi, *Architecture as Space* (New York: Horizon Press, 1957), p. 27.

25. Douglas Brenner, "Good-by to All That," (*Architectural Record,* May 1985), p. 142.

26. A *lacunar* is a ceiling, particularly one of the ancient Roman type made up of sunken panels.

27. Donald Hoffmann, *Frank Lloyd Wright's Fallingwater* (New York: (Dover Publications, 1978), p. 17.

28. Edgar Allan Poe, "The Pit and the Pendulum" in *The Complete Poems and Stories of Edgar Allan Poe* (New York: Alfred A. Knopf, 1970), p. 444.

29. David R. Coffin, *The Villa d'Este at Tivoli* (Princeton: Princeton University Press, 1960), p. 28.

30. Ibid., p. 19.

31. W. B. Dinsmoor, *The Architecture of Ancient Greece* (New York: W. W. Norton, 1975), p. 168.

32. A. W. Lawrence, *Greek Architecture* (Harmondsworth, Middlesex: Penguin Books Ltd., 1957), p. 172.

33. This phenomenon is commonly experienced at cocktail parties where one has the ability to pick out a particular conversation amidst the din and chaos of many people talking at the same time.

34. Sam Seibert with Meggan Dissly, "Starck's View of Design," *Newsweek,* November 28, 1988, pp. 88–90.

35. Phil Patton, "Starck Reality," *New York Magazine,* October 31, 1988, pp. 44–52.

36. Ashvaghosha, *The Awakening of Faith* (Chicago: Open Court, 1900), p. 55.

CHAPTER 5

LIGHT: SPACE DEFINITION

Light is the most important single component in the definition of space or the manifestation of form. Without light, there is no perceived visual space. Although humans employ all their senses in one way or another, visual perception dominates. The quality of light in an architectural space directly affects the definition as well as the quality of the space itself. Interior Architecture is developed with lighting to reinforce the architectural space. The lighting, whether it is produced naturally, electrically, or chemically, expands the viewer's perception and awareness of physical, emotional, psychological, and spiritual dimensions of the space. Creative lighting is the key to effective visual perception. Human beings are sensitive to brightness, intensity, contrast, and color.

The human eye is often compared to a camera in that each has a light-sensitive plane upon which an inverted image is focused through a light-controlling lens. In the eye, the light-sensitive plane is the retina; in the camera it is the film located at the focal plane. The crystalline lens of the eye controls the amount of light with an automatic iris; the camera lens uses an iris diaphragm.

Image formation in (A) the pinhole eye, (B) the compound eye, and (C) the human eye, for two targets X and Y.

DIAGRAM OF THE HUMAN EYE.

Although the eye is frequently compared to a camera, focusing an image is quite different in each. A camera is focused by adjusting the distance between lens and film; the eye is focused by changing the shape of its gelatinous lens: more like a sphere for closer objects; becoming flatter as distance of the object increases. Drawing by Jennifer Ehrenberg.

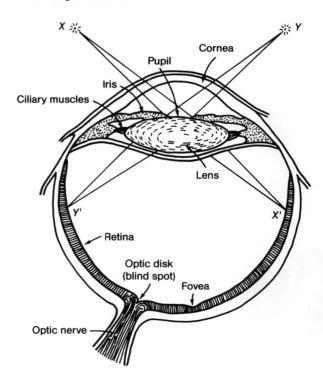

But the eye is not a mechanical camera; it is a living organ featuring un-cameralike perceptive characteristics and continuously automatic adaptive abilities that react to changes in lighting conditions and levels. The eye does not produce a picture in the brain, but it feeds the brain "with information coded into neural activity—chains of electrical impulses—which by their code and the patterns of brain activity, represent objects."[1] The brain continuously organizes sensory data into objects; this presents the intrinsic problem of perception. With minimal visual cues, the brain seeks and organizes discern-ible, if not meaningful, objects. Cartoonists depend upon this perceptual ability. Many times people see objects that really are not there, such as animals in cloud formations or a man's face in a full moon.

The act of seeing involves many sources of information beyond purely visual.

It generally involves knowledge of the object derived from previous experience, and this experience is not limited to vision but may include the other senses: touch, taste, smell, hearing, and perhaps also temperature or pain. Objects are far more than patterns of stimulation: objects have pasts and futures; when we know its past or can guess its future, an object transcends experience and becomes an embodiment of knowledge and expectation without which life of even the simplest kind is impossible.[2]

Perceiving space is a more complex situation. Here one has a collection of objects within a shell or enclosure, all of which have pasts and futures. How one perceives this collection or any part of it depends largely on its relative visibility. The three- and four-dimensional aspects of space require certain lighting conditions to manifest themselves to the viewer. The effectiveness of visible space or space-time depends directly on appropriate and creative lighting. To be properly illuminated is the art of Interior Architecture.

With the widespread use of electricity at the beginning of the twentieth century, lighting interior space no longer depended on sunlight or chemical combustion such as torches, candlelight, and gaslight. Electric illumination finally made it possible to turn night into day with an ease hitherto unexperienced by architects and designers.

Electric light became so easy to use, in fact, that light could be put anywhere. Concern for scientific illumination levels and their mathematical tables to create ideal task light levels began to dominate the designer's concern with lighting. The development of the cost efficient fluorescent fixture led to a standardization of commercial lighting, which seemed to fit the image of the anonymity of the Modern Movement. Creative lighting, which reinforced, expanded, or transformed interior space, became a rare occurrence, especially for commercial and public space. Lessons to be learned from historical uses of natural light were ignored or forgotten in the quest for scientific calculation of ideal lighting for the workplace or the perfection of lighting systems, mass produced for the ubiquitous suspended ceiling gracing the curtain-walled high-rise office building.

NATURAL LIGHT

The creative use of natural light in interior space can offer many ideas for electric light applications. Likewise, artists, theatrical set designers, and photographers use light to develop and shape their art; ideas from these sources also apply to interior lighting. The following series of historical case studies exemplifies models of lighting and defining space primarily through natural light—particularly from the importance of the direction of light, the quality of light, and special aspects of light.

HYPOSTYLE HALL, KARNAK, EGYPT

In ancient Egypt, natural light was often introduced into interior spaces by high, clerestory windows near the roof. In the great Hypostyle Hall at Karnak (ca. 1312–1301 B.C.), the central axial path featured a ceiling supported by columns higher than the level of the two adjacent colonnaded side halls. This difference in height between the two roofs created vertical space that was covered by stone grills that admitted beams of light to penetrate the darkness of the temple and illuminate the polychromed surfaces.

DETAIL OF CLERESTORY WINDOWS, HYPOSTYLE HALL, TEMPLE OF AMMON, KARNAK, EGYPT, 1530–323 B.C.

The clerestory windows of the higher central axis were made of stone grills with regularly spaced slits to create a diffused illumination of the axial hall. Photograph by John Kurtich.

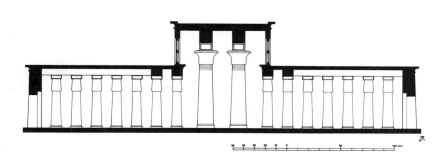

TRANSVERSE SECTION THROUGH A TYPICAL HYPOSTYLE HALL, SUCH AS THAT FOUND AT THE TEMPLE OF AMMON, KARNAK, EGYPT, 1530–323 B.C.

This diagrammatical section based on the Egyptian hypostyle hall configuration clearly shows the location and subsequent lighting results from the clerestory window. Drawing by John Kurtich.

PALACE OF KNOSSOS, CRETE

When interior spaces were located deep within an architectural complex, such as many of the rooms of the palace of Knossos, Crete (ca. 1600 B.C.), illumination from above was necessary. The Minoans built large vertical shafts that penetrated the palace for several floors, bringing natural light and ventilation into the deepest recesses, and light reflected off the shaft walls would illuminate the interiors of the adjacent spaces. The Minoans also employed an architectural light filtering system, using layers of screening colonnades particularly on south and east exposures. The "Queen's Megaron" (reconstructed by Sir Arthur Evans (1851–1941) in 1910 had an outer screen consisting of a

DETAIL OF COLUMNS AND PILLARS AS LIGHT CONTROL, "QUEEN'S MEGARON," KNOSSOS, CRETE, CA. 1600–1400 B.C.

The bright light court is shielded through a series of architectural filters consisting of, first, a colonnade of inverted round columns, followed by a wall of pillars resting on a continuous parapet. Photograph by John Kurtich.

"QUEEN'S MEGARON," KNOSSOS, CRETE, CA. 1600–1400 B.C.

The lively frescoes, reconstructed here, actually represent two different periods of decoration which the archaeologists uncovered, the rosette pattern being newer. Photograph by John Kurtich.

colonnade of round, inverted columns, followed by an inner screen wall of large rectangular openings occurring in repetitive measurement, giving the effect of a colonnade of square pillars connected by a low, continuous parapet of the same thickness at the floor. The lighting inside the resulting room is soft and even, without the heat of the harsh Cretan sunlight. The actual bathing chamber was an adjacent interior room, lit only by one rectangular opening in the wall separating it from the outer room. The light here was softer yet, but adequate for the intended activity.

STOA OF ATTALOS, ATHENS, GREECE

The classical Greek stoa used a principle similar to the Minoan palace to control light from the side —colonnades screening a deep porch, which sheltered the open shops within. The reconstructed Stoa of Attalos, Athens (originally built 159–138 B.C., reconstructed A.D. 1953–1956 as the Agora Museum), gives the modern visitor an accurate picture of light quality of this building type. The outer colonnade is the first line of defense against the hot, bright sun, but allows a filtered light to

freely penetrate the deep porch. Shadow patterns from the columns on the floor change throughout the day, enriching the visual field. A second row of columns, half as many as the first, support the center of the span of the deep porch. The inner back wall is lined with commercial shops that have generous rectangular openings, allowing a soft, uniform illumination, totally protected from the glaring Athenian sun and heat.

ATRIUM HOUSE, POMPEII AND HERCULANEUM, ITALY

The Romans developed the atrium house for providing natural light and ventilation in an otherwise closed-off, self-contained building structure. The best examples of this type of house are at Pompeii and Herculaneum (ca. 200 B.C. to A.D. 79). The principal rooms of the house surrounded a central space, the atrium, which was open to the sky. Natural light would illuminate the atrium through a rectangular opening called the *complu-*

vium, through which rain water would fall to be collected directly below it in a catch basin called the *impluvium*. The Romans expanded the Minoan light shaft into a usable space that became the central focus, organizing the plan of the house. More elaborate atrium houses had peristyle gardens surrounded by additional rooms. This plan created a private internal sunlit space for family living and entertaining.

TEMPLE OF MERCURY, BAIA, ITALY

When the Romans developed the dome, they usually left a round skylight or oculus in the center of the dome for illumination of the space. The most spectacular surviving example is the Pantheon of Rome (see Chapter 4 for a discussion of this building), but a more typical example of the oculus is found in the so-called Temple of Mercury at the Baia Baths (A.D. 46–138 onward) overlooking the Bay of Naples south of Rome. The shaft of light from the oculus is the primary source of illumi-

ATRIUM, HOUSE OF THE VETTII, POMPEII, ITALY, CA. A.D. 62–79.

The impluvium clearly mirrors the compluvium above it, expressing the function of a catch basin to its open skylight above. Photograph by John Kurtich.

nation. It creates a dynamic hot spot on a light-colored surface, which radiates reflected light throughout the rest of the space. Such illumination dramatizes the contrast between the static architectural space with kinetic sunlight.

HADRIAN'S VILLA, TIVOLI, ITALY

Hadrian's Villa, Tivoli, (A.D. 118–138), featured a cryptoporticus, which was a covered, underground means of passage between one building of the palace complex with another, permitting people to walk in cool air during the warmest hours of the day. The cryptoporticus was located underneath the perimeter of a large rectangular pond surrounded by a portico of fluted columns. Exactly below the portico is the cryptoporticus with loopholes each corresponding to the intercolumniation above. The loopholes, open to natural light, not only illuminate the buried passage with soft light but emphasize, by means of reflected light, the structural vaulting that creates the openings.

ROTUNDA, "TEMPLE OF MERCURY," THE BAIAE THERMAE, BAIA, ITALY, CA. A.D. 46–138 ONWARD.

The oculus of a dome creates a very strong focusing device for the sun to be projected within the domical space, dramatizing the movement of light throughout the day. Photograph by John Kurtich.

CRYPTOPORTICUS OF THE SWIMMING
POOL, HADRIAN'S VILLA, TIVOLI,
ITALY, A.D. 126–134.

*The vaulting is dramatically highlighted
by the light openings which also produce
a strong stepping-stone path of light on
the ground. Photograph by John
Kurtich.*

CENTRAL SANCTUARY, S. COSTANZA,
ROME, ITALY, A.D. 330 (CONVERTED
INTO A CHURCH IN 1256).

*The Christian mysteries are reinforced
with the relatively intense light of the
central sanctuary and its altar as opposed
to the relatively dark, surrounding
ambulatory. Photograph by John
Kurtich.*

S. COSTANZA, ROME, ITALY

Dramatic natural light emphasized the unworldly
or heavenly nature of the interior of early Christian
churches in contrast to their modest exteriors.
S. Costanza, Rome (ca. A.D. 350), originally built
as a mausoleum for Constantina, Constantine's
daughter, became a church in 1254. It is a centrally
planned building with its nucleus higher and
larger than the surrounding vaulted ambulatory.
The heart of the building is flooded with natural
light through windows in the tall drum supporting
the dome while the ambulatory is in semi-darkness.
When its interior polychromed mosaic
decoration was totally intact, it had a shimmering
vision of heavenly divine light focused on the centralized
space.

SANTA SABINA, ROME, ITALY

Santa Sabina, Rome (A.D. 422–432), treated natural light in a similar manner, although this church is basilican in plan. Santa Sabina is characterized by a central, high-ceiling nave, with single smaller aisles on each side, and a deep apse. Clerestory windows flood the nave with natural light while the side aisles remain relatively dark. Originally the walls of the nave were richly decorated with colored marble revetment and mosaic panels, which caused a dematerialization of the surface, while the side aisles remained plain and dark, giving more emphasis to the bright upper half of the nave, the receptacle of divine light.

SAN LORENZO, FLORENCE, ITALY

In contrast to Santa Sabina's dark aisles, San Lorenzo, Florence (1425 onward) by Filippo Brunelleschi (1377–1446), developed a more balanced lighting responding to the Renaissance focus on humanism. The spatial hierarchy in church interiors dramatically shifted during this time. Basilican plans were expanded by the addition of chapels along the central nave. The nave retained the brightest lighting through high clerestory windows modulated by the columnar rhythm. The smaller scaled aisles were illuminated by round windows high in the vaults, reinforcing the calculated perspective scheme. Below these windows, chapels were framed by arches illuminated only by reflected light and candlelight. The lighting created a hierarchy that reinforced the scale changes of the great church into a volume of multiple human experiences.

NAVE, SAN LORENZO, FLORENCE, ITALY. FILIPPO BRUNELLESCHI, 1421–1460.

Humanistic concerns of the Renaissance modified the contrast between the brightly lit central nave and dim side aisles. Photograph by John Kurtich.

NAVE AND SIDE AISLE, S. SABINA, ROME, ITALY, A.D. 425.

Early Christian basilican churches were characterized by brightly lit naves and altars because this represented the path to salvation. Photograph by John Kurtich.

CEILING AND DOME OF SAN CARLO
ALLE QUATTRO FONTANE, ROME,
ITALY. FRANCESCO BORROMINI,
1638–1641.

*The lantern of the dome is the principal
focus of light, dramatizing the theatrical
orchestration of light manipulation in the
Italian Baroque church. Photograph by
John Kurtich.*

SAN CARLO ALLE QUATTRO FONTANE, ROME, ITALY

The open and dynamic character of seventeenth century Italy was the basis of the Italian Baroque; the making of its form of life visible and manifest was through persuasion. The architecture of the Church became a theatrical setting, using light and color to intensify the experience of the worshipper. The most original architect of the Italian Baroque was Francesco Borromini (1599–1667), who created a new conception of space. His invention of the undulating wall gave a new flexibility to interior space, and his treatment of light aimed at an illusory effect of depth. ". . . it is above all a 'guided' light, an instrument that can bring out the characteristics of a structure by augmenting their perceptibility, a factor of *claritas* that, more than anything else, is logically coherent and has the capacity to identify the synthetic connections."[3] In his San Carlo alle Quattro Fontane, Rome (1638–1641), Borromini used light to

VAULTS, MASJID-I-JAMI, ISFAHAN, IRAN, CA. 1072–1629.

The multi-domed and vaulted areas of this mosque could be illuminated only from above, through the oculi of each dome. Photograph by John Kurtich.

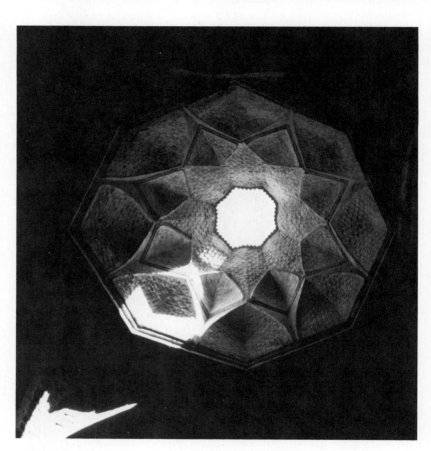

VAULT DETAIL, MASJID-I-JAMI, ISFAHAN, IRAN, CA. 1072–1692.

Detail of an octagonal oculus of one of the domes. Photograph by John Kurtich.

emphasize the dipping and swelling of the walls as though they were pliable. The relatively dark interior allows light to burst into it through the lantern, illuminating and softening the contours of the superimposed moldings. This makes the domed core inseparable from the chapels; the interior is made to run smoothly together.

MASJED–I–JOMEH, ISFAHAN, IRAN

Similar lighting occurs in the centers of small domical vaults of the Seljuk quincunxes of Masjed-I-Jomeh, Isfahan, Iran (ca. eleventh century A.D.). The domes are in series, creating a rhythmic pattern of light and dark. These domes

WINDOW DETAIL, ALI QAPU PALACE,
ISFAHAN, IRAN, EARLY SEVENTEENTH
CENTURY.

*The deep frames of the narrow windows
served as an effective light filter for the
space within the palace. Photograph by
John Kurtich.*

CEILING SKYLIGHT, ALI QAPU
PALACE, ISFAHAN, IRAN, EARLY
SEVENTEENTH CENTURY.

*The Persians took advantage of their
skills of geometric tracery to create a
fantasy of form and light with their
skylights. Photograph by John Kurtich.*

are illuminated by oculi. They might be round or square, depending on the geometry of the individual vault, but the light projects its pattern on the interior as well as illuminating the intricate brick masonry patterns of the vault. The integrated lighting system dynamically illuminates the interior, with high contrast dark and light, creating an intimate human experience.

ALI QAPU, ISFAHAN, IRAN

Another quality of light is achieved within the Pavilion of Ali Qapu, Isfahan (1589–1627), the royal residence of Shah Abbas I. The majority of the rooms are naturally lit from the side, but through carefully designed masonry screens placed within deep openings, the quality of light

INTERIOR STREET, QAYSARIYA (GRAND BAZAAR), ISFAHAN, IRAN, EARLY SEVENTEENTH CENTURY.

The Grand Bazaar is literally acres of covered space with opportunity for natural light to come from above only. Oculi furnish linear patterns of light to guide the shopper through the maze of spaces. Photograph by John Kurtich.

that finally penetrates is soft and reflected. As the direct light strikes the crust, an exaggeration of energy is generated. This light dematerializes the walls and ceiling, which feature geometric, highly colored cutouts covering the surfaces with various spatial levels of design and information.

BAZAAR, ISFAHAN, IRAN

Isfahan's central bazaar (built during the reign of Shah Abbas I, 1589–1627) uses a series of identical oculi in a row of domical vaults, which form one of the main concourses of the covered market. For the better part of midday, the sun projects a pattern of the oculi on the floor, reinforcing the axial nature of the concourse. The poetic streams of

light lead the visitor through this intriguing series of spaces filled with visions, smells, and sounds of the mysterious Middle East.

JOHN SOANE RESIDENCE, LONDON, ENGLAND

The Breakfast Parlour by John Soane (1753–1837) in his London residence (1792–1834), carried the idea of the central domical skylight to a more complex development. The room was designed as a domed canopy space within a larger cubical volume. The domed canopy was supported on four columns, independent of and some distance from the enclosing walls of the overall space. A circular opening in the middle of the domed can-

DETAIL OF THE BREAKFAST PARLOUR
CANOPY DOME, SIR JOHN SOANE
RESIDENCE, LINCOLN'S INN FIELDS,
LONDON, ENGLAND. SIR JOHN
SOANE, 1812.

*The inner space of the breakfast parlour
culminates in the lantern of the dome
which admits light through stained glass
panels in the vertical well of the lantern.
Photograph by John Kurtich.*

opy allowed light, but the light was filtered through a perforated drum that defined this circular hole as a vertical light well. The enclosing walls of the larger volume were washed with light from rectangular skylights directly above them but hidden by the central canopy cover. The combined effect further emphasized the space-within-a-space and separated the canopied space from the larger enclosing space.

INDUSTRIAL REVOLUTION

It was not until the latter part of the eighteenth century during the Industrial Revolution that iron and glass building technology made it possible to create larger expanses of skylight than Minoan light shafts, Roman compluvia, and domical skylights. These new glass skylights also protected the interior space from adverse weather. The challenge of new building types in the nineteenth century, such as museums, stock exchanges, department stores, banks, and libraries required illumination from above due to deeper ground plans and a need for escape from visual environmental distractions.

The glass skylight developed during the nineteenth century to fantastic dimensions. It became an indispensable part of almost all building types, eliminated direct contact between the interior spaces and the outer world, and transformed the atmosphere of the space. Sunlight, the play of sharp shadows and reflections, gave way to a softer, more neutral light—studio lighting. Northern exposures became fashionable. Nature was replaced by the artificially created mood of the "indoor Orient." As an extension of this trend, branches of the applied arts, interior decoration, and plant cultivation thrived as never before.[4]

PADDINGTON STATION, LONDON, ENGLAND

Top lighting was the most common way to illuminate the great train sheds that began to appear, first in England, when train transportation became widespread. London's Paddington Station II (1852–1854), by Isambard Kingdom Brunel (1806–1859) and Matthew Digby Wyatt (1820–1877), not only reinforces the linear path of the train shed with a wide, axial skylight, but con-

nects parallel sheds with skylights at right angles. This plan creates luminous transcepts that open up the interior space to the sides, relieving the monotony of the long tunnels.

PASSAGE DU CAIRE, PARIS, FRANCE

Covered pedestrian and shopping arcades were an outgrowth of the same iron and glass technology. Again the primary illumination was a continuous

INTERIOR STREET, PASSAGE DU CAIRE, PARIS, FRANCE, 1798–1799.

Industrial Revolution technology transformed consumer shopping facilities by developing galleries and arcades, the predecessors to the contemporary interior shopping mall. Photograph by John Kurtich.

TRAIN SHED, PADDINGTON STATION, LONDON, ENGLAND. I. K. BRUNEL AND M. D. WYATT, 1852–1854.

Nineteenth century glass and iron train stations were marvels of engineering which led to competition among the industrial nations to achieve the greatest unsupported roof span. Photograph by John Kurtich.

skylight above. This building type was invented by the French, and one of the earliest surviving examples is the Passage du Caire, Paris (1798–1799). The plan of the arcade conforms to the street patterns beyond it so that the glass-covered passage follows a 45°/45° right triangle path incorporated with a longer linear passage.

GALLERIA VITTORIO EMANUELE II, MILAN, ITALY

The development of the arcade building type culminated with the Galleria Vittorio Emanuele II, Milan (1865–1867), a new pedestrian, glass-covered street that linked the Piazza del Duomo with the Piazza della Scala. At the midpoint of this passage was a shorter cross-street which, at the crossing, created a rotunda about 105 feet in diameter covered by a glass dome. In addition to the natural daylight, the arcade was originally illuminated at night with six hundred gas jets, the number of which could be increased to two thousand for special occasions. Here was a major interior space of

CROSSING, GALLERIA VITTORIO EMANUELE II, MILAN, ITALY. G. MENGONI, 1865–1877.

By the mid-to-late nineteenth century, entire streets could be covered with glass and iron, freeing city dwellers from capricious or inclement weather. Photograph by John Kurtich.

a city, protected from the weather and lighted from above by means of a continuous glass roof. The interior was richly adorned with paintings, sculpture, and mosaics, making it a favorite central gathering place for the citizens of Milan then as it is today.

BIBLIOTHEQUE NATIONALE, PARIS, FRANCE

The library had to be rethought as a building type during the nineteenth century, because of the increased production of books. Stack storage for books began to take up more and more room, changing the earlier tradition of stack and reading room being one and the same. Henri Labrouste (1801–1875) solved the problem of separating the two areas very elegantly in his Bibliotheque Nationale, Paris (1858–1868), particularly with respect to lighting. Labrouste designed the reading room as a square containing sixteen slim cast-iron columns supporting spherical vaults, each of which had round openings at the top in the manner of the Pantheon. This design ensured that all the reading desks were equally well lighted. Immediately behind the reading room was the large stack room in five levels to accommodate 900,000 books. This entire part of the library was covered with a glass ceiling. Gridiron floors of cast iron allowed the natural light to permeate every level of the stack room.

DULWICH GALLERY, LONDON, ENGLAND

As museums became more popular and widespread during the nineteenth century, they too employed the skylight as a principal means of illumination. The oblong skylight was used in the Dulwich Gallery, London (1811–1814), by Soane (1753–1837); its use reinforced the three-dimensional quality of the galleries. Nearly a century and a half later, a flat-domed, large circular skylight was the central illumination for the helix-shaped Guggenheim Museum designed by Wright, New York (1956–1959). This building culminated the centralized circular space of the

DETAIL OF VAULTING, THE READING
ROOM OF THE BIBLIOTHEQUE
NATIONALE, PARIS, FRANCE. HENRI
LABROUSTE, 1862–1868.

*The oculi of the spherical vaults provide
a series of down-lights for the benefit of
the library patrons. Photograph by John
Kurtich.*

PUBLIC GALLERY AREA, DULWICH
COLLEGE, THE PICTURE GALLERY AND
MAUSOLEUM, LONDON, ENGLAND.
SIR JOHN SOANE, 1811–1814.

*The large rectangular skylights of the
galleries provided an even illumination
throughout the space. By permission of
the Governors of Dulwich Picture
Gallery.*

CENTRAL ROTUNDA AND RAMPS,
SOLOMON R. GUGGENHEIM MUSEUM,
NEW YORK, NEW YORK. FRANK
LLOYD WRIGHT, 1956–1960.

*The skylight is the central focus and
termination of the great spiral ramp.
Photograph by John Kurtich.*

Romans with the skylight technology of the Industrial Revolution, combining the perimeter he-
lical circulation ramp with the gallery exhibition
space.

ILLUMINATION

For designers, the illumination of interior space is
the most challenging task and the most creative.
When the sun sets, the environment is plunged
into natural darkness unless some other kind of
lighting is supplied. Until the electric light was
developed in the nineteenth century, such illumination was based on the chemical combustion of
organic materials or fossil fuels. A major technological advance was the candle, which introduced
the concept of the wick to control the burning
rate of animal or vegetable waxes. The candle
begot the candelabra and chandelier, enhancing
interior light with crystal prisms and providing
decorative elements for their own sake. Candle

CHANDELIERS, GALERIE DES GLACES,
PALAIS DE VERSAILLES, FRANCE.
FRANÇOIS MANSART, 1678–1684.

*The shimmering, glittering magnificence
of the Galerie des Glaces depended upon
thousands of points of brilliant candle
flames multiplied by reflecting crystal
prisms and mirrored walls. Photograph
by John Kurtich.*

ELEVATION/SECTION OF BOUGIE
ELECTRIQUE LIGHT FIXTURE, FIRST
FEATURED FOR OUTDOOR LIGHTING AT
THE EXPOSITION UNIVERSELLE DE
PARIS, 1878.

*This lamp revolutionized the way cities
would be illuminated. Courtesy of The
Art Institute of Chicago.*

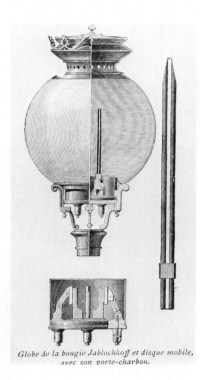

*Globe de la bougie Jablochkoff et disque mobile,
avec son vorte-charbon.*

illumination was no longer confined to visibility concerns but became the primary means of creating exciting visual effects.

OIL AND GAS ILLUMINATION   Oil lamps became common during the eighteenth and early nineteenth centuries due to improved combustion design and the development of reflectors to concentrate the light. They had the advantage of portability and of producing brighter and longer lasting light. Gas lighting was a major development of the nineteenth century due to production and distribution of coal gas to urban centers. Such lighting provided constant and controllable illumination. Fixtures evolved into an important art form, becoming models for some electric light devices. Gas lighting, through street lamps, revolutionized the illumination of cities, turning night into day on the most important streets.

Lighting by combustion had serious disadvantages. The most obvious was danger from fire. A second drawback was the soot and other dirty residue left from combustion. Burning wax, oil, and gas all produced characteristic smells that

did not necessarily enhance the environment. Gas lighting demanded considerable servicing and trimming and it could only be installed in areas that could manage its heat production and need for ventilation.

ELECTRIC   INCANDESCENT   ILLUMINATION   The invention of the incandescent electric lamp, about 1870, dramatically changed the illumination of the human-designed environment. Thomas Edison (1847–1931) in the United States and Sir John William B. Swan (1828–1914) of England were simultaneously developing and demonstrating the new light source. The earliest light bulb of each inventor used a carbon filament contained in the vacuum of a glass light bulb. A major improvement following these early demonstrations was the development of the tungsten filament in the early twentieth century. Because tungsten had a very high melting point, lamps using it could run at a higher temperature and produce greater and whiter light for the same amount of electricity required of the carbon filament. Electrical power became a major energy

RENDERING OF PROJECTOR LAMPS
AT THE TOP OF THE EIFFEL TOWER,
PARIS, FRANCE. GUSTAVE EIFFEL, 1889.

*The Eiffel Tower culminated the
structural virtuosity of the nineteenth
century, and its crowning glory was the
use of the new electric as projecting
searchlights radiating from its summit.
Courtesy of The Art Institute of Chicago.*

DETAIL OF ARC ELECTROLIER IN HALL
OF ARCHES, MANUFACTURES
BUILDING, COLUMBIAN EXPOSITION,
CHICAGO, ILLINOIS. GEORGE B. POST,
1893.

*The Chicago Columbian Exposition
made the electric light a priority for
interior illumination, as witnessed by the
enormous hanging coronas of the
Manufactures Building. Courtesy of
The Art Institute of Chicago.*

source for the industrialized world, allowing safe and clean electric light to replace gaslight. The bright, naked light bulb produced glare, however. This led to the necessity of new decorative fixtures and lampshades, permitted now by the improved safety and cleanliness of the electric light bulb.

ELECTRIC LIGHTING AT NINETEENTH CENTURY INTERNATIONAL EXPOSITIONS

The French international expositions of the nineteenth century became the first showcase of electric light, starting with the Exposition Universelle, Paris, 1878. Scholars regard this exposition as the beginning of "a great upsurge in lighting systems." Paris featured the carbon based electric candle, or the *Bougie electrique,* as the modern and celebratory way to illuminate the streets of the central city to glorify the exposition.

The Exposition Universelle, Paris, 1889, was the first fair to be illuminated by electricity; for this reason it was also the first fair to remain open at night. Thousands of electric bulbs illuminated

the new Eiffel Tower, and strings of lights outlined the pavilions or garlanded the landscaping of the fair grounds. This electric illumination was furnished by 1,150 arc and 10,000 incandescent lamps. Increasingly elaborate lighting became a major feature of the subsequent expositions that followed the 1889 Paris fair.

The World's Columbian Exposition, Chicago, 1893, used over 5,000 arc lamps and about 90,000 incandescent lights to illuminate its buildings and grounds. Architects were now being asked to design their pavilions with electric illumination as part of the design aesthetic. The most impressive interior electric lighting was that of the central nave of the Manufacturers Building. This space, 1,300 feet long by 368 feet wide by 202 feet high, was lighted by five giant coronas. The central fixture was the largest at 75 feet in diameter and carrying 102 arc lights, hung in two concentric circles. The other four coronas were each 60 feet in diameter, each carrying seventy-eight arc lights, also hung in two concentric circles. These immense fixtures included attached walkways for lamp trimmers to maintain the lights.

COMMERCIAL ARCHITECTURE.   ROMANESQUE ORNAMENT.

THE MONTAUK BLOCK.

PERSPECTIVE RENDERING OF THE
MONTAUK BLOCK, CHICAGO,
ILLINOIS. BURNHAM AND ROOT,
1881–1882.

*In the spirit of the progressive design of
high rise architecture, the Montauk
Block featured built-in electric wiring,
anticipating the eventual primacy of
electric lighting and mechanical devices.
Courtesy of The Art Institute of
Chicago.*

DETAIL OF MAIDENS BEARING TORCH
LIGHTS IN THE HEADHOUSE OF UNION
STATION, ST. LOUIS, MISSOURI.
THEODORE C. LINK, WITH LOUIS
MILLET, 1891–1894. RESTORED BY
HELLMUTH, OBATA AND KASSABAUM,
INC., 1984–1985.

*Imaginative design of the period took
advantage of the electric light to enhance
and transform interiors in a totally
integrated way. Photograph by John
Kurtich.*

THE MONTAUK BLOCK, CHICAGO, ILLINOIS

The Montauk Block, designed by Burnham and Root in 1881, Chicago, was an early commercial project in which the proprietors, in the scientific spirit of the times, demanded that electric wiring for lighting be built into the structure. This request was unique, because it was at least a year before electric power mains were available for the building.

HEADHOUSE, UNION STATION, ST. LOUIS, MISSOURI

Many interior spaces of the early twentieth century exploited the naked electric light bulb with its glowing filament as a major decorative element as well as the source of light. Louis Millet (1855–1923), who designed the interiors with Louis Sullivan (1856–1924) for the Trading Room of the Chicago Stock Exchange and with Theodore C. Link (1850–1923) for the Headhouse of St. Louis'

MAIN HALL OF THE RESTAURANT OF
THE EXHIBITION, DARMSTADT,
GERMANY. JOSEPH MARIA OLBRICH,
1901.

*Olbrich's sparse chandeliers reinforce the
dining room's characteristic arched
windows and harmonize with the
graceful furnishings. Courtesy of The
Art Institute of Chicago.*

Union Station, employed early electric lights for
illumination and decoration.

The Grand Hall of the Headhouse, with its
65 foot high barrel vaulted ceiling, was illuminated by skylights and clerestory leaded-glass
windows by day. A variety of electric lights were
integrated into the architecture to articulate the
bold forms while embellishing the delicate decorative motifs. The polychromed color scheme
was developed by Millet (see Chapter 8 for details
of the restoration of the Grand Hall) to exhibit

their correct hues when illuminated by the golden
glow of carbon filament bare bulbs.

A band of exposed light bulbs, located between the vaulted windows and the balconies,
provided a glitter of light, circumscribing the hall.
This lighting, interrupted by the colossal vaults,
accentuated the space's rhythmic quality. In the
1984 restoration, freestanding multihead lamps,
inspired by street lights, were installed on the
main floor to provide intimate lighting for the
central lobby.

NIGHT VIEW OF EXTERIOR OF THE
HALL OF SCIENCE, CENTURY OF
PROGRESS, CHICAGO, ILLINOIS. PAUL
PHILIPPE CRET, 1933.

*Neon lighting was a new breakthrough
in architectural illumination,
particularly with its ability to outline
form and space in a range of colors.
Courtesy of The Art Institute of
Chicago.*

Celebrating the newly created electric technology, Millet designed seven maidens in relief, framing the terminus of the vault. Bearing glowing torches in outstretched arms, these figures were transformed into goddesses of light. Within the arches were twin golden statues offering the gift of light represented as suspended illuminated globes.

HAUPTRESTAURANT, DARMSTADT, GERMANY

Joseph Maria Olbrich (1867–1908) was commissioned in 1899 to design the Kunstler-Kolonie at Darmstadt, a group of artists' houses and exhibition halls. The Hauptrestaurant, located in one of the halls, was built to accommodate four hundred people on two floors, linked by a central staircase. The timber-framed gabled structure was completed in 1901, enclosing a long, narrow dining room that was completely done in white with ornamental stripes on the walls. The simple, open room was illuminated by a series of medieval-inspired chandeliers, supporting two rings of hanging electric lamps. The delicate, circular forms, with minimal decoration, contrasted the plain white ceiling form and restaurant interior. Tables along the perimeter walls were illuminated by bracketed fixtures that extended the language of the chandeliers. The design of the lighting provided a balanced illumination while relating well

to the delicacy of the furnishings. A powerful series of colorful Tiffany windows, depicting the Roman god Bacchus by Hans Christiansen, contrasted the beautiful white room and became the focal point.

THE CENTURY OF PROGRESS, CHICAGO, ILLINOIS

In keeping with the late nineteenth century tradition of showcasing the latest in lighting technology at world's fairs, the Century of Progress Exposition, Chicago, 1933, featured a new kind of illumination in addition to incandescent and arc lighting. The Hall of Science Building was lit with neon and other rare-gas tubes. Neon gas produced red light when sealed in a clear tube while being charged with electric current; mercury gas furnished blue light in a clear tube; green was achieved by mercury gas in a yellow tube; yellow was produced by helium in a yellow tube.

THE RAINBOW ROOM, ROCKEFELLER CENTER, NEW YORK, NEW YORK

The Rainbow Room received its name in 1934 from the RCA Victor Color Organ that transformed music into colored light. The reflected light formed rainbows of color onto the spectacular domed ceiling of the room. The room

DANCE FLOOR AREA, RAINBOW ROOM, ROCKEFELLER CENTER, NEW YORK, NEW YORK. REINHARD AND HOFMEISTER; CORBETT, HARRISON AND MACMURRAY; HOOD AND FOUILHOUX, 1931–1940. RESTORED BY HUGH HARDY, HARDY HOLZMAN PFEIFFER ASSOCIATES, 1987.

Lighting creates a rotunda-like central space combined with the sparkle and elegance reminiscent of Versailles. Photograph by John Kurtich.

DINING AREA, RAINBOW ROOM, ROCKEFELLER CENTER, NEW YORK, NEW YORK. REINHARD AND HOFMEISTER; CORBETT, HARRISON AND MACMURRAY; HOOD AND FOUILHOUX, 1931–1940. RESTORED BY HUGH HARDY, HARDY HOLZMAN PFEIFFER ASSOCIATES, 1987.

The use of individual candles on the dining tables is essential to create the necessary intimate scale within this grand and complex space. Photograph by John Kurtich.

opened October 3, 1934, on the sixty-fifth floor of the RCA Building, centerpiece of the newly constructed Rockefeller Center, New York. Its swank interior became an overnight success for dining, dancing, and romancing.

The symmetrical room, with views of the Manhattan skyline on three sides, is dominated by a circular dance floor, mirrored by a corresponding shallow dome. The radial-patterned wood floor is the focal point of the room, surrounded by carpeted terraces with dining tables. The dance floor is illuminated by two rings of multicolored cove lights that circumscribe the dome above. Suspended from the center of the dome, an ele-

gant crystal chandelier recalls the prismatic glitter of preelectric lighting. This glittering quality is repeated by smaller chandeliers and wall sconces on the perimeter of the room. The dramatic effect of the bold cove lights is softened by the romantic sparkle of the crystal fixtures. Candles on the tables bring the scale of the chandeliers down to the most intimate level of dining and conversation. The enclosing walls of the room are alternating views of the patterned lights of the Manhattan skyline with mirrors reflecting the view of the room. The Rainbow Room is a harmonious balance between grand scale theatrical lucency and intimate glow.

FLUORESCENT LIGHTING

In 1939, New York and San Francisco simultaneously held world's fairs. Each fair introduced fluorescent lighting as the new state-of-the-art illumination technology. In the U.S. Steel Pavilion of New York's World of Tomorrow, the ribs of the pavilion's dome were outlined with fluorescent tubing. The Petroleum Building used fluorescent lighting as indirect illumination, which produced an illusion of the building's horizontal elements floating in space. San Francisco's Golden Gate Exposition featured multicolored effects to illuminate its architecture, using 2,400 pink, blue, gold, and green fluorescent tubes mixed with about 10,000 colored floodlights hidden in troughs or buried in landscaping. Instead of portraying the utopian future of New York's World of Tomorrow, San Francisco created a fantasy world of Asian, Central American, and Pacific Basin exhibition palaces and courtyards. Each court was a separate entity of mood and color. The Court of the Moon and Stars was illuminated in blue-greens and purples. The Court of the Seven Seas was predominantly apricot, combined with a harmonious yellow on set-back sections of the walls. Fluorescent paint was applied to sculptural niches, which were then bathed with invisible ultraviolet light, creating dramatic luminosity and deep shadows.

Fluorescent lighting revolutionized the illumination of interiors, particularly in commercial applications. The fluorescent tube could produce more light more cheaply than an equivalent incandescent lamp. Other advantages of the fluorescent lamp included longer life, less heat per unit of lucency, and lower surface brightness than the corresponding incandescent lamp. Early fluorescent lamps, however, were much noisier than their incandescent counterparts, due to required ballasts that provided correct starting voltage as well as current limitation and circuit protection. The fluorescent lamp did not produce a full color spectrum, and its initial resulting light quality was cold and flat. Faulty tubes could produce irritating flicker. In spite of these disadvantages, fluorescent lighting became the predominant way to illuminate commercial interiors, leading the way to integrated and luminous ceilings.

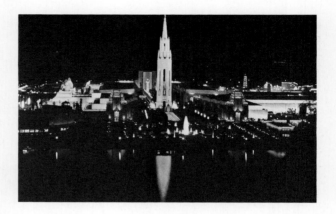

AERIAL NIGHT VIEW OF THE GOLDEN GATE EXPOSITION, SAN FRANCISCO, CALIFORNIA, 1939.

The fluorescent light was a revolutionary breakthrough in the evolution of electric lighting, being capable of producing more light for less cost than incandescent. Courtesy of The Art Institute of Chicago.

Fluorescent technology now permitted the architect and interior designer to create a ceiling as an interior sky or a continuous plane of light. A leader in this development was Skidmore, Owings & Merrill (SOM), who designed a highly integrated ceiling system for the Union Carbide Building, New York (1960), currently Manufacturers Hanover Trust. SOM's system transcended the conventional luminous ceiling because it combined lighting with air-conditioning, sound control, and unlimited flexibility of wall partitions. Union Carbide had more than 800,000 square feet of ceilings in its building complex, and this new system unified the interiors throughout, fulfilling the client's desire to alter office layout overnight without disturbing lighting levels, air distribution, and acoustical control.

CEILING SYSTEM OF THE UNION
CARBIDE BUILDING, NEW YORK,
NEW YORK. SKIDMORE, OWINGS
AND MERRILL, 1960.

*The fluorescent light was easily
adaptable to the concept of the integrated
ceiling system, which allowed a new
flexibility in office design. Photograph
by Ezra Stoller Associates.*

EERO SAARINEN'S INTERIOR ARCHITECTURE

Eero Saarinen's (1910–1961) early work showed a developed interest in defining interior space to reflect the experimental structure of his architectural envelope. Saarinen's design palette included natural light and electric illumination as equal to steel and concrete in shaping space. His innovative work led to pushing all the components of architectural design to their limits. Past critics have focused on his structure and exterior form giving, ignoring his perhaps more important contribution to Interior Architecture. Saarinen's buildings were created for the function of the interior space, and his use of light transcended its practical raison d'être to become a sculptural presence.

Saarinen's pair of buildings for Massachusetts Institute of Technology, Cambridge, 1955, the Kresge Auditorium and the Chapel, were criticized at the time of their completion for their lack of relationship to each other and to the plaza they occupy. Their exteriors belie their real value, which is the interior space.

The Kresge Auditorium was an experiment in thin shell concrete, a pure geometric form one-eighth of a sphere, supported on three points. The interior is articulated within the structure to create a broad, triangular space, focusing on the stage at one of the shell's vertices. This shell's interior is shaped to accommodate the needs of a concert hall

through terraced radial seating focusing on the stage, which is surmounted by suspended, reflective, acoustical panels. Further shaping of the auditorium is accomplished with a layer of acoustical clouds that also provide general illumination. This directionally focused space is contrasted by a continuous cove light, broken only at the stage, which reestablishes the true shape of the enclosing shell. This contrast clearly and powerfully articulates the juxtaposition of structure and function. Here, Saarinen achieves light as structure.

The Chapel, on the other hand, explores the mystical quality of natural light, supplemented by electric illumination. The 125-seat cylindrical sanctuary is sited within a circular moat of water, accessed by a bridge. Upon entering the Chapel, one is immediately drawn to the altar, which is located on the far side of the space, showered by natural light reflecting off Harry Bertoia's (1915–) suspended sculptural screen.

A subtler kinetic effect is introduced through more sophisticated architectural details. The brick cylinder walls undulate on the interior, transforming the shape. These undulations are generated as radiations from the highlighted off-center altar. Corresponding to this rhythm, a series of arches in the exterior shell were formed to admit perimeter up-lighting. This detail reveals the true purpose of the moat, which is to reflect light from the pool to the bottom of the interior walls. This

INTERIOR, KRESGE AUDITORIUM,
M.I.T., CAMBRIDGE,
MASSACHUSETTS. EERO SAARINEN,
1954–1955.

Saarinen used cove lighting to visually reinforce the thin shell structure of the auditorium, which is otherwise evident only from the exterior. Photograph by John Kurtich.

PLAN, KRESGE CHAPEL, M.I.T.,
CAMBRIDGE, MASSACHUSETTS. EERO
SAARINEN, 1955.

Electric light is used to subtly enhance and reinforce the unusual manipulation of natural light. By permission of The M.I.T. Museum.

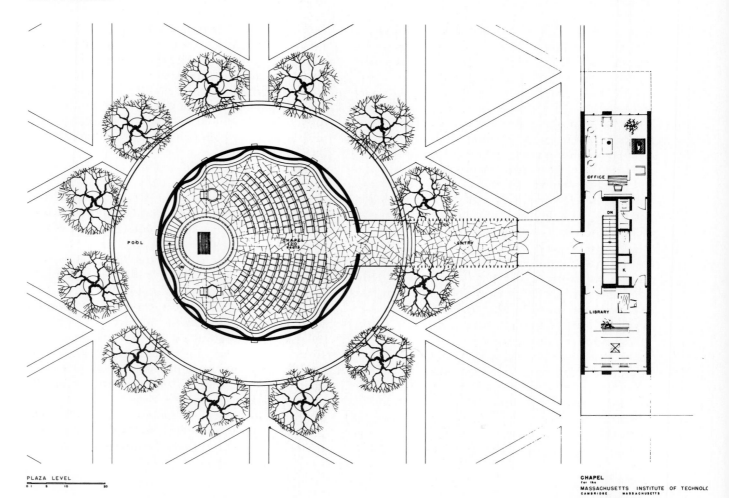

PLAZA LEVEL

CHAPEL
for the
MASSACHUSETTS INSTITUTE OF TECHNOLC
CAMBRIDGE   MASSACHUSETTS

EERO SAARINEN & ASSOCIATES
ARCHITECTS

ANDERSON & BECKWITH
ASSOCIATE   ARCHITECTS

OCTOBER 14, 1953

INTERNATIONAL TERMINAL, TRANS
WORLD AIRLINES, J.F. KENNEDY
INTERNATIONAL AIRPORT, NEW
YORK, NEW YORK. EERO SAARINEN,
1956–1962.

*Saarinen again combines natural light
with electric light to explain and
reinforce the unusual shell structure of
the terminal. Photograph by John
Kurtich.*

mirrored light emphasizes the sensuous quality of
the undulations and the rich texture of the brick.
In addition, quivering light from the agitated
water infuses an ethereal effect.

Saarinen's most sculptural building, the
TWA Terminal at JFK International Airport,
New York (1956–1962), is a study of mass and
void defined by light. This reinforced concrete
shell structure, with its robust curvilinear forms
and intersecting peripheral buildings, utilizes
monumental scale and sweeping forms to create
three-dimensional spaces charged with movement. Natural light illuminates the spaces from
the huge perimeter curtain walls and linear skylights. The skylights, supplemented by electric
illumination, define the major structural intersections, dramatizing the purpose of the building.
Saarinen was very successful at creating an airport
terminal that embodies the spirit of travel through
emotional architectural forms reinforced by integrated lighting.

KRAMER PENTHOUSE,
NEW YORK, NEW YORK

Illumination of spaces by borrowing natural and
electric light from adjacent spaces is a neglected
method of lighting. This concept was employed
by Michael Kalil (1944–1991) as a thematic approach to illuminating the interior of the Kramer
residence, New York (1990). He described his design as ". . . how to light a space by using the
space next to the space you want to light."[5] To
achieve this, Kalil adapted the principle of the sun
coming through a window by employing hidden
incandescent lighting. A trough of perimeter
lighting terminating with a cubic lighting device,
illuminates the fireplace wall from above, flooding the surface with warm, irregular levels of illumination, reminiscent of shimmering sunlight.
This essentially makes a wall act as a window.

STANLEY KORSHAK AT THE CRESCENT,
DALLAS, TEXAS

The brilliantly illuminated stair of Stanley Korshak at the Crescent, Dallas, Texas (1986), a
three-story contemporary specialty store, establishes an exciting focal point, while uniting the
various departments at the main entrance. Him-
mel/Bonner, Chicago architects, with Wheels-
Gerstoff-Shanker, New York lighting designers,
collaborated to create this cylindrical stair which
acts as a knuckle to resolve the transition of two
colliding geometries of the existing building complex. The dynamic stair was conceived as a floating sculptural form, illuminated by back lit walls
of translucent glass.

To achieve this floating effect, a steel structure, supported by eight vertical tubes, were
placed behind the glass wall. On the back side of
the wall, a cavity was formed to support vertical

Main floor, Stanley Korshak at the Crescent, Dallas, Texas. Darcy Bonner, Himmel/Bonner Architects, 1986.

A vertical shaft of light defines the vertical circulation, its brilliance spilling into the main space of the store. Photograph by R. Greg Hursely.

Detail of stairwell, Stanley Korshak at the Crescent, Dallas, Texas. Darcy Bonner, Himmel/ Bonner Architects, 1986.

Lighting the container for the stairs dramatizes the kinesthetic experience of vertical circulation. Photograph by R. Greg Hursely.

fluorescent fixtures and a catwalk to allow for re-lamping and maintenance. The steel grate catwalk, structure, and lighting were carefully modeled to prevent any shadowing or hot spots. Two sheets of sandblasted glass sandwiched a layer of milky film to thoroughly diffuse the light. These faceted panels, joined by silicone, formed the backdrop for the cantilevered stair.

The stair was cantilevered from the eight tubes, utilizing flat steel supports welded to hidden steel stringers. The steel stringers support heavy, pre-cast terazzo treads, formed in an L-Shape. This achieves an open riser effect, allowing reflected light to glow onto the tread. The open handrails are a combination of steel, mahogany, and sandblasted glass, providing an intricate silhouette against the back lit glass. Further accentuation of the lighting is achieved by employing highly polished black granite in patterns that reflect light.

VIVERE, CHICAGO, ILLINOIS

Robust and whimsical lighting dramatizes the enigmatic series of spaces in Vivere, Chicago, Illinois (1990), a renovated dining room of the Italian Village restaurant complex. Designer Jordan Moser (1958–) conceived the restaurant as a hand-crafted Italian Baroque experience, filled with provocative textures, forms, and lighting. The glowing golden skin of the space appears to be a magnification of living tissue. The sensuous, curvilinear forms accelerate and heighten the diners' senses. Illumination is integral to these forms, defining space, accenting textures, and enhancing the symbolic language of the interior.

The strongest thematic symbol is the spiral. For Moser, the spiral form conveyed his sense of the owner's family heritage and tradition. Three generations have owned and operated this restaurant complex, spiralling from the original founder. Various details are derived from this form, in two and three dimensions. The spiral is the basis for four columns, defining the main dining room. These whimsical, corkscrew forms are illuminated from their interior, mocking the column's structural integrity. The columns visually support an entablature, which is perforated by a rhythmic pattern of hand-blown glass lights. This ensemble frames a gigantic, suspended chandelier, which is cut out of an old boiler head. A radiating spiral on the chandelier is defined and articulated by a back lit, leaded glass pattern. Finally, to scale down the space for intimate dining, suspended conical luminaires create a series of vignettes in concert with the dining tables and their adjacent mirrored *faux* windows, decorated with elaborate period drapery.

Without the benefit of any exterior views or natural lighting, Vivere is alive through the assembly of unpredictable shapes and surfaces, illuminated by custom incandescent lighting fixtures. The mystic of its inventive imagery is intended to make each of the 120 seats a unique visual experience by focusing on complex and idiosyncratic details. Moser has succeeded in fusing incandescent light with exotic materials to produce a vivid dining adventure.

THE MASTERS OF LIGHT

Light was a major creative force in the work of four twentieth century architects, particularly in the way light defined and shaped their interior spaces: Le Corbusier (1887–1965), Louis I. Kahn (1901–1974), Alvar Aalto (1898–1976), and Frank Lloyd Wright (1867–1959).

Sunlight and shadows were primary ingredients with which Le Corbusier worked. He said:

The human animal is strongly affected by sunlight: This response is rooted in the inmost nature of the species . . . Light and forms, specific intensities of light, successive spaces—these all act on our sensibility, producing physiological sensations that scholars have recorded, described, classified, and specified. This horizontal and this vertical, this harshly serrated line or this gentle undulation, the closed and centered form of a circle or a square—these all work strongly on us, characterize our creations, and determine our sensations.[6]

Kahn stated his belief with a strong poetic vision:

"I said that all material in nature, the mountains and the streams and the air and we, are made of Light which has been spent, and this crumpled mass called material casts a shadow, and the shadow belongs to Light."[7]

Aalto was concerned about the quality of light.

. . . But one item that is most often ignored or in any case neglected is the quality of the light. What do we mean by the light's quality? Light exists for man, a phenomenon he needs without interruption at his disposal. Properly adapted quality is in other words much more important in this case than in the case of objects whose contact with humans is merely temporary. We meet here the same phenomenon as everywhere else: an acceptable perfection from a purely technical viewpoint —fixtures, their movable parts, their methods of manufacture, etc., have received their rational treatment but

Main dining area, Vivere,
Chicago, Illinois. Jordan Moser,
1990.

*A world of light and spiral fantasy
surround the diner in a space untouched
by natural light. Photograph by John
Kurtich.*

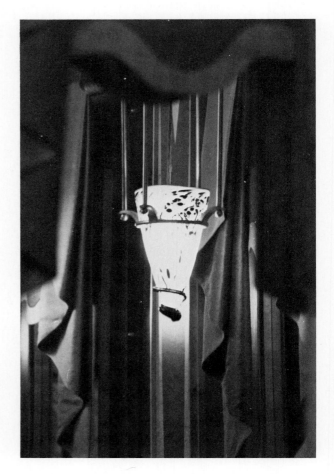

Lighting detail, Vivere, Chicago,
Illinois. Jordan Moser, 1990.

*Hanging light fixtures form a
cadence for the rhythm of dining tables
and corresponding draped mirrors.
Photograph by John Kurtich.*

from many different viewpoints, their main task, lighting as man's good servant, its adaptability for good vision, and in general its quality in relationship to man, has fallen behind. In this field, if anywhere, people have tried to improve upon this lack with inappropriate glued-on forms.[8]

The integrated use of light was central to Wright's work. He especially valued sunlight.

The more we desire the sun, the more we will desire the freedom of the good ground and the sooner we will learn to understand it. The more we value light, the more securely we will find and keep a worthwhile civilization to set against prevalent abuse and ruin. Because of light, the cave for human dwelling and work, for play and toil, is at last disappearing.[9]

LE CORBUSIER

To Le Corbusier (1887–1965) natural light was the basic requirement for architectural space. "To him even a cavern only exists, architecturally speaking, as a result of the sun."[10] As he was a painter as well as an architect, Le Corbusier considered natural light very carefully in his architectural projects, developing an artist's philosophy about light and color. "I use light abundantly, as you may have suspected; light for me is the fundamental basis of architecture. I compose with light."[11]

An early commission that exercised Le Corbusier's concern with natural light was the Maison Ozenfant, Paris, France (1923). Amédée Ozenfant (1886–1966) was a painter who founded an aesthetic movement in 1916 called Purism. This Purist philosophy demanded a return to a balanced, harmonic environment through elegant, economic, geometric forms. Ozenfant had an important influence on Le Corbusier at this time, and together they published a book in 1918, *Après le Cubisme*. Being a painter himself, Le Corbusier understood the importance of indirect natural light for a studio. Ozenfant's studio was on the top floor of his house and was lighted with large side windows overlooking a reservoir and a skylight made up of sawtooth factory windows that subsequently filtered the toplight through an interior smoked glass ceiling.

During the 1920s, Le Corbusier designed a series of artists' studios and private villas, which allowed him to develop his Five Points of a New Architecture (see note 23 in Chapter 4 for further discussion of the five points). Briefly, the five points are *piloti* (support pillars), *plan libre* (free plan), *façade libre* (free facade), *fenêtre en longueur* (strip window), and *toit-jardin* (roof garden).

The *façade libre* (free facade) allowed the *fenêtre en longueur* (strip window) to be placed anywhere, its length not dictated by the structure. Since this would increase the amount of natural light that could be admitted into a building, such horizontal strip windows became standard features in his houses and villas. Two commissions in particular were designed for art collectors, the Maison La Roche, Paris, France (1923–1924), and the Villa Stein/de Monzie, Garches, France (1926–1927).

The Maison La Roche was designed as a box raised on *piloti* with one outwardly curved wall. The spatial sequence began with a triple height entry hall that offered the participant optional

GALLERY, MAISON LA ROCHE. PARIS,
FRANCE. LE CORBUSIER AND PIERRE
JEANNERET, 1923–1924.

*The clerestory windows provided
relatively even illumination while
maximizing useable wall space for
hanging paintings. Photograph by
John Kurtich.*

routes to terminate either in a ramped gallery or an outdoor roof garden.

> *In the entrance hall we find over-lapping blocks of space which are lit from behind, thus always suggesting something beyond. Instead of the eye and mind being abruptly halted by edges and contained surfaces, they are led continuously on in exploration, never quite comprehending the mystery of layered and veiled space.*[12]

The glazing of the high strip windows that achieved this veiled spatial sequence were so detailed that they seemed to allow surfaces to flow in and out, not dissimilar to the enigmatic Purist paintings Le Corbusier was producing during this period. The light in the space was designed to illuminate and dramatize Le Roche's extensive collection of modern art. "In Maison Le Roche formal and colouristic contrasts are dramatized by the ever-changing point of view, a procession through spaces and volumes that Le Corbusier called 'promenade architecturale.' "[13]

The Villa Stein/de Monzie, Garches, France (1926–1928), was designed to house a major collection of Matisse as well as function as a suburban villa outside of Paris. The resulting building combined Le Corbusier's interest in ocean liners with abstract spatial arrangements influenced by

Purist painting. The villa, located on a narrow, long parcel of land, was designed with two principal facades, the entrance and the garden. The midsection of the entrance facade is characterized by two narrow bands of ribbon windows that extend for the entire width of the building. The arrangement of the garden facade is the reverse; narrow bands of wall separate much larger, higher strip windows that allow natural light deep into the villa. However, one portion of this facade is a double height open terrace covered only by the continuation of the roof line, penetrating the enclosed volume of the villa with natural light and ventilation.

The Villa Savoye, Poissy–sur–Seine, France (1929–1931), exemplified Le Corbusier's Five Points of Architecture (see Chapter 4 for the four-dimensional discussion of the Villa Savoye). Here, the *piloti* clearly separated the base from the *piano nobile* living quarters. Strip windows, both glazed and unglazed, illuminated equally the enclosed living room and the adjacent open terrace. The terrace and roof garden so boldly opened up the villa from the top that natural light and fresh air penetrated everywhere. Le Corbusier's use of color in this villa proclaims his Purist background. "White paint on *pilotis* and on the main

FRONT VIEW, VILLA STEIN/
DE MONZIE, GARCHES, FRANCE.
LE CORBUSIER AND PIERRE
JEANNERET, 1926–1928.

*The narrow strips of windows of the
front facade stretch from corner to corner,
making a taut, machine-like elevation.
Photograph by John Kurtich.*

REAR VIEW, VILLA STEIN/DE MONZIE,
GARCHES, FRANCE. LE CORBUSIER
AND PIERRE JEANNERET, 1926–1928.

*The rear facade doubles the height of the
strip windows, correspondingly
narrowing the infill walls. These
windows allow south light to permeate
the living quarters. Droits de
reproduction percus par la SPADEM.
Copyright 1991 ARS N.Y./
SPADEM.*

box stands out sharply against the green walls of the undercroft, the pink and blue of the curves on top."[14]

In the 1930s, Le Corbusier invented the *brise-soleil* for window openings to control the intense light and heat gain of hot climates.

One day, while I was considering Mediterranean problems, . . . my head full of these buts and ifs, the solution came to me: install, in front of the glass skin, a device regulated by the sun's daily path as it varies between the solstices and equinoxes. The "brise-soleil," as an architectural event, was born.[15]

After World War II, the *brise-soleil* became a characteristic part of Le Corbusier's architectural vocabulary.

The Unité d'Habitation, Marseilles, France (1947–1952), represented Le Corbusier's statement of individual and communal living in the same complex. Two-story-high apartments interlocked with each other around interior "streets" on every third floor. Each apartment had natural light from both the east and west, which was controlled by the now highly developed *brise-soleil* loggia. The Mediterranean sun penetrated the deepest part of each apartment.

Le Corbusier used natural light not only to define space within but also to generate sculptural entities without. Many of his exterior sculptural forms were created to specifically channel natural light to define and transform interior space. The Chapel of Notre Dame du Haut, Ronchamp,

ROOF GARDEN ADJACENT TO LIVING AREA, VILLA SAVOYE, POISSY-SUR-SEINE, FRANCE. LE CORBUSIER AND PIERRE JEANNERET, 1929–1931.

The roof terrace garden which services the main living quarters is open to the sky but enclosed with the same strip windows (unglazed) as the living spaces (glazed). Photograph by John Kurtich.

DRAWING OF THE PRINCIPLE OF THE *BRISE-SOLEIL*. LE CORBUSIER, LATE 1930s.

The sun-shading device was a sculptural opportunity made up of framed balconies filled with integrated sun control elements weaving light and shade into rich patterns. Droits de reproduction percus par la SPADEM. Copyright 1991 ARS N.Y./SPADEM.

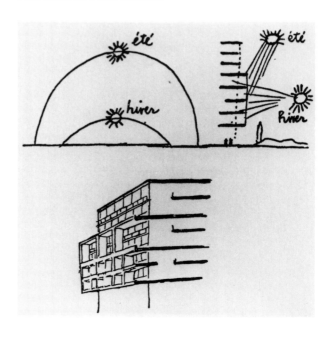

UNITÉ D'HABITATION, MARSEILLE, FRANCE. LE CORBUSIER, 1947–1952.

This apartment complex was Le Corbusier's first finished project realizing his brise-soleil *design. Photograph by Garret Eakin.*

PERSPECTIVE DRAWING OF TYPICAL APARTMENT ARRANGEMENT, UNITÉ D'HABITATION, MARSEILLE, FRANCE. LE CORBUSIER, 1947–1952.

The interlocking split level design allowed natural light to penetrate deep into the apartment from both sides of the building, receiving morning and afternoon sunlight, all controlled by the brise-soleil. *Droits de reproduction percus par la SPADEM. Copyright 1991 ARS N.Y./SPADEM.*

● Une cellule normalisée : le feu, le foyer.

France (1950–1955), exemplifies the importance of light to Le Corbusier's interior design.

> *Light is the key and the light lights up the forms. And these forms have a power of emotion due to the play of the proportions, the interplay of unexpected, startling relations, but also by the intellectual play of the underlying reasoning—their authentic birth, their ability to last, structure, know-how, hardihood, even temerity, play—of real things that are essential things, the constituent elements of architecture.*[16]

At the Ronchamp chapel, light was used in specific ways to define the space and emphasize the mysteries of Christianity. First, it clarified the asymmetrical structure of the building from within. A band of natural light separates the curving, arched roof from the walls, revealing the facts that the shell form of the roof rests on massive pylons expressed on the exterior and that the walls are nonstructural infill. This use of light also works to lift the otherwise heaviness of the roof as it reacts to the play of light.

Second, a dramatic focus was created from the light coming through openings in the south wall of the chapel. The punched out fenestrations are smaller at the exterior of the wall and flare out to larger rectangles as they plunge through the wall material. Panes of vividly colored glass, some with symbols and designs, cover the openings at the exterior face. This glass actually transforms the light by both heightening its value and softening its intensity with color. The light, in turn, defines and enhances the materials. The rough concrete frames vibrate and channel rays of colored light through the space as the sun passes its vivid rays through the south wall. The bursts of color and sparkle contrast dramatically with the general lower ambient light level of the chapel.

Third, indirect light from three smaller adjacent chapels extended the space of the main chapel and intensify the mystical atmosphere of the spatial complex. These tiny sanctuaries are each defined by an individual tower that is well expressed on the exterior of the building. Each tower collects its own light in a specific way, gently reflecting the light down its hollow core. The east and west facing towers produce indirect light, which varies in intensity as the sun changes its position relative to the earth; the tower bringing in east light, which is also underneath the pulpit, is tinted red and on its inside surface, creating a contrasting atmosphere when the morning sunlight pours into the tower opening. The north facing tower provides constant illumination.

Finally, a rectangular window on the east wall behind the altar of the main chapel illuminates a statue of the Virgin. Early morning worshippers face a brilliantly backlit image, silhouetted against the sky. The eastern sunlight produces a dramatic shaft of light through this opening, dominated by the presence of Our Lady of the Height. Le Corbusier sensitively utilized natural light to provide a powerful sense of mystery and effective modulation of space and form.

Sainte-Marie-de-la-Tourette, the Dominican monastery overlooking Eveux sur l'Arbresle, France (1957–1960), was Le Corbusier's interpretation of the traditional courtyard plan of a monastic complex. The Dominicans had an extremely restricted budget, which impelled Le Corbusier to feature the creative use of natural light as the major design element. He expanded his architectural vocabulary by inventing new light controlling elements in addition to the *brise-soleil* loggia, which now were used to define the monks' cells. For the public seminar spaces, library, and enclosed walkways, he designed floor-to-ceiling glazed openings apportioned by unequally spaced vertical concrete mullions, which he called *ondulatoires*.

As he did in the chapel at Ronchamp, Le Corbusier used natural light to clearly define all parts of the monastery's church. Each of the spatial components (the public worship area, the monks' worship area, the sanctuary, and the sacristy) had specific illumination and color. The rectangular volume and height of the ceiling of the public worship area and the monks' worship area are defined by vertical and horizontal light slots respectively. The amount of admitted light is minimal enough so that the feeling of Christian mystery is maintained but is bright enough to clearly define the boundaries of the large volume.

Lighting for the sanctuary is as contrasting to the illumination of the worship areas as the sanc-

MAIN SANCTUARY, CHAPELLE NOTRE-DAME-DU-HAUT, RONCHAMP, FRANCE. LE CORBUSIER, 1950–1955.

The separation of the shell roof and heavy walls is more clearly visible from the interior with the band of natural light separating these elements, making the ceiling seem to hover above the space. Photograph by John Kurtich.

SOUTH WALL, CHAPELLE NOTRE-DAME-DU-HAUT, RONCHAMP, FRANCE. LE CORBUSIER, 1950–1955.

The openings of the south wall pierce the fortress-like thickness with truncated shapes, emphasizing the rough texture of the wall material with the brilliant colors of the painting-like glazing. Photograph by John Kurtich.

LIGHT TOWER, CHAPELLE NOTRE-DAME-DU-HAUT, RONCHAMP, FRANCE. LE CORBUSIER, 1950–1955.

This tower's opening faces north, gathering an even light throughout the day and providing an even-tempered, calm effect for the chapel below. Photograph by John Kurtich.

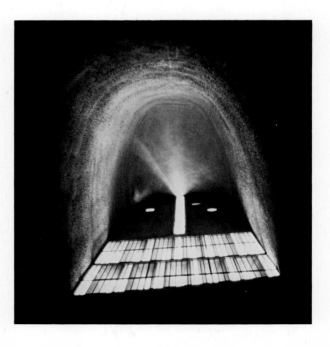

EAST WINDOW DETAIL WITH THE
VIRGIN, CHAPELLE NOTRE-DAME-DU-
HAUT, RONCHAMP, FRANCE.
LE CORBUSIER, 1950–1955.

*The statue of the Virgin can rotate 180
degrees within the window to face either
the congregation inside the sanctuary or
the thousands of pilgrims who gather
twice a year for an outdoor mass.
Photograph by John Kurtich.*

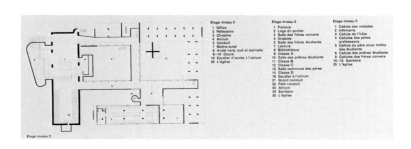

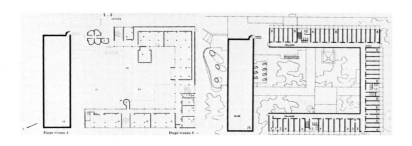

PLAN, COUVENT DE LA TOURETTE,
EVEUX-SUR-L'ARBRESLE RHONE,
FRANCE. LE CORBUSIER, 1957–1960.

*Three levels of the plan show the
complex nature of this monastery, an
ideal community built on stilts and
pillars, hovering over an Arcadian
landscape. Droits de reproduction percus
par la SPADEM. Copyright 1991
ARS N.Y./SPADEM.*

ONDULATOIRES, COUVENT DE LA
TOURETTE, EVEUX-SUR-L'ARBRESLE
RHONE, FRANCE. LE CORBUSIER,
1957–1960.

The ondulatoires *were designed
by Yannis Xenakis, composer
and architect, in accordance with
Le Corbusier's* Modulor *proportions,
calling it "musical glazed rhythms."
Photograph by John Kurtich.*

MAIN CHAPEL, COUVENT DE LA
TOURETTE, EVEUX-SUR-L'ARBRESLE
RHONE, FRANCE. LE CORBUSIER,
1957–1960.

*The main chapel is stark and primitive,
reminiscent of early Christian churches,
however lit dramatically in strategic
places such as the side altars and
sacristy. Photograph by John Kurtich.*

tuary's spatial free form is to the strict rectilinear boundaries of the worship areas. Three powerful "light cannons" perforate the sanctuary's ceiling, distributing direct light (see Chapter 6 concerning the colors employed within the cannons) over this space. The light cannons are expressed on the exterior as three truncated cones, each angled in a different direction to capture the continually moving sunlight and illuminate the holy place within.

A different lighting scheme illuminates the sacristy. A set of seven equally-angled, prismatic-shaped skylights floods a bright red-orange sacristy with diagonal light. The light, intense south light, can be seen from the worship areas as brilliant polygons of hot light, symbolizing the holy contents of this space, the sacred vessels, and vestments.

Le Corbusier, the painter, definitely influenced Le Corbusier, the architect, particularly in the use of light and color. Le Corbusier had an artist's eye and sensitivity to spatial composition and sequence that was controlled and amplified by the use of natural light.

LOUIS I. KAHN

Of the four master architects discussed here, Louis I. Kahn (1901–1974) was the most philosophical about the use of natural light in his architecture. He could not conceive of architectural space without natural light.

A space can never reach its place in architecture without natural light. Artificial light is the light of night expressed in positioned chandeliers not to be com-

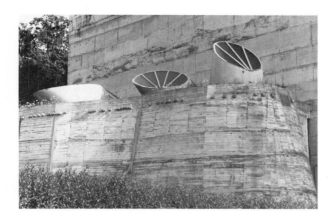

LIGHT CANNONS, COUVENT DE LA
TOURETTE, EVEUX-SUR-L'ARBRESLE
RHONE, FRANCE. LE CORBUSIER,
1957–1960.

*The three light cannons each capture a
different angle of the sun, successively
illuminating the altars within the
monastery. Photograph by John
Kurtich.*

SACRISTY LIGHT PRISMS, COUVENT
DE LA TOURETTE, EVEUX-SUR-
L'ARBRESLE RHONE, FRANCE.
LE CORBUSIER, 1957–1960.

*The sacristy's skylights are so aligned as
to capture direct sunlight at the equinox.
Photograph by John Kurtich.*

*pared with the unpredictable play of natural light . . .
The structure is a design in light. The vault, the dome,
the arch, the column are structures related to the character of light. Natural light gives mood to space by the
nuances of light in the time of the day and the seasons
of the year as it enters and modifies the space.*[17]

Kahn considered natural light to be the life-
giving force to architecture. Natural light constantly changes color as the day proceeds from
sunrise to sunset. Thus, Kahn placed great emphasis on the significance of the window and how
it gave the space its vitality. In his design of the
Weiss House, Norristown, Pennsylvania (1948–
1949), Kahn turned the entire south wall of the
house into huge floor-to-ceiling double-hung
windows, with one sash in each window glazed
the other filled with waterproofed plywood. The
plywood panels could effectively block sky glare

when placed in the "up" position. When the
glazed portion of the windows are raised to the
"up" position, particularly on a clear night, the
patterns of the stars would become part of the
interior design.

As Kahn continued experimenting with the
window, he developed the "keyhole" window, a
design that would maximize the usable wall space
without sacrificing openings for natural light. His
Tribune-Review Building, Greensburg, Pennsylvania (1959), featured, on the upper part of the
wall, large, wide panes of glass that were connected to vertical slits of glass at human level. The
proportions of the windows placed at each of the
four facades responded directly to the type of natural light that fell on them. For instance, the north
facade had the largest rectangles and slots, while
the west facade featured T-shaped narrow vertical

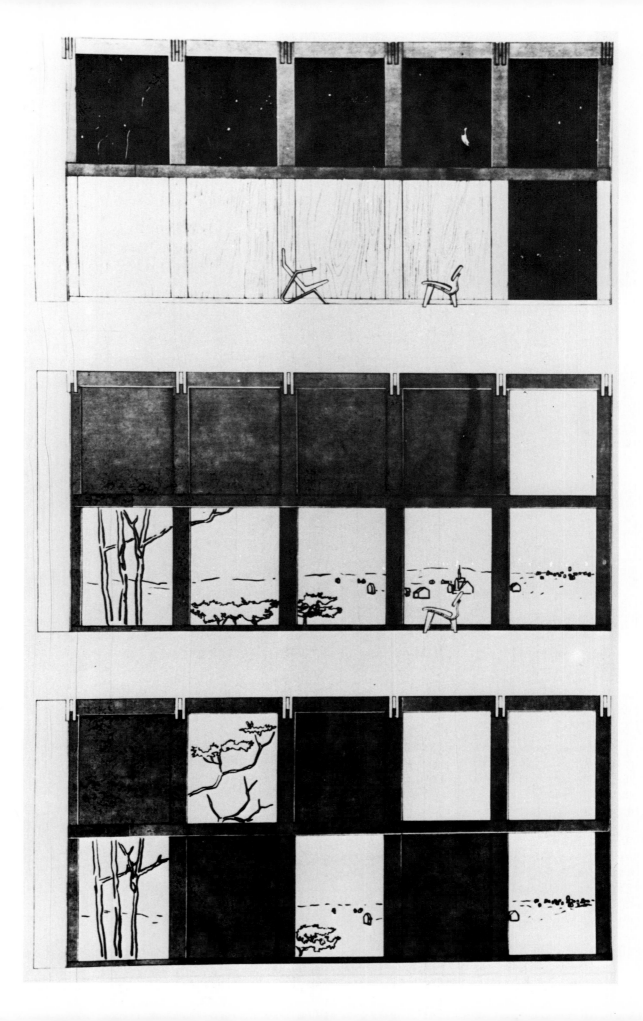

KEYHOLE AND "T" WINDOWS ON
THE EXTERIOR, TRIBUNE REVIEW
PUBLISHING COMPANY BUILDING,
GREENSBURG, PENNSYLVANIA. LOUIS
I. KAHN, 1958–1962.

*This exterior northwest corner clearly
shows Kahn's response to the difference
between western light (narrow vertical
and high horizontal slits) and northern
light (large upper rectangles upon
narrower vertical slots). Courtesy of
John Ebstel.*

KEYHOLE AND "T" WINDOWS ON
THE INTERIOR, TRIBUNE REVIEW
PUBLISHING COMPANY BUILDING,
GREENSBURG, PENNSYLVANIA. LOUIS
I. KAHN, 1958–1962.

*An interior view of the northwest corner
shows how furniture can be easily
arranged against walls without blocking
the openings for natural light. Courtesy
of Cengiz Yetken.*

LIVING ROOM WINDOW SCHEME,
WEISS HOUSE, NORRISTOWN,
PENNSYLVANIA. LOUIS I. KAHN,
1948–1949.

*The giant double-hung window design
created a flexible system of altering the
perceptible space of the interior, not only
through light control but view control.
The Louis I. Kahn Collection,
University of Pennsylvania and
Pennsylvania Historical and Museum
Collection.*

and horizontal slots to better control the late-day western light. The slotted window design, or "keyhole" as it would be known in future projects, maximized placement of furniture against exterior walls while limiting the visual clutter from the exterior. Furthermore, the high bay glazing ensured appropriate illumination deep into the office interior and provided adequate visual relief from within.

Kahn used indirect light with great mastery in his First Unitarian Church, Rochester, New York (1959–1961). The building complex consists of schoolrooms and offices that enclose a great central space, the sanctuary itself. The surrounding auxiliary spaces are illuminated indirectly through bays in the exterior walls. The walls

EXTERIOR, FIRST UNITARIAN CHURCH AND SCHOOL, ROCHESTER, NEW YORK. LOUIS I. KAHN. 1959–1969.

The light wells of the sanctuary are a major compositional element of the exterior massing of the building. Photograph by Don Kalec.

SANCTUARY, FIRST UNITARIAN CHURCH AND SCHOOL, ROCHESTER, NEW YORK. LOUIS I. KAHN, 1959–1969.

The quality of light from the ceiling wells washes the brick walls with a pervasive luminosity. Photograph by Don Kalec.

themselves become active with light. The central sanctuary is illuminated by four large light wells located in each of the four corners, the remaining ceiling slab taking the shape of a giant cross. The sunlight that enters the light wells is diffused throughout the space by the way it strikes the walls. Direct light openings would have caused disturbing glare from the contrast between the bright outside and relative dim inside.

The Erdman Hall Dormitories, Bryn Mawr, Pennsylvania (1960–1965), use a similar scheme. Large central spaces with light wells or scoops are surrounded by bedroom clusters that receive their light through bay windows in the sides of the complex. The central space, used as a dining hall, has an overall glow from the diffused light entering through four corner light wells. This glow subtly changes the color of the interior space as the natural light goes through its daily and seasonal cycles.

Kahn became interested in the idea of filtering light through external screens when he was exploring designs for the U.S. consulate in Luanda, Portuguese Angola (1959). He adapted

PUBLIC SPACES (A. DINING HALL, B. ENTRANCE HALL, AND C. LOUNGE), ERDMAN HALL DORMITORY, BRYN MAWR COLLEGE, BRYN MAWR, PENNSYLVANIA. LOUIS I. KAHN, 1960–1965.

The three central public spaces are animated by an everchanging diffused natural light from ceiling light wells, similar to the First Unitarian Church in Rochester. Photographs by John Kurtich.

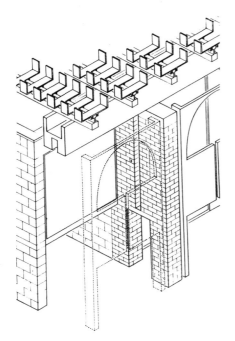

ISOMETRIC DETAIL, UNITED STATES CONSULATE BUILDINGS PROJECT, LUANDA, ANGOLA. LOUIS I. KAHN, 1959–1962.

Kahn's development of light control through external screens began with this project. Reproduced with permission from Perspecta 7: The Yale Architectural Journal, *1961, "Kahn," p. 22.*

his keyhole window idea as a freestanding filter to screen the sun's intense glare. He thought that each window should face a wall that would take sunlight and reflect it into the interior spaces. As these screens seemed to be like ruins,[18] Kahn developed the concept of containing a building within a ruin, or wrapping ruins around buildings, all for the sake of controlling natural light. Although the consulate was never built, Kahn kept exploring the concept.

Kahn had close feelings about Greek columns, particularly in terms of light:

Once in class—and he attended class—in explaining that structure is the maker of light I introduced the idea of the beauty of the greek columns in relation to each other and I said the column was no light—the space was light.

But the column feels strong not inside—the column—but outside the column. And more and more the column wants to feel its strength outside and it leaves a hollow inside, more and more, and it becomes conscious of the hollow.

And if you magnify this thought the column gets bigger and bigger and bigger, and the periphery gets thinner and thinner and inside is a court.[19]

Kahn explored the idea of enlarging a hollow column with a thin periphery, which then became the filter for the light entering it. Early schemes of the Salk Institute lecture halls were buildings surrounded by three-dimensional ruins. These freestanding walls were square in plan when surrounding a circular building and circular in plan when surrounding a square building. The Mikveh Israel Synagogue Project for Philadelphia, Pennsylvania (1961) used large hollow columns inserted into the exterior walls at intervals. Such a nonstructural cylinder would admit light into it from the outside, diffuse the light within the cylinder walls, and filter the resultant light into the synagogue interior.

The National Assembly Building, Dacca, Bangladesh (1964), realized a structural centerpiece for controlling light. The building itself became a hollow column with perforated walls. The top of the building was designed as a cylinder with circular openings divided inside by radial sections, also with circular openings, all serving to bring in natural light and filter it through all the adjacent sections.

The ruin became fused into the structure in Kahn's Suhrawardy Central Hospital, Dacca (1962–1974). Here, three-dimensional arches form an arcaded screen that both catches the sunlight and filters out the glare for the inner hallway.

Kahn achieved metaphysical light for the interiors of the Kimbell Museum, Fort Worth, Texas (1966).

No space, architecturally, is a space unless it has natural light . . . I am designing an art museum in Texas. Here I felt that the light in the rooms structured in concrete will have the luminosity of silver. I know that rooms for the paintings and objects that fade should only most modestly be given natural light. The scheme of enclosure of the museum is a succession of cycloid vaults each of a single space, 100 feet long and 23 feet

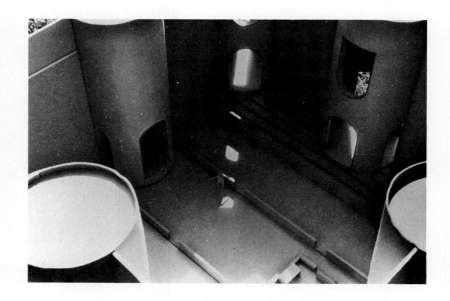

MODEL, MIKVEH ISRAEL SYNAGOGUE PROJECT, PHILADELPHIA, PENNSYLVANIA. LOUIS I. KAHN, 1961–1972.

Light control screens evolved into three-dimensional light filters, here as large hollow columns with discrete openings to control and diffuse exterior natural light. The Louis I. Kahn Collection, University of Pennsylvania and Pennsylvania Historical and Museum Commission.

MODEL, NATIONAL ASSEMBLY
BUILDING, DACCA, BANGLADESH.
LOUIS I. KAHN, 1962–1982.

*The entire building became a light filter,
starting with its top, which was outfitted
with geometric radial partition cut-outs,
serving as internal filters. Photograph by
William Christensen.*

CEILING DETAIL, KIMBELL ART
MUSEUM, FORT WORTH, TEXAS.
LOUIS I. KAHN, 1966–1972.

*Kahn refined the light filter so that
natural light could illuminate museum
galleries without damaging the works of
art which were sensitive to sunlight.
Photograph by Pamela M. Olecky.*

wide, each forming the rooms with a narrow slit to the sky, with a mirrored shape to spread natural light on the side of the vault. This light will give a glow of silver to the room without touching the objects directly, yet give the comforting feeling of knowing the time of day.[20]

The ability of light to change mood was of key importance to this museum. Kahn felt that it was important for the quality of light to reveal special characteristics of the displayed art, and that this would be ever-changing with the mutability of sunlight.

One of Kahn's last projects, the Hurva Synagogue Project, Jerusalem (1968), uses light as if it were a building material. The floor plan reveals a square within a square—an outer stone structure surrounding an inner concrete one. The outer structure is made up of 16 pylons, four on each side, that filter the sunlight. The interior faces of the pylons have niches that function in the candle service, a tribute to the celebration of the divine symbolism of light. A concrete structure is within

the pylons; this supports the roof and defines the inner sanctuary. Here, the ruin becomes the building itself, because the glare filtering pylons are part of the very fabric of the whole complex.

Kahn's architectural career could be summed up as an evolutionary process in the use of natural light, starting with the physical characteristics of light as determining architectural space to the mystical properties of light creating both structure and space. Kahn never compromised his ideals about light; he was truly a poet who worked with light as his creative medium.

So this is a kind of invention that comes out of the desire to have natural light. Because it is the light the painter used to paint his painting. And artificial light is a static light—you see?—where natural light is a light of mood. And sometimes the room gets dark— why not?—and sometimes you must get close to look at it, and come another day, you see, to see it in another mood—a different time, you see, to see the mood natural light gives, or the seasons of the year, which have other moods.[21]

SECTION AND SKETCHES, HURVA SYNAGOGUE PROJECT, JERUSALEM, ISRAEL. LOUIS I. KAHN, 1968.

This project, if built, would have culminated Kahn's quest for the element of light achieving a building material status. Light was the very essence of the design, both natural and candle. The Louis I. Kahn Collection, University of Pennsylvania and Pennsylvania Historical and Museum Commission.

ALVAR AALTO

Alvar Aalto (1898–1976) was preoccupied with ruins as they related to his building designs. He believed that his buildings could not be judged until they were at least fifty years old. There is a certain quality about Aalto's buildings, as if they had been aged in advance, a kind of metaphor for ruins, which is reinforced by his use of materials. Aalto preferred brick, stone, wood, and tile to the more commonly used concrete, stucco, steel, and glass that dominated contemporary European architecture of the 1920s and 1930s. Aalto's choice of materials would show their age less dramatically and more predictably than the technological materials of the early twentieth century. The textural surface quality and color of brick, stone, wood, and tile were enhanced and dramatized by the play of natural light, which was essential to all of Aalto's architecture.

Aalto was strongly influenced by the quality of light of Finland. The Finnish landscape is characterized by the undulating curves of the sea coast, the contours of the hills, and the play of light and shade through the many forests. The winter is at least six months with very short days, only four hours of daylight at the winter solstice. This lengthy darkness influenced the desire to achieve maximum reflection of light in interiors, creating a characteristic whiteness that prevails in Aalto's furniture and architectural details. Aalto introduced natural light into his interior spaces as a major criterion for interior environmental quality.

Light and sun. Under extreme conditions one can no longer leave the dwelling's access to the sun to chance. Light and air are such important preconditions for living that the haphazard conditions that prevail today must be changed. The norms would not only require that each dwelling get sun; the angle of incidence should also be decided, to, let us say, one degree's leeway. The sun is a source of energy; but only if we use it in a scientific way and in exact quantities will it become, under all circumstances, a positive factor for the biodynamic concept that involves the family's and the single individual's life within the dwelling's walls. In a

AURORA BOREALIS.

Aalto was influenced by Finland's frequent phenomenon of the mystical aurora borealis (northern lights), evidenced by his curvilinear shapes in pavilions, furniture, and vases. Courtesy of Martin Guth.

BALCONY, TUBERCULOSIS
SANATORIUM, PAIMIO, FINLAND.
ALVAR AALTO, 1929–1933.

*The sanatorium was built to maximize
its exposure to natural sunlight. Its
general shape reflected Finland's natural
landscape and natural sloping hills.
Photograph by Kevin Harrington.*

fifty-square-meter dwelling we don't have, in this regard, the slightest margin to be left to chance, nor can we afford to allow the sun's and the light's energy to remain unused. And at the same time we have to eliminate the inconveniences that these same factors, under unfavorable circumstances, can lead to.[22]

A natural phenomenon that occurs in Finland is the aurora borealis, the nothern lights. The basic shape of the visible northern lights is a gentle arc. This aurora occurs in the earth's magnetosphere when electrons from sunspot activities are carried by gusts of solar wind to interact with the magnetic field. Some displays of northern lights pulsate or flare up in the latter half of the night, supplemented by glowing, multicolored cloud-like formations. Thus, not only is the Finnish landscape replete with influential forms and features that are illuminated and seasoned by almost continuous sun during the midsummer and almost continuous darkness during midwinter, but the night sky itself periodically glows with sheets, arcs, curtains, and clouds of light and color of the aurora borealis. The influence of these lights is evident in Aalto's interiors, furniture, and accessories design.

In 1929, Aalto won first place in a design competition for the Tuberculosis Sanatorium, Paimio, Finland. The prevailing theory for treating tuberculosis was to remove the patient from the polluted urban environment and isolate him in a space designed to maximize absorbing solar rays and fresh air. The building Aalto designed was essentially in three parts: the ward or patient block facing south, which was linked by a central entry to the communal block, which was connected to the service block by a circulation passage. Aalto wanted to make the separation of the various activities highly visible. He was also particularly sensitive to the plight of the patient.

When I received the assignment I was myself ill and therefore had the opportunity to make a few experiments and find out what it really felt like to be sick. I became irritated at having to lie horizontal all the time, and my first observation was that the rooms were designed for people who were upright and not for those who lie in bed day in and day out. Like moths to a lamp my eyes were constantly drawn to the electric light

in the room, which was absolutely not designed for bedridden patients. The room conveyed neither balance nor calm. I therefore decided to plan the patients' rooms in such a manner as to provide a restful atmosphere for the bedridden patient. . . .[23]

Aalto concentrated the sunning activity of patients by locating suntraps at the end of each corridor floor. The suntrap complex was seven stories high with the top level of the deck continuing across the entire length of the patients' wing.

In another competition, Aalto won the commission for the Municipal Library at Viipuri, Finland (now called Vyborg in the former USSR) (1927–1935). He employed a carefully designed roof-light system consisting of a series of evenly spaced lens roof-lights, which brought natural light into the library's reading room. Each skylight consisted of a conical concrete tube 6 feet in diameter with a thick jointless round piece of glass sealing off the top. The cones were so constructed that sunlight always entered indirectly. The light reflected off the interior surfaces of the cones, bringing reflection and diffusion of light over a wide area. The skylights contained a system of wall-washer fixtures that would duplicate the same light quality day or night. Aalto saw it as making "a contract between the book and the reader."[24]

The main problem connected with a library is that of the human eye. A library can be well constructed and can be functional in a technical way even without the solving of this problem, but it is not humanly and architecturally complete unless it deals satisfactorily with the main human function in the building, that of reading a book. The eye is only a tiny part of the human body, but it is the most sensitive and perhaps the most important part. To provide a natural or an artificial light that destroys the human eye or that is unsuitable for its use, means reactionary architecture even if the building should otherwise be of high constructive value.[25]

The Viipuri Library featured in its lecture room a wooden acoustic ceiling in the form of a planar sine curve with every other trough raised to only half amplitude. The ceiling is constructed of clear pine strips that form the contours and create a horizontal curtain of wood that relates directly to the windows, the lowest drape or curve lining up with each mullion. The draped

READING ROOM, VIIPURI LIBRARY, VIIPURI, FINLAND. ALVAR AALTO, 1927, 1933–1935.

The concept of the skylight lens system became a common Aalto lighting device. He desired the same light quality whether the source was the sun or electric light. Permission by the Museum of Finnish Archives of Architecture, Helsinki, Finland.

AUDITORIUM, VIIPURI LIBRARY, VIIPURI, FINLAND. ALVAR AALTO, 1927, 1933–1935.

The wooden acoustic ceiling was directly influenced by the aurora borealis, particularly the "curtain aurora" variation. Permission by the Museum of Finnish Archives of Architecture, Helsinki, Finland.

ceiling seems to represent a sculptural interpretation of the drapes of light that frequently occur with the aurora borealis, known as the "curtain aurora." Although the ceiling was designed primarily to control the acoustics of a long, narrow space, it gave Aalto the opportunity to experiment with acoustical treatment through curvilinear wooden forms, dramatically transforming the otherwise rectangular volume of the space.

The "curtain aurora" became the main design feature of his Finnish Pavilion for the New York World's Fair (1939). Aalto entered the competition held for the design of this pavilion; he presented three separate schemes. He won not

MAIN FLOOR, FINNISH PAVILION, NEW YORK WORLD'S FAIR OF 1939, NEW YORK, NEW YORK. ALVAR AALTO, 1939.

The "curtain aurora" was again employed as the main design concept. Installed vertically as it would normally be experienced in the Finnish landscape, the wooden drapery dominated the space. Ezra Stoller © Esto. All rights reserved.

only the first prize, but the second and third prizes as well. The final version incorporated the undulating vertical curtain plywood screen-wall forming an exhibition space arranged diagonally in a rectilinear shell. The battened, curvilinear wall rose to the full height of the interior, leaning out over the viewers as the northern lights dominate the Finnish landscape.

The Villa Mairea, Noormarkku, Finland (1938–1939), was a commission that gave Aalto the opportunity to combine all his current ideas about design into a single structure. The villa was a courtyard solution, the open court idea being a direct functional response to the Finnish climate, where, particularly in the winter, much time had to be spent indoors with very few hours of daylight. This villa was designed not just as an open plan within itself, but the interior of the living area opened into the adjacent "room" of the garden. By the same token, the garden was made to intrude into the living area, serving as a daylight filter between the merging interior and exterior spaces.

This deliberate blurring of the boundaries of interior spaces with the surrounding landscape brought about a special light quality that, during the long sunlit days of summer, established an ideal living environment for the otherwise short summer season. The relationship between the external and internal spaces represented the Finns' romantic connection between themselves and their land of forests.

Aalto designed the village center of Saynatsalo, Finland (1950–1952) as a larger scale version of the Villa Mairea. A series of interconnected buildings consisting of offices, library, council chamber, and staff flats and some shops surround a raised courtyard. The courtyard is approached from the forest village by both a paved stairway adjacent to the dominating council chamber and by boarded earth steps opposite the council chamber. Aalto did not intend that the courtyard be a piazza or town square as much as it was the open-air extension of the surrounding buildings' interiors. The sensitivity to precious natural light guided this design decision.

PLAN, VILLA MAIREA, NOORMARKKU, FINLAND. ALVAR AALTO, 1937–1939.

The plan shows an integration of the house with the courtyard garden to maximize natural sunlight, achieving a blurring of inside and outside space. Alvar Aalto Foundation.

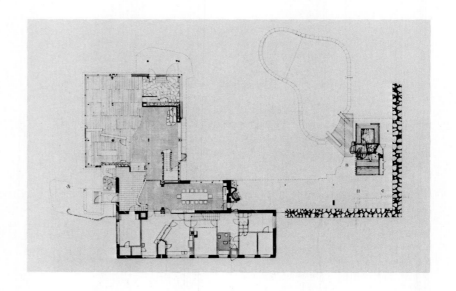

VILLAGE CENTER COURTYARD,
SAYNATSALO, FINLAND. ALVAR
AALTO, 1950–1952.

*The scheme for the village courtyard is
similar in concept to the Villa Mairea,
again for the consideration of
maximizing natural sunlight.
Photograph by Kevin Harrington.*

LOWER PORCH, STOA OF ATTALOS II,
ATHENS, GREECE, CA. 150 B.C.
(RESTORED A.D. 1953–1956 AS THE
AGORA MUSEUM).

*The ancient Greek stoa is an analogous
treatment of natural light to the village
center building cluster. Photograph by
John Kurtich.*

BRICK STAIRWAY TO COUNCIL
CHAMBER, SAYNATSALO, FINLAND.
ALVAR AALTO, 1950–1952.

*The way light enters the main stair to
the council chamber articulates a series of
patterns and defines wall and floor
textures as a continuation of the outside
passageways. Photograph by Kevin
Harrington.*

Windows flanking connecting corridors open up the surrounding buildings to the central court. The courtyard itself is alive with natural vegetation, and plants are introduced into the interior corridors to blur the distinction between inside and outside. The windows are articulated with wooden posts that form a continuous pergola, which, when illuminated with sunlight, flood the interior space in a similar manner to the Greek stoa, such as the Stoa of Attalos, Athens. In fact, the ensemble is a modern interpretation of the Greek agora, particularly in the way the surrounding buildings relate to natural light with rhythmic shadows of the posts articulating the floors and interior walls. The main stair to the council chamber continues this feeling of light and articulation, but the posts become shadow-casting beams in the ceiling directly connected to a band of clerestory windows.

The National Pensions Institute, Helsinki, Finland (1952–1956), was another commission Aalto obtained by winning a competition. It consisted of a bank complex with offices organized about two connecting courts, one square and one rectangular. The heart of the institute is the interviewing hall rather than the courtyards.

The interviewing hall is lighted with large, multifaceted skylight lenses in the ceiling. These skylights are triple glazed with the top layer sharply inclined like jagged mountain peaks to prevent snow accumulation. Aalto wanted to create an interior space in a cold climate that would, lightwise and colorwise, be similar to the open skies of more southern latitudes.

Aalto designed the Academic Bookshop (extension to the Stockmann Department Store), Helsinki (1966–1969), as top-lit interior courts. Again, he was searching for ideal interior environments. The store is an interior street with various galleries; the predominant lighting comes from lantern lights above, in order to bring every lumen of sunlight into the deep interiors, which are far from the window walls.

Aalto's use of light to shape and define space was based on sensitive pragmatism. The quality of light was everything to Aalto.

INTERVIEWING HALL, NATIONAL PENSIONS INSTITUTE, HELSINKI, FINLAND. ALVAR AALTO, 1952–1956.

The high, distinct skylights create an expansive ceiling in the Interviewing Hall, opening up the space and belying the harsh climate in which the building exists. Photograph by Kevin Harrington.

Not only ever-increasing mechanization but also our own actions estrange us from nature. We see how road construction destroys nature to a certain extent. And on closer inspection we find similar phenomena in all branches of the architectural profession. We have created, for example, better and better forms of artificial lighting. Our electric light is much more practical than our grandfathers' oil lamps or wax candles. But is the quality of this light really better than what we obtained from the old sources? In fact it is no better at all. Nowadays we use a sixty- to eighty-watt light bulb when we wish to read at a certain distance from the light source. Our grandparents managed with two candles.

EXTERIOR DETAIL OF SKYLIGHTS,
INTERVIEWING HALL, NATIONAL
PENSIONS INSTITUTE, HELSINKI,
FINLAND. ALVAR AALTO, 1952–1956.

*The steepness of the skylight discourages
snow accumulation and maximizes
intake of natural light. Photograph by
Kevin Harrington.*

ACADEMIC BOOKSHOP, HELSINKI,
FINLAND. ALVAR AALTO, 1966–1969.

*This space is a considerable distance
from exterior walls with windows; it
depends on the skylights for the natural
light it receives. Photograph by Kevin
Harrington.*

*Even incandescent light is no longer good enough; high-
intensity fluorescent lights have been introduced which
give an inconstant light with excessive amounts of blue.
We are using more light for the same task as before,
because the physical and psychic qualities of light are no
longer satisfying. . . .*[26]

FRANK LLOYD WRIGHT

Light was a central objective to the designs of
Frank Lloyd Wright (1867–1959). The use of materials was integral in the organic approach of

Wright. How light affected these materials was
therefore of prime importance. Not only did
Wright promote natural light in his projects, but
he understood the need for balance between natural light and artificial light.

*Proper orientation of the house, then, is the first
condition of the lighting of that house; and artificial
lighting is nearly as important as daylight. Daylighting
can be beautifully managed by the architect if he has a
feeling for the course of the sun as it goes from east to
west and at the inevitable angle to the south. The sun*

is the great luminary of all life. It should serve as such in the building of any house.

As for all artificial lighting, it too should be integral part of the house—be as near daylighting as possible. In 1893, I began to get rid of the bare light bulb and have ever since been concealing it on interior decks or placing it in recesses in such a way that it comes from the building itself; the effect should be that it comes from the same source as natural light.[27]

In 1889, Wright designed and built his first house, the Home and Studio, for himself and his wife in Oak Park, Illinois. For the next twenty years he experimented with his home through remodeling and additions, which eventually developed into what is known as the Prairie style. The handling of light was a basic consideration in his designs. His 1895 dining room addition was his first total environment in which he used ribbon

DINING ROOM, FRANK LLOYD WRIGHT HOME AND STUDIO, OAK PARK, ILLINOIS. FRANK LLOYD WRIGHT, 1889.

Wright believed in the proper balance between natural light and electric light; his dining room achieves this with the combination of ribbon windows and the overhead light fixture which disguises the electric light source. Photograph by John Kurtich.

MEZZANINE OF DRAFTING ROOM, FRANK LLOYD WRIGHT HOME AND STUDIO, OAK PARK, ILLINOIS. FRANK LLOYD WRIGHT, 1898.

Wright used his own house to experiment with spatial ideas, particularly with the treatment of light, both natural and electric. Photograph by John Kurtich.

windows for both vista and light. This natural light was balanced by a large rectangular light fixture covered with a decorative ceiling grill, located above the dining room table defining the central eating area. The studio, studio entrance hall, and library were added between 1898 and 1905, admitting light through high windows around the walls in the studio and library and skylights in the entrance hall and library. The design for the two-level, octagonal studio workroom was the genesis for the schemes of the Larkin Building, Unity Church, Johnson Wax Administration Building, and the Guggenheim Museum. An electric light hung over each drafting table on the lower level to balance the natural light that came through the higher windows under the octagonal roof.

Wright's use of the cruciform or "windmill" plan was characteristic of his Prairie houses. He placed the hearth as the center of the house and extended the rooms as arms of the windmill or crosses from this chimney core. By grouping rooms together, Wright eliminated needless hallways and achieved a flexible system of open planning hitherto unknown. With this layout, he could get natural light into the rooms from three sides.

The ribbon window was utilized in many of Wright's Prairie houses because it provided natural light befitting the horizontal thrust of the spaces created by the organic massing of the building. In the Boynton House, Rochester, New York (1908), the ribbon windows of the dining room are reflected on the opposite wall as glass-doored cupboards, increasing the feeling of spaciousness and light through mirror image and reflection. The Robie House, Chicago (1909), used the ribbon window idea as the principal light source to unify the living and dining rooms, which were separated by a see-through central fireplace. The rhythm of the windows is further emphasized by the globular light fixtures that occur on dropped soffits above the windows, centered on wooden ribs aligned with the window mullions. The cantilevered overhang of the roof on the south facade, while much less than the west and east facades, shades the glass during the summer. "In fact it is *exactly* sufficient—the sun stands tall in summer in Chicago's latitude, and at mid-day on Midsummer day, the shadow of the eaves just kisses the woodwork at the bottom of the glass in the doors to the terrace."[28]

A further enhancement of lighting in the dining rooms of both Boynton House and Robie House was achieved with Wright's design of the dining room furniture. In both rooms, a central table with high-backed chairs created a room within a room for the diners. On each of the four

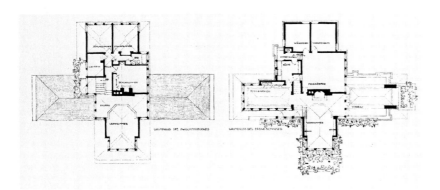

PLAN, ISABEL ROBERTS HOUSE, RIVER FOREST, ILLINOIS. FRANK LLOYD WRIGHT, 1908.

This is a classic Prairie cruciform plan which maximized the opportunity for natural light to reach all interior spaces from several directions simultaneously. Courtesy of The Art Institute of Chicago.

DINING ROOM, E. E. BOYNTON RESIDENCE, ROCHESTER, NEW YORK. FRANK LLOYD WRIGHT, 1908.

The ribbon window is used in this dining room not only to emphasize the horizontal nature of the space but to provide an opportunity to mirror it on the non-window side with similarly proportioned glass cupboards, increasing the sense of space. Photograph by Don Kalec.

SEE-THROUGH FIREPLACE FROM THE LIVING ROOM, ROBIE HOUSE, CHICAGO, ILLINOIS. FRANK LLOYD WRIGHT, 1906–1909.

The ribbon window as a unifying design feature is further reinforced with the "window" of the see-through fireplace. Photograph by John Kurtich.

DETAIL OF DINING ROOM TABLE, E. E. BOYNTON RESIDENCE, ROCHESTER, NEW YORK. FRANK LLOYD WRIGHT, 1908.

The integrated light fixture at the four corners of the dining room table was an ingenious method of making the dining experience more intimate through light. Photograph by Don Kalec.

corners of the table, Wright designed a light fixture to extend and crown the vertical supports of the table, further reinforcing the intimacy of the dining experience.

During Wright's Prairie house phase, he designed several nondomestic commissions, the most outstanding being the Larkin Building and Unity Church. The Larkin Company Adminis- tration Building, Buffalo, New York (1904), was designed as a complex of offices surrounding a four-story central atrium and topped by a huge skylight. All the offices were open to this central shaft of light and air. A double row of custom electric light fixtures further illuminated the desks placed at the bottom of this central well.

Unity Church, Oak Park, Illinois (1906), was

DETAIL OF GLAZED TRELLISES,
EDGAR J. KAUFMANN, SR., RESIDENCE
"FALLINGWATER," OHIOPYLE,
PENNSYLVANIA. FRANK LLOYD
WRIGHT, 1935.

*The blurring of inside and outside was
successfully achieved through the
manipulation of natural light control.
Photograph by John Kurtich.*

the first building in which Wright developed multidirectional movements of space. Lighting was achieved in the Temple portion by high clerestory windows on all four sides and a coffered skylight that covered the entire roof.

> *Flood these side-alcoves with light from above: get a sense of a happy cloudless day into the room. And with this feeling for light the center ceiling between the four great posts became skylight, daylight sifting through between the intersections of concrete beams filtering through amber glass ceiling lights, thus the light would, rain or shine, have the warmth of sunlight. Artificial lighting took place there at night as well. This scheme of lighting was integral, gave diffusion and kept the room space clear.*[29]

Wright had a clear vision about how important light was to his interior spaces. Two remarkable commissions in the mid-1930s allowed him to demonstrate his mastery of natural light, particularly by its enhancement of the textures of the building materials. The Kaufmann residence at Bear Run, Pennsylvania (1935–1937), otherwise known as Falling Water, was designed to blur the boundary between inside and out (see Chapter 4 for the four-dimensional description of this house). By extending the house into the landscape both visually and structurally, Wright maximized daylight within the house without sacrificing control. Overhead trellises of porches became glazed trellis-skylights as they continued as the roof construction for interior spaces.

The other great commission of the 1930s was the Johnson Wax Administration Building, Racine, Wisconsin (1936). Wright designed the building complex so that a person could "feel as though he were among pine trees breathing fresh air and sunlight."[30] The artificial forest Wright created out of concrete columns with flat, broad capitals is bathed in light, which pours through the space between the columns infilled with Pyrex glass tubing. The same tubing is used to create a continuous clerestory around the perimeter wall.

MAIN OFFICE FLOOR, S. C. JOHNSON AND SON ADMINISTRATION BUILDING, RACINE, WISCONSIN. FRANK LLOYD WRIGHT, 1936.

The column, not the perimeter wall, is the structural system which supports this building. Wright made this very clear by the way he used natural light to illuminate the separation of perimeter wall and ceiling. Photograph by John Kurtich.

Summary

The creative control of light is critical to the Interior Architect. Not only must it be deployed to maximize functional needs and human comfort, but its contribution to the perception and aesthetic experience of interior space is predominant and profound. Light is vital to architectural space in two ways. It is the medium by which space and form are defined and perceived. It is also a medium that has the ability to command its own aesthetic experience. Light can suggest place. Light can accentuate or heighten the character of a space. Light can guide human movement through space, its beckoning power can lead one from dimness to brightness or suggest continuity of space beyond a corner or visual obstruction.

So-called white light is really a mixture of radiant energies of certain varying wave lengths, any wave of which when isolated is referred to as a "color." Therefore light and color are really inseparable. Not only does Interior Architecture encompass all aspects of illumination, it also embodies the application and manipulation of color through control of the wavelength of any light energy illuminating an interior, the materials employed in structuring the interior, the surface treatment through applied pigment of any part of the interior, and the furnishing of the interior.

NOTES

1. R. L. Gregory, *Eye and Brain: The Psychology of Seeing* (New York: McGraw Hill, 1966), p. 7.

2. Ibid., p. 8.

3. Paolo Portoghesi, *The Rome of Borromini* (New York: George Braziller, 1967), p. 381.

4. Johann Friedrich Geist, *Arcades: The History of a Building Type* (Cambridge, Mass.: MIT Press, 1983), p. 22.

5. Jim Murphy, "A Moss Garden," *Progressive Architecture,* September, 1990, pp. 104–109.

6. Le Corbusier, *Précisions sur un État Présent de l'Architecture et de l'Ur-banisme* (Paris: Vincent, Freal & Cie, 1960), p. 74.

7. John Lobell, *Between Silence and Light* (Boulder, CO: Shambhala Publications, Inc., 1979), p. 22.

8. Goran Schildt, *Sketches: Alvar Aalto* (Cambridge, Mass.: MIT Press, 1985), p. 49.

9. Don DeNevi, "Masters of Light: Frank Lloyd Wright," *AIA Journal,* (September, 1979), p. 65.

10. Stanislaus von Moos, *Le Corbusier: Elements of a Synthesis* (Cambridge, Mass.: MIT Press, 1980), p. 99.

11. Le Corbusier, *Précisions sur un État Présent de L'Architecture et de l'Urbanisme* (Paris: Vincent, Freal & Cie, 1960), p. 132.

12. Charles Jencks, *Le Corbusier and the Tragic View of Architecture* (Cambridge, Mass.: Harvard University Press, 1973), p. 68.

13. William J.R. Curtis, *Le Corbusier: Ideas and Forms* (New York: Rizzoli, 1986), p. 72.

14. Ibid., p. 95.

15. Jacques Guiton, ed., *The Ideas of Le Corbusier on Architecture and Urban Planning* (New York: George Braziller, 1981), p. 55.

16. Le Corbusier, *Texts and Sketches for Ronchamp* (Jean Petit, 1965), no page numbers.

17. Richard Saul Wurman and Eugene Feldman, eds., *The Notebooks and Drawings of Louis I. Kahn* (Philadelphia: Falcon Press, 1962).

18. In Kahn's exploratory designs of screen walls with punched out keyhole-shaped openings separated from the actual walls that defined the interior space, he recalled ruins in which remnants of walls with yawning holes disclosed a vacuity beyond. This thought evolved into the concept of wrapping an entire building with an outer shell of "ruins," which would serve as a light and heat filter, controlling the intensity of direct sunlight in an architectural manner.

19. "Louis Kahn: Statements on Architecture," *Zodiac* 17 (1967), p. 57.

20. Neil E. Johnson, *Light is the Theme: Louis I. Kahn and the Kimbell Art Museum* (Fort Worth: Kimbell Art Foundation, 1975), p. 15.

21. Alexandra Tyng, *Beginnings: Louis I. Kahn's Philosophy of Architecture* (New York: John Wiley, 1984), p. 176.

22. Goran Schildt, ed., *Sketches: Alvar Aalto* (Cambridge, Mass.: MIT Press, 1985), p. 32.

23. Ibid, p. 131.

24. Paul David Pearson, *Alvar Aalto and the International Style* (New York: Whitney Library of Design, 1978), p. 122.

25. Goran Schildt, ed., *Sketches: Alvar Aalto* (Cambridge, Mass.: MIT Press, 1985), p. 78.

26. Ibid, p. 131.

27. Frank Lloyd Wright, *An American Architecture* (New York: Horizon Press, 1955), p. 102.

28. Reyner Banham, *The Architecture of the Well-tempered Environment* (Chicago: University of Chicago Press, 1984), p. 121.

29. Edgar Kaufmann and Ben Raeburn, *Frank Lloyd Wright: Writings and Buildings* (New York: Meridian Books, 1960), p. 78.

30. Jonathan Lipman, *Frank Lloyd Wright and the Johnson Wax Buildings* (New York: Rizzoli, 1986), p. 51.

CHAPTER 6

Color: Emotional Character

Interior Architecture incorporates color to establish and define the human character of its spaces. The simple application of color has the power to reinforce or destroy architectural volumes, emphasize or balance objects in space and create tension or calm immediately in a room. A well balanced color scheme can be one of the designer's most challenging tasks, involving knowledge in theory, physiology, and lighting. The use of color is always subjective, affected by personality, taste, and history. Most human beings have some sort of color vision, even those who are described as "color blind." Color blindness is the inability to differentiate certain color hues that the majority of people can distinguish clearly. People with normal color vision probably do not see color exactly the same, but there is a general consensus as to what color is being perceived. Any particular color associated with an object is a result of what happens when light strikes the object. The human visual process interprets the stimulation of light reflected from the object, producing the sensation of color.

The Physiology of Color

Color is a very complicated subject in that it has both a scientific basis and a perceptual reality, each of which is independent of the other. Visible light is the source of color. This light is a very small constituent of the electromagnetic spectrum, which includes at its high end X rays and gamma rays and at its low end microwaves and radio waves. All of this energy travels at the same speed (186,000 miles per second), but the length and frequency of the waves distinguishes one energy from another. The longest visible wavelength (red light) is 0.00007 cm, and the shortest (violet) is about 0.000035 cm. The human eye rarely, if ever, sees any color of a single wavelength, but rather it sees a mixture of many wavelengths, which produce a sensation that the brain interprets as a color.

Wavelengths of visible light carry information to the human visual system, which then assigns colors to objects viewed in conjunction with other kinds of clues. There is a reconstruction in the brain that might not exactly replicate the actual color of the object. For instance, if the brain knows it is perceiving a "white" handkerchief, this object will look white in sunlight, white in yellowish incandescent light, or white under red illumination. This is called *color constancy*. Color photography is not nearly as generous in its interpretation of color as the human eye/brain combination. Color film is manufactured specifically for a particular light source, such as daylight (5400°K), tungsten (3200°K) and photoflood (3400°K). If the film is not used with its proper light source (without correction filters), color distortion results in the finished photograph.

The nature of the material of the object also makes a difference in terms of perceived color.

A given color, such as red, *may have a large number of different appearances.*
—It may be filmy and atmospheric like a patch of crimson sky at sunset.
—It may have volume to it like a glass of red wine.
—It may be transparent like a piece of cellophane.
—It may be luminous like a stop light or a lantern.
—It may be dull like a piece of suede.
—It may be lustrous like a piece of silk.
—It may be metallic like a Christmas tree ornament.
—It may be iridescent like the gleam of an opal.
It is wholly conceivable that all such red colors could be made to match each other and thus be identical as far as instrumental measurements and physics were concerned. Yet in personal experience, each of the reds would be different, each would have a beauty of its own, an effect *that would be unique.*[1]

The perception of color, which is thus governed to a large degree by the material characteristics of a given object, is an important design tool for the designer. Sensitivity to the effect of one kind of material versus another of the same color demands skill, familiarity, and experience with a range of materials as well as the lighting conditions that would illuminate them. Combining materials and objects of different colors complicates the design issue. The understanding of color and its most effective use is paramount to achieving successful and distinguished interior spaces.

THE OPTICS OF COLOR

Mastery of the optics of color is important in order to use color most creatively. Humans have the propensity to visually balance a given color impression through their eye/brain perception system. If they are subjected to a prolonged view of a single intense color illuminating an object, a strain develops which, when the color is eliminated, results in an afterimage of this object colored in its opposite hue or complementary color.[2] This pure optical illusion has been used very effectively in theatrical productions. A related effect can be achieved with shadows cast from colored light sources. For instance, if an object is illuminated with a strong greenish-blue light, casting its shadow on an adjacent wall, the shadow will be a faded reddish-orange. The color of the shadow exists only in the eye/brain of the observer as an optical illusion.

When juxtaposing colors side by side or assigning one color to be the background for another, interaction of color occurs. Color hues as background can influence neutrally colored figures by appearing to tint them with the complementary color of the background. Color hues as figures can be made to appear more brilliant as their background darkens. Identical figures of a certain color value can be altered lighter or darker by reaction to their backgrounds as they vary. Entire books have been written on the interaction of color, such as M. E. Chevreul's *The Principles of Harmony and Contrast of Colors* (New York: Van

Nostrand Reinhold Company, 1981), Josef Albers's *Interaction of Color* (New Haven: Yale University Press, 1963), Johannes Itten's *The Art of Color* (New York: Van Nostrand Reinhold Company, 1961), and Ellen Marx's *Optical Color & Simultaneity* (New York: Van Nostrand Reinhold Company, 1983). The designer needs to be conversant with such studies in order to fully exploit the potential of color in architectural space.

An area of color manipulation that has not been fully explored or exploited in architectural interiors is the use of colored light on a colored surface. This type of color modification has been standard fare for theater since the beginning of controlled stage lighting. Designers for the stage have always had to consider not only the surface colors of their sets and costumes but also the colors of the lighting. The visual result of colored light on a colored surface is a consequence of subtractive mixing.[3] Because of the variables involved (countless pigments available to be applied to a given surface lit by infinite variations of colored light in terms of hue and intensity), experimentation and testing of various pigments with colored light compared to the same pigments with white light is necessary for the designer to develop invaluable color notes.

THE PSYCHOLOGY OF COLOR

It is known through experience that color affects mood. Psychologists have tried to test this idea in a scientific way, but no real conclusive results substantiate a scientific theory. Comparing subjective responses to color produce contradictory conclusions. But human responses to color cannot be ignored. Various designers and architects throughout history have established certain rules of color that seem to work well for them but do not necessarily provide universal truths about the appropriate use of color. Culture and society contribute their bias to color. It is illuminating to see how color has been used in past cultures and what rules are followed at any given time.

In the subsequent historical survey, examples are chosen for their emphasis of color as a primary

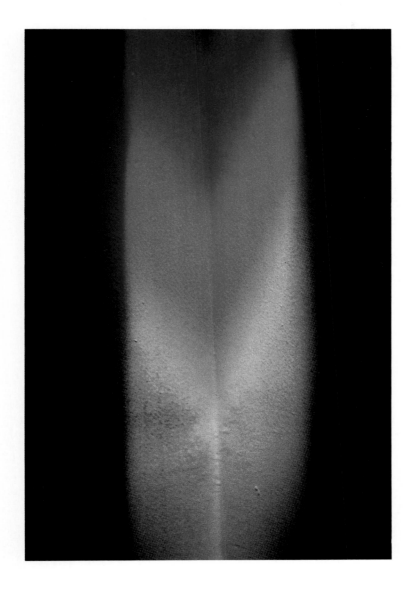

COLOR SPECTRUM OF LIGHT.

Visible light in varying wave lengths creates sensations which are interpreted through the eye to the brain as color. Photograph by John Kurtich.

feature of the interior space. This emphasis is achieved by one of four ways: applying paint or coloring agent to a neutral surface; employing naturally colored materials as the finished surface; using colored light either by passing natural light through colored transparent or translucent materials; artificial illumination with some means of coloration; or a combination of any of these.

LASCAUX CAVE, FRANCE

Throughout the history of humanity's quest for shelter and ceremonial spaces, color has been an important element. The availability of any given or desired color was always determined by accessible materials, existing technology, and the pervading culture. Paleolithic cave paintings represent the earliest surviving example of transforming interior space through color. The cave at Lascaux, France (ca. 20,000 B.C.), consists of two main "halls" and a connecting passage between them, the walls and roofs of all chambers covered with paintings of horses, deer, bison, bulls, cows, and other figures. The artists of these paintings had limited pigments available to them: red and yellow ochre, iron and manganese oxides, mud, soot, and calcite.

CATAL HUYUK, TURKEY

The neolithic town of Catal Huyuk, Turkey (ca. 6000 B.C.) featured an architecture of rectangular houses and shrines following a standard plan in layout, size of bricks, heights of panels and doorways. The houses were grouped around terraces rather than a street system. Entry to a typical house was provided by a hole in the roof, which also served as a ventilation shaft for the hearth. Because each house had its own walls and roof level different from those of the surrounding buildings, natural light could be brought in through a series of small windows placed just below the eaves. The interior walls of these buildings were covered with elaborate wall paintings and plaster reliefs, using a full range of pigments. Red, brown, and yellow ochre were derived from iron oxides; blue and green came from copper ores, mercury oxide provided deep red; manganese produced mauve or purple; lead grey came from galena; black was obtained from soot. Not only were the walls painted but also the plaster reliefs, clay statuettes, panels, posts, doorways, benches, platforms, and architectural or decorative details of the houses and shrines.

ANCIENT EGYPT

The ancient Egyptians produced a highly colored architecture as a result of climate and geography. The intense, bright sunlight and the hot, dry atmosphere contributed to the development of sur-

PREHISTORIC CAVE PAINTING OF TWO BISON, CUEVAS DE ALTAMIRA, SPAIN, CA. 12,000 B.C.

Cave dwellers painted their interiors with natural pigment images in early attempts to civilize and personalize their homes. Courtesy of The Art Institute of Chicago.

THE ROOM OF PILLARS, NORTH WALL, MASTABA OF MERERUKA, SAQQARA, EGYPT, CA. 2500–2350 B.C.

The limestone figures of Mereruka, carved in bas-relief, are unified to his statue in the niche through the use of bold colors. Photograph by John Kurtich.

face decoration of bright colors. The availability of natural materials such as clay, limestone, sandstone, syenite, and red granite helped to determine the basic color palette. The Egyptians favored earth colors in the reddish, yellow, and brown hues. The development and use of copper and its oxidation produced intense blue hues. Malachite produced a sharp green and carbon provided black. These pigment sources were mixed with a binder that produced a kind of tempera paint that has a remarkable permanence and radiance to this day.

> *The architecture of the Egyptians is thoroughly polychromatic,—they painted everything; therefore we have much to learn from them on this head. They dealt in flat tints, and used neither shade nor shadow, yet found no difficulty in poetically conveying to the mind the identity of the object they desired to represent.*[4]

The Egyptians used mainly primary colors separated by black, white, or tan outlines, inside and outside of their buildings. The capitals of their columns took vegetable forms such as flower buds, open flowers, or groups of flowers, all richly colored. One can still see such remains in the surviving columns of the Hypostyle Hall, Temple of Amon, Karnak (ca. 1312–1301 B.C.).

ANCIENT MESOPOTAMIA

Another type of polychromed interior was developed in the fourth millennium B.C. civilization of Mesopotamia, centered around the city of Uruk, Iraq. The geography of this region dictated the use of clay bricks as the primary building material; thus the inhabitants developed kiln baking and colored glazes to protect the clay from seasonal rains. Certain available minerals provided colors, such as tin for white, antimoniate of lead for yellow, and copper for red-brown. Early temple architecture featured a patterned system of polychromed wall treatment by employing hundreds of thousands of colored clay cones, similar to clay nails, embedded in the wall plaster, their heads painted black, red, and white. The designs seem to have been derived from woven reed matting. The Eye Temple at Brak, Iraq (ca.

COLOR PALETTE, EGYPTIAN NO. 3, BY OWEN JONES, 1856.

The Egyptians employed intense color interior architecture contrasting their monochromatic desert environment. The flat, bright patterned colors gave delicacy and meaning to the simple forms. Courtesy of The Art Institute of Chicago.

3200 B.C.) "exhibited the brilliant polychromy of the Jemdet Nasr period, for the outer face of the north wall was decorated with a colored cone mosaic and the inner with rosettes of white marble, black shale and red limestone."[5]

MESOPOTAMIAN ZIGGURATS

The ziggurat was the principal religious structure of Mesopotamian society; it was a broad tower made up of stepped terraces, crowned with a temple. Each of the terraces was a different color, believed to be linked to each of the planets of the solar system. The ziggurat at Ur, Iraq (ca. 2125 B.C.) had four concentric walls, respectively from bottom to top, black, red, gold, and blue. The Temple of the Seven Spheres at Bers Nimroud had seven terraces colored black, orange, red, yellow, green, blue, and white.

THE GATE OF ISHTAR, BABYLON, IRAQ

The great Gate of Ishtar, Babylon, Iraq, was a spectacular polychromed monument of seven huge towers, built by Nebuchadnezzar (601–560 B.C.). It was covered with blue-glazed bricks that

CLAY CONES, THE WHITE TEMPLE, URUK (WARKA), IRAQ, CA. 3500–3000 B.C.

The colored ceramic cones set in the plaster walls not only polychromed the interior but produced a harmonious texture. Photograph by John Kurtich.

DETAIL, ISHTAR GATE, BABYLON, IRAQ, 601–560 B.C.

The golden lions formed of fire-glazed bricks created a permanent integrated image in the famous landmark. Photograph by John Kurtich.

formed the background for various animals in contrasting glazed colors. There were yellow bulls, silver dragons, and golden lions, all shimmering against the blue setting. Similar bricks were used for the exterior and interior walls of his nearby palace.

THE PALACE OF DARIUS I, SUSA, IRAN

The Persians, united under Cyrus the Great in 555 B.C., became the predominant culture in the Near East. Their use of color in architecture combined some Egyptian ideas with those of Mesopotamia. They applied color by using glazed bricks, painted stucco, and naturally colored materials. A frieze of archers from the Palace of Darius I, Susa, Iran (522–486 B.C.), illustrates Persian color very well. Blue-green background supported life-size archers who wore robes of yellow with blue rosettes or white with blue and yellow adornments. Their headgear and shoes were yellow. They had green and brown quivers, white bows, and white-tipped yellow arrows. Archaeologists, reconstructing the palace, believe that this frieze may have flanked the stairway, as the archers were bodyguards to the king.

THE PALACE AT KNOSSOS, CRETE

The palace at Knossos, Crete (ca. 1600 B.C.), was a building complex alive with color. The characteristic inversely tapered column was painted red with black trim at the base and capital. These columns supported ochre-painted beams that framed walls filled with lively frescoes. The frescoes were painted on wet stucco and were either rendered on a flat surface or in light relief. Female figures were white; males were reddish-brown. The Minoans' extensive color palette was made of the following materials: red from ferric oxide or red lead; yellow from ochre; pale greenish blue from crystalline silicate of copper; white from gypsum; green from malachite; black from carbon. Red seemed to dominate most of their interior spaces as it was used as background or on blank walls. The so-called throne room at Knossos, as reconstructed by Sir Arthur Evans (1851–1941), foremost archaeologist of Knossos exemplifies the use of red.

DETAIL OF FRIEZE DEPICTING A PERSIAN WARRIOR, PALACE OF DARIUS I, SUSA, IRAN, 522–486 B.C..

Color is the contained energy of these relief figures which were the life-sized guardians of the King of Kings. Photograph by John Kurtich.

DETAIL OF NORTH "LUSTRAL BATH," PALACE AT KNOSSOS, CRETE, CA. 1600 B.C.

The top lit colonnaded stairwell was brightly painted to articulate the forms and celebrate the natural illumination. Photograph by John Kurtich.

ANCIENT GREECE

The classical Greeks (from the Archaic Period, seventh century B.C., onward) painted their temples and statues. The purists of the eighteenth century were shocked when traces of color were discovered on the remains of ancient buildings and statue fragments.

> . . . an unknown author describes the sculpture of a freshly unearthed Greek pediment: "Flesh, reddish in tone; globe of eyes yellow, iris green, with a hole in the centre filled with black; black outlines to eyebrows and eyelids; hair and beard bright blue at time of excavation, which disintegrated later into a greenish tone; circle of brown around the nipples. [6]

Greek temples and tombs were painted to emphasize architectural details and refinements. Typically, decorative patterns and moldings, such as egg-and-dart, maeander, palmettes, or leaf patterns, would be painted to reinforce the carved marble. Red and blue were common colors. The Acropolis Museum in Athens, Greece, has preserved a number of archaic Greek (seventh to fifth centuries B.C.) architectural fragments which preserve some of these painted surfaces. The tradition of Greek polychrome wall painting has been lost except for some examples found in a handful of Macedonian tombs, discovered in the mid-to-late twentieth century. The Lafkadia Tomb (second half of the fourth century B.C.), uncovered in 1966, has a well-preserved facade upon which deep blue was used for the background of a low relief frieze; on panels flanking the central door to the tomb were found polychromed full human figures.

DOMESTIC GREEK HOUSES, OLYNTHUS

The classical Greeks appear to have preferred broad areas of their interiors in saturated colors. Archaeological excavations at Olynthus, a city in northern Greece (last third of the fifth century B.C.), have uncovered many houses whose interior walls were painted in bright shades of yellow and red, sometimes contrasted with textured zones or black areas.

EXTANT IONIC CAPITAL, SHOWING TRACES OF PAINT, FROM AN UNKNOWN BUILDING, CA. FIFTH CENTURY B.C., STOA OF ATTALOS II, ATHENS, GREECE.

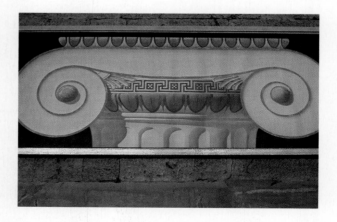

RENDERING OF SAME EXTANT IONIC CAPITAL, RESTORED, SHOWING THE POLYCHROMED AREAS.

Although few good examples exist, the Greeks used vivid color to polychrome their temples. Bright paints were applied to emphasize the forms and produce flat patterns. Photograph by John Kurtich.

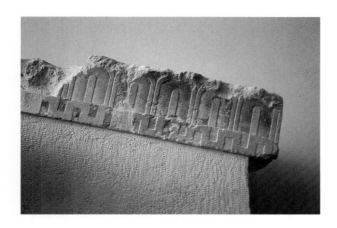

DETAIL OF THE "OLIVE TREE PEDIMENT" OR "TROILUS PEDIMENT," FROM A SMALL ARCHAIC BUILDING, ACROPOLIS, ATHENS, GREECE, CA. 570–560 B.C.

The alternating reds and blues of the incised relief design above the meander pattern have been well preserved, giving a rich and animated dignity to the architecture. Photograph by John Kurtich.

DETAIL OF PORCH, THE ACADEMY, ATHENS, GREECE. THEODOR HANSEN, 1859–1885.

Nineteenth century neo-classic architecture idealized the polychrome techniques of ancient Greek architecture. Photograph by John Kurtich.

In the "House of Many Colors," the *andron* (banqueting room) was found to have on its floor a raised border of lime cement, painted yellow. This surrounded a central square area paved with a mosaic. The baseboard of the wall was molded plaster painted blue. The wall above was red. The *andron* was considered the most important room in the house and had to be entered via an anteroom which had similar wall treatment of blue baseboard, but the wall was a rich burnt orange.

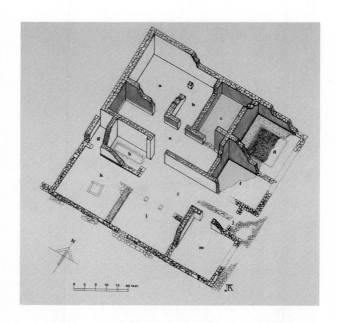

PLAN OBLIQUE, PARTIALLY RESTORED, OF THE "HOUSE OF MANY COLORS," OLYNTHOS, GREECE, LAST THIRD OF THE FIFTH CENTURY B.C.

The Greek's love of polychrome not only applied to the sunlit exteriors but to interior rooms washed with full rich color. Legend for the plan: a.& b. sleeping or loom rooms c. unknown use from evidence d. andron (banqueting room) e. room with altars f. anteroom to andron g. bathroom with tub h. kitchen with cooking trench i. court j. corridor k. oecus (center of domestic activities, with central hearth l. covered court, open to court "i" m. pitheon (storage below floor level). Drawing by John Kurtich.

FRAGMENT OF ETRUSCAN TEMPLE PEDIMENT WITH RAKING SIMA CROWNED WITH PIERCED CRESTING, CA. FOURTH–THIRD CENTURY B.C.

Similar to the Etruscan tomb interiors, the temples were brilliantly colored with elaborate terra cotta roof decorations of lotus and palmette motifs and painted meander patterns on the revetment planks below the sima. Photograph by John Kurtich.

ETRUSCAN TOMBS, ETRURIA, ITALY

The ancient Etruscans used color extensively in their built environment, as evidenced by terra cotta architectural remains and painted tomb interiors. They applied color to their architecture by means of pigment, terra cotta, and tile. Some of their tombs were built to represent interiors of Etruscan houses, such as the Tomb of the Reliefs, Cerveteri, Italy (fourth century B.C.), complete with sloping ceiling, which appears to be supported by a central beam and pillars. Realistic reproductions of household artifacts rendered in

color stucco covered the beams and pillars. Painted tombs, such as the Tomb of the Leopards, Tarquinia, Italy (second quarter, fifth century B.C.), featured walls covered with a continuous frieze of colorful banqueting and dancing human figures. The geometrically patterned ceiling was sloped, forming a truncated pediment on the end walls that highlighted two painted leopards in confrontation. Etruscan artists used both mineral and vegetable pigments. Chalk furnished white, reds came from iron oxides, lapis lazuli provided blue, charcoal made black. They achieved a sophisticated degree of half tones and blended color,

FRESCO OF FOOD ON TABLE IN
PERSPECTIVE, POMPEII, ITALY. A.D.
FIRST CENTURY.

*Fully rendered image of a table setting
with a draped background. Photograph
by John Kurtich.*

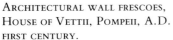

ARCHITECTURAL WALL FRESCOES,
HOUSE OF VETTII, POMPEII, A.D.
FIRST CENTURY.

*Murals in full color within architectural
frames gave a three-dimensional energy
to the Roman house. Photograph by
John Kurtich.*

as well as gradations of color from one surface to another. They established a technique and a tradition for wall painting that were later refined by artists of Rome and Pompeii.

ANCIENT ROMAN DOMESTIC HOUSES

The interiors of the ancient Roman atrium house (prior to 79 A.D.), so well preserved at Pompeii and Herculaneum, were dominated by vivid wall paintings, mosaics, and painted stucco reliefs. Romans used pigments consisting of earth colors, mineral colors, and vegetable and animal dyes. These included yellow ochre (earthy clay containing iron ore); red earths; lemon-yellow orpiment (native arsenic trisulfide); Melian white from Melos; green chalk; vermilion made from cinnabar; black soot mixed with size; black charcoal; blue (combining sand, flowers of natron, and copper filings); burnt ochre; green verdigris (treating copper with vinegar); white lead; purple (obtained from the porphyra shellfish or from dyeing chalk with madder root and with hysginum); malachite green; and indigo blue.[7]

According to recent research, the technique of the Pompeian wall paintings must have been as follows: First two or three carefully prepared layers of limestone, mixed with sand and calcite, were applied to the walls. The background of the picture was painted first and left to dry, whereupon the figures and ornaments were added. The colours were mixed with soapy limestone and some kind of glue to act as a medium, and were rendered shiny by waxing. By these means the paintings acquired great durability and brilliance.[8]

Pictorial content consisted of architectural features, architectural scenes, trompe l'oeil views, mythological themes, landscape scenes, gardens, birds, animals, fish, vegetables, fruits, and large compositions of human figures.

THE MAUSOLEUM OF GALLA PLACIDIA, RAVENNA, ITALY

Early Christian church interiors were alive with colored marbles and mosaics, thanks to the availability of such material from ruined pagan temples and palaces that served as a convenient quarry. The exteriors were generally plain and unadorned, a complete contrast to the profuse colors of rich marbles and mosaics applied to the interior. An example of this duality of inside/outside is the Mausoleum of Galla Placidia, Ravenna, Italy (ca. A.D. 425). The exterior was built of plain red brick, with a series of blind arcades as the only ornament. The interior is like entering another world, so different is the wall and ceiling treatment. The lower part of the interior walls was covered with translucent yellow Sienese marble. The upper walls, vaults, and central dome were

EXTERIOR, MAUSOLEUM OF GALLA PLACIDIA, RAVENNA, ITALY, A.D. 420.

completely covered with mosaics, still largely intact today. Small windows covered with alabaster slabs filter colored light into the space, amplifying the mystery and magic of this interior. Architecture and mosaics are integrated so well that not only do the architectural elements provide the opportunity for ornamental development but the ornament accentuates the architecture.

HAGIA SOPHIA, ISTANBUL, TURKEY

The premier church of this era to use mosaic technique to create interior religious spaces that could transcend normal earthly concerns and visions was the Hagia Sophia, Istanbul, Turkey (A.D. 532–537). Colored stones, gold, and painting techniques produced a shimmering skin, which, when combined with natural lighting effects,

would dematerialize the interior space and assist the worshipper in experiencing heaven. Although its surface treatment was largely destroyed or covered over when it was converted into a mosque in 1453, the few surviving mosaics give an idea of what the interior might have been like.

THE CATHEDRAL OF NOTRE DAME, CHARTRES, FRANCE

The great Gothic cathedrals of France used color and light together to proclaim a vision that symbolized the spiritualized space of western Christianity. Rather than natural light illuminating the shimmering surfaces of colored mosaics and gold as in Byzantine churches, the French Gothic cathedrals were illuminated with colored light through large stained glass windows that dema-

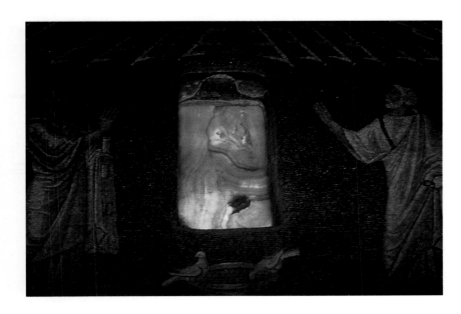

INTERIOR DETAIL OF ALABASTER WINDOW, MAUSOLEUM OF GALLA PLACIDIA, RAVENNA, ITALY, A.D. 420.

The interior architecture contrasted the austere exteriors with colored decoration in mosaics and alabaster. Photographs by John Kurtich.

terialized the very walls themselves. The Cathedral of Notre Dame, Chartres, France (1194–1260), became the epitome of a space transformed by stained glass windows. The colors were actually few—blue, red, some yellow and green, white, and a brown, which might also appear deep purple. The unearthly light achieved by these windows constantly changed with the sun, time of day, and weather conditions (see Chapter 4 for a discussion of the four-dimensional aspects of Chartres Cathedral).

Light entering the interior is not clear daylight, which would produce shadow, highlight, and plastic effects, but light washed with many hues and diffused throughout the interior. Drawing space into a continuity, this light emphasizes distances, intensifies the vertical, increases the apparent length of the church from the entrance to altar. Consequently, the outer skin of the church is transformed into zones of space and light.[9]

MEDIEVAL STAINED GLASS Medieval glaziers were able to produce a certain range of colors in glass, such as blue, green, yellow, brown, and purple, by varying the amounts of manganese and iron added to the melted glass. Beechwood ash

STAINED GLASS DETAIL, ABBEY OF
SAINT DENIS, FRANCE, 1137–1144.

*Medieval stained glass was particularly
vivid, partly due to the handmade
imperfections. Photograph by John
Kurtich.*

seems to have been the source of this manganese/ iron mixture, as the ash was the flux to promote the fusion of all ingredients. Red and other types of blue were produced by adding copper. Although these glaziers had crude kilns and relatively unsophisticated materials, they were able to produce stained glass, the luminosity of which has never been equaled in modern times, using sophisticated and scientific methods. The radiance of medieval windows is partially due to imperfections and bubbles in the glass, which seems to be able to capture sunlight, reprocessing it to produce the shimmering polychromed effervescence that made the interior space transcendent.

THE CATHEDRAL, SIENA, ITALY

The development of church architecture in Italy during the Medieval period relied almost exclusively on colored marbles and inlaid stone for both exterior and interior decorative treatment. The interior of the cathedral at Siena, Italy (ca. A.D. 1226–1380) is a fantasy of horizontal black and white marble stripes on the walls and col-

umns set off by an incredible polychromed marble mosaic floor. The mosaics are divided into fifty-six pictorial representations, covering the entire floor area of the cathedral. These panels depict stories from the Bible, the Virtues, the Sibyls, and Allegories. An example of the paintinglike quality of the mosaic work is the panel of the History of Fortune or Hill of Virtue, designed by

NAVE, CATHEDRAL, SIENA, ITALY,
1226–1380.

*The integral color banding was produced
by alternating layers of black and white
marble. This technique emphasized the
column shapes while imparting an
electrifying energy to the space.
Photograph by John Kurtich.*

PAVIMENTO DEL DVOMO DI SIENA

Bernardino Pintoricchio (1454–1513) in 1504 and executed by Paolo Mannucci in 1506. The scene features a black sky, red mountains, and greenish-gray sea. Human figures are delineated in grays and whites, with touches of reddish-brown, green, black, and yellow for costume highlights.

PERSIA

Coinciding with medieval Europe, in Persia, the use of tile and mosaic faience became a refined architectural feature. Because of climatic conditions of the region, painted surfaces and designs might not remain in prime condition for more than several generations. Tile and mosaic faience, on the other hand, seem to keep their original color and brilliance eternally. The tradition of fired, glazed bricks continued from the cultures of the ancient Middle East, but with improved techniques the Persians achieved a thin, tough tile that gave greater architectural flexibility. They learned that different colors reach their optimal luster at different firing temperatures.[10] The color palette included blue from cobalt, purple from manganese, greenish turquoise from copper, dark brown from oxides of iron and manganese, yellows, and rose pinks. A thousand years of Persian mosque building with these colored tiles culminated in the Masjid-i-Shah, Isfahan, Iran (1612–1638). The outer portal and the four ivans of the mosque courtyard are encased in shimmering glazed dark blue and golden yellow tiles. The dome of the sanctuary is enveloped with intricate blue and yellow arabesques. Much of the design found in these tiles, which tended to cover entire curvilinear surfaces of vaults and domes, inside and out, were inscriptions from the Koran.

RENDERED PLAN OF FLOOR PAVEMENT DESIGNS, CATHEDRAL, SIENA, ITALY, 1266–1380.

The rich mosaic floor patterns articulate the structural bays and represent various religious teachings and events important to the Church. Museo dell'Opera Metro Politana, Siena.

EXTERIOR SANCTUARY DOME, MASJID-I-SHAH, ISFAHAN, IRAN, 1612–1638.

The Persian use of glazed tiles to clad architecture resulted in highly colorful and permanent surface treatments. Photograph by John Kurtich.

TROMPE L'OEIL PAINTING IN RENAIS-SANCE ITALY With the discovery of linear perspective in Renaissance Italy, painting took on a new relationship with architecture. Painting became a device to visually extend space (see the discussion of perspective in Chapter 3), particularly when it achieved trompe l'oeil status through linear perspective. Walls of rooms and sometimes entire rooms were painted in full color to visually extend or distort the actual space (see the discussion of trompe l'oeil as a means of achieving the fourth dimension in architectural space in Chapter 4). There are many examples of this type of interior treatment, particularly in Italian late Renaissance, Mannerist, and Baroque buildings. Many of the interiors of Andrea Palladio's villas have their walls and ceilings completely covered with architectural trompe l'oeil and decorative paintings that interact with the actual architecture. Color is the main organizing force, reinforcing illusionistic architectural elements that frame various mythological scenes. The Villa Almerico–Valmarana (La Rotonda), Vicenza, Italy (1565/1566–1569), with its symmetrical plan of a central circular domed hall and four corridors leading to the four entrances, is filled with such painting, begun from the time the villa was completed and continued into the seventeenth and eighteenth centuries by various artists.

The use of color is a vivid contrast to the relatively plain plastered exterior.

THE CHURCH OF SANT' IGNAZIO, ROME, ITALY

The entire ceiling of the nave of the Church of Sant' Ignazio, Rome, Italy (1688), painted by Andrea Pozzo (1642–1709), celebrates the Glory of St. Ignatius and the Society of Jesus. The painting dominates the space and expands the architecture of the space upward into an infinite heaven. The use of color amplifies the trompe l'oeil effect and clearly defines the architectural elements, both painted illusions and actual.

THE ROYAL CHÂTEAU, FONTAINEBLEAU, FRANCE

The Italians influenced the use of color in French Renaissance interiors. Francis I (1515–1547) brought to his court Italian artists who richly rendered interiors of the royal chateau at Fontainebleau. Il Rosso (1494–1540), known as Maitre Rous or Fiorentino, was responsible for the Francis I Gallery (1530) where he blended painting and sculpture to achieve a radiant interior. The pre-

CENTRAL ROTUNDA, VILLA ALMERICO-VALMARANA (LA ROTONDA), VICENZA, ITALY. ANDREA PALLADIO, 1565/1566–1569. STUCCOES IN THE CUPOLA AND CEILINGS BY RUBINI, RUGGERO BASCAPE, AND DOMENICO FONTANA, 1581. LOWER FRESCOES BY DORIGNY, 1680–1687.

Trompe l'oeil paintings cover the interior of the central rotunda, expanding the space into mythical worlds and times. Copyright 1991, G. Paolo Marton.

CEILING OF THE NAVE, SANT'IGNAZIO, ROME, ITALY. CARLO MADERNA, 1626–1650.

This illusionistic painting dramatizes the verticality of the cathedral, drawing one into a provocative dream world. Photograph by John Kurtich.

DETAIL OF THE GALERIE DE FRANÇOIS I, PALAIS DE FONTAINEBLEAU, FONTAINEBLEAU, FRANCE. GILLES LE BRETON, 1528–1540. INTERIOR DECORATION OF THE GALERIE BY ROSSO.

The French, influenced by the Italians, combined sculpture with painting in elaborate detail to decorate their interior surfaces. Photograph by John Kurtich.

dominant color was the rich brown of natural wood from coffering of the ceiling, paneling highlighted with gilt on the lower walls, and unadorned herringbone flooring. At eye level, a large continuous frieze of separate polychromed paintings framed by elaborate sculptural casings animated the entire space with elegance and radiance. This gallery marked the beginning of the French Renaissance in architecture.

THE CHÂTEAU AT VAUX–LE–VICOMTE, FRANCE

The splendor of Versailles was made possible by a trio of artists, architect Louis Le Vau (1612–1670), painter/interior decorator Charles Le Brun (1619–1690), and landscape architect Andre Le Notre (1613–1700), who were originally engaged by Nicolas Fouquet (1615–1680) to create his chateau, Vaux-le-Vicomte (1656–1661). The surviving interiors of le Salon des Muses and la Chambre du Roi each feature remarkable painted ceilings in which Le Brun masterfully blended painting and sculpture to a high art. Color is all-important in le Salon des Muses, as Le Brun captured a freshness and sensuality that he never again achieved after he moved to Versailles. Le Brun established a style of interiors in la Chambre du Roi that virtually became the model for Versailles. Each separate piece of the interior, whether it was movable furniture and hangings or fixed paneling and molding, became part of a holistic statement of the space. The ceiling was made alive with sculptural stuccowork, balanced with painting. Gilded crown molding, gold brocade paneled walls, gilt balustrades and furniture, and a florid Savonnerie carpet completed the space as a golden room designed for the Sun King. It is small wonder that Louis XIV (1638–1715), angered by a palatial setting more splendid than his own, imprisoned Nicolas Fouquet and engaged the artists to build Versailles in Vaux-le-Vicomte's image.

CEILING DETAIL, ROOM OF THE
MUSES, CHÂTEAU DE VAUX-LE-
VICOMTE, FRANCE. LOUIS LE VAU,
1657–1661. INTERIORS BY CHARLES
LE BRUN.

*This vivid original painted relief
represents Le Brun's mature work prior
to his contributions to Versailles.
Photograph by John Kurtich.*

ROYAL SUITE, CHÂTEAU DE VAUX-LE-
VICOMTE, FRANCE. LOUIS LE VAU,
1657–1661. INTERIORS BY CHARLES
LE BRUN.

*Rich, flamboyant color, with excessive
use of gold, created a powerful political
statement in rooms intended to intimidate
visitors. Photograph by John Kurtich.*

CHAMBRE DU ROI, LE PALAIS DE
VERSAILLES, VERSAILLES, FRANCE,
1701.

*Louis XIV employed opulent colors and
decoration to enhance his image of
supreme power and wealth. Photograph
by John Kurtich.*

BIBLIOTHEQUE DE LOUIS XVI, LE
PALAIS DE VERSAILLES, VERSAILLES,
FRANCE. DESIGNED BY JACQUES
GABRIEL AND EXECUTED BY ANTOINE
ROUSSEAU, 1774.

*Louis XVI preferred a more restrained
and subtle use of color and form which
led to the eventual neo-classical
movement in France. Photograph by
John Kurtich.*

THE ROYAL CHÂTEAU, VERSAILLES, FRANCE

Versailles became the model for royalty throughout Europe for the next century. Interiors featured much gilt, mirrors, tapestries, colored
marbles, stucco work, paintings, and various textiles. Predominant colors, in addition to gold,
were green, powder green, crimson red, and rose
beige. During the reign of Louis XV (1715–1774),
a number of pastel shades became fashionable.
Madame de Pompadour (1721–1764), mistress to
the king for almost twenty years, virtually controlled French art and taste. The desire for smaller

rooms and apartments, furnished with elegantly
detailed furniture and objets d'art, required sophisticated and muted colors never before used.
"New to the art of decoration . . . are the pastels
and lush tones of Powder Pink, Apple Green,
French Lilac, Oriental Gold, Sevres Blue, Rose
Pompadour, Pompadour Blue, and French Turquoise."[11] Under the short reign of Louis XVI
(1754–1793), interest in the classical past, brought
about by Greek and Roman excavations, simpli-
fied French royal interiors. The color palette essentially stayed the same as that of Louis XV, but
furnishings and decorative moldings became more
delicately straightforward and spiritually classical.

OSTERLEY PARK HOUSE, MIDDLESEX, ENGLAND

The interiors of Robert Adam (1728–1792) dominated English interior architecture during his lifetime. He used color deliberately and creatively to define certain decorative ideas. He used it to imitate other kinds of materials, such as antique Greek vases or Wedgwood ceramics.[12] Color was also the unifying element for his interiors; through color Adam could relate his furniture to the shell of the room by repeating similar colors and motifs on the walls and ceilings as on the furnishings. His very original Etruscan Dressing Room at Osterley Park House, Middlesex, England (1761–1780), is a visit through eighteenth century eyes to the antique world of Greece, Rome, and Etruria. Attic red vase painting was the influence for the terra cotta and black figures and trellis work on the pale sky-blue walls and ceiling. Paintings in the medallions referred to Trojan War themes, since it was believed that the Etruscans were descendants of the Trojans. The chairs were designed by Adam, the frames of which were painted to correspond to the border designs on the walls and around the windows.

THE RESIDENCE OF SIR JOHN SOANE, LONDON, ENGLAND

The period between the death of Robert Adam (1792) and the beginning of the reign of Queen Victoria (1837) was known as the Regency in England. As in France during the same time, things Greek and Roman became dominant in design. John Soane (1753–1837), in his own house (see Chapters 1, 3, and 5), featured Pompeiian red as the dominant color for his dining room and library complex. By trimming the moldings of the walls with a complementary green, the red walls became particularly vibrant.

THE PAVILION, BRIGHTON, ENGLAND

England in the Regency had a worldwide empire that included possessions in the Far East. John Nash (1752–1835), a contemporary of John Soane, designed for the Prince Regent a pre-Victorian Oriental fantasy at Brighton known as the Pavilion (1815–1821). Stylistically appearing as a hybrid Chinese-Indian concoction, the Pavilion was a stage-set complex built of brick, timber, and iron. The interiors were done by John Crace (1754–1819) and Sons, with Robert Jones collaborating with Frederick Crace (1779–1859) in the final phase. Chinese red and gold wallpaper scenes dominated the fantastic domed Music Room, with giant green dragons and snakes appearing in the corners as though they were peeling away the wall. The room was lit by nine exotic flowerlike chandeliers hanging from glittering, bangle-encrusted chains. The space was designed for night use, to be artificially lit, which would enhance the Arabian Nights palace effect to the fullest and permit the strongest enrichment of the prevailing colors of the space through tinted lighting.

DETAIL OF LIBRARY, SIR JOHN SOANE RESIDENCE, LINCOLN'S INN FIELDS, LONDON, ENGLAND. SIR JOHN SOANE, 1812.

The Pompeiian red reinforces the richness of the natural wood details and is complementary to the brass hardware. Photograph by John Kurtich.

MUSIC ROOM, ROYAL PAVILION, BRIGHTON, ENGLAND. JOHN NASH, 1815–1821.

The Chinese red and gold color scheme emphasizes the oriental aura prevailing in this great domed room. Photograph by John Kurtich.

CROSSING, CRYSTAL PALACE, LONDON, ENGLAND. INTERIOR COLOR BY OWEN JONES, 1851.

The structural parts were painted multiple colors, forcing the observer to mix the strips and details when viewing the whole. Courtesy of The Art Institute of Chicago.

OWEN JONES

Owen Jones (1809–1874) published his classic *The Grammar of Ornament* in London in 1856; it quickly became the most important Victorian reference book on the use of color and ornament. Jones was the Superintendent of Works for the London Exhibition of 1851, and he decorated the interior of the Crystal Palace, the edifice that held the exhibition. He chose for the iron columns, stripes of blue, red, and yellow, which, when seen from a distance, appeared as a dynamic bluish-gray field. Jones's method of creating color mixing in the eye or mind of the observer was precursory to the development of pointillism[13] in painting, championed by Georges Seurat (1859–1891) in France.

WILLIAM MORRIS

William Morris (1834–1896) was influenced by Jones's *The Grammar of Ornament,* particularly the section on medieval color. He particularly deplored the machine technology of his time that produced crude, synthetic, artificial dyes and colors. This technology adversely affected contemporary art and architecture, in his opinion. Morris believed that art should return to that of handicraftsmen, such as during the Middle Ages. He preached against the current dyeing practice of his day, arguing that the best and most beautiful colors could be produced only by the time-tested, handicrafted methods prior to the Industrial Revolution. In 1858, Morris wrote:

Then came . . . one of the most wonderful and most useless of the inventions of modern chemistry, that of the dyes made from coal-tar, producing a series of hideous colours, crude, livid—and cheap,—which every person of taste loathes, but which nevertheless we can by no means get rid of until we are able to struggle successfully against the doom of cheap and nasty which has overtaken us.[14]

JOHN RUSKIN

John Ruskin (1819–1900) was a contemporary of William Morris and also believed in the use of "natural" color in architecture. He felt that applied color, such as found in numerous Italian Renaissance and Baroque exteriors and interiors, was always inferior to the color of natural materials. He argued that nature provided one system for the form of any of its creations and a separate system for the color arrangement. He pointed out that the spots on a leopard have no relationship to its anatomical system, nor do the stripes of a zebra. Thus he presented his theory of architectural color: "Let it [color] be visibly independent of form. Never paint a column with vertical lines, but always cross it. . . . and in sculptured ornaments I do not paint the leaves or figures . . . of one color and their ground of another, but vary both the ground and the figures with the same harmony."[15]

VIOLLET–LE–DUC

Eugene Viollet-le-Duc (1814–1879) was a French contemporary of John Ruskin and his adversary in theories of architectural restoration (see Chapter 1 for a more detailed discussion of the differences between Viollet-le-Duc and Ruskin concerning restoration). Viollet-le-Duc despised the fact that architecture and painting had become very separate disciplines in the nineteenth century. He said that the architect "neither conceived nor realized the effect which painting was to produce on the surfaces which he prepared" and the painter's attitude was that such surfaces were "pieces of canvas stretched in a studio far less convenient than his own."[16] When Viollet-le-Duc re-

ELEVATION OF THE "ARMOIRE DE NOYON" FROM *DICTIONNAIRE RAISONNÉ DU MOBILIER FRANÇAIS*, BY M. VIOLET-LE-DUC, 1858.

Pure colors were avoided in favor of more vivid and complex secondary and tertiary hues. Courtesy of The Art Institute of Chicago.

stored Notre Dame, Paris, France (1845–1864), he added his version of wall murals based on the latest nineteenth century archaeological evidence that an unpainted Gothic church interior was actually a rare occurrence. Viollet-le-Duc used vivid colors, based on the prevailing confident nineteenth century scientific method. He calculated through the rationale of "colour harmony"[17] a color scheme that was probably not actually the way the medieval artisan originally colored the interiors. Viollet-le-Duc used secondary[18] and tertiary[19] colors much more than the primaries.[20]

ANILINE DYES   The nineteenth century development of coal-tar dyes, known as aniline dyes, created bright, strong colors such as malachite green, fuchsine (brilliant bluish-red), ungreenable black, spirit blue, and safranine red. The cochineal insect, dried and crushed, produced crimson. The combination of a solution of potassium ferrocyanide with ferric salt made Prussian blue.

THE BELLE EPOQUE

At the turn of the twentieth century, Paris was the center of fashion and decorative arts. This period was known as the "Belle Epoque" and was proclaimed by the Exposition Universelle of 1900. Art Nouveau was a predominant style, and electricity, the new invention, lit the pavilions. Iridescent glass shimmered its rainbow hues, imitating the colors of peacock feathers, which themselves became a popular design theme. Interiors featured pastel colors interacting with asymmetrical furniture constructed with exotic woods. However, this delicate world of refined colors and manners was jolted in 1909 by the Ballets Russes of Sergei Diaghilev (1872–1929), the sets and costumes of which were dominated by brilliant primary colors in exotic combinations. The sudden revolution in the use of color in the West was further jolted by the revolution in music by the same company when it presented *Le Sacre du Printemps* (1913) by Igor Stravinsky (1882–1971). (See Chapter 4 for further discussion of the impact of this ballet on the Western world.) The color shift not only affected architecture and interiors, but it brought prominence to such artists as Pablo Picasso (1881–1973), Georges Braque (1882–1963), Robert Delaunay (1885–1941), Henri Matisse (1869–1954), Juan Gris (1887–1927) and Maurice Utrillo (1883–1955), all of whom at one time or another designed costumes and sets for the Ballets Russes.

SET DESIGN FOR "LES ORIENTALES," BALLETS RUSSES, PARIS, FRANCE, 1909.

The sets' vital use of primary colors shocked the prevailing sensibilities of the period. Courtesy of The Art Institute of Chicago.

ANTONI GAUDÍ

During this same revolutionary period, Antoni Gaudí (1852–1926) developed his own style of architecture, which was integrated with color, both inside and out. He used natural bricks of mixed colors, glazed brick, ceramic tiles, heavily em-

EXTERIOR DETAIL, TEMPLE OF THE SAGRADA FAMILIA, BARCELONA, SPAIN. ANTONI GAUDÍ, 1884–1926.

The cast-in-place glazed ceramic decoration gave dynamic texture to his idiosyncratic forms and symbols. Photograph by Garret Eakin.

bossed papier mâché tiles, pressed stucco, stone rubble, wrought-, cast-, and meshed-iron, ivory, marble, gilded metal, inlaid wood, stained glass, blue-green slate, glass mosaics, and paint. His unfinished masterpiece, the Church of the Sagrada Familia, Barcelona, Spain (1883–1926), was intended to be extensively colored. Gaudi presented a model of the church at the Paris Exhibition of 1910. Green was the proposed color of the Portal of Hope facade, to symbolize the Nile Valley. Burnt sienna was to color the Portal of Faith, recalling the desert sands of the Holy Land. Radiant blue was intended for the center Charity door, depicting a Bethlehem night. Gaudí wanted to use yellow, red, and orange symbolizing the yellow light of God bonded to the crucified red of Jesus through the orange intercession of the Holy Ghost. He planned to divide the nave into two color zones: white and gold, symbolizing joy, would dominate the right aisle; the left aisle would be purple and black, expressing mourning.

RUDOLPH STEINER

Rudolph Steiner (1861–1925) integrated color in his architecture for spiritual and idealistic reasons. He was the founder of the Anthroposophical Society and believed in a transcendental province beyond physical reality concerning humanity's relationship to a spiritual world filled with higher truths. He was convinced that architecture was the link to access this spiritual world and believed in "making the whole building as if possessed of a soul."[21] He designed a twin-domed wooden meeting hall at Dornach, Switzerland, known as the first Goetheanum (1913–1920). The plan consisted of two circular rotundas of unequal size, which overlapped each other. The larger rotunda was the seating area facing the smaller, which was the stage. Architecture, sculpture, and painting were fully integrated in this building. The interior of the larger dome was painted with colors that abstractly recounted the architraves. Colored glass windows let natural light into the space in a sequence from west to east of green, blue, violet, and pink. The building exemplified fully developed Expressionism.

LOBBY, THE GOETHEANUM, DORNACH, SWITZERLAND. RUDOLPH STEINER, 1924–1928.

The projection of colored light through bright stained glass windows was intended to dematerialize the interior surfaces. Photograph by John Kurtich.

CLASSROOM, THE GOETHEANUM, DORNACH, SWITZERLAND. RUDOLPH STEINER, 1924–1928.

Goethe's theory of color produced an expressionistic application of transparent colors that freed the pigment from architectural constraints. Photograph by John Kurtich.

On New Year's Eve, 1922–1923, the first Goetheanum burned. A larger second Goetheanum (1924–1928) was built on the same site out of concrete. The auditorium was trapezoidal rather than circular. The color of the interior primarily comes from light through four colored glass windows of green, blue, violet, and pink (as in the first Goetheanum). However, Steiner's intent was, through the quality of the color, to make the walls transparent. He wanted "to free colour from gravity, to experience colour as an independent element, to make colours eloquent." [22] Steiner developed his theory of color for architecture, using Johann Wolfgang von Goethe's *Theory of Colours,* [23] as a departure point. This included the investigation and experimentation of transparent paint and its application and the production and application of plant colors.

THE 1920s

Color in the mid-twenties, particularly in France, became subdued, partially a reaction to the Oriental brilliance of the Ballets Russes and some-

what of a response to the aftermath of World War I. The Exposition des Arts Decoratifs, Paris (1925) was dominated by a style now labeled "Art Deco." Art Deco interiors featured a palette of blacks and whites, gold, gray, silver, and beige. As the Modern Movement grew, Art Deco gave way to more machine-inspired interiors. Designers such as Jean-Michel Frank (1895–1941) favored whites and beiges to color his minimalist interiors, accented with custom furniture made from rare woods (such as Brazilian rosewood, black pearwood, and Macassar ebony) and exotic furniture finishes (such as straw marquetry, gypsum mica, and white shagreen).

FRANK LLOYD WRIGHT

Frank Lloyd Wright (1867–1959) believed that architecture should grow out of the ground as a plant does, thus his theory of "organic architecture." Interiors should express their material existence in their natural colors and textures, as much as possible, but be in harmony with one another. In describing the building of Taliesin, Spring Green, Wisconsin (1911), Wright says:

ENTRY DETAIL, FRANK LLOYD WRIGHT RESIDENCE, TALIESIN, SPRING GREEN, WISCONSIN, 1925.

Wright believed in using materials in as natural a state as possible, such that their integrity and raw beauty would not be compromised. Photograph by John Kurtich.

Inside floors, like the outside floors, were stone-paved or if not were laid with wide, dark-streaked cypress boards. The plaster in the walls was mixed with raw sienna in the box, went on to the walls "natural," drying out tawny gold. Outside, the plastered walls were the same but grayer with cement. But in the constitution of the whole, in the way the walls rose from the plan and the spaces were roofed over, was the chief interest of the whole house. The whole was all supremely natural.[24]

LE CORBUSIER

Le Corbusier (1887–1965) was very influenced by the natural beauty and simplicity of the indigenous houses of the Greek islands. White-washed and gleaming under the hot Aegean sun, these humble dwellings were alive with ideas that would blossom in Le Corbusier's work throughout his career. He noted, particularly, how the Greeks used color. They often accented their doors and windows with bright, primary colors, which actually affected the color and quality of

EXTERIOR WINDOW DETAILS, UNITÉ D'HABITATION, MARSEILLE. LE CORBUSIER, 1952.

The interior walls of Le Corbusier's brises-soleil *were brightly painted to soften the hot Mediterranean light. Photograph by Garret Eakin.*

PORCH DETAIL, PHIRA, THERA, GREECE, EARLY TWENTIETH CENTURY.

The Minoan influence on the use of pure pigment color in these modest dwellings is evident. Contrasting the hot sun with rich, colored interiors provided relief to the eye. Photograph by John Kurtich.

light coming into their houses. Sometimes entire walls of exterior porches were painted a solid color to contrast with the whiteness of the rest of the structure. The Greeks have maintained a tradition of applied color to their vernacular buildings going back to their ancient polychromed temples, which were human-scaled sculptures in the landscape.

THE UNITÉ D'HABITATION, MARSEILLES, FRANCE

Le Corbusier (1887–1965) used his Greek inspiration for the window treatment of his Unité d'Habitation, Marseilles, France (1952). Employing a variation of his *brise-soleil* (see Chapter 5 on a discussion of the *brise-soleil*), Le Corbusier de-

ALTAR, MAIN CHAPEL, COUVENT DE LA TOURETTE, EVEUX-SUR-L'ARBRESLE RHONE, FRANCE. LE CORBUSIER, 1960.

The reflected light is colored as it passes through the "light cannons," dramatizing the openings. Photograph by John Kurtich.

signed a thick sun break, the vertical walls of which were painted in bright primary colors of red, yellow, and blue. This sun break would directly affect the quality and color of light entering the building, just as in the Aegean island houses. He achieved a similar effect of producing natural colored light by painting the insides of his "light cannons" for the Monastery of La Tourette, Eveux-sur-l'Arbresle, France (1953–1957).

THE DE STIJL MOVEMENT

Le Corbusier (1887–1965) was also influenced by the Neoplasticist ideas of the De Stijl movement (1917–1931) in the Netherlands. De Stijl (see Chapter 3 for a spatial discussion of the Schröder House and Chapter 7 for Rietveld's red/blue chair) valued colored planes as a means of spatial dislocation. In 1924 Theo van Doesburg (1883–1931) published: ". . . In this way architecture gets (insofar as is possible from a constructional point of view—the task of the engineers!) a more or less floating aspect that, so to speak, works against the gravitational forces of nature."[25] Color was used in interiors to articulate space. This articulation included a control of natural light to create joviality, brightness, and glow. The followers of De Stijl believed in a symbiosis and harmony between architects and painters. Gerrit Rietveld (1888–1964) felt that space was the architect's medium, and if he chose to use color it was to serve his architectural space. The architect colors the planes and surfaces "to limit space in such a way that they reflect the incident light, thus making the space visible, and making the light visible as a result of its reflection by the materials used."[26]

WORKING–CLASS HOUSING, PESSAC, FRANCE

Le Corbusier (1887–1965) designed an experimental working-class community at Pessac, near Bordeaux, France (1926). Although many political, bureaucratic, and technical problems prevented Pessac from realizing the original vision

Axonometric drawing, "Maison Particulière," by Theo van Doesburg and Cornelis van Eesteren, 1923.

The De Stijl Movement applied color to thin planes to energize their compositions. Courtesy of The Art Institute of Chicago.

and intent of Le Corbusier, he achieved initial success with the use of color for these houses. Eiler Rasmussen visited the site in 1926 and said

Le Corbusier's architecture has, in my opinion, never been more clearly expressed than in his last work: the Pessac housing settlement near Bordeaux. The black-and-white illustrations give only a faint impression of this elegant world. The foundations of the houses are black, the walls alternately sienna brown, bright blue, bright aquamarine, white, bright yellow or grey. The various sides of the houses are not the same colour; one side for example is dark brown, the other bright green, and these colours meet directly at the corner; this is perhaps the strongest way of making the walls appear immaterial. The impression is strange and fantastic, but not chaotic. All these highly coloured surfaces with green plantings spaced in an architectonic order are placed in rows and arranged along axes. All the windows are standardized and made of the same materials. Imagine the whole settlement inhabited, the roof gardens overgrown with live vegetation, gaily coloured washing flapping in the wind of the service yards, while children run about playing. Is this then the architecture of tomorrow? [27]

THE VILLAS OF LE CORBUSIER

During Le Corbusier's (1887–1965) modernist villa period of the 1920s and early 1930s, he developed a color vocabulary only now being appreciated, partly because his villa interiors were initially published in black and white. With the restoration of the Maison la Roche, Paris, France (1923), and the Villa Savoye, Poissy-sur-Seine, France (1931), one can see how Le Corbusier used color planes for his interior spaces. The curved studio of Maison la Roche (now the headquarters of the Fondation Le Corbusier) has provocative walls of blue, brown, gray, and white. The living room of the Villa Savoye (now a historic monument) has the west wall blue, the short south wall rust orange, the exposed chimney of the fireplace burnt sienna, and the floor tawny gold tile, set in an otherwise white space with ribbon windows on the west and north walls, and floor-to-ceiling glass doors on the majority of the south wall.

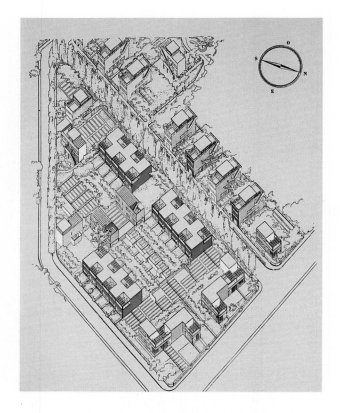

PLAN OBLIQUE, QUARTIER MODERNE FRUGES, PESSAC, FRANCE. LE CORBUSIER, 1926.

Le Corbusier's painterly attitude made compositional sense out of this repetitive complex, using a language of color. Droits de reproduction percus par la SPADEM. Copyright 1991 ARS N.Y./SPADEM.

GALLERY, MAISON LA ROCHE, PARIS, FRANCE. LE CORBUSIER AND PIERRE JEANNERET, 1923.

Bold contrasts in color emphasize the most elegant shapes. Photograph by John Kurtich.

LIVING ROOM, VILLA SAVOYE, POISSY-SUR-SEINE, FRANCE. LE CORBUSIER AND PIERRE JEANNERET, 1929–1930.

Le Corbusier used contrasting colors to separate parts of his architecture; i.e., chimney from columns, or west from south wall. Photograph by John Kurtich.

THE HEIDI WEBER PAVILION, ZÜRICH, SWITZERLAND

The most brilliantly colored building Le Corbusier (1887–1965) designed was the Heidi Weber Pavilion, Zürich, Switzerland (1961–1965). A steel truss umbrella roof covers a sequence of spaces that are formed by arranging primary-colored porcelainized steel panels with plate glass panels in modular proportions. The resulting color permeates the inside as well as the outside, foreseeing a new interest in color and high technology during the next decades.

EXTERIOR, CENTRE LE CORBUSIER, LA MAISON DE L'HOMME, ZÜRICH, SWITZERLAND. LE CORBUSIER, 1967.

Porcelainized steel panels in primary colors dramatize this playful pavilion. Photograph by John Kurtich.

THE GERMAN PAVILION, BARCELONA, SPAIN

Instead of applying color to interior walls, Ludwig Mies van der Rohe (1886–1969) relied on the color of the materials he used in his interiors, accented by carefully chosen or designed fabrics and furnishings. His German Pavilion, Barcelona, Spain (1929, restored 1986) is a study of rich and sumptuous colors, finishes, and flowing space. The focus of the pavilion is provided by a free-standing wall of rare onyx dorée, whose swirling veined colors vary from white to deep gold. The glass walls that enclose the pavilion are greenish, offset by brilliant red drapery. White kid leather chairs and ottomans rest on a solid black carpet. Structural clarity of the space comes from chrome-plated, cross-shape steel columns. An

German Pavilion, Barcelona, Spain. Ludwig Mies van der Rohe, 1929. Restored by Christian Ciricil, Fernando Ramos, and Ignasi de Sola-Morales, 1986.

Mies van der Rohe preferred the rich quality of natural materials to provide color and texture to his timeless spaces. Photograph by Don Kalec.

outdoor pool lined in black glass features a bronze woman created by Georg Kolbe (1877–1947). The background for the sculpture is a wall of dark green Tinian marble, whose veining merges with the vegetation of cypress and conifers, which constitute the landscaping. The entire composition, inside and out, is a symphony of colored opulence, stunning the beholder with polished reflections that multiply and magnify the richness of the spaces and reinforces the free flow of movement throughout.

ELSIE DE WOLFE

Elsie de Wolfe (1865–1950) loved color, and her book, *The House in Good Taste* (1913), devoted a whole chapter to it. She preached that one must first learn color from nature, particularly regarding the background color versus the accent. She used this axiom as her point of departure concerning the use of color.

We must decide our wall colors by the aspect of our rooms. Rooms facing south may be very light gray, cream, or even white, but northern rooms should be rich in color, and should suggest warmth and just a little mystery . . . For south rooms blues and grays and cool greens and all the dainty gay colors are charming . . . For north rooms I am strongly inclined to use the panel-

ing in our native American woods, that are so rich in effect, but alas, so little used. I hope our architects will soon realize what delightful and inexpensive rooms can be made of pine and cherry, chestnut and cypress, and the beautiful California redwood.[28]

From that point she would advise "building" a room around some special piece, such as a special rug, an old print, an antique chair, an heirloom vase. This would give her direction for color accents. The use of colorful chintz to finish

"WRITING CORNER OF CHINTZ BEDROOM." ELSIE DE WOLFE, *THE HOUSE IN GOOD TASTE*, NEW YORK: THE CENTURY CO., 1913. COLOR PLATE FACING P. 83. (RYD13.1 D52)

Elsie de Wolfe employed chintz to enliven her rooms with cheerful color and pattern. © 1991 The Art Institute of Chicago, All Rights Reserved.

off the room was a de Wolfe trademark. She argued that it was much better to use a good chintz than an inferior silk. Rooms full of color, but logically organized with background walls and trim in harmony with special pieces, are all brought together with bright, patterned chintz.

> *. . . you enter a little dressing-room that is also full of color. Here are the same cream walls, the dull red carpet, the old blue silk shades on lamps and candles, but the chintz is different: the ground is black, and gray parrots and parquets swing in blue-green festoons of leaves and branches . . . You can imagine how impossible it would be to be ill-tempered in such a cheerful place.*[29]

RUBY ROSS GOODNOW WOOD

Ruby Ross Goodnow Wood (1880–1950) followed Elsie de Wolfe's book with her own book, *The Honest House* (1914). In it were specific rules about the use of color for interiors. The wall was a critical area, and her advice was strict and direct: "The fundamental principle of mural decoration is: Walls are backgrounds. Keep that in mind and you cannot go far wrong."[30] She thought that blue was the nicest color, but not for walls. She felt that green and red had been misused so much that they should not be used at all for walls. She argued that yellow was the most pleasant color for walls because it would be hard for the occupant to become gloomy in a yellow environment. She disliked yellow-green, but felt that it would be used by anyone who could handle color properly. Orange was a magnificent color to her, but it had to be used carefully and sparsely. She deliberated that white was the most difficult of all to use for walls; she contended that white was too cold, too immediate, too much glare. "White may be softened and mellowed by mixing a little yellow with it, and it becomes cream or ivory or buff, suave and aristocratic. But dead white walls are never pleasant."[31]

LUIS BARRAGAN

Luis Barragan (1902–1988) used large areas of white in his architecture, both interior and exterior, in order to set off the planes of vibrant color he employed to create truly poetic drama. The rich tapestry of his Mexican homeland of rugged terrain, adobe buildings, bold colors, and the intense "white" sunlight greatly influenced his work. Barragan believed in an "emotional architecture," one of beauty and serenity. With his design for the Chapel for the Capuchinas Sacramentarias del Purisimo Corazon de Maria, Tlalplan, Mexico (1952–1955), Barragan was able to create his special brand of architecture through his dazzling use of light and color.

The sequestered nuns pray for the forgiveness of the sins of the world. Instead of providing a somber setting for the nuns, Barragan created a bright haven for their religious rites. The chapel glows. A warm luminous yellow pervades the interior, creating a feeling of hope and optimism. The roughly textured walls are painted a light yellow with a rich honey-colored wooden plank floor. The surfaces are lit from two natural light sources. Light enters from the back of the chapel through a lattice wall. Using the concrete screen wall, Barragan intensified natural shadow conditions by painting the interior wall deep yellow while the inside of the squares was painted a light yellow. This technique created a sunny illusion even on an overcast day. The other light source shined through a golden glass window, hidden from view, onto a large freestanding cross, casting a dramatic shadow on the altar. The designer deliberately concealed the light source to create special lighting effects to heighten the mystical quality of the chapel. All materials are simpatico with Barragan's sunny theme. Flames from the candles intensify the interior's warm ambience while the golden altar adds to the chapel's radiance. Barragan artfully combined both light and color as his strongest design tools.

THE OFFICES OF GOLDMAN SOKOLOW COPELAND, NEW YORK, NEW YORK

North light, reinforced by two shades of cool lavender, established the soothing atmosphere for the engineering firm of Goldman Sokolow Copeland (New York, 1985) by Peter Gisolfi Architects. The hectic pace created by completion deadlines in this fifty-person consulting engineer-

OFFICE INTERIOR, GOLDMAN
SOKOLOW COPELAND, NEW YORK,
NEW YORK. PETER GISOLFI
ASSOCIATES.

*Cool lavender establishes a calming
atmosphere while the terra cotta tones
provide a warm balance. Photograph by
Jon Naar.*

HOUSERMAN SHOWROOM, PACIFIC
DESIGN CENTER, LOS ANGELES,
CALIFORNIA. VIGNELLI ASSOCIATES
WITH DAN FLAVIN, 1982.

ing firm required a concept incorporating a calming environment. The architect envisioned a highly organized plan reinforced by color.

The walls and ceiling of the main workroom were painted a pale lavender, accented by a deeper shade of lavender on the trim moldings and columns. Initially, the engineers opposed this color scheme. The architect, being sensitive to this reaction, reviewed the project after six months and discovered that the unorthodox pastel color treatment proved successful in instilling a serene setting. He found that even though the space was acoustically hard, the color scheme encouraged lower noise.

To balance the cool palette, a shade of warm terra cotta was employed to announce the change from one space to another. This color scheme was inspired by the Minoan red columns and blue walls used at Knossos. The purposeful use of such color was unconventional, transcending the boundaries of the physical space and creating a psychologically comforting atmosphere.

THE HAUSERMAN SHOWROOM, LOS ANGELES, CALIFORNIA

In the Hauserman Showroom at the Pacific Design Center, Los Angeles, California (1982), Masimo (1931–   ) and Lella Vignelli collaborated

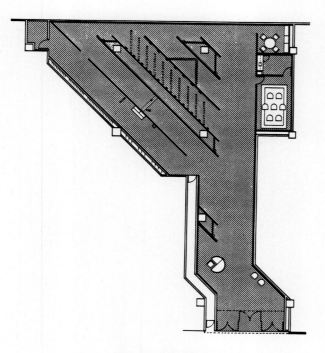

TW Best, Chicago, Illinois. Eva Maddox, 1987.

Bold forms in space accentuated by brilliant contrasting colors provide a magnetic focal point to this retail space. Photograph by Jon Miller, Hedrich Blessing.

Plan of Houserman Showroom. Vignelli Associates.

This showroom of moveable partitions was dramatized by the infusion of colored light reflected off of glossy surfaces. Photograph by Toshi Yoshimi.

with artist Dan Flavin (1933–). The purpose of the showroom was to display a rather ordinary product—movable partitions—within a work of art. The oddly shaped enclosure of this showroom was neutralized by painting the wall light beige to match the wall panels and bleached oak flooring. The monochromatic palette created a continuous envelopic screen, blurring edges. Colored fluorescent light was employed to illuminate the wall system and dematerialize the volume. A series of parallel walls at a 45° angle provided "light" corridors illuminated by different arrangements and colors of fluorescent fixtures. One corridor consisted of yellow and pink light; another was green and yellow; the third corridor was all blue. The surrounding walls were used as reflectors to mix the colors and their intensities. Mirrors on the end wall extend further the illusive quality of the space.

As one moves through the space, the color mixing constantly changes from bold color to gentle pastels. The designers created a highly fluid space that is greatly affected by an individual's viewing position. A bright yellow passageway is relieved at the end by a cool green slice of light. An emerald green composition relieved by a counterpoint of yellow reverses the experience. The spectacular changes and surprises that occur throughout the showroom keep one constantly exploring while being totally intrigued by the simplicity of the concept. Letting the wall panels act as the artist's canvas, the designers were able to create a piece of art through the magical medium of colored light.

T. W. BEST NEWSSTAND, CHICAGO, ILLINOIS

The traditional image of a newsstand is dark, cramped, and undistinguished. The challenge that faced Eva Maddox, Eva Maddox Associates, with

T. W. Best/Eastern Lobby Shops Chicago, Illinois (1988), was to take a standard newsstand and supply it with a new highly charged marketable image. The 1100 square feet of retail space with an active corner location was transformed by its spatial organization, form, and bold strokes of primary color.

The perimeter of the space was painted black, providing a high contrast to a series of brightly painted and overscaled volumetric forms. An inverted red cone, a bright blue frame, and perforated yellow screens established an engaging composition, activating the store from floor to ceiling. A brilliant green tube was threaded through the black perimeter display cases, providing a piercing accent upon which signage could be hung. The large, brightly colored elements draw the shopper into the space, while the products displayed hold their attention in the newsstand.

Maddox's choice of color was not pale or subtle. She preferred the vibrant, intense color of magazine covers, candy wrappers, and paperback books that infused the interior with energy and excitement. This animation through color made T. W. Best memorable, upsetting the traditional image of the newsstand and giving her client a marketing edge through design.

PAUL FLORIAN APARTMENT, CHICAGO, ILLINOIS

Bright, vibrant color is used to accentuate and dramatize the architectural forms of the Paul Florian apartment, Chicago, Illinois (1986), by Florian Wierzbowski Architecture. The minimalist design strategy (see Chapter 3 for the three-dimensional discussion of the scheme) sought to maintain an open flowing feeling in the small second story space. Entry is via a gray painted wood stair leading to a curious yellow column and angled red soffit at the top. The red form visually draws one into the main room—a white gabled space with blue roof trusses. The red, twisted soffit caps the kitchen and provides for a loft bedroom above.

To balance the electric red soffit, muted apple green is applied to the long horizontal wall enclosing the stair, bathroom, and closets. The green surface is proportionally much larger than the red soffit, thereby creating a soothing contrast. To further add detailed contrast, delicate black furniture, countertops, and accent details boldly silhouette the space.

The architects have very economically made a small space seem much larger and brighter through the use of bold color on architectural form. The colors not only dramatize but inject compositional interest and surprise into the smallest of the rooms.

SUMMARY

Color has many values in a given culture. It can symbolize a nation, a college, an athletic team. It can arouse emotions. The color palette of any given culture has always been governed by available materials, level of technology, and socio-political perceptions and ideals. Throughout history, color could be consciously manipulated in a certain manner to achieve desired results.

Designers and architects must be educated to appreciate the power of color. The choice of a color or combination can ruin or make an interior, regardless of how wonderful the design. The visualization of color in a space can be difficult as compared to seeing a detail or proportion that can easily be studied on paper. It is often safer to work in neutral tones or black and white, not unlike the typical drawings designers make. Unfortunately this can lead to solutions without the full potency color can add. The illusive ability to see color in space can best be gained through experiment and experience.

Architects tend to be conservative with their use of color, whereas interior designers and decorators are much more experimental, boldly integrating color. This disparity between the professions is in part due to the designer's ability to consider an interior in total, including fabrics,

INTERIOR VIEW OF PAUL FLORIAN
APARTMENT, CHICAGO, ILLINOIS.
FLORIAN/WIERZBOWSKI
ARCHITECTURE, 1986.

*The use of color redefines and enlarges a
small series of spaces into dramatic and
bright living quarters. Photograph by
John Kurtich.*

finishes, and furnishings. It is difficult to select color without reviewing all elements of the space. Usually fabrics and furnishings are not a part of the architect's palette.

Color must be integral to the conception of the space. Its wealth has long been overlooked by architects. Color communicates. It is sometimes indispensable in differentiating between form and content. It is an expedient way to create hierarchy. It is effective in reinforcing a focal point. It is a dynamic means of introducing energy into a space. Such energy influences human feelings. People are most affected by color energy, even though these elements are the hardest to quantify. Color can have a most powerful affect on Interior Architecture.

NOTES

1. Faber Birren, *Creative Color* (New York: Van Nostrand Reinhold Company, 1961), p. 60.

2. "One theory maintains that the nerve ends on the human retina (rods and cones) are tuned to receive any of the 3 primary colors (red, yellow, or blue), which constitute all colors.

"Staring at red will fatigue the red-sensitive parts, so that with a sudden shift to white (which again consists of red, yellow, and blue), only the mixture of yellow and blue occurs. And this is green, the complement of red." (from *Interaction of Color* by Josef Albers, (New Haven: Yale University, 1963), p. 23.

3. There are two ways of explaining color mixing: additive and subtractive. Additive mixing refers to the blending of the three primary colored lights of red, green, and blue, which when mixed in equal parts produce "white" light. All other colors of the spectrum can be produced by varying the intensities of these three primaries.

Subtractive mixing refers to the combination yellow, magenta, and cyan (colors, each of which are initially produced from the overlapping of two primary colored lights). When these three colors are mixed in equal parts, they produce black (or the absence of light). Pigments are compounds that absorb very particular wavelengths of visible light and appear to the eye as a particular color. If pigments of the entire range of spectral hues are mixed, the result is again black.

4. Owen Jones, *The Grammar of Ornament* (London: Messrs Day and Son, 1856), p. 24.

5. Stuart Piggott, ed., *The Dawn of Civilization* (New York: McGraw-Hill, 1961), p. 88.

6. Tom Porter, *Architectural Color* (New York: Whitney Library of Design, 1982), p. 10.

7. For a more detailed description of Roman pigments and how they were prepared, see Vitruvius, *The Ten Books on Architecture* (New York: Dover Publications, Inc., 1960), Book VII, chapters 7–14.

8. Gisela Richter, *A Handbook of Greek Art* (London: Phaidon Press Ltd., 1959), p. 285.

9. Christian F. Otto, *Space Into Light* (Cambridge, Mass.: The MIT Press, 1979), p. 21.

10. According to Arthur Upham Pope (*Persian Architecture,* New York: George Braziller, 1965), 800°C is needed for lead glazes; about 1600°C for tin and cobalt glazes. Multicolored tiles are generally fired at 1050°C but do not give individual colors their maximum brilliance.

11. Faber Birren, *Color for Interiors, Historical and Modern* (New York: Whitney Library of Design, 1963), p. 45.

12. The ceramics developed by Josiah Wedgwood during this time were revolutionary. He successfully formulated a ceramic that maintained the same color throughout the material. It was named jasperware, and it depended on barium sulphate for its quality. Color was produced by adding metallic oxides, such as cobalt for blue. Upon this base, he would decorate the surface with designs and figures in white ceramic relief.

13. Pointillism is a method of painting by which the laws of color vision are applied to painting technique. Small, even-size spots of pure color pigment are employed in a mosaiclike fashion to create the painting, allowing the viewer to mix and blend, through color juxtaposition signals to the brain via the eye, all the intended colors of the artist. A problem with this technique is the proper viewing distance to have all colors blend or fuse satisfactorily. The characteristics of different hues change with different viewing distances, so that one viewing point cannot achieve ideal optical color mixing.

14. Aymer Vallance, *William Morris: His Art, His Writings, and His Public Life* (London: Studio Editions, 1986), p. 98.

15. John Ruskin, *The Seven Lamps of Architecture* (New York: Farrar, Straus and Cudahy, 1961), p. 133.

16. Eugene Viollet-le-Duc, *Dictionnaire Raisonné* (Paris: Bance, 1858), p. 249.

17. Owen Jones in his *Grammar of Ornament* (London: Messrs Day and Son, 1856) established "scientific" rules concerning color harmony. Proposition 18 details this set of rules:

The primaries of equal intensities will harmonise or neutralise each other, in the proportions of 3 yellow, 5 red, and 8 blue,—integrally as 16.

The secondaries in the proportions of 8 orange, 13 purple, 11 green,—integrally as 32.

The tertiaries, citrine (compound of orange and green), 19; russet (orange and purple), 21; olive (green and purple), 24;—integrally as 64.

It follows that,—

Each secondary being a compound of two primaries is neutralised by the remaining primary in the same proportions: thus, 8 of orange by 8 of blue, 11 of green by five of red, 13 of purple by 3 of yellow.

Each tertiary being a binary compound of two secondaries, is neutralised by the remaining secondary: as, 24 of olive by 8 of orange, 21 of russet by 11 of green, 19 of citrine by 13 of purple.

18. Webster's New International Dictionary defines a secondary color as follows: "A secondary color is formed by mixing any two primary colors in equal or equivalent amounts."

19. Webster's New International Dictionary defines a tertiary color as follows: "A tertiary color is produced by the mixture of two secondary colors. Such a mixture must include all the elements necessary to produce white (in practice, gray), and a tertiary color is hence merely some primary or secondary color dulled with gray, as russet or olive."

20. Webster's New International Dictionary defines primary colors as follows: "Primary colors are the principal colors of the spectrum (Newton's seven were red, orange, yellow, green, blue, indigo, and violet), esp. certain fundamental colors by the combination of which (color mixture) any other color can be produced."

21. Rudolph Steiner, *Der Baugedanke des Goetheanum,* (Stuttgart: Verlag Freies Geistesleben, 1958), p. 52. (See *Expressionist Architecture* (New York: Praeger, 1973) by Wolfgang Pehnt.)

22. Rudolph Steiner, *Colour* (New York: Anthroposophic Press, 1935), p. 86.

23. Goethe believed, as did Aristotle of ancient Greece, that yellow and blue were the two primary colors. All color was produced by the interaction between light and darkness, yellow being the first color to materialize when white began to be darkened and blue the first color to emerge when darkness (black) became lightened.

24. Edgar Kaufmann and Ben Raeburn, ed., *Frank Lloyd Wright: Writings and Buildings* (New York: Meridian Books, 1960), p. 179.

25. Theo van Doesburg, "Towards a Plastic Architecture," *De Stijl,* VI, 6/7 (1924), p. 78–83.

26. Paul Overy, Lenneke Büller, Frank den Oudsten, and Bertus Mulder, *The Rietveld Schröder House* (Cambridge, MA: MIT Press, 1988), p. 71.

27. Steen Eiler Rausmussen, "Le Corbusier, the Architecture of Tomorrow?," *Wasmuths Monatshefte für Baukunst* 10 (1926), p. 382 ff. Translation Serenyi.

28. Elsie de Wolfe, *The House in Good Taste* (New York: The Century Co., 1913), p. 77 ff.

29. Ibid, p. 83.

30. Ruby Ross Goodnow, *The Honest House* (New York: The Century Co., 1914), p. 179.

31. Ibid, p. 180.

FURNITURE PLAN OF BEDROOM,
HOUSE E.1027, CAP-MARTIN
ROQUEBRUNE, FRANCE. EILEEN
GRAY, 1926–1929.

*Courtesy of The Art Institute of
Chicago.*

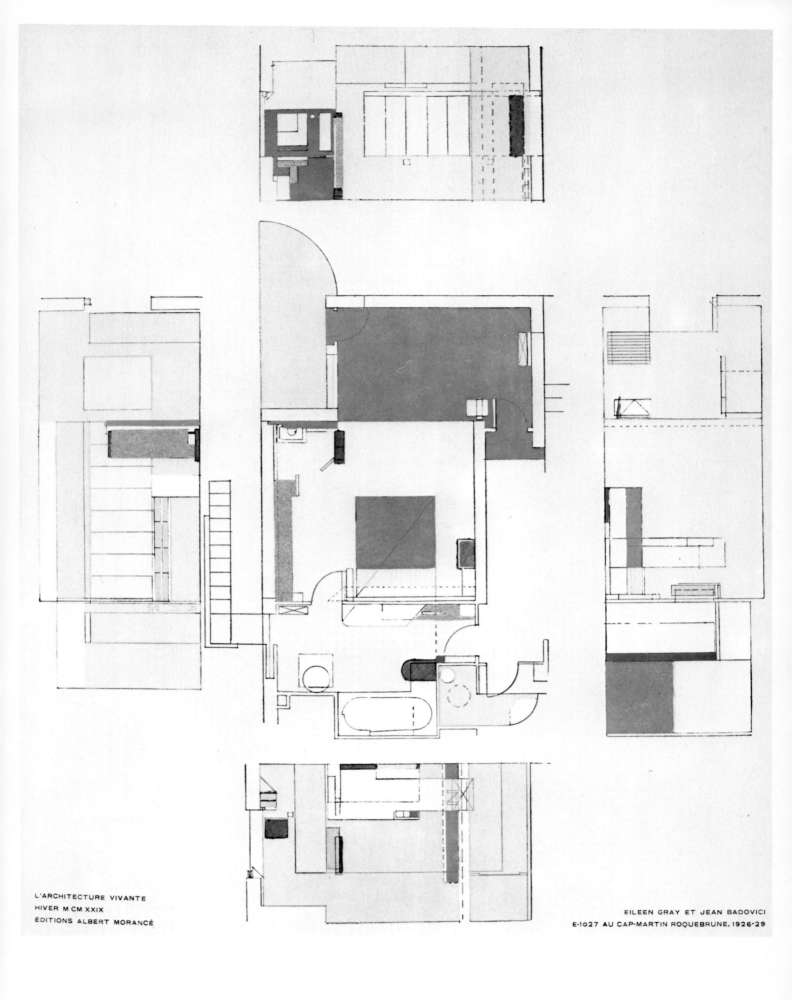

L'ARCHITECTURE VIVANTE
HIVER M CM XXIX
ÉDITIONS ALBERT MORANCÉ

EILEEN GRAY ET JEAN BADOVICI
E·1027 AU CAP·MARTIN ROQUEBRUNE, 1926·29

CHAPTER 7

FURNISHINGS: INTIMATE HUMAN COMFORT

The focus of the foregoing discussion about Interior Architecture has primarily been spatial—the development of the third dimension, the experience of the fourth dimension, and the necessity of light and color to define and extend the spatial spectrum. Another central issue is the furnishing of the interior and how these contents relate to their enclosure.

ATTITUDES ABOUT FURNISHINGS: ARCHITECTS VERSUS DESIGNERS

Furniture is essential to humanity's daily existence. Because people live with furniture day and night, its intimate connection with them makes it an extension of their personalities and tastes. The design of furniture has never been the exclusive activity of any single profession; architects, designers, artists, engineers, craftspeople, carpenters, and talented amateurs have all designed furniture. Interior Architecture focuses on the concept that furniture is a key factor in architecturally integrated interiors. Furniture not only provides a means for the functions of living and working but should also enhance, extend, and enrich interior space. In 1895, Mackay Hugh Baillie Scott (1865–1945), one of William Morris's followers, said

It is difficult for the architect to draw a fixed line between the architecture of a house and the furniture. The conception of an interior must necessarily include the furniture which is to be used in it, and this naturally leads to the conclusion that the architect should design chairs and tables as well as the house itself. Every architect who loves his work must have had his enthusiasm dampened by a prophetic vision of the hideous furniture with which his client may fill his rooms, and looks all the more incongruous as the rooms themselves are architecturally beautiful.[1]

Not everyone agreed that it was ideal for the same person to design a building and all its contents. In 1898, Adolf Loos (1870–1933), Viennese architect and critic, had such a point of view.

I am an opponent of the trend that considers it to be especially desirable that a building has been designed along with everything in it—down to the coal scoop— by the hand of one architect. I am of the opinion that the building can have a rather monotonous appearance as a result. All individuality is lost in the process.[2]

These two prominent, contemporaneous practitioners pointed out the dilemma of the potential pitfalls of completing interior space.

Very few architects or designers are able to design and execute the complete environment, from the shell of the enclosure to the smallest detail of furnishing within. The range of design decisions is extensive, including architecture, mechanical, lighting, equipment, color and materials, furnishings, window treatments, art, and accessories. Their training has traditionally separated the enclosure from the contents, making both professional groups inadequately prepared to accomplish complete interiors. It is unfortunate, but understandable, that this polarization has occurred between the two professions, leaving prejudice and insensitivity to one another. In general, architectural education has biased its graduates to believe that they are above interior designers. They are conditioned to draw a line between the two disciplines. Developing a mutual respect in the future will depend on the proper education to sensitize the divergent groups. The new profession, Interior Architecture, seeks to dissolve the limiting boundaries and unite architecture and interiors. Presently, the completion of interior space is a major portion of work for architects and designers. How they go about their job reveals two general approaches.

The Architect's Approach to Completion of Interior Space

When traditionally trained architects design interiors, they strive to develop an overall statement, concept, or view, usually through careful planning, detailing, and coordinating of furnishings of the interior. Although this method of approach is sanctioned, especially for commercial interiors, it can inhibit spontaneity. The flow of spontaneous ideas should be allowed to affect the project in any stage of its development. Unfortunately, the current professional methodology inhibits on-site creative alterations.[3] Architects are trained to be consistent with their design language in the name of "purity." This attitude can lead to predictable solutions. Their specialized education makes them care more for the architectural enclosure than the contents of the interior. Architects generally do not understand comfort; in fact they are trained to place aesthetics over comfort, especially regarding furnishings. They tend to suppress their own design personalities in favor of neutral components and classic furniture. They are well trained to work geometrically and have strongly developed three-dimensional concerns, yet their sources tend to be limited.

The Designer's Approach to Completion of Interior Space

In contrast, most residential designers and decorators work piecemeal. Because they have no rigid, overall plan, they work more intuitively, discovering possibilities room by room and detail by detail. Spontaneity is a component of their work method, making design decisions and alterations natural throughout the process. Decorators, in particular, care less for "purity"; they tend to be eclectic, which enables them to achieve rich vignettes of interior space. The nature of the vignette approach makes it effective only from certain viewpoints, fragmenting the perception of the whole. Many designers care little for the architectural enclosure and tend to isolate their interiors from any integration with it. They strongly emphasize visual and tactile comfort, however. Fabrics, finishes, and accessories are major means of expression. Designers often have a greater sensitivity to the interior and how it will be used. Their designs also express personalities either of themselves or their clients. They are not trained to visualize in three dimensions; the two-dimensional surface has greater importance to their designs.

The Approach of Interior Architecture

Interior Architecture seeks to combine the positive attributes of both the architect and the interior designer to achieve holistically completed interior space. Interior Architecture ties all the elements of the design problem together. A well-educated designer understands the importance of three-dimensional enclosure and two-dimensional surface, functional furniture and decorative objects, natural light and electric lighting, constraint and color, planar surface and patterned relief, technology and tradition. The conscious understanding of all elements that complete a space and how they relate is central to good design.

Historical Perspectives

ANCIENT EGYPTIAN FURNITURE

Furniture preserved from ancient Egypt is from the wealthy and royal classes. The remarkably dry climate of Egypt and the burial customs of including furniture in the tombs of the rich have preserved many examples of wooden furniture from the earliest dynasties of the Old Kingdom (ca. 3000–2130 B.C.), the Middle Kingdom (ca. 2130–1580 B.C.) and the New Kingdom (ca. 1580–332 B.C.).[4] Furniture was a status of the rich; the peasants sat and slept on reed mats directly on the floor. In comparing surviving furniture of Queen

Hete-pheres (Fourth Dynasty, 2565–2440 B.C.) to that of Tutankhamun (Eighteenth Dynasty, ca. 1351–1347 B.C.), the difference of a thousand years did not provide a serious change in design. Mirroring Egyptian society, furniture was very conservative. The Egyptian bed represented a design well suited for the climate and environment. The sleeping platform of the bed was elevated by its frame from the ground, the sleeping surface made of flexible webbing, such as cord or thongs, to support the body, permitting air circulation about the occupant. The bed was of light construction with a footboard but no headboard. A wooden headrest served as a "pillow." A type of folding bed for traveling was discovered in Tutankhamun's tomb, a forerunner of the early nine-teenth century Napoleonic camp beds. The Egyptians developed seating in the form of thrones, chairs, and stools. Two types of seating have been identified with the beginnings of the Old Kingdom. One was based on wicker construction, usually with square legs and some kind of bracing with bent wood; these were usually in the form of stools (no backs). The second type appears to be derived from bed design, made of a frame and legs carved to resemble a bull's legs. Lion's legs became popular later. When seating had backs, those of ordinary chairs were commonly of slats. Finer chairs would have solid wood panels, sometimes curved and decorated with inlaid strips of precious materials such as ebony or ivory.

WOODEN CHAIR, ANCIENT EGYPT, NEW KINGDOM, DYNASTIES XVIII-XXX, 1580–332 B.C.

The rudimentary furniture of ancient Egypt, well preserved within tombs, was a symbol of wealth and prestige. Photograph by John Kurtich.

ANCIENT GREEK FURNITURE

Examples of ancient Greek furniture have not survived to the modern world as they were usually made either of wood, which eventually disintegrated or burned, or bronze, which was melted down and reused during times of stress. However, common pieces of furniture and household articles have been frequently referred to in ancient literature, and numerous examples have been depicted in surviving vase paintings, reliefs, statuettes, and sculptural groups. The study of Greek furniture reveals the classical world's outlook and approach to art. The Greeks evolved and materialized their furniture as they did their architecture, ceramics, and sculpture. They developed only a few types, such as chairs, stools, couches, tables, and chests, and were interested in perfecting these

MARBLE RELIEF OF KLISMOS, ANCIENT GREECE, CA. FIFTH CENTURY B.C.

The ancient Greeks developed their furniture over generations in their consistent search for perfection. The klismos is an elegant icon of the culture's interest in non pretentious comfort. Photograph by John Kurtich.

REPRODUCTION OF KLISMOS BY T. H. ROBSJOHN-GIBBINGS, MANUFACTURED BY SARIDIS S. A., ATHENS, GREECE, 1990.

The modern klismos is sturdy, light weight, and without superfluous decoration. It is a structure that expresses its function—to support and transfer weight to the earth. Photograph by John Kurtich.

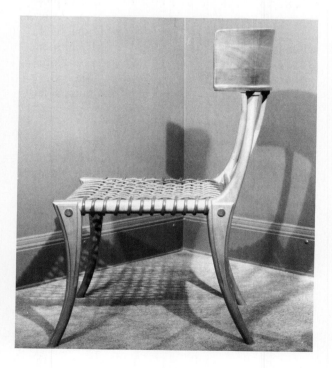

in a continual evolution, rather than perpetually inventing new designs or forms. These furniture types became standard not only within the Greek world but were adapted by the Romans throughout their empire until at least the fourth century A.D. The piece of furniture most characteristically Greek was the light chair with back, designed to be comfortable and to be used informally. Known as the *klismos,* it was usually undecorated. Its main features were a curved back and plain, curved legs; its beauty depended solely on proportion and line. This chair was usually but not exclusively depicted as part of the furnishings of women's apartments.

ANCIENT ROMAN FURNISHINGS

Roman furniture is generally an elaboration of Greek. From the reign of Augustus (27 B.C.) onward, furniture and furnishings became more luxurious and ostentatious. The custom of dining on couches was borrowed from the Greeks, but Roman couches became more lavish, eventually adding a back, predating the modern sofa. Examples of furniture and wall paintings depicting Roman interiors have been preserved at Pompeii and Herculaneum, illustrating a luxurious lifestyle, which was an echo of how the emperors must have lived. In rich patrician houses, Romans developed rooms for specific uses. The *triclinium* was the room dedicated to dining, and a large

ANCIENT ROMAN TRICLINIUM, POMPEII, ITALY, A.D. FIRST CENTURY.

The triclinium or dining room was specially designed for comfort, conversation, serving, and maintenance. The U-shape affords views while focusing on the centered food and drink. Photograph by John Kurtich.

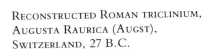

RECONSTRUCTED ROMAN TRICLINIUM, AUGUSTA RAURICA (AUGST), SWITZERLAND, 27 B.C.

This reconstruction is furnished with opulent cloth coverings and pillows, necessary for comfort during lengthy banqueting. Photograph by John Kurtich.

town house or villa might have more than one, such as a space used during warm weather which opened onto peristyle gardens. A typical furniture arrangement of a triclinium consisted of couches orthogonally arranged on three adjacent sides of a central dining table. The U-shaped arrangement allowed for service to the central table without disturbing the diners, and this directional array permitted the dinner guests to enjoy an open view of the rest of the villa. Many such rooms had permanently built couches of brick covered with stucco, with either a similar brick table built in place or an open space for a portable table to be placed. The comfort of these brick couches depended upon pillows and thick cloth coverings. The Romans valued dining as an important social activity.

WESTERN EUROPEAN MEDIEVAL FURNISHINGS

Examples of western European furniture from after the fall of the Roman empire to about the fourteenth century are not very plentiful. Seats of honor or thrones have been depicted in some manuscripts and sculptural pieces. The early Middle Ages was a time of movement and unrest; even kings and landowners had nomadic tendencies. There was always the problem of obtaining enough food to feed large households, which resulted in moving people to the source of food

more often than bringing the food to a fixed place. The most common portable furniture type of this period was the chest, which could be used for storage as well as transporting possessions. If such a chest were flat, it could also be used for seating, a table top, or even a bed. One of the earliest chests was made from convenient lengths of hollowed large tree trunks, slicing the side designated as the top to serve as the lid. Permanent furniture of this period tended to be built in. The thick walls of the defense-minded medieval architecture provided opportunities to construct shelves and storage within such walls. Seating was often built into the walls, either directly or as part of the paneling system.

ISLAMIC FURNISHINGS

The desert and nomadic origins of the early Islamic civilizations (ca. A.D. seventh to twelfth centuries) of the Middle East precluded most wooden furniture. Small chests were more common and might be richly decorated with inlaid woods and ivory. Islamic furnishings consisted largely of textiles. Carpets, bolsters, pillows, mattresses, and hanging fabrics to create privacy and alter lighting conditions prevailed. People lived intimately with textiles, sitting, eating, entertaining guests, and sleeping on the many varieties of brightly colored fabrics and stuffed cloth

LATE MEDIEVAL CHEST, DURHAM, ENGLAND, CA. FOURTEENTH CENTURY.

The chests served as transportable vaults for possessions and doubled as seating, tables, or beds, to elevate the user off the cold floors. Courtesy of The Art Institute of Chicago.

LIVING AREA, BAGHDAD KIOSK,
TOPKAPI SARAYI, ISTANBUL, TURKEY,
1638.

*The Middle East led the way in the
obsessive use of soft furniture made from
fabrics, textiles, rugs, and pillows.
These furnishings not only provided for
comfort, privacy, warmth, and shelter,
but were readily mobile. Photograph by
John Kurtich.*

furnishings. Textiles were easily packed and transported. They were unbreakable. Carpet production flourished, and the relationship between patterns of rugs and textured ornamentation of architecture was extremely close. Patterned brick-work of Iranian mosques had the textile quality of knitting or weaving. The use of colored tiles as surface decoration derived from this obsession with textiles as if this architectural adornment were the very clothing of the structure.

ITALIAN RENAISSANCE FURNISHINGS

Church interiors of fifteenth century northern Italy led the way to a major change in domestic furnishings, which eventually spread throughout western Europe and England. Architects of these new churches had influence, if not control over interior furnishings, favoring a rebirth of classical motifs from ancient Rome. This design trend soon spread to domestic furnishings. Marble Roman sarcophagi became a model for ornate wooden chests, known as a *cassone,* the most elaborate single piece of furniture in a sixteenth century Italian household. Such chests were the repository of the bride's dowry, symbolizing the marriage chest and the merging of family fortunes. The *cassone* mutated into the *cassapanca,* which was a chest turned into seating by adding a back and armrests on its top, another predecessor of the sofa. Opulent textiles from the Islamic world, such as Turkish carpets, were highly prized, not as rugs on the floor but as tablecloths or wall hangings. Unlike the ancient Romans, who dedicated a particular space for dining, the wealthy of the Italian Renaissance dined in whatever room seemed convenient or appropriate for the occasion; this was made possible by the portability of their furniture.

ITALIAN RENAISSANCE *CASSONE* SHOWING THE PROCESSION OF BACCHUS AND ARIADNE, FLORENCE, ITALY, CA. 1475.

Cassones were typically elaborate, containing important possessions while expressing family pride. The Metropolitan Museum of Art, Rogers Fund, 1916. (16.155)

ITALIAN RENAISSANCE *CASSAPANCA,* FLORENCE, ITALY, THIRD QUARTER OF THE SIXTEENTH CENTURY.

The evolution of the cassone *or chest into the seating form of the* cassapanca *was a natural progression of efficient use of a major piece of furniture. The Metropolitan Museum of Art, funds from various donors, 1958. S(58.19a,b).*

TRADITIONAL JAPANESE FURNISHINGS

The distinguishing feature of the traditional Japanese interior is its floor-level orientation. There is no development of raised furniture for seating and reclining. Other furniture, such as chests or cabinets, have no legs or stands. Everything remains low, within easy reach of anyone sitting on the floor. This approach to furniture has traditionally been integrated with a systemized interior that exists within a standard architectural frame. The development of the Japanese interior led to an attitude called *shitsurai,* which means "from the floor up." Tatami mats establish the dimensions of the interior floor plan; these mats are a standard size (approximately 3 feet by 6 feet) and interlock in various arrangements. Matching dimensions in the vertical plane through fusuma and shoji screens determine the walls of the interior. The functional furniture of such a space is absorbed into the architecture, allowing the space to serve many activities, unlike Western architecture where there are specific rooms for specific uses. In the West, an interior space is named by its function, such as *bedroom, dining room, kitchen.* In Japan, interior spaces are designated by their location, such as *okuzashiki* (the inner room), or *nakanoma* (the middle room), rather than by function. Such spaces have the multiple uses of sleeping, family get-together, eating, and working.

This directly affects the furnishings. Built-in storage for low, simple, movable tables, cushions, and sleeping mats provide the ultimate in flexibility.

LOUIS XIV FURNISHINGS

The furniture and their interior settings during the long reign of Louis XIV of France (1638–1715) were a product of a state-supported organization that designed and manufactured practically all branches of the decorative arts, the *Manufacture Royale des Meubles de la Couronne.* Jean-Baptiste Colbert (1619–1683), chief minister to Louis XIV and Superintendent of Finance and Buildings was responsible for this institution, and its success was accomplished by its first director, Charles Le Brun (1619–1690). Le Brun was a discovery of Nicolas Fouquet (1615–1680), Superintendent of Finance in 1653, who built himself a lavish château, Vaux-le-Vicomte, setting up workshops to supply everything for the palace. Upon its completion, Fouquet entertained Louis XIV and so generated the king's envy that Fouquet was imprisoned for embezzling state funds. Louis then appropriated the talents of Le Brun and his entire staff to create his court at Versailles. Through the output of furniture, tapestries, and decorative arts from the royal workshops, Le Brun created a na-

Interior, replica of main room of a Japanese home with an adjoining room and a garden, with furniture and accessories, Workshop of Mrs. James Ward Thorne, mixed media, Gift of Mrs. James Ward Thorne, 1962.456. front

The anthropomorphic proportions of the tatami *establish a module which generates the proportions of rooms and enclosures.*

GALERIE DES GLACES, LE PALAIS DES VERSAILLES, VERSAILLES, FRANCE. JULES HARDOUIN-MANSART AND CHARLES LE BRUN, 1678–1687.

Louis XIV's great halls were lavish in scale and material, filled with uncomfortable furniture intended to intimidate visitors. The expression of power and wealth through architecture and furnishings took on new meaning during his reign. Photograph by John Kurtich.

DETAIL OF LAMP BEARER, GALERIE DES GLACES, PALAIS DES VERSAILLES, VERSAILLES, FRANCE. JULES HARDOUIN-MANSART AND CHARLES LE BRUN, 1678–1687.

The statuary bearing the heavy light fixture symbolized well the Sun King's command that the people serve him. Photograph by John Kurtich.

tional style that glorified Louis XIV and his court, making it the standard of taste and elegance for the rest of Europe. Le Brun conceived the interior as a unified design made up of the painted ceiling, the mouldings, the tapestries, the furniture, and the sculptural fittings. His greatest achievement was the Galerie des Glaces, Versailles (1684). This 235-foot-long space features seventeen arched windows facing the gardens that illuminate on the opposite wall an equal number of shallow recesses infilled with Venetian mirrors. The brilliance of the space is unified by free-standing gilt candlesticks and three rows of crystal chandeliers hanging from the ceiling. Originally the hall had solid silver furniture designed by Le Brun, which was later melted down to help pay for the various expensive wars the king engaged in during his long reign.

ANDRÉ-CHARLES BOULLE

André-Charles Boulle (1642–1732) created individual pieces of furniture for Louis XIV (1638–1715), the prime purpose of which was to glorify and exalt the Sun King. His furniture made a very strong political statement—a material representation of the strength of the monarchy embodied in one person only, the King. Boulle's elaborate appointments exemplified Louis's royal philosophy: "l'État c'est Moi." The furniture was a metaphor for absolute monarchy and expressed the same status and importance as the great palaces that housed the pieces. Such furniture was not designed for comfort but for splendor and glorification. Rich and exotic materials, intricately combined in complicated designs, were trademarks of Boulle's cabinets, commodes, desks, clock-cases, pedestals, and mirrors. Boulle had training and experience in cabinetmaking, painting, architecture, engraving, bronze work, and marquetry. Through his genius, cabinetmaking became an elaborate art in which France dominated Europe. Boulle was most famous for his technique of brass and tortoise shell marquetry. Application of different materials such as metal and animal products to wood subjected the resulting furniture to warping and misshaping from changes in temperature and humidity. To overcome this problem, he designed gilt-bronze mounts and reinforcements, which transcended their original purpose and became an essential part of the aesthetic character of the furniture. Boulle is well known for the development of the commode, originating as a variation of the bureau but with drawers extending the entire width. His marquetry magnified the curved nature of the furniture, amplifying the current fashion of minimal rectilinearity and severity.

ROBERT ADAM

Robert Adam (1728–1792) considered himself as the master designer whose work encompassed every detail of the interior from the plastered ceiling decoration to the pattern on the carpet. Although he designed totally new buildings, inside and out, Adam is primarily known for his interiors. His designs for the ceilings, walls, chimney pieces, drapery, carpets, and furniture were conceived as a whole statement; this practice, coupled with a prolific output of work, made him the tastemaker of his era. His influence was felt not only throughout England but his work became the model for the Federal Style in America. John Soane (1753–1835), in a speech to students of the Royal Academy, appreciated Adam's importance: "To Mr. Adam's taste in the Ornaments of his Buildings, and Furniture, we stand indebted inas-much as Manufacturers of every kind felt, as it were, the electric power of this Revolution in Art."[5] The interiors of Osterley Park House, Middlesex, England (1761–1780) provide an excellent example of Adam's holistic method as the house still retains most of its original contents (see Chapter 1 for additional discussion of Osterley Park House). Adam's treatment of ceilings is often a key to his method of completing an interior. Not only did he introduce a variety of new designs with his ceilings, but he generally coordinated the floor design to echo the ceiling, such as the entrance hall, Osterley Park House. The mirroring of the floor to the ceiling in this room does so without duplicating the motif. Although the compositions are the same, the details of each are

COMMODE. ANDRÉ-CHARLES
BOULLE, CA. 1710–1732.

*The Boulle commode was designed to
glorify the Sun King; it had little
functional value. The Metropolitan
Museum of Art, The Jack and Belle
Linsky Collection, 1982. (1982.60.82)*

quite different; this technique was typical of Adam for establishing a strong relationship between the two parts of the interior. Adam's furniture designs were conceived two dimensionally and have that bias upon execution. Wall furniture (such as tables, commodes, girandoles, and mirrors) and decorative pieces (such as pedestals, tripods, and urns) dominate his interiors. He designed furniture for a specific room and a particular place in that room. The furnishings would, in addition, relate to the architectural decorations, ornamentation, and paintings of the room. The pier glass mirror, designed in 1777 for Osterley Park House, is divided into vertical sections, which meet the edge of a table in front of it, matching exactly and continuing the vertical divisions with the legs of the table. The bottom of this mirror has ornamental festoons and elaborated divisions that seem really to belong to the table. When seen as an elevation drawing, it is not always possible to tell where the mirror ends and the table begins.

THE HALL, SYON HOUSE, MIDDLESEX, ENGLAND. ROBERT ADAM, 1761–1762.

Robert Adam contributed a clarity in dialogue among all parts of the enclosure and components of the space in many of his interiors. Typical is this mirroring of design motif without repetition of the floor and ceiling patterns. Courtesy of The Art Institute of Chicago.

DESIGN FOR MIRROR AND SIDEBOARD, SYON HOUSE, ISLEWORTH, ENGLAND. ROBERT AND JAMES ADAM, 1762–1769, 1773.

The mirror is visually received by the table below while being celebrated by flanking candelabra. The relationship between the parts is refined and deliberate, resulting in a unified eloquence. Courtesy of The Art Institute of Chicago.

THE SHAKER COMMUNITY

Shaker design is a quiet yet powerful example of holism in harmony. The American religious sect was established in 1774, with their most prolific designs being created between 1820 and 1845. They lived communally in large "families," men separated from women. Isolated from the outside world, they worked in a variety of trades to foster independence. Their independence freed the craftsmen of current styles to create practical objects relying on simplicity and proportion as the guiding aesthetic.

Shaker design aesthetic was influenced by their fanatic lifestyle devoted to God and work, rejecting material possessions. Learning to live communally required sharing, cooperation, and patience, placing the group above individuals. They believed in cleanliness and order, avoiding excess and luxury. Their founder, Mother Ann, considered work to be as important to the spirit as to the production of goods, saying, "Do all your work as though you had a thousand years to live, and as you would if you knew you must die tomorrow."[6] This ideal established a high level of craftsmanship regardless of the significance of the object or task. The raising of a barn was as important as the turning of a knob. The Shaker desire to maintain clean and ordered interiors resulted in creative relationships between their architecture and furnishings. Built-in storage in the form of cabinets, dressers, desks, and wardrobes was common, eliminating clutter and the need for cleaning below the units. The unadorned cabinetry was usually designed for a specific purpose using the pattern and proportion of drawers and doors to create a composition. The Shakers disdained any form of decoration, relying on multiple wood species, stains, and color to develop interest and detail. Employing oak, walnut, cherry, and maple simultaneously in a cabinet created subtle distinctions and variety in what may have been an ordinary functioning unit. Staining was common as well as painting surfaces in pure colors such as bright blue, cherry, and canary yellow.

The Shakers' use of built-in cabinetry was integral to their concepts of space and how it was used. They are probably the first group in America to employ built-ins in their architectural spaces —not until the Modern Movement did the concept gain such widespread acceptance. The desire to maintain clean and orderly rooms led the Shakers to devise organizing systems affecting the Interior Architecture and furnishings. A hanging system of wooden rails and pegs allowed furnishings to be attached to the wall, clearing floors. Ladder-back chairs, clocks, and lanterns were designed to be attached to the peg rails. The furnishings were lightweight, economical, and minimal. Unaffected by the outside styles of their time, the Shaker craftspeople produced spare, beautifully proportioned objects that were an expression of their religious beliefs and lifestyle.

LIVING ROOM, C. 1800, SHAKER COMMUNITY HOUSE, WORKSHOP OF MRS. JAMES WARD THORNE, MIXED MEDIA, C. 1930–1940, 22.9 x 55.2 x 62.5 CM, GIFT OF MRS. JAMES WARD THORNE, 1942.498. FRONT.

The Shaker aesthetic is driven by function, economy, and the obsession for cleanliness. © 1990 The Art Institute of Chicago, All Rights Reserved.

KARL FRIEDRICH SCHINKEL

Karl Friedrich Schinkel (1781–1841) produced work that celebrated the unity of the opposites. His work was

> not the harmony of the classical style in contrast to the spiritualisation of the gothic expression, not the symmetrical austerity in contrast to relativised order, but the mutual conditioning of classicism and romanticism, of order and coincidence, of absolute austerity and complete freedom. It is the "coincidence of the opposites" and not their isolation that results in the complete, the living Gestalt . . . It is the intellectual unity of the things in their formal diversity.[7]

Schinkel used history as a way to evolve and perfect architectural ideas. His architecture, interiors, and furniture were not only concerned with function, but primarily with the generality and universality of ideas. He felt that because history was a rich source of ideas, it should be taught as a living tradition. However, he firmly believed that "History has never copied previous history . . . Every epoch has left behind its own style of architecture. Why should we not try to find a style for our own?"[8]

Schinkel's furniture designs had an enormous impact in central Europe during the mid- and late decades of the nineteenth century. Using both

TENT ROOM, SCHLOSS CHARLOTTENHOF, POTSDAM, GERMANY. KARL FRIEDRICH SCHINKEL, 1826.

The image of a mobile campaign tent is reinforced by the lightweight furniture. Photograph by Anders Nereim.

Gothic and Classical vocabularies, he produced pieces always with a fresh, inventive approach. One of his most ingenious designs was a *secrétaire à abattant* (made for King Friedrich Wilhelm III in 1826) in which he melded the two vocabularies in the same piece. Closed, the secretaire is a powerful architectural statement featuring a pair of imposing Ionic columns nearly the height of the 6-foot console. Open, the desk reveals a glowing, delicate set of Gothic arches forming the drawers and a writing surface of intricate, geometric marquetry. Obviously Schinkel understood the traditions of both the Gothic and Classical.

In the Tent Room at Schloss Charlottenhof, Potsdam (1830), Schinkel created a totally original interior featuring classical-inspired furniture integrated into a fantasy environment. The beds, windows, and doors were draped in blue-and-white-striped linen twill with the walls and ceiling covered in a matching paper. The seats and stools were upholstered in similar linen fabric with a modified Greek key design to accent and distinguish the furniture from its surroundings. Schinkel's furniture and interiors represented the best of the Biedermeier style, the name of which was derived from two comic characters, Biedermann and Bummelmeier, who epitomized the optimistic boorishness and cheerful unrefinement of middle-class Germans from about 1815–1848. Biedermeier furniture represented a transition between the severe classicism of the Napoleonic Empire style and the tasteless overindulgence and factory-produced virtuosity of late nineteenth century furniture. Schinkel managed to successfully combine the delicacy of neo-classicism with the functional and comfort qualities of Biedermeier.

WILLIAM MORRIS

William Morris (1834–1896) was interested in recreating a national style, which had been lost through the English obsession of importing foreign art, furniture, and fabrics.

> *. . . for us to set to work to imitate . . . the degraded and nightmare whims of the blase and bankrupt aristocracy of Louis XV's time seems to me merely ri-*

diculous. So I say our furniture should be good citizen's furniture, solid and well made and workmanlike and in design should have nothing about it that is not easily defensible, no monstrosities or extravagances, not even of beauty, lest we weary of it.[9]

Morris rejected the Industrial Revolution because the manufacturing process eliminated the craftsman. He felt the medieval era was England's richest period of design and craftsmanship, produced by the guild system. By studying the methods and aesthetic of medieval times, Morris thought he could establish the basis of a new English style.

> *. . . if we do not study the ancient work directly and learn to understand it, we shall find ourselves influenced by the feeble work all around us, and shall be copying the better work through the copyists and without understanding it, which will by no means bring about intelligent art. Let us therefore study it wisely, be taught by it, kindled by it; all the while determining not to imitate or repeat it; to have either no art at all, or an art which we have made our own.*[10]

Morris studied architecture and painting, but he was most recognized as a pattern maker. In collaboration with architect Philip Webb (1831–1915), Morris built his famous Red House, Bexley Heath, Kent, England (1859–1860). He found ready-made furniture unacceptable for his new home, compelling Webb to design most of the furnishings. The drawing room on the first floor was dominated by a settle (a long wooden bench with a back and arm rests) designed by Webb. This common piece of furniture was made uncommon by integrating it into the wall and flanking it with pictures depicting a romantic story of Sir Degravaunt painted by Edward Burne-Jones (1833–1898). The back of the settle was replete with bookshelves rather than a solid panel. The modulation of the back was repeated above by cabinets complete with medieval-inspired iron hinges. Crowning the composition was a bracketed cornice, articulated by twelve coats of arms, again expressing Morris's love of medieval imagery. The brilliant integrated composition, combining art, architecture, and furnishing elements, epitomized the emerging Arts and Crafts movement of the late nineteenth century. This collabo-

RED HOUSE, BEXLEYHEATH, KENT, ENGLAND. PHILIP WEBB, 1859–1860.

The Red House was a complete expression of William Morris's rejection of industrialization in favor of handmade craft. Photograph by Charlotte Wood from Red House *by Edward Mollamby, New York: Van Nostrand Reinhold, 1991, plate 9.*

rative experience led to the founding of the decorating firm, Morris, Marshall, Faulkner and Co. (1861), an organization of artists, architects, and craftsmen established to design, produce, and distribute Morris's vision of English style. This vision is summed up in his attitude about architecture.

> *Noble as that art is by itself, and though it is specially the art of civilisation, it neither ever has existed nor ever can exist alive and progressive by itself, but must cherish and be cherished by all the crafts whereby men make the things which they intend shall be beautiful and shall last somewhat beyond the passing day. It is this union of the arts, mutually helpful and harmoniously subordinated one to another which I have learnt to think of as Architecture.*[11]

ANTONI GAUDÍ

Antoni Gaudí (1852–1926) created extraordinary architecture, interiors, and furniture as a result of his desire to produce poetic metamorphoses of natural forms, working according to natural laws.

His interest in nature was in three-dimensional forms, differentiating him from the two-dimensional and bas-relief attributes of the Art Nouveau movement at the end of the nineteenth century, with which he is sometimes connected. Gaudí's philosophy unified his architecture with his furniture; he was holistic in his approach to any project or commission. He was able to work freely and completely with ceramics, stained glass, wood, plaster, brick, concrete, stone, and ironwork. He felt that to use a material to its fullest extent was to honor it. The Casa Batlló (1904–1906) was a total remodeling project completed by Gaudí to a rather ordinary house built between 1875 and 1877. He reorganized the interior spaces, added a fifth floor for servants, and renewed the entire facade in a smoky blue-gray, with the upper portion rendered in a blue and green ceramic, impregnated with disks. George Collins refers to the facade as the "bubbly surface of a Mediterranean wave spreading over a rocky beach."[12] Gaudí made the exterior relate to the interior through color, curvilinear forms, and un-

CASA BATILLO, BARCELONA, SPAIN.
ANTONI GAUDÍ, 1904–1906.

*Gaudí's interiors were idiosyncratic,
charged with energy that was generated
by his fluid designs and rich materials.
Courtesy of The Art Institute of
Chicago.*

dulating surfaces. The central lightwell/staircase was rendered with pale gray-blue tiles at the ground level, becoming bright blue at the upper floors. He created special furniture and light fixtures as part of the total design. His simple wooden chair had allusions to the eyes, feet, and body of an animal; this piece is typical of the power inherent in his furniture of symbolism and structure simultaneously. Circular depressions in the back of the chair resemble the ears of an animal and allow it to be picked up easily by the user's thumbs. Gaudi's vocabulary of forms, in his furniture as well as his architecture, had its roots in nature, evolving from natural forms. In using this resource, he made the forms his own, full of variety, energy, animation, and vitality.

CHARLES RENNIE MACKINTOSH

Charles Rennie Mackintosh (1868–1928) did not consider his interiors and furniture designs less important than his complete buildings. His output of furniture, over four hundred pieces, represents his concern for the human occupant. Like Eileen Gray, Mackintosh designed very specific furniture, such as game tables, high back chairs, abstract clocks, and sculptural lighting fixtures. Many of Mackintosh's designs suffer from the "architect's syndrome," that is to say, the aesthetic of a given piece might outweigh its function or comfort. A chair might be a marvel to look at, integrated with all other aspects of an interior, but comfort-wise it could be a disaster to sit on. An example of such a chair is the high, spindly back seating designed for the Willow Tea Rooms; the chair seen as a group arrangement was meant to metaphorically represent a forest of young willow trees as opposed to being designed for comfort. If his chairs were upholstered, such upholstery was minimal, never deep or comfortable. Most important to Mackintosh was the conception of an interior space as a whole; all furniture and minor elements had to relate to this vision. His wife, Margaret Macdonald Mackintosh (1865–1933), collaborated with him in his best interiors. The White Bedroom of Hill House, Helensburgh (1902–1903), was designed as a total environment

to fulfill more than one function. Although it was primarily the clients' bedroom, the bed was located in one part of the L-shaped plan to distinguish its separate identity from the sitting room nature of the rest of the space. The bed area was spatially enhanced by a vaulted ceiling and a matching curved bay containing a curved window with curved shutters. The sitting room portion had additional windows with curtains designed and embroidered by his wife. The entire bedroom and all of its fitted furniture was painted white. Mackintosh introduced two high-backed "ladder" chairs, painted black, to express visual, geometric punctuation and indicate by their position a change of function in the space from sleeping to sitting. Fernando Agnoletti described the bedroom as ". . . the exotic bloom of a strange plant, not made but grown, not sensuous but chaste, not floating like a dream, but firm and decisive like the poetical vision of a fact that is expressed in the only possible art form . . . "[13]

THE WIENER WERKSTÄTTE

The Vienna Secession (beginning in 1897) was Austria's version of the Arts and Crafts movement. It was originally started by nineteen artists, not to challenge older traditions such as similar movements were doing in Paris and Munich, but to achieve a new expression of the rising power of the middle class during the Industrial Revolution. "In Munich and Paris the intention of the Secessions has been to replace the 'old' art with a 'new' art . . . No, with us it is different. We are not fighting for and against the traditions, we simply don't have any."[14]

Credit for beginning this movement in architecture and design is given to Josef Maria Olbrich (1867–1908), Koloman Moser (1868–1918), and Josef Hoffmann (1870–1956). They persuaded Otto Wagner (1841–1918), Austria's leading architect, to join the Secession, giving it national credibility. Josef Hoffmann was inspired by Charles Rennie Mackintosh (1868–1928) and his group in Glasgow to form a workshop in Vienna; in 1903, along with Koloman Moser and banker Fritz Waerndorfer, Hoffmann established the

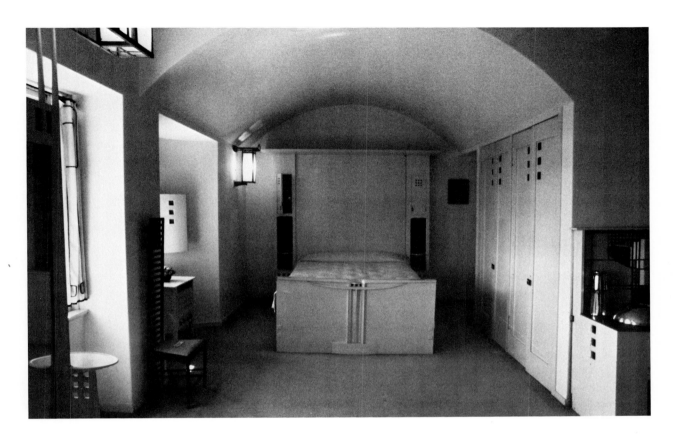

WHITE BEDROOM, HILL HOUSE,
HELENSBURGH, DUMBARTONSHIRE,
SCOTLAND. CHARLES RENNIE
MACKINTOSH AND MARGARET
MACDONALD, 1902–1903.

*Mackintosh's signature patterned squares
create a strong dialogue among the
furnishings, doors, cabinets, shutters,
and light fixtures, resulting in
harmonious unity. Photograph by
May Hawfield.*

DINING ROOM, PALAIS STOCLET,
BRUSSELS, BELGIUM. JOSEF
HOFFMANN, 1905–1914.

*The grand symmetrical dining room
unifies the enclosure with the furniture
through repetition of texture, color,
materials, and pattern. Courtesy of The
Art Institute of Chicago.*

Wiener Werkstätte. Although its initial inspiration came from the Arts and Crafts movement, the workshop did not continue the British movement's prevailing medieval tradition; instead Hoffmann and his collaborators became the new arbiters of European taste. Similar to the ideals of the Bauhaus, this workshop created a center for artists and craftsmen to produce functionally oriented objects as pieces of fine art.

The furnishings of Hoffmann's greatest architectural achievement, the Palais Stoclet, Brussels, Belgium (1905–1911), resulted from his Wiener Werkstätte. The axially planned building was comprised of a series of discrete spaces oriented to a great hall. From the hall, a splayed vaultlike entry connects to one end of the long, thin dining room, suggesting a safe and special place. The dining room's walls are clad in buff colored Paonazzo marble with long buffets of dark Portovenere marble and Macassar wood. Above the buffets are mosaics by Gustave Klimt (1862–1918), the "Dancer" (expectation) and, on the opposite wall the "Pair of Lovers" (fulfillment). The freestanding wood table accommodating twenty-two diners is set on a deep brownish-olive patterned rug surrounded by a fine checkerboard marble floor. This marble matches the wall and binds the room together with subtle excitement. Simple wood chairs, upholstered with black leather and brass buttons, are tooled with gold relief repeating the gold color of the room molding, light fixtures, and candlestick holders. The room terminates in a wedgelike bay window, complete with a small black marble fountain as a focal point. The fountain has a fish mouth and is crowned by a sculpture by Michael Powolny (1871–1954). Four ceramic versions of the same sculpture are displayed in the vestibule recalling the entrance. All the elements and materials of the room are composed as a whole respecting the overall scheme of the residence, yet having a distinct clarity of its own. The use of pattern on pattern, Klimt's mosaic art, and the framing of materials, express the architect's Byzantine influence. The dining room is a brilliant example of Hoffmann's control of pattern and high contrast with constant dialogue among all components of this purposeful room.

FRANK LLOYD WRIGHT

Frank Lloyd Wright (1867–1956) believed in the concept of an organic architecture; to him this meant a

"natural architecture—the architecture of nature, for nature . . . Architecture which is really architecture proceeds from the ground and somehow the terrain, the native industrial conditions, the nature of materials and the purpose of the building, must inevitably determine the form and character of any good building." [15]

This philosophy prevailed in Wright's interiors and furnishings as he required such to express the character of the architectural whole. Wright designed both built-in and freestanding furnishings that were creatively interwoven into the fabric of his interiors.

His earliest known example of a totally integrated interior was the dining room of his Oak Park house, converted in 1895 from the original 1889 kitchen. The room featured a horizontal band of continuous windows further reinforced by horizontal paneling. This interior shell was then dramatized and balanced by the verticality of eight high-backed chairs, which would enclose the diners within a smaller intimate space around the dining table. This eating area was clearly defined by the screenlike wall created by the elongated backs of the chairs. Criticism of the lack of comfort in Wright's chairs is legend, although not everyone agrees that the element of comfort was ignored.

In Don Kalec's thoughtful study on Prairie School furniture, interesting design considerations were brought to light.

This is not to say that comfort was not an important item; but they [the Prairie School architects] knew that one man's comfort may be another man's back ache. The high straight backed dining chairs which appear so strange today were designed for a society where women were corseted from knee to shoulder blade, and men stood as if they had a poker strapped to their backs. When they sat down to eat, they sat straight and tall; "correctness," manners and moral values were more important than comfort. [16]

Wright's furniture was consistently ingrained to specific interior spaces and represented his or-

Dining Room, Frank Lloyd
Wright Home and Studio, Oak
Park, Illinois. Frank Lloyd
Wright, 1889.

Wright contrasted horizontal and
vertical elements to develop drama
within the unified space. Photograph
by John Kurtich.

ganic idealism through the choice and execution of a particular material—wood. He understood and respected the nature of wood, avoiding carved ornamentation, paint, inlay, or complicated joinery. His resulting furniture is characterized by simple, severe, rectilinear forms that emphasize his interest in geometry. The geometrical approach became most uncompromising in his chair designs, the importance of which was not comfort but the extension and reinforcement of the interior space they occupied. The spatial revolution created by Wright cannot be overemphasized. He developed and perfected an open, flowing interior where built-in and freestanding furniture controlled a new discipline of defining, arranging, and directing the spatial movement and composition.

GREENE AND GREENE

Like Mackintosh and Wright, Greene and Greene [Charles Sumner Greene (1868–1957) and Henry Mather Greene (1870–1954)], architects, were masters of complete Interior Architecture. They were most influenced by the simple functionalism of the craftsman movement and the joinery details of oriental timber construction. The Greenes worked in natural finished woods expressing the construction in three-dimensional details. They articulated wall and ceiling surfaces in wood to scale the enclosure to the furniture. A conscious relationship of scale, material, and detail between the furniture and architecture created a pleasing unity. The architects produced a prolific amount of custom furnishings to complete their architecture. This production would not have been possible without the close association of artists and craftspeople of the area. Beautifully refined quality furnishings built of wood, glass, and metal are typical of the Greenes' work. Unlike Mackintosh and Wright, the Greenes viewed chairs as a place for someone to comfortably sit instead of allowing the overall effect to determine the design. This attitude, coupled with the architects' desire to work in the shops with the craftspeople and personally finish many of the pieces, produced highly original and humane furnishings.

Trademark details such as the square wood pegs were a direct result of understanding the craft of construction. The pegs allowed the furniture makers to construct joints with screws that had slotted washers to allow for expansion and contraction. This construction helped eliminate warping and splitting of the solid wood by allowing movement, which the Greenes favored over veneered construction. Also, greater freedom of expression was achieved in art glass windows by working with the artists. Making varied weight in the lead came was difficult with the traditional construction techniques. The Greenes devised a way of overlaying flat sheets of lead that could vary in width to extend the limitations of leading glass. This allowed the artists to be more expressive with organic forms and profiles. As Henry Greene said, "The whole construction was carefully thought out, and there was a reason for every detail. The idea was to eliminate everything unnecessary to make the whole as direct and simple as possible, but always with the beautiful in mind as the final goal." [17]

The Gamble House, built in 1908 in Pasadena, California, is considered the best residential achievement executed by the Greenes. The two-story wood structure with attic was asymmetrically planned for the wealthy Gamble family. The individual common areas of living and dining rooms are axially symmetrical whereas the private bedrooms are asymmetrical in composition. This basic planning approach lends formality to common areas while creating a casual feeling in the private rooms. The house is unified by the use of natural wood for floors, trim, beamed ceilings, and furniture. A language of details is consistently developed throughout the residence, reinforcing the unity at a tertiary scale. Within that unified framework is surprising variety that makes the house come to life. The beamed ceiling changes in scale and pattern from room to room. The living room is executed in teak, while the dining room is mahogany and a bedroom is white cedar. Within the individual rooms rigorous consistency of materials, detail, furniture, and lighting is developed. The San Domingo mahogany dining room encloses a beautifully shaped Honduras mahogany table and chairs designed by the architects. The table's cross-timbered base is joined by ebony splines and pegs. It is designed to anchor the table with cantilever supports without separating even when expanded to double its size. The wood shapes and ebony peg details are repeated in the room's moldings, cabinetry, and light fixtures. The shape of the table top is reproduced in the leaded glass cabinets above the fireplace. The overall consistency in this room is remarkable, especially in the dialogue created between the enclosure and furnishings. This house is full of surprises and interest yet maintains a settling unity.

LIVING ROOM, DAVID R. GAMBLE
HOUSE, PASADENA, CALIFORNIA.
GREENE AND GREENE, 1908.

*The "inglenook" or chimney corner is
beautifully scaled by expressing the
joining of elements or by reducing the
size of elements to create intimacy and
interest. Photograph by Don Kalec.*

DETAIL OF STAIRWAY, DAVID R.
GAMBLE HOUSE, PASADENA,
CALIFORNIA. GREENE AND GREENE,
1908.

*The highly articulated stair, with a
handrail reflecting the tread and riser
rhythm, forms a space for seating at the
bottom. Photograph by Don Kalec.*

DE STIJL

In 1917, Theo van Doesburg (1883–1931) published in the Netherlands the first issue of a magazine called *De Stijl* (The Style), which propounded a theory called Neoplasticism. This idea represented a reality housed in the principle of an absolute abstraction that eliminated any reference to objects of nature. It was visually expressed with straight lines and right angles, featuring dissimilar rectangular planes of primary colors arranged in patterns of dynamic asymmetry. Led by artists and architects such as Piet Mondrian (1872–1944), Gerrit Rietveld (1888–1964), and J. J. P. Oud (1890–1963), De Stijl became an influential movement. These visionaries sought harmony through abstract means, which might appear to be antinature, but they were exploring a new visual style to create a new style of living.

Van Doesburg and Rietveld were responsible for translating Neoplasticism into the third dimension through their furniture and architecture. Rietveld's most famous chair, *the rood/blauwe stoel* (red/blue chair), was the physical manifestation of the philosophy of De Stijl; the chair was intrinsically a dissertation on the nature of space. To quote Rietveld's intentions, "If, for a particular purpose, we separate, limit, and bring into a human scale a part of unlimited space, it is (if all goes well) a piece of space brought to life as reality. In this way, a special segment of space has been absorbed into our human system." [18] His chair had similar compositional qualities to Wright's earlier Prairie School interiors in that it allowed space to flow through the object and thereby eliminate its isolation in space. Its abstract qualities make it equally as strong as a piece of sculpture as a functional seating apparatus. The question of comfort has been raised, but Rietveld was aware of comfort as a relative thing, to be defined in terms of a specific activity. His red/blue chair was designed to give firm support to the human occupant.

Rietveld's major architectural piece, the Schröder House, Utrecht, Netherlands (1923–1925), was the development and realization of a spatial complex following the abstract and structural principles of his furniture. The final effect was creating an architecturally sized Neoplastic

RED/BLUE CHAIR. GERRIT RIETVELD, 1918.

Rietveld's severe abstraction of anthropomorphic form resulted in a chair that symbolized the De Stijl movement. Photograph by John Kurtich.

sculpture. The house featured built-in furniture so integrated that it became almost indistinguishable from its architectural surroundings (see Chapter 3 on a further discussion of the Schröder House and Chapter 6 for color.)

ELSIE DE WOLFE

Elsie de Wolfe (1865–1950) is considered the first professional decorator in the United States, establishing her practice in 1905. Up to this time, the upholsterers and manufacturers of furniture had been the arbiters of taste for interior space. Mass-produced collections of furniture were readily available, matched in style and coloration, to produce the acceptable taste of the day. Upholsterers not only provided upholstery services but also purveyed draperies, rugs, wall coverings, furniture finishes, and even such architectural components as windows, fireplaces, and molding details. These mass merchants, oriented to the middle class, provided little cultural or creative influence for those who had more refined taste. Although the architect created some of the most elegant interior spaces for the upper classes, he was not in-

volved with the selection and placement of furniture, art, and accessories. He simply relied on the shape of the room to determine its completion through furnishings. De Wolfe's background as an actress in the theatre provided her with an artistic vision of interior space well beyond the current practice of the early twentieth century. In contrast to the current, dark, opulent, and cluttered look, she relied on the question of suitability to guide her design decisions.

The new popularity of chintz helped build Elsie's reputation as a tastemaker, but it was really only one aspect of her more general move toward a curiously dainty form of functionalism. It was not the functionalism of the Bauhaus, the adaptation of industrial design for the modern home, but rather a quiet insistence on furnishing a house with things that were practical as well as pretty. The bright colors and exotic patterns of the chintz stilled the passion for ribbons and tassels, whatnots and knickknacks that the previous generation had needed to enliven the dark interiors of their rooms, and so a good deal of the clutter could be removed. If you had light curtains instead of heavy draperies that cut off the sun, you didn't need gilding to brighten the gloom. If you had upholstery that didn't get greasy and matted, you didn't need doilies to protect it. If tables and chairs were light enough to move at will, you re-

TRELLIS ROOM, COLONY CLUB, NEW YORK, NEW YORK. ELSIE DE WOLFE, 1913.

The Trellis Room was influenced by Roman images. The trellises enclose the room, becoming at once columns, cornices, and furniture. Courtesy of The Art Institute of Chicago.

quired only half as many. And if you followed these ideas, you had an interior that was radically different from the prevailing mode.[19]

Elsie de Wolfe rejected overly ornamental interior treatment; she preferred the simplicity and the dignity of the architectural space in relation to the furnishings. "In other words, the architecture of the room becomes its decoration."[20]

Her first major work as a decorator was the Colony Club, New York (1906), the first American clubhouse for women. The innovative treatment of the Trellis Room was most influenced by the knowledge of historic examples employing trellis in their decorative schemes. She drew upon such sources as Roman frescoes and Pompeiian mural paintings depicting ancient gardens and Moorish expressions of trellises found at the Alhambra, Granada, and the Great Mosque at Cordoba. The long narrow room was filled with light, illuminating the bright green and white pattern of trellis covering all of the walls. These trellises were modulated to form panels integrating lighting and to support living plants. Trellis-columns were treated classically with base, shaft, and capital decoration. The gardenlike effect was complete with a fountain, red tile floors, and light, wooden furniture repeating the trellis effect. Elsie de Wolfe had the ability to create a sense of place through decoration and historic reference.

RUBY ROSS GOODNOW WOOD

Ruby Ross Goodnow Wood (1880–1950) was a disciple of Elsie de Wolfe and worked as her ghostwriter for *The House in Good Taste* (1913). Wood's contribution to interior design was her own book, *The Honest House* (1914). In contrast to de Wolfe's book, which focused on upper-class style and fashion, Wood's interest was in educating the growing middle class about good residential design. Her book, written in simple yet thoughtful language, surveyed the various problems of selecting, designing, building, and furnishing smaller homes and residences. Informing homeowners who could not afford professional design assistance about good design was its purpose. Wood's practical advice with specific ex-

amples influenced not only the do-it-yourself amateur but professional designers and architects as well. Her book is divided into twenty-four chapters discussing practical issues, such as the value of an architect, building, plan arrangements, and materials and roofs. Aesthetic considerations are explained in chapters on color, good taste and common sense, proportion and balance, interior design, decoration of walls, window treatments, and furniture. Throughout this book she gives us a sense of the continuity of the house by discussing historical precedents. Finally, she writes about what other authors avoid—what elements make a house into a home. In the furniture chapter, Wood discusses the reality of furnishing a home on a budget. She supports the traditional way of completing a home by collecting pieces over a period of time.

If you start out with the determination to have mahogany furniture only, or oak, or walnut, or whatever you may like, your house will be absolutely unobjectionable, but you won't have very much fun with it. If, however, you have a few pieces of furniture that you love too much to give up, and you have to search and search for every new thing you buy so that it will be friendly with the old things, your house will be a much pleasanter place to live in.[21]

She goes on to describe the four basic types of furniture available in 1914. First, wooden furniture that is finished naturally and only uses its color and grain for decoration. Second, painted or lacquered pieces such as Colonial or Chinese. Third, upholstered furniture in tapestries, leather, or chintzes. Fourth, lightweight furniture built of reeds, rattan, and other materials. Today we can add significantly to those four types by including furniture employing plastic, glass, metal, cardboard, and so forth. "You can associate furniture of each of the first four classes pleasantly in one room, if the design and color are in harmony."[22] This simple idea has had a great influence on residential design in America, resulting in what we call eclectic design. Not only did Wood favor collecting different kinds of furniture over a period of time but also gave advice on how to relate the various pieces together as workable interior. "The Oriental lacquer furniture and the Occidental painted furniture are not friendly, just as oak and mahogany are usually unfriendly, but any one of the decorated woods may be combined with any one of the stained and waxed woods if the selection is made carefully." [23]

LUDWIG MIES VAN DER ROHE

Architecture and furniture were the same for Ludwig Mies van der Rohe (1886–1969). As he developed the skeletal steel structure covered with a curtain wall skin for his high-rise buildings, he likewise designed furniture with a clean, high-quality elastic steel as the skeleton, the skin then attached to the frame. The German National Pavilion at the Barcelona International Exposition, Spain (1929) was the physical realization of Mies van der Rohe's ideas of interior space. He believed that "the shaping of space with structure is the true task of architecture. The building is not the work of art—the space is." [24] The open plan of the Pavilion extended to the adjacent exterior space; the two were inseparable. By using polished marble as partitions and enclosing walls of green glass, the resulting free-flowing space was further enhanced by reflections of what a visitor had just seen or spectral images of space yet to be experienced. Mies designed special furniture in keeping with this spatial complex, creating unity of building and furniture. The furniture was grouped about a central onyx screen to be primarily used for the opening ceremonies featuring the king and queen of Spain. A table holding a golden book was placed against the onyx screen flanked by two ottomans; two identical chairs for the use of the king and queen were placed at right angles to the onyx screen. Opposite the chairs against a double paneled wall containing a light source was placed a larger table for champagne. Additional ottomans were carefully positioned about the Pavilion. The designs of this group of furniture, now named "Barcelona," survived the Pavilion, which was dismantled after the close of the exposition. In 1986, it was reconstructed as a permanent building.

The Barcelona chair and ottoman became a standard furnishing for many of Mies's later interiors. Werner Blaser has summarized the special qualities of this chair. "The Barcelona chair, for example, seems to grow out of the floor with an easy bound and yet it contrasts with it. The chair doesn't actually 'stand' anymore; it lends ease and

GERMAN PAVILION, BARCELONA, SPAIN. LUDWIG MIES VAN DER ROHE, 1929. RESTORED BY CRISTIAN CIRICI, FERNANDO RAMOS, AND IGNASI DE SOLA-MORALES, 1986.

Mies van der Rohe's masterful extension of interior to exterior space created eloquently minimal enclosures for his steel and leather seating. Photograph by Don Kalec.

elegance to the act of sitting and eliminates the sense of heaviness and rigidity."[25] Mies designed his furniture as part of the structural relationship with his interiors. He considered the entire spectrum from the building shell to the furniture all part of an artistic statement of technique, form, and material. He repeated many times: "Architecture is not only linked to its objectives, but also to the materials and methods of its construction."[26]

LE CORBUSIER

Le Corbusier (1887–1965) believed that "the sphere of architecture embraces every detail of household furnishing, the street as well as the house, and a wider world still beyond both."[27] His treatment of interiors divided furnishings into two classifications: built-in storage and cupboards based on a standard unit (casier standard) that could be located within the wall or act as a partition

PAVILION DE L'ESPRIT NOUVEAU, EXPOSITION DES ARTS DECORATIFS DE 1925, PARIS, FRANCE. LE CORBUSIER, 1925.

Le Corbusier saw free standing furniture as sculpture in space, always in composition with the built-in elements and enclosing volume. Droits de reproduction percus par la SPADEM. Copyright 1991 ARS N.Y./ SPADEM.

between one space and another and freestanding pieces such as chairs and tables, which he considered as sculpture in an overall composition. The built-ins would be containers for any type of storage, maximizing the free space for arranging those pieces of furniture that have direct contact with the human body. This philosophy of furniture is summed up as the sense of geometric precision (storage units) juxtaposed with the plasticity of sculptural forms (freestanding units).

One of Le Corbusier's earliest complete interiors was his Pavillon de L'Esprit Nouveau for the International Exposition of Decorative Arts, Paris (1925). Here he demonstrated built-in cabinets with freestanding pieces of furniture. In addition to his designs for the storage units and tables, he used Thonet's circular bentwood chairs for the first time, exclaiming: "We have introduced the humble Thonet chair of steamed wood, certainly the most common as well as the least costly of chairs. And we believe that this chair, whose millions of repo Americas, possesses a nobility of its own."[28] The fact that Thonet's chairs worked so well as sculpture in space inspired Le Corbusier to design (in collaboration with Charlotte Perriand [1903–], who worked in his atelier) tubular steel chairs, such as the *fauteuil grand confort* (1928) and an armchair with pivoting backrest (1928). The *chaise-longue à réglage continu*, which Le Cor-

busier designed in 1928, also paid tribute to Thonet's renowned bentwood rocking chair of 1860. The chaise longue had a fixed supporting structure for the human occupant, an anatomically shaped undulation covered with pony hide, which was attached to a long curve, allowing for various positions to be fixed on the substructure of the molded base. Although the angle of recline would have to be fixed before the person reposed, the position chosen would be firm and stable. This chaise longue epitomized Le Corbusier's theory of rationalism and functionalism, summed up in his metaphor, "a chair is a machine for sitting in."[29]

MARCEL BREUER

Marcel Breuer (1902–1982) was trained at the Bauhaus in Weimar, Germany, entering the school in 1920, a year after it was founded. He was with the first group of architecture, design, and painting students whose artistic spirits and identities would be shaped and molded by the Bauhaus. The Bauhaus (1919–1933) initially had the following aims, quoting Walter Gropius (1883–1969):

The Bauhaus strives to bring together all creative effort into one whole, to reunify all the disciplines of practical art—sculpture, painting, handicrafts, and the

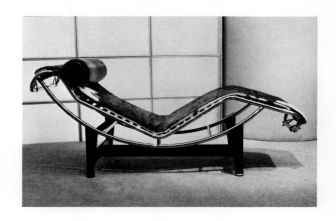

CHAISE-LONGUE. LE CORBUSIER WITH CHARLOTTE PERRIAND, 1927–1929.

The chaise-longue is a rational expression of a stable structure supporting an anatomically correct lounge that is simply adjustable. Photograph by John Kurtich.

crafts—as inseparable components of a new architecture. The ultimate, if distant, aim of the Bauhaus is the unified work of art—the great structure—in which there is no distinction between monumental and decorative art. The Bauhaus wants to educate architects, painters, and sculptors of all levels, according to their capabilities, to become competent craftsmen or independent creative artists and to form a working community of leading and future artist-craftsmen. These men, of kindred spirit, will know how to design buildings harmoniously in their entirety—structure, finishing, ornamentation, and furnishing.[30]

Breuer remained at the Bauhaus until 1928, starting out as a student and ending as the head of the furniture workshop when the Bauhaus moved to Dessau.

His initial chair designs were of wood, with obvious influence from Gerrit Rietveld (1888–1964) and the De Stijl movement. In 1925 Breuer began to experiment with tubular steel chair designs after observing the impressive strength and lightness of his tubular steel bicycle, particularly the way in which the material could be bent into a handlebar and support one or more riders with ease. He developed a club armchair out of tubular steel and stretched fabric that became known as the Wassily chair (after Wassily Kandinsky [1866–1944]). The chair was meant for the home, a daring idea for a time when Arts and Crafts ideals were being practiced. The Wassily chair is somewhat ungainly, similar in spirit to the red/blue chair of Rietveld. However, Breuer was interested in achieving the sense of a sitting apparatus suspended above the ground, floating the occupant in pure space. This notion led him to develop the modern cantilever chair. He was always very concerned about comfort and believed that structural resilience was more important in comfortable seating than upholstery or padding on stiff frames. The following sums up Breuer's attitude about furniture: "A piece of furniture is no willful form but, rather, a necessary component of our surroundings. In itself impersonal, it derives its meaning only from the manner in which it is used, which is to say, in the framework of a total plan."[31]

ALVAR AALTO

Alvar Aalto (1898–1976) designed chairs that expressed two primary things: a form that was a direct response to a human being's anatomy while sitting and a shape that reflected the appropriate use of the material. The primary idea behind Aalto's philosophy of design can be summed up in his own words: ". . . since architecture covers the entire field of human life, real functional architecture must be functional mainly from the human

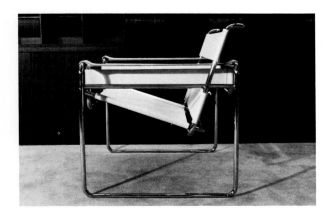

WASSILY CHAIR. MARCEL BREUER, 1925.

Conceptually, this chair was viewed as a structure which suspends its occupant in the air. Photograph by John Kurtich.

SCROLL CHAIR. ALVAR AALTO, 1934.

The Scroll chair is an honest expression of the bending properties of Finnish birch plywood. The chair is lightweight, yet very sturdy. Photograph by John Kurtich.

point of view.''[32] Aalto's designs start with humanity's needs, combining function and material to produce furniture both physically comfortable and visually beautiful. Aalto's native Finland, with its characteristic cold and dark winters and its abundant birch forests, influenced his designs, which became counter to the developments in France and Germany. The cold tubular steel used by Breuer, Le Corbusier, and Mies van der Rohe was inappropriate for the harsh Finnish climate. Thonet's use of beech was of interest to Aalto, particularly in the way the material could be bent in three dimensions, yet this wood was not plentiful in Finland. It was natural for Aalto to develop furnishings using native birch, whose characteristics were very much different than beech. He found that birch, being much stiffer, was better bent in two dimensions. The 1929 Scroll Chair, designed for the Paimio Sanitarium, was completely made of laminated bent birch. Still being manufactured, this classic Aalto design, with its delicate, lightweight profile, reflects his inspired humanism.

EILEEN GRAY

Attitudes about furnishings of various individual architects and designers, as well as design movements, are an invaluable source of ideas to illuminate the ideals of Interior Architecture. Eileen Gray (1879–1976) was one of those rare people who could design the entire package of space from siting and exterior shell to all the furniture and rugs for the interior (see Chapter 1 for additional discussion of Eileen Gray's work). Her early background in designing lacquer screens and furniture and weaving original rugs and carpets prepared her for creating complete interiors when she began architectural studies and explorations in 1924.

In her house, the Tempe a Pailla, Castellar, France (1932–1934), the balance of the inside to the outside was very important. Since she felt that the furnishings and details should be part of the entire organization of the architecture, she was compelled to design all of the furniture for this house. Due to the small size of the house (approximately 1000 square feet) she was forced to be inventive with her built-in and freestanding furniture. Furniture had to serve many functions: a metal seat could be transformed into a stepladder, her dining table could be altered by either reversing its top (one side was cork and the other zinc) or putting the table on its side and lowering it into a coffee table. In the bathroom she designed a piece that could be a towel holder, a small stepladder, or a seat. Her storage chests had hinged drawers that allowed them all to pivot out and

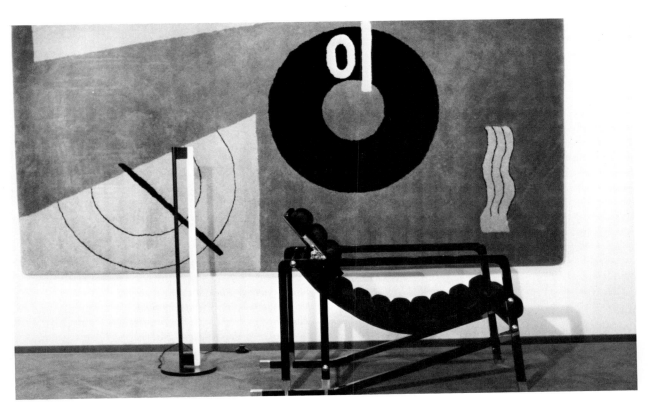

TRANSAT CHAIR, 1924–1930. RUG
FOR HOUSE E.1027, 1929. TUBE
LAMP, 1930. EILEEN GRAY.

*Eileen Gray made poetry out of
function—expressing her passion for
discovering, designing for, and solving
human needs. Photograph by John
Kurtich.*

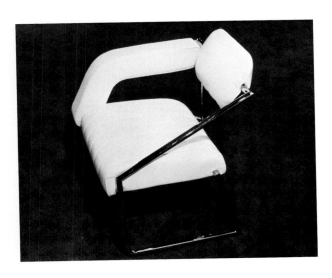

NONCONFORMIST ARMCHAIR. EILEEN
GRAY, 1926–1928.

*The design illuminates the necessity for
furnishings that are for individual needs,
not simply for mass production.
Photograph by John Kurtich.*

reveal their contents simultaneously. Her cupboards, made of metal, served as architectural dividers and screens. False ceilings were employed to hide more storage space; access to this space was through an opening covered with a folding perforated metal grid.

The main bedroom had a ceiling oculus that could be manipulated from the bed to control entering daylight as though an eclipse of the sun were occurring; the size of the circular glass opening was controlled by a counterbalanced circular shield. She not only oversaw all of the upholstery but also designed and had the fabrics and rugs woven. Today there is a vast interior products industry that offers tremendous choice to the designer. It is no longer necessary to design everything for an interior, but the coordination of these choices becomes highly complex. Eileen Gray demonstrated a talent for design of a variety of products, a goal worthy of study in the contemporary world of manufactured choice.

PIERRE CHAREAU

Pierre Chareau (1883–1950) was a prolific architect who intimately understood interior space and its contents. His designs for cabinetry, beds, sofas, lounge chairs, side chairs, desks, dressing tables, dining tables, light fixtures, vanity mirrors, carpets, and accessories were all creatively conceived as a part of the architectural whole. Space was viewed as three distinct components: the volume, the permanent fixtures, and the furnishings. To Chareau, the permanent fixture was the missing link between architecture and furniture; it established the unity of the space. Unlike most architect-designed furniture of the time, which was unrelated to its context and could be placed anywhere, Chareau's designs were uniquely related to their space. Furniture was in dialogue with the volume.

In the Dalsaces' apartment, Paris, France (1923), Chareau created a volumetric relationship between the ceiling and wall with an over-scaled pyramidal cornice. The cornice scaled the room and established a data line at which the wall covering, drapes, and bookshelves terminate. This allowed Chareau to change the surface treatments without losing unity. The curving cornice engages the permanent bookcase, forming a corner in the room. Nestled in the corner, an oval chaise longue complete with throw pillows and flanked by a built-in end table and a freestanding floor lamp completed the composition. The lamp with onyx shades became a vertical counterpoint for the chaise and balanced the dominant bookcase. The sensitivity to human use and comfort was beautifully achieved with his manipulation of architecture and furniture. Chareau balanced geometric and organic forms, smooth and tactile surfaces, massive and intimate volumes, horizontal and vertical elements, and massive and human scales, to achieve ensembles rich with human appeal.

JEAN-MICHEL FRANK

Jean-Michel Frank (1895–1941) used a studied knowledge of history as the basis of his interiors and furniture. His designs relied on refinement of proportion and balance, rationally conceived as a totality. Practicing in collaboration with Adolph Chanaux (1887–1965) during the development of the Modern Movement with its characteristic machine aesthetic, his inspiration was grounded in the ideas and techniques of the past.

The principles were proportion, space, form and matter. For both, harmony of the forms came first. The balance of a piece depended strictly on the association of the various elements. There was a subtle relationship between the length of a sofa and that of the mantelpiece, which in turn related to the dimensions of the windows, the height of the ceiling or the spacing of doors.[33]

Frank used history as the foundation of his ideas. He owes a debt to eighteenth century France for its heightened awareness of scale and the use of materials. He revived straw marquetry and shagreen, historically used to cover small objets d'art. He covered walls and furniture with straw marquetry, giving his interiors a unique golden richness. Shagreen, the skin of the small dogfish shark, became veneer for various pieces of furniture. Some of his lamps made reference to vases of ancient Egypt. His **X**-stools were influenced by furniture designs of the archaic Greek period. His furnishings often included the very pieces that inspired his work, thereby establishing a dialogue between the past and present.

LIVING ROOM, THE DALSACES' APARTMENT, PARIS, FRANCE. PIERRE CHAREAU, 1923.

Chareau's brilliant integration of functions and forms in elegant composition made him one of the great designers of the early twentieth century. Courtesy of The Art Institute of Chicago.

LIVING ROOM, THE NOAILLES
APARTMENT, PARIS, FRANCE. JEAN-
MICHEL FRANK, 1929.

*The minimal interior is made grand
through the use of rich, exotic materials:
vellum wall covering, straw marquetry
tables, leather seating, silk curtains,
bronze doors, and shagreen cover tables.
Courtesy of HOUSE BEAUTIFUL,
September 1929.*

The grand salon of the town house of the Vicomte and Vicomtesse de Noailles, Paris (1932), clearly illustrates his genius. Sheathed in walls of tawny vellum, the room expresses the artist's skillful control of natural materials. The random quality of the vellum's grain is modulated by the regularity of the grid. Although the room is modern, its proportions suggest the monumentality of an earlier time. The room represented the epitome of his personal style in that it contained tables and screens of straw marquetry, oversize seating in white leather, low tables in shagreen or bronze, unadorned silk curtains, bronze doors, a mica-covered mantelpiece, and lamps in rock crystal or ivory sheaves. Such specialized furnishings were produced for Frank by an extensive and exclusive work force. In collaboration with other studios and artists, he realized their contribution to his unique interiors. Although he allowed such artists as the Giacometti brothers to create sculptures and lighting fixtures for him, Christian Berard (1902–1949) to paint the designs for upholstery and carpets, and Emilio Terry (1890–1972) to generate ideas for furniture, their individual efforts depended on Frank's vision to realize their artistic contribution to the whole.

BILLY BALDWIN

Billy Baldwin (1903–1984) was considered by many as the dean of American decorators. Baldwin avoided a personal style in favor of expressing his clients' personalities. He said, "The essence of client and decorator is we." [34] Baldwin felt personal ego got in the way of designing for someone else's use. Having his work not recognizable as a Baldwin interior was a primary goal. Like many decorators, he worked in plan only to establish circulation and arrange the functions of a room: Yet he knew the best laid plans never worked in actuality as well as they do on paper. Working with the physical room, trusting the logic of his eye was Baldwin's methodology. He felt the eye was the best protection against the possible pitfalls of decorating a room from an intellectual or purist point of view. No matter how well a room is studied on paper or mentally visu-

alized, there are always possibilities for error. "Only your eye can tell you what you will be happy with. Today, thank goodness we are more concerned with the personal than with perfection." [35]

Being flexible and expecting change was Baldwin's rule when arranging rooms. This philosophy predominates the interiors of a house in southern Arizona designed by the architectural firm Ford, Powell, and Carson of San Antonio, Texas. "The concept of the architecture was to create the illusion that we had found a tiny old Spanish hilltown and, by connecting all the parts, created a house." [36] Baldwin's treatment of the interiors was to relate to the rough and barren vastness of the landscape and at the same time to provide relief and security from it. The rooms featured floors paved with Mexican tiles, white plastered walls, and exposed, rough-hewn wooden beams. The eclectic furnishings in most of the rooms were colors of the landscape. Baldwin used the landscape and architecture as the basis of his decorating concept. The interiors had an inward orientation to create a haven from the expansive, uninhabited view. The structure changed levels and volumes, evoking a medieval feeling.

Baldwin saw the master bedroom suite as a counterpoint to the rest of the house. "I tried to create a sheik's tent in the Sahara: enveloping, sensuous, removed from the slightly austere surroundings." [37] Upon entering the room, one is overwhelmed with a lush texture and pattern of multicolored paisleylike wall covering and fabric. The bed is within a canopied enclosure, complete with operable drapes, not unlike the bed of a medieval castle. Instead of keeping out the cold, the drapes protect the sleeper from the tumultuous Arizona dawn. The drapes are lined with a voluptuous golden fabric, illuminated with reading lights, which create a separate, intimate chamber. Tactile pleasure predominates the suite through soft and hard material contrasts. A linen-velvet sofa and slipper chairs share the room with marble tub and bathroom appointments. Baldwin's genius in creating personal spaces lay in his sensitivity to existing conditions and his willingness to work with these surroundings. Visual and physical comfort was always his major objective in completing the interior.

CHARLES AND RAY EAMES

The furniture of Charles (1907–1978) and his wife Ray (1915–1988) Eames represents a perfect balance between art and technology. He was most noted for his chairs, as they revolutionized standards of comfort combined with mass production in furniture in the years following World War II. Eames collaborated with Eero Saarinen (1910–1961) in 1941 at the Cranbrook Academy of Art to produce a prize-winning solution for seating, using plywood shells molded in two directions. The double curvature of the shell provided impressive strength combined with lightness, and the shape was easily contoured to the human body for maximizing comfort. Because the current molding process was so expensive, Charles and Ray spent their spare time during the war years developing inexpensive plywood molding processes, which resulted in a new design of plywood stretchers and splints for the U.S. Navy. After the war, Charles further developed and refined the molding process to produce a series of chairs that became as much a part of the post-World War II interior as the European tubular steel chairs of Mies van der Rohe, Breuer, and Le Corbusier had been of the post-World War I interior.

Charles and Ray designed for themselves a house in Pacific Palisades, California (1949), that featured factory-produced materials. The result was a successful marriage between the artist and the technocrat. Their furniture reinforced and completed the interior spaces. The nature of their furniture was that it did not need to be formally arranged or aligned but could be dispersed or clustered, which gave it admirable flexibility for many types of interiors.

In 1956 Eames designed his famous lounge chair and ottoman, which was truly a comfortable chair resulting from a new form. The lounge was constructed of three laminated rosewood shells padded with black leather cushions filled with just the right mixture of goose down, latex foam, and duck feathers. The three shells were joined with

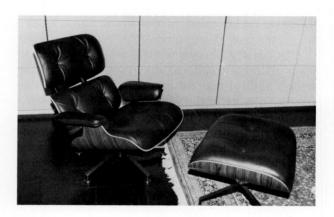

LOUNGE CHAIR AND OTTOMAN, CHARLES EAMES, 1956.

The well known Eames lounge chair and ottoman are beautifully related in form, detail, and material, producing a luxurious and comfortable sculpted composition. Photograph by John Kurtich.

aluminum connections, the ensemble mounted on a five-pronged metal swivel base. With the accompanying ottoman of similar design, the pair provided a luxuriously comfortable chaise. This chair and ottoman could either dominate any furniture grouping or they could be arranged in groups of their own kind; the overall sculptural shape did not demand formal or fixed placement.

CARLO SCARPA

The architectural poet of the twentieth century was Carlo Scarpa (1906–1978). His body of executed work contains profound examples of spatial, visual, and tactile poetry that transcend the ordinary and the commonplace. His attitude about furnishings was direct and consistent with the rest of his work.

Furnishings are necessary, hence the corollary: Concern yourselves with furnishings, with their pres-

ervation, and above all their beauty, something that seems an absolute must for our profession. Just as we provide for our necessities, so it seems logical to provide for beauty, something which we humans have always felt a need for. Originally the cavemen would decorate their caves before furnishing them; it is undeniable that though we have no furnishings made by cavemen we do have wonderful, esthetic, decorative forms.[38]

Scarpa's work is deeply embedded in the tradition of the craftsman. His inventive experimentation with details and materials resulted in fresh relationships, which in turn established a new and inspiring architectural language. In the chapel for the Brion Tomb at the cemetery of San Vito d'Altivole, Italy (1969 onward), Scarpa produced an architectural interior rich with metaphorical and allegorical references. Concrete was the main material, but its combination with marble, granite, onyx, bronze, gold leaf, and wood make manifest the complexity of the metaphorical experience. To visit the chapel is to be introduced into profound mysteries encompassing life and death. The symbols created in the architecture are strongly reinforced by juxtaposition of unlikely materials and an obsessive attention to details. Scarpa cre-

ated two rich paths from which the visitor can enter the chapel. A sequence of architectural places and details unfold as one crosses the moat surrounding the structure. The moat itself is a microcosm of the underworld, filled with mysterious structures buried in murky water; these structures echo the building above, providing experiential simultaneity of two worlds, the past/future or underworld and the present or overworld. One entry is guarded by concrete double doors, elegantly framed in bronze and set into perfectly balanced hinges that belie the actual weight of the portals. The other entry is more indirect, bringing the visitor into an antechamber featuring a receptacle for holy water. An open arch consisting of nearly a whole circle allows access to the chapel proper. The altar dominates the space.

Its stark geometrical figure is not only enriched by almost imperceptible patterns that complicate its severe outline, but also ruffled by the play of light focused on it. The metallic form is lit not only from above, as mentioned, but also by two contiguous floor-to-ceiling apertures in the walls. These two marble antae capture the natural reflection of the water surrounding the base

BRION CEMETARY CHAPEL, SAN VITO D'ALTIVOLE, ITALY. CARLO SCARPA, 1969.

Scarpa's interiors contain intense beauty expressed in meaningful forms. His obsession with the smallest detail is a moving testimony of the passion in his work. Photograph by John Kurtich.

*of the tempietto as if to evoke a Venetian atmosphere.
The interplay between the voids and solids, between the
material fullness of the concrete and the chromatic effects
of the marble or the transparency of the onyx, make the
chapel one of the most complete works produced by
Scarpa, and the one most exemplary of this tendency to
counterpoint.*[39]

Throughout the interior of the chapel, Scarpa is constantly interrelating inside with outside, reminding the visitor of the relationship between the overworld with the underworld, life with death. "To endure life . . . this is always the first duty of every living creature. Illusion loses all its value if it hinders us from doing this . . . *Si vis vitam, para mortem.* If you want to be able to endure life, be ready to accept death."[40]

MEMPHIS

In 1981, the design group called Memphis exhibited its first collection of furniture during the Milan Furniture Fair. Ettore Sottsass (1917–), architect and industrial designer, was one of the leading innovators of the group; he and his associates were dissatisfied with the results of the Modern Movement. Andrea Branzi (1928–), spokesman for the group, established its aims.

(1) Putting behind the myth of the 'unity' of a project and concentrating on a free discontinuity of parts with respect to the whole. (2) The search for a new linguistic 'expressive' quality as a possible solution to the enigma of design and as a possible new meaning. (3) Recycling all possible idioms now in circulation within the experience of our lives. (4) Recuperating decoration and color as signs of freedom and nobility of creative invention. (5) Going beyond ergonomic limits and concentrating on an affective relationship between man and his things.[41]

Like the furniture of Boulle during seventeenth century France, Memphis's furniture made a political statement. But unlike Boulle, the new statement was a criticism of social hierarchies and their power structures, which was manifested in pieces of furniture that would juxtapose unlikely materials, such as a costly, exotic wood with cheap plastic laminate. The idea was to disrupt the visual symbols of power connected to expensive

materials and the perceived tackiness associated with humble materials and garish colors. Memphis took this a step further by using its designs to unsettle commonly held perceptions of status interiors by establishing a disparity between furnishings and environment. Individual pieces also would confront the public with metaphors for the disturbing, hyperactive, unpredictable contemporary world. Such strong design statements have been criticized as impractical or uncomfortable furniture, but the philosophy of Memphis is to challenge humanity into questioning how it lives in the contemporary unstable world. Sottsass says

"CARLTON ROOM DIVIDER," ETTORE SOTTSASS, MEMPHIS MOVEMENT, 1981.

The jarring forms of Memphis force one to reexamine traditional concepts of furniture and ultimately how the contemporary person lives in a chaotic world. Courtesy of The Art Institute of Chicago.

Memphis furniture is very intense, and . . . it can only live with very intense people, with highly evolved and self-sufficient people. Self-sufficient because I am thinking of evolved people as people who know how to run their lives properly in society without having themselves protected by any institution, even a cultural one. It is up to each one of us to decide whether we are intense enough to undertake the reevaluations Memphis demands.[42]

CHARLES PFISTER

Charles Pfister (1949–1990), San Francisco, demonstrated remarkable versatility in his interior spaces. Always holistically conceived and executed, his designs ranged from large corporate office landscapes with custom designed furniture systems (the Weyerhaeuser Corporation, Tacoma, Washington, 1971), to eclectic, Beaux Arts public spaces rich with rotundas and peristyles linked together by axial allées (the Grand Hotel, Washington D.C., 1986). He expressed a sleek, pristine setting through geometric motifs and highly reflective materials such as lacquer and stainless steel for the Knoll International Showroom, Paris, France (1981). The Knoll Showroom

was a particularly interesting challenge since it is the producer and repository of many of the most famous and prestigious furniture pieces of the twentieth century. Pfister chose to use mirror reflection as a major wall treatment (see Chapter 3 on three-dimensional development of the Knoll Showroom), making it as legitimate a furnishing device as the mirrored walls of the Galerie des Glaces at Versailles. The Baroque gardens of Versailles were mirrored in the grand hall, expanding its interior space to the seventeenth century notion of infinity. Pfister used mirrors as an interior device not only to increase the exposure and display viewpoints of Knoll's famous furniture but to fragment the interior into manageable zones of concentration, without losing the sense of the whole. The furnishings of this showroom are truly the articulated mirrors, creating a stage for the most effective display of the furniture.

THE LANDAHL GROUP

The Landahl Group, headed by Greg Landahl (1947–), Chicago, has a unique talent of relating their interiors directly to the architectural shell containing them. The Landahl Group's work is

KNOLL INTERNATIONAL INC. SHOWROOM, PARIS, FRANCE. CHARLES PFISTER, 1981.

The mirrored risers dematerialize the stair and intensify the act of ascent. Photograph by John Kurtich.

OFFICES OF DRIEHAUS RESSEARCH
ASSOCIATES, CHICAGO, ILLINOIS. THE
LANDAHL GROUP, INC., 1982.

*The serrated desk corner is directly
related to the portals which ultimately
draw from the overall highrise footprint.
This system of miniaturization creates a
solidly grounded concept for the design.
Photograph by Jim Norris.*

concerned with forming interior space that has a
direct relationship to the structure and language
of the enclosing architecture. In Landahl's commission for the offices of Driehaus Research Associates (1982), located in 3 First National Plaza
Building, Chicago (1981), he developed a design
that is a microcosm of the building in which it
resides. The form of the high-rise office building
is characterized by a multiplicity of vertical bay
windows. This stepped shape provided the basis
for the planning and detailing of the furnishings.

The central reception room is dominated by a
twin zigzag mahogany desk. The sawtooth motif
is continued into the frames of the surrounding
portals that lead to the private offices. A terrazzo
and bronze border echoes the portal frame and
emphasizes the threshold. This intricate detail is
miniaturized and repeated in the rich mahogany
furniture throughout the suite. The tops of the
desks elaborate the rhythmic pattern with a polished bronze marquetry separating the mahogany
from a more luxurious redwood burl working

surface. The final diminution of bay window form occurs in the cast bronze base of the owner's custom computer cover.

PHILIPPE STARCK

The concern for completing interior space holistically through thoughtful and well-designed furnishings is exemplified in the work of a number of contemporary young designers and architects. Philippe Starck (1949–) combines theatrical drama with straightforward, cost-conscious use of materials. The key idea of his Café Costes Paris, France (1987), was to "be as handsome, barn-like and melancholy as the railway station buffet in Prague."[43] He feels that the consumer society must end because of the earth's limited resources; spaces must be built to endure as well as be comfortable. He says: "Real modern design has to be the kind of thing that you can live with for years, and which your grandmother can put up with when she comes to stay without feeling uncomfortable or humiliated."[44] The dominant feature of the interior of Café Costes is a central, oversized staircase flanked by two large cylindrical columns. This feature serves more as a giant piece of ornamental furniture as its function is to access a very small mezzanine. The stair widens as it ascends, creating a reverse perspective effect, which compresses the space and draws attention to the stair structure. Starck fills the main floor and mezzanine with shiny curved chairs and petite pedestal tables, leaving a wide approach to the staircase, which echoes the reverse perspective path on the floor design.

SUMMARY

Furnishings define the function of interior space. Good furnishings enhance the pleasure of occupying the space. Exceptional furnishings express conceptual ideas that transcend the utilitarian. Extraordinary furnishings merge with the architecture of the space and are vital to its definition. The terms "good," "exceptional," and "extraordinary" do not necessarily relate to the size of the budget. Large or unlimited budgets can, in fact, be detrimental to creativity. One might think of furnishings as an essential palette for the Interior Architect to humanize space.

In some cases, furnishings are much stronger than the architectural space that they occupy. Traditionally, interior decorators have this strength; they can create exciting vignettes. They are fascinated with the people who will occupy the space, their moods, their personal belongings, their need for comfort, atmosphere, color, light, texture. These practitioners are not inhibited by the dogma of current, formal, design education. This encourages an intuitive freedom, resulting in fresh and spontaneous ideas. Not being preoccupied with a consistent design language and its detailing, the decorator breaks rules, often arriving at energetic solutions. With no architectural training, the decorator relies primarily on color, materials, and furnishings to transform the space. Their work, at its best and worst, parallels stage set design. Strong set design is based on a narrative, giving it cohesion. Nevertheless, the impermanent, superficial quality of the stage set impairs the perception of substance.

Most interior designers have been trained in either home economic departments or design schools. Their sense of architectural history influences their work, giving them a stronger understanding of space. Their concept of furnishings tends to be more sympathetic to the architectural whole. Rather than working in fragmented vignettes, they create within the interior a cohesive sense of place. They appreciate and know furniture from the classic to the avant garde and the subtle messages they impart. Their professionalism has made them aware of the importance of the furnishings in relation to the architectural finishes and details. Having very limited architectural training, designers are often excluded from the early stages of architectural development of the enclosure. Missing this opportunity can compromise the successful completion of a holistic interior.

Architects have little formal training in the history, selection, or design of interior furnish-

ings. They have studied architects (such as Frank Lloyd Wright and Le Corbusier), who, as a matter of course, designed not only buildings but their contents as well. This concept is generally well-founded in their education, yet when it comes to applying these principles, most architects fall short. The prevailing extremes in attitude about furnishing the interior are: the architect is fully capable of doing it all, or, it is someone else's job. Few architects are actually talented (or even interested) enough to complete interior spaces. Some architects dream of designing their own chair that would bear their name. This limited, egotistical attitude has little to do with the development and completion of interior space.

Architects are generally insensitive to fabrics, finishes, color, lighting, and objects of art. They relate better to architectural materials such as steel, concrete, and wood, and technical elements such as plumbing and ventilation. They are well trained to integrate all of the building systems and construction materials. Unfortunately, this ability to integrate does not continue to the interiors and their furnishings.

On the other hand, many young architects have found that interiors commissions are more plentiful and accessible than building projects. The successful ones have overcome their educational deficiencies and learned to appreciate the design of interior space. In recent years, the major architectural journals have started devoting entire issues to interiors, illuminating the creative work of these emerging practitioners. These architects represent a new, balanced profession that appreciates the intimacy of interior space as well as the architectural form that encloses it.

This new profession is Interior Architecture. It seeks to synthesize the parallel development of architects, interior designers, and artists. These individual talents have long been segregated, yet great interior space throughout history has been the result of integration. Interior Architecture is the cross-fertilization of these disciplines.

CAFE COSTES, PARIS, FRANCE.
PHILIPPE STARCK, 1984.

The three-legged chairs were designed to ease serving access in the dense Parisian cafe. Photograph by John Kurtich.

NOTES

1. Marian Page, *Furniture Designed by Architects* (New York: Whitney Library of Design, 1980), p. 8.

2. Adolf Loos, *Spoken into the Void: Collected Essays 1897–1900* (Cambridge, MA: The MIT Press, 1982), p. 27.

3. Frank Lloyd Wright, in the process of building Unity Temple, made hundreds of changes to the construction contract so that he could perfect the interior. Wright saw the value of making alterations to his design as a result of seeing the actual spaces take shape. These relationships could not be seen in drawings.

4. The dates in the text are the traditional dates, rounded off, for the Old Kingdom, Middle Kingdom, and New Kingdom, not taking into account the so-called intermediate periods, which were times of unrest and change between the major groups of dynasties. A more precise chronology reads:

    Predynastic Period—5200–3050
    Early Dynastic Period (dynasties 1–2)—3050–2686
    Old Kingdom (dynasties 3–8)—2686–2160
    First Intermediate Period (dynasties 9–11)—2160–2040
    Middle Kingdom (dynasties 11–13)—2040–1633)
    Second Intermediate Period (dynasties 14–17)—1786–1558
    New Kingdom (dynasties 18–20)—1558–1069
    Third Intermediate Period (dynasties 21–25)—1069–656
    Saite Renaissance (Dynasty 26)—664–525
    Late Dynastic (dynasties 27–31)—525–330
    Alexander's Conquest—332

(Note: the above chronology is from *Ancient Egypt,* edited by Gilbert M. Grosvenor (Washington D.C.: National Geographic Society, 1978), p. 249.

5. Sir John Soane, *Lectures on Architecture* (London: Publication of Sir John Soane's Museum, no. 14, 1929), p. 180.

6. Quoted in Edward D. Andrews, *The People Called Shakers* (New York: Dover Publications, 1953), p. 24.

7. Oswald Mathias Ungers, "Five Lessons from Schinkel," (*Free-Style Classicism,* Charles Jencks, ed., London: Architectural Design, 1982), p. 24.

8. A quote of Schinkel's from Martin Filler, "Karl Friedrich Schinkel, Designer: The Architect's Furniture," (*Casa Vogue,* July/August 1985, no. 165), p. 88.

9. Marian Page, *Furniture Designed by Architects* (New York: Whitney Library of Design, 1980), p. 58.

10. From a lecture by William Morris, "The Lesser Arts" (1877) in Joanna Barham and Jennifer Harris, ed., *William Morris and the Middle Ages* (Manchester, U.K.: Manchester University Press), p. 39.

11. Quote by William Morris from Nikolaus Pevsner, "William Morris and Architecture," *Studies in Art, Architecture and Design, Volume Two, Victorian and After* (New York: Walker and Company, 1968), p. 110.

12. George Collins—a verbal quote (Columbia University, discussion, New York, 1967).

13. Fernando Agnoletti, "The Hill-House Helensburgh," *Deutsche Kunst und Dekoration,* Vol. VI, no. 1 (Marz 1905), p. 337.

14. Robert Waissenberger, "Ver Sacrum und die Abneigung gegen den Pro-vinzialismus," *Ver Sacrum* (Wien: Wien Kultur, 1983), p. 9.

15. Edgar Kaufmann and Ben Raeburn (selected by), *Frank Lloyd Wright: Writings and Buildings* (New York: Meridian Books, 1960), p. 280.

16. Donald Kalec, "The Prairie School Furniture," (*The Prairie School Review,* V. 1, no. 4, 1964), p. 10.

17. Marian Page, *Furniture Designed By Architects* (New York: Whitney Library of Design, 1980), p. 123.

18. Gerrit Rietveld, "Levenshouding als achtergrond von mijn werkD" (View of life as a background for my work), lecture delivered at the Stedelijk Museum, Amsterdam, 27 June 1957, trans. in Theodore M. Brown, *The Work of G. Rietveld, Architect* (Utrecht: A. W. Bruna & Zoon, 1958), p. 162.

19. Jane S. Smith, *Elsie de Wolfe: A Life in the High Style* (New York: Atheneum, 1982), p. 109.

20. Elsie de Wolfe, *The House in Good Taste* (New York: The Century Company, 1913), p. 26.

21. Ruby Ross Goodnow with Rayne Adams, *The Honest House* (New York: The Century Company, 1914), p. 198.

22. Ibid, p. 198.

23. Ibid, p. 198.

24. Werner Blaser, *Mies van der Rohe: Furniture and Interiors* (New York: Barron's 1982), p. 7.

25. Ibid, p. 12.

26. Ibid, p. 10.

27. Marian Page, *Furniture Designed by Architects* (New York: Whitney Library of Design, 1980), p. 184.

28. Charles-Edouard Jeanneret Gris, *Almanac d'Architecture Moderne* (Torino: Bottega d'Erasmo, 1975), p. 31.

29. Charles Jencks, *Le Corbusier and the Tragic View of Architecture* (Cambridge, MA: Harvard University Press, 1973), p. 82.

30. Hans M. Wingler, *The Bauhaus* (Cambridge, MA: The MIT Press, 1978), p. 32.

31. Howard Dearstyne, *Inside the Bauhaus* (New York: Rizzoli, 1986), p. 99.

32. Göran Schildt, ed., *Sketches: Alvar Aalto* (Cambridge, MA: The MIT Press, 1985), p. 76.

33. Leopold Diego Sanchez, *Jean-Michel Frank* (Paris: Editions du Regard, 1980), p. 18.

34. Billy Baldwin, *Billy Baldwin Decorates* (New York: Holt, Rinehart and Winston, 1972), p. 10.

35. Ibid, p. 16.

36. Ibid, p. 30.

37. Ibid, p. 37.

38. Francesco Dal Co and Giuseppe Mazzariol, *Carlo Scarpa: The Complete Works* (New York: Rizzoli, 1985), p. 282.

39. Francesco Dal Co and Giuseppe Mazzariol, *Carlo Scarpa: The Complete Works* (New York: Rizzoli, 1985), p. 64.

40. Sigmund Freud, *Civilization and its Discontents* (New York: W. W. Norton & Co., 1962), p. 50.

41. Richard Horn, Memphis: *Objects, Furniture, and Patterns* (Philadelphia: Running Press, 1985), p. 17.

42. Ibid, p. 25.

43. Philippe Starck quotation in Charles Clifford, "Cafe Costes," *The World of Interiors,* July/August 1985, p. 80.

44. Philippe Starck quotation in Maurice Cooper, "The Designer as Superstar," *Blueprint,* April 1987, no. 36, p. 21.

CHAPTER 8

Preserving the Past: Preservation, Restoration, Renovation, and Adaptive Reuse

Humans seem to need a sense of being connected to the past so that they have a confidence that there will be a future. Many older buildings offer qualities that are difficult or impossible to reproduce today. Prime locations, quality craftsmanship, elaborately detailed woodwork, gracefully proportioned rooms, authentic historic styles, and materials rich with the patina of age all contribute to what makes these buildings valuable. Older buildings have acquired a collage of narrative that a new building does not contain. This quality immediately engages one's imagination concerning the previous layers of events that took place within the walls. One is constantly reminded of the positive aspects of past eras implied by surviving details and spaces. The reassuring experience of turning a cast brass doorknob attached to a solid four-panel mahogany door and entering an original Victorian room with its parquet floor, three-piece baseboard, paneled wainscoat, papered walls, crown molding, and plaster ceiling triggers images of the past. Such exposure contrasts with the general lack of character of current building materials and methods. Experiencing the past through these older buildings inspires an emotional response that enhances and enriches the substance of contemporary life.

Historic interiors are a primary resource for new Interior Architecture. The educational value of visiting preserved interiors cannot be underestimated for the design professions as well as for the general public. There is no substitute for this direct personal experience. Historic architectural space imprints the most vivid personal memory, allowing the viewer the closest opportunity of experiencing an actual moment of history. The impact of this kind of understanding can only fertilize the designer's palette and cultivate the public's appreciation. The most sophisticated photographic, electronic, or holographic media cannot replicate the reality of being there. This reality is perpetuated by sustaining significant spaces through preservation, restoration, renovation, and adaptive reuse.

Preservation

Preservation is the act of maintaining all or any part of a building in order to ensure its historic significance. Several categories of older buildings can be considered. The most refined and abstract is the preservation of an architectural landmark installed in a museum. Usually this edifice is a single, prominent interior space or an exterior architectural monument or fragment. When the architectural landmark can be preserved and restored in situ, the building becomes a museum itself, frozen in a particular time or era. This second category is the most ideal as the building maintains its relationship to its original site as well as between its inside space and outside shell. Another category is the preservation of a historical building, which, instead of becoming a museum, functions with contemporary needs and life without compromising its historical and physical features. Finally, there is the adaptive reuse of an older building; here, the original shell of the building might be preserved, but the interior would be totally new. All of these categories require that designers have a sensitive historical approach to how the interiors relate to the building as a whole.

PRESERVATION WITHIN THE MUSEUM
European museums of the nineteenth century were particularly interested in collecting and preserving architectural monuments and fragments found through extensive archaeological excavations in Greece, Turkey, and the Middle East.

The Staatliche Museen, Berlin (also known as the Pergamon Museum) featured spectacular reconstructions, in full scale with the actual fragments, of the central passage of the Great Gate of Ishtar from Nebuchadnezzar II's Babylon (605–563 B.C.), the Agora of Miletus (150 B.C.), and the Great Altar of Zeus of Pergamon (180–160 B.C.). These exterior monuments require huge gallery spaces to house and protect them from the climate of northern Germany. The viewer has the experience of leaping through time when passing, for instance, through the Great Gate of Ishtar and emerging on the other side into the middle of the Miletus agora.

Such architectural reconstructions were not common in most museums because they took up a great deal of space. It is even rarer to find architectural reconstructions of interior space. "Period" rooms are common in European and American museums, but they represent stage sets in order to display a variety of authentic furniture of a given period. Even the furniture collection might not necessarily be from the same place. In any case, the space itself is usually totally fabricated to form the proper setting for the furniture and objects.

PRESERVATION IN SITU   Museum preservation replaces the original context and vitality of any architectural reconstruction. The result is an artificial environment attempting to emulate the original space but isolating it from its former

PROCESSIONAL WAY AND ISHTAR GATE, BABYLON, IRAQ, 605–563 B.C. RECONSTRUCTED AT THE PERGAMON MUSEUM, BERLIN, GERMANY, 1899–1930.

The bold Ishtar Gate in its deep blue glazed brick and rich emblematic patterns, echoes the imperial might of Nebuchadnezzar's Babylon. Photograph by John Kurtich.

ALTAR OF ZEUS, PERGAMON, TURKEY, 197–159 B.C. RECONSTRUCTED AT THE PERGAMON MUSEUM, BERLIN, GERMANY, 1888–1930.

This great altar was renowned for its dynamic, high relief sculpture, which told the story of the Gigantomachy or the battle between the Olympian gods and the giants. Photograph by John Kurtich.

INTERIOR VIEW OF LOBBY AND MAIN
OFFICE SPACE, JOHNSON WAX
ADMINISTRATION BUILDING, RACINE,
WISCONSIN. FRANK LLOYD WRIGHT,
1936.

*To provide a bright and open work area
in the administration building, Wright
replaced structural walls with a forest of
elegantly tapering columns. Photograph
by John Kurtich.*

human vigor and function. A rare form of continuously preserved architecture, outside the confines of a museum mentality, is the S. C. Johnson
and Son Administration Building, Johnson Wax
Company, Racine, Wisconsin (Frank Lloyd
Wright, 1936). This superlative example of a distinguished design has maintained its original architectural integrity. The complex has functioned
as the corporate headquarters, continuously preserving Wright's innovative concept of a totally
designed office complex.

RESTORATION

Restoration is the act of returning the building in
some manner to a condition deemed appropriate
after it has been set aside to be "preserved." The
Rotunda of the University of Virginia, Charlottesville 1822–1826 (Thomas Jefferson (1746–
1826), suffered a Beaux Arts "restoration" by
Stanford White (1853–1906) after a devastating
fire in 1895. White eliminated one of Jefferson's
original floors, drastically changing the Dome

Room. From 1973 to 1976, the Rotunda was restored to Jefferson's initial plans with its oval-
shaped lower rooms, hourglass-shaped halls,
unique double-curved staircases, and magnificent
Dome Room, replete with accurate materials and
methods of finish.

RENOVATION

Renovation is the act of renewing and updating
older buildings' original uses to satisfy contemporary needs. The renovation of the Richard Carrigan residence, Chicago, Illinois (1983), by
Anders Nereim (1947–) and Stuart Cohen
(1942–) was inspired by the work of Sir John
Soane (1753–1837). The 1890s Victorian town
house had been remodeled over the years with
little remaining evidence of its initial character.
The architects found some trim of the period in
the front hall that had a robust personality. Drawing upon this find, the designers developed the
language for all the interior detailing, which recalled the original spirit of the house.

INTERIOR VIEW OF FIRST FLOOR, THE ROTUNDA, UNIVERSITY OF VIRGINIA, CHARLOTTESVILLE, VIRGINIA. THOMAS JEFFERSON, 1822–1826. RESTORED BY FREDERICK D. NICHOLS AND FRANCIS L. BERKELEY, JR., 1953–1976.

As a result of not masking the oval-shaped walls of the meeting rooms, the curved hallways create highly active and unexpected space. Photograph by John Kurtich.

INTERIOR VIEW OF DOME ROOM, THE ROTUNDA, UNIVERSITY OF VIRGINIA, CHARLOTTESVILLE, VIRGINIA. THOMAS JEFFERSON, 1822–1826. RESTORED BY FREDERICK D. NICHOLS AND FRANCIS L. BERKELEY, JR., 1953–1976.

The Dome Room, crowning the Rotunda, was originally designed by Jefferson as the University's library. Photograph by John Kurtich.

INTERIOR VIEW OF LIVING AND DINING ROOMS, RICHARD CARRIGAN RESIDENCE, CHICAGO, ILLINOIS. STUART COHEN AND ANDERS NEREIM, 1983.

Mysterious shafts of light framing the entrance to the dining room expand the space both vertically and horizontally. Photograph by Nick Merrick, Hedrich-Blessing.

With this detailing established, an intricate sequence of spaces was created, employing the ideas of Soane. The oval dining room visually divided the first floor, implying a complete room when in reality it was merely a doorless connection between the living room and the den. Columns framed this spatial sequence, recalling Soanian interposition. Located at the threshold between the dining room and the den was a narrow, two-story shaft, partially filled by opposing second-story bays, recalling the typical Chicago gangway between two houses. The renovation was not authentic to the original design, yet the spirit was recreated in a sympathetic language.

Adaptive Reuse

Adaptive reuse is the interjection of an entirely new function into the shell of an older building. The Chicago Children's Museum, Chicago, Illinois (Banks/Eakin, 1989), occupies 23,000 square feet of space in North Pier Chicago, a former loft-style warehouse. The two-story museum was carefully designed to fit into the columnar structure while contrasting the modest contemporary building materials of dry wall, vinyl tile, and carpet with the original heavy timber construction. All the new walls avoided the existing column grid, defining a series of symmetrical circulation spaces. These spaces are energized by a black and white patterned tile floor, illuminated by simple strip fluorescent fixtures with colored gel sleeves, emphasizing movement. This implied movement leads to a two-story "heart space," connecting the two levels via a steel stair and bridge. The exhibition spaces surround this central space. In contrast to the active circulation, the exhibitions are in asymmetrical rooms, carpeted and illuminated by incandescent track lighting, creating a quieter and more contemplative atmosphere.

The ability to combine the new with the old requires a special creative sensitivity. Of all the categories of preserving the past, adaptive reuse demands more design attention. The practitioner of Interior Architect, trained to resolve contemporary problems while maintaining a respect for history, must exercise the vision and responsibility to recognize and protect unique architecture.

The Architectural Value of the Past

The decline of new construction in recent years has helped the public to refocus on the important resources older buildings contain. Certain construction techniques, superior craftsmanship, and the choice of fine materials used in many older buildings are proving to be economically unfeasible to duplicate. Many older buildings are already located on desirable sites, while others could pro-

INTERIOR VIEW OF CHICAGO CHILDREN'S MUSEUM, CHICAGO, ILLINOIS. BANKS/EAKIN, 1990.

The carefully detailed interiors of this museum quietly reveal the universal message of adaptive reuse: respect for the past can only enhance the present and the future. Photograph by William Kildow.

vide the opportunity to "seed" the redevelopment of an urban area if they were properly renovated. No longer is it generally cheaper to demolish an older, structurally sound building and erect a new one in its place. Many older buildings have important historical or architectural significance in addition to functional or commercial use. Federal, state, and municipal laws favorably affect the process of historic preservation and rehabilitation through tax credits, grants, and subsidies.

The older building has a history of its existence in space. In addition, it might also represent an interesting historical style or composite of styles. Considering the building's rehabilitation, the designer must have a keen, intelligent understanding of all histories associated with the building. Careful and thorough research is necessary. Primary sources of research begin with a diligent investigation of the building itself, amplified by studying records found in courthouses, historical societies, libraries, and title guaranty companies as well as letters, postcards, diaries, inventories, and such. Secondary sources comprise any published material, such as news stories, magazine articles, and advertisements related to the building. Peripheral sources would include other buildings by the same architect, building codes at the time, trade catalogs, architectural handbooks, and tax laws.

Existing conditions of the older building must be thoroughly analyzed. The analysis is necessary for a proper evaluation of what needs to be done or what can be done. The evaluation would include the historical or architectural significance of the building, the size of the building and its room disposition, the condition of the building's structure and mechanical systems, the location of the building, and the building's economic potential.

MUSEUM PRESERVATION

F. W. LITTLE LIVING ROOM

The Metropolitan Museum of Art, New York, New York, has preserved the living room of the Francis W. Little house, designed by Frank Lloyd Wright (1867–1959) from 1912 to 1914. The in-

INTERIOR VIEW OF LIVING ROOM, FRANCIS W. LITTLE RESIDENCE, DEEPHAVEN, MINNESOTA. FRANK LLOYD WRIGHT, 1912. RECONSTRUCTED IN THE METROPOLITAN MUSEUM OF ART, NEW YORK, NEW YORK, 1972.

Wright provided great expanses of windows in the fifty-five-foot living room in response to the original site's dramatic views of Robinson Bay and the surrounding countryside. Photograph by John Kurtich.

stallation is located in the museum to simulate the original siting of the room within the house with a view to Central Park. This location allows natural light from the south to illuminate the room installation; the original room was open to natural light from both the south and the north, balancing the light quality. The museum had to imitate the northern exposure with fluorescent lighting, which actually deadens that side of the space when compared to natural light.

When visitors approach this exhibit, they can see the original materials and details of the exterior construction and peer through the art glass windows to the restored interior. This creates a richer sequence from outside to inside through the original entrance. The Metropolitan Museum transcended the "period" room installation practiced by most museums up to this time; it achieved an exciting spatial experience for museum visitors. Unfortunately, once they enter the living room, they are confined to one area by roped barriers, not being able to experience other viewpoints of the space.

This room was never completely furnished by the original designs of Frank Lloyd Wright because the owners had leftover furniture from an earlier house that Wright had designed for them. For a major room such as this, Wright would have had complete control as opposed to allowing his clients to diminish the consistent quality he envisioned. Furthermore, this is not considered one of Wright's best examples of Interior Architecture. His special floor design was never executed to echo the geometric pattern of the ceiling. The print table, though extraordinarily beautiful, was not designed for this room. Visitors are actually deceived to believe that this is an accurate, unified design by Frank Lloyd Wright. This fact, coupled with the problematic, constrained viewing position, questions the validity of using this room as the major example of Prairie School architecture in New York. Is this room so precious that it could not be fully experienced by the public? Would it not be wonderful if the Metropolitan Museum had reproduced one of Wright's greatest interior spaces, complete with duplications of all the furnishings? This would allow the public a rare opportunity of experiencing an interior by an American architectural genius.

SULLIVAN'S TRADING ROOM

The Art Institute of Chicago, Chicago, Illinois, does allow the public to experience a restored, major interior by Adler and Sullivan. When the Art Institute agreed to house the remains of the Chicago Stock Exchange Trading Room, designed in 1893 (demolished in 1972), it decided to reconstruct the entire room, using as many genuine architectural fragments as could be salvaged from the original building. John Vinci (1937–   ) was commissioned to reconstruct and restore the room as a major, permanent installation within the museum's new addition being designed by Skidmore, Owings & Merrill (1976).

The Trading Room originally was on the second floor of the Stock Exchange Building, a large space measuring 64 by 81 feet, with a 30-foot high ceiling and a 16-foot deep gallery running the length of the west wall. Large double-hung windows provided natural light on the east wall, which overlooked LaSalle Street, and the south wall, which faced an alley separating the building from its nearest neighbor. The ceiling was covered with colored art glass, illuminated from above by special skylights. Because there were eleven more stories of offices above the Trading Room, the skylights were so designed that natural light could filter in through third floor lunettes in the east and south facades and through shed roofs of prismatic glass on the north and south walls.

Vinci's original proposal was to reconstruct the room on a second floor level in the Art Institute, oriented exactly as it had been in the Stock Exchange with natural light coming in from the east and south. Because of the complexity of the building program for the entire museum addition, it was decided to locate the Trading Room reconstruction on the first floor. However, the room was rebuilt in its correct orientation, receiving a new lease on life through proper use of natural light.

Vinci had exactly four months to research and salvage the room prior to the building's demolition. His research resources consisted of careful and thorough exploration of the building itself through producing measured drawings and photographic documentation. Although a basic floor plan of the space existed, there were no other extant drawings. He found a rendering in *Harper's Magazine,* two photos of the interior, and one photo of it after it was remodeled into a bank. Photometric drawings were produced for him by another firm; they turned out to be inaccurate because the photometric firm assumed that the building was built square. Instead of trusting their instruments, which were telling them that the room was not square, they "corrected" their findings to produce a plan with true right angles. It was not until Richard Nickel (1928–1972) produced a careful photographic collage of the Trading Room ceiling before it was dismantled, that it

INTERIOR VIEW OF TRADING ROOM,
CHICAGO STOCK EXCHANGE,
CHICAGO, ILLINOIS. ADLER AND
SULLIVAN, 1893–1894.
RECONSTRUCTED IN THE ART
INSTITUTE OF CHICAGO, CHICAGO,
ILLINOIS BY VINCI-KENNY,
ARCHITECTS, 1976–1977.

*The level of decorative articulation
found in the Trading Room was
exceptional for commercial space during
the late 1890's. Adler and Sullivan,
American, partnership 1883–1895,
Chicago Stock Exchange Trading
Room, reconstructed in The Art
Institute of Chicago, 1893–1894
(demolished 1972), scagliola, gilded
plaster, stained glass, terracotta,
wood, etc. The reconstruction and
reinstallation of the Trading Room was
made possible through a grant from the
Walter E. Heller Foundation, and its
president, Mrs. Edwin J. Decosta,
with additional gifts from the City of
Chicago, Mrs. Eugene A. Davidson,
The Graham Foundation for Advanced
Studies in the Fine Arts, and Three
Oaks Wrecking. © 1990 The Art
Institute of Chicago, All Rights
Reserved.*

was discovered the room was not a true rectangle. In fact, the Trading Room was out of square by 18 inches and was reconstructed as such.

Vinci's philosophy in reconstruction and restoration is analogous to a mathematical problem: find the knowns and solve the unknowns. Eighty percent of the cast iron was recovered by the original building and reused in the reconstruction. Forty percent of the plaster castings are original and one bay of the stencils. Due to subsequent remodelings, several unknowns needed to be solved, such as the original material of the floor and the shape and color of the base of the columns. A wooden floor was chosen (rather than the marble, which was extant at the time of the building's demolition and representative of later remodeling) because it was more logical for acoustical reasons and not out of line with its period. The column bases (removed due to the remodeling process) were reconstructed from the very few photographs available of the original space. The richly stenciled walls and ceiling utilized at least fifty-two colors and most had to be reproduced.

LaSalle Street entrance arch, the Chicago Stock Exchange, Chicago, Illinois. Adler and Sullivan, 1893–1894.
Reconstructed and installed at The Art Institute of Chicago, Chicago, Illinois by Skidmore, Owings and Merrill, 1977.

The current location of the entrance arch as a garden fixture annihilates the original strength of Sullivan's arch as an entry portal. Photograph by John Kurtich.

The entrance arch of the Chicago Stock Exchange Building was also salvaged by the Art Institute. Vinci's proposal was to reconstruct it as an entry into the new wing of the museum and subsequently the Trading Room, maintaining the physical and spiritual connection between the entrance of the Stock Exchange Building and its primary interior space, the Trading Room. Unfortunately, the architects for the building addition did not agree, and their will prevailed. The entry arch was reconstructed as a freestanding monument in a sunken area of the landscaping in front of the new wing of the museum, oriented 90° from its original position, standing depressed in the ground, lonely and detached.

The Trading Room is a living installation, not treated as a precious object to be peered into from a distance. Its current use as a reception room, performance space, and banquet hall resembles its original use as a trading room, full of people, noise, and energy.

IN SITU RESTORATION

WRIGHT HOME AND STUDIO

Many problems exist when an older building is to be preserved and restored on its original site. In the case of the Home and Studio of Frank Lloyd Wright, Oak Park, Illinois, originally designed in 1889, the building had gone through extensive remodelings and additions, continuing until as late as 1925. Basic decisions had to be made as to how the Home and Studio would be restored, particularly what period it would portray. The year 1909 was finally chosen as this represented the condition of the building complex at the peak of Wright's first twenty years of professional practice. The Frank Lloyd Wright Home and Studio Foundation acquired the property in 1974 to preserve and restore this unique architectural monument. Architect Donald Kalec (1935–   ) was chosen as the director of research and resto-

INTERIOR VIEW OF DINING ROOM, FRANK LLOYD WRIGHT HOME AND STUDIO, OAK PARK, ILLINOIS. FRANK LLOYD WRIGHT, 1889. RESTORED BY DON KALEC AND THE FRANK LLOYD WRIGHT HOME AND STUDIO FOUNDATION, 1977–1980.

A. BEFORE RESTORATION.

B. AFTER RESTORATION.

The interior restoration of the dining room, reconstructed from historical photographs, required the re-creation of the recessed ceiling lighting fixture, the leveling and retiling of the floor, restoring the art glass windows, and the applying of linen to the walls and ceiling. Photograph by John Kurtich.

ration. A long and careful evaluation of the building had to be made to determine the scope of the project.

Primary research materials including studying the "footprints" of the building itself, scruti-

nizing approximately two hundred existing historical photographs of the interior and exterior, analyzing the surviving original working drawings (a complete set did not exist), interviewing surviving family members who lived in the house, researching property records, and reading surviving correspondence, which included descriptions of the Home and Studio, either as fact or as future planning.

Secondary research included studying other Wright buildings of the same vintage (for surviving details unique to Wright as well as decorative features), other non-Wright buildings of the same period (for general construction techniques and stock items), and published articles in magazines contemporary with the period, such as *House Beautiful* and *Architectural Record*.

Peripheral research comprised studying trade catalogs of the period (for plumbing fixtures, lighting fixtures), carpenter's journals (for framing and construction techniques), and surveying salvage yards (for surviving standard hardware of the period). An interesting fact that turned up from this sort of research: The barrel vault used in the playroom was a standard wood construction technique for the period, a wood frame system with plaster infill. Wright took advantage of available standard details whenever it suited his aesthetic requirements.

Since the decision was made to restore the house faithfully to its 1909 condition, everything done to the building after that time had to be eliminated, even if the alterations had been done by Wright himself. A basic rule was established that all removed material had to be recorded with measured drawings and photographs. This careful documentation was necessary to be responsible to scholarship and justification of design decisions made.[1]

Hard data for restoration accounted for about 85 percent of the Home and Studio. When something had to be restored for which no information existed, the rule was to keep the solution as simple as possible. The temptation to "play" Frank Lloyd Wright had to be avoided; such newly designed items should not attract attention. The challenge of furnishing the Home and Studio accurately was met with the help of the historic photos. About six hundred objects were identified from these photos by a special committee whose on-going job was then to collect them to complete the furnishings.

WRIGHT'S DANA HOUSE

Frank Lloyd Wright (1867–1959) designed the lavish Dana House, Springfield, Illinois (1902–1904), for Susan Lawrence Dana (1862–1946), who wanted an appropriate and impressive place to entertain politicians, socialites, and distinguished visitors from abroad. She was also very active in women's rights during the early twentieth century and pursued studies and research in metaphysics and religious cults, all of which required her hosting meetings and gatherings at her house. Wright was given *carte blanche* in terms of design and budget and described his approach to the house as "A home designed to accommodate the art collection of its owner and for entertaining extensively, somewhat elaborately worked out in detail."[2]

The design of the house had to incorporate an earlier Victorian structure, starting out as an expansion of the original house but finally swallowing it totally as well as consuming much of the property the house stood on. Wright was required by Mrs. Dana to preserve part of the original house—her father's Victorian study, complete with marble fireplace and old family photos. The new design featured a cruciform plan, and Wright created for the first time several two-story-high interior spaces, including a dramatic barrel-vaulted dining room. Wright designed the details of every aspect of the house, including art glass, lighting fixtures, furniture, carpets, draperies, mural decorations, woodwork, friezes, and tilework. ". . . it is possible to argue that Mrs. Dana's open purse had proved a danger to Wright as well as an opportunity; the note of excess is struck again and again in what amounts, after all, to a gargantuan folly—a sort of Springfield San Simeon."[3]

Mrs. Dana closed her house in 1928 due to the depletion of her inherited wealth and subsequent inability to maintain the estate. The house was saved from demolition in 1944 when it was purchased by the Charles C. Thomas Publishing Company for their executive offices. The house and its contents were then purchased in 1981 by the state of Illinois to be preserved and restored as

a landmark monument of the Illinois Historic Preservation Agency. Hasbrouck Peterson Associates of Chicago, Illinois, was hired to do a detailed restoration study, and Wilbert Hasbrouck (1931–   ) subsequently served as restoration architect.

Similar to the restoration of the Frank Lloyd Wright Home and Studio, a definite year had to be decided upon to restore the house. Hasbrouck chose 1910 because "the house was at the peak of its viability (then). The little things that made the house a home were in place, and it had attained the patina of use by 1910."[4] Luckily many photographs had been taken of the house during that year, so there was a rich source of research docu-

mentation. However, the photographs could not determine the original colors of painted surfaces and wood finishes. Scientific inspection and analysis was necessary with more than 250 samples of paint.

The eighty-six years between the house's construction and its definitive restoration had witnessed alterations or removal of some of Wright's designs on the facade. Missing pieces or fragments had to be carefully researched and replicated. Even the mortar joints of the exterior brick walls had to be taken back to Wright's original deeply raked joints.

The restored Dana House represents an important, multilayered historic monument for Illi-

VIEW OF INTERIOR DETAILS OF DINING ROOM AND BALCONY ABOVE, DANA HOUSE, SPRINGFIELD, ILLINOIS. FRANK LLOYD WRIGHT, 1902–1904. RESTORED BY WILBERT HASBROUCK, 1987–1990.

The restoration of a Wright interior is very complex because it involves research and analysis of a variety of interdependent elements, including plaster friezes, murals, art glass, metal work, custom furniture, unique light fixtures, rugs, and special finishes. Photograph by Don Kalec.

nois social and architectural history. Mrs. Dana was a prominent Illinois socialite as well as a pioneering suffragette. The house preserves two periods of history: the Victorian study of Mrs. Dana's father, Rheuna Lawrence, who was mayor of Springfield; and a major commission for Frank Lloyd Wright during his early Prairie School years while he was perfecting his style, philosophy, and spatial dynamics.

JEFFERSON'S MONTICELLO

Wright's Home and Studio was an important experiment in developing a uniquely American residential vernacular. He was not the first person,

however, to take on this challenge. About one hundred fifty years earlier, Thomas Jefferson (1743–1826) was experimenting with the same idea in his own home "laboratory," Monticello. He designed this home using modified classical language to express the new American democracy. Rejecting Georgian elitism, he favored classical reference for the young republic, which embodied the ideal political structures of ancient Greece and Rome.

Jefferson grew up in an environment that encouraged a Renaissance approach to all things. Anything was a possibility. Although he was formally trained as a lawyer, architecture was a lifelong passion. Jefferson's architectural ideas were

influenced by his European travels when he was the U.S. Minister to France (1785–1789). Buildings such as the Hôtel de Salm (1783–1786) in Paris, the Column House at the Desert de Retz (1774–1789) outside of Paris, and the Maison Carrée (A.D. 4) in Nimes inspired his subsequent designs for the Virginia State Capitol (1789–1798), the University of Virginia (1822–1826) at Charlottesville, and Monticello (1769–onward). While in Europe, he purchased a complete set of Andrea Palladio's *I Quattri Libri del' Architettura* (1570), which became a reference textbook for his buildings.

Monticello is uniquely sited on a hilltop overlooking Charlottesville. The house was begun in 1769 and was developed and constructed over the next fifty-four years. Jefferson thought of his house as an architectural laboratory where he could experiment with new ideas at all scales, from the building shell itself to the furnishings within the interior. Jefferson was truly a holistic designer. His house was a reflection of his genius, summed up in his statement: "Architecture is my delight, and putting up and pulling down, one of my favorite amusements."[5]

Jefferson's first version of Monticello, heavily influenced by Palladio, broke with the predominant colonial architecture. The house had a two-story temple front, similar to Palladio's Villa Pisano (1552/1553–1555), Montagnana, Italy.

When he returned from his French mission in 1789, he decided to remodel his house based on the Hotel de Salm. He tore down the existing two-story temple front in order to make Monticello appear as though it were a one-story house without sacrificing the second and third floors. Doubling the size of the house, he relegated all service areas, such as the kitchen, to below the first floor. The major living spaces and Jefferson's living quarters were on the first floor, with the dome room, bedrooms, and storerooms on the second and third floors.

Jefferson's first floor suite was designed as a group of private rooms containing a library, cabinet (study), solarium, and bedroom. He was influenced by the French alcove bed that he observed at the Column House, le Desert de Retz. When he applied this idea to Monticello, he positioned his bed within a thickened wall separating the bedroom and the cabinet. This wall also contained a stair leading to a closet above the bed. The unique position of the bed allowed him access to either room and to maintain the axial alignment of the fireplace and the windows. Intimacy was created in this otherwise high-ceilinged house by carving a room through the wall for the bed.

After Jefferson's death, debts caused his heirs to sell Monticello. A history of absentee owners with poor caretakers led to the decline of the estate. It was sold to the Thomas Jefferson Memorial Foundation in 1923, a nonprofit organization dedicated to saving this extraordinary architectural landmark.

The restoration of Monticello is typical of most national treasures, freezing a moment in time, attempting to establish authenticity. Unfortunately, people are misled into believing that such restorations represent a past reality. Jefferson was building Monticello for over fifty years, putting it in a constant state of flux. The influence of his travels and his desire for architectural experimentation caused Jefferson to constantly reevaluate and modify the structure. Furthermore, Jefferson was not a trained architect, but he learned by doing. The enlightened era in which he lived encouraged the educated man to pursue a multitude of interests and careers. Jefferson was the third president of the United States, author of the Declaration of Independence, ambassador to France, a lawyer, a musician, an architect, an interior decorator, an inventor, a landscape designer, and a revolutionary politician, to name a

INTERIOR VIEW OF THOMAS JEFFERSON'S ALCOVE BED FROM THE DRESSING ROOM, MONTICELLO, CHARLOTTESVILLE, VIRGINIA. THOMAS JEFFERSON, 1793–1809.

Leaving no detail to chance, Jefferson created all of his own curtain designs as seen in the elegant draping of his bedroom in crimson damask, lined in green, and trimmed with golden fringe. Photograph by May Hawfield.

few. The original Monticello reflected its owner's complex personality with its visionary plan, unique interior spaces, and numerous mechanical inventions. Knowledge of this history raises the question of how one captures the vitality of the period through restoration. The usual restorative approach exploits the frozen moment, idealizing the architectural past. This idealization limits the depth of understanding, producing a false sense of reality.

RICHARDSON'S GLESSNER HOUSE

The J. J. Glessner House, Chicago, Illinois (1885–1886) by Henry Hobson Richardson (1838–1886) is another example of a house museum. It was restored mainly from primary research and evidence. The architect's working drawings of floor plans and elevations as well as his specifications existed intact. Although the house was not built exactly as specified by the drawings, the Chicago architectural firm of Perkins & Will provided as-built drawings. In addition to the drawings, the Glessners kept bills from the construction firm, bills for fixtures, and a complete set of weekly journals in a diary format. The original textiles

were preserved (now kept at the Art Institute of Chicago). The house itself provided the archaeological evidence for original colors, wallpaper, and materials that still existed in fragments hidden behind moldings or forgotten corners.

The restoration policy of the Glessner house was to restore it to the first five years of the use of the house. The administration of the restoration is done through a House and Collections Committee. The curator, Elaine Harrington, worked with this committee and its advisory architect. Although her training is in art history and museum curatorship, Elaine Harrington has a remarkable, sensitive approach to the problems of Interior Architecture with respect to restoration.

Through her careful research, it seems that Mrs. Glessner was very much influenced by a book called *The House Beautiful* by Clarence Cook (1881). This book, subtitled "Essays on Beds and Tables, Stools and Candlesticks," featured designs and attitudes of Colonial Revival, Japanese, Gothic Revival, and William Morris. What details could not be found from primary research could be filled in with information from this book. However, not all original architectural details and fittings were missing from the house. Much of

INTERIOR VIEW OF FIRST FLOOR BEDROOM, J. J. GLESSNER HOUSE, CHICAGO, ILLINOIS. H. H. RICHARDSON, 1885–1886.

Built in 1886, the massive thirty-five room Romanesque style house of rough-hewn granite, effectively shields the quiet serenity of the interior from the urban site. Photograph by John Kurtich.

Richardson's decorative moldings, panels, doors, frames, and other details of wood were intact. Many of these wood pieces had suffered badly during the nearly one hundred years between construction and restoration; they needed serious rehabilitation to bring them back to their original beauty and finish.[6]

The Glessner House was one of Richardson's last commissions. Construction had hardly begun before he died. Since the house represents one of his most mature residences, its preservation is very important. He was known for his rusticated granite exteriors, rounded arches, and Romanesque details. He strived for a combination of massiveness and repose. He believed that:

> *in Romanesque art only, and in those early Renaissance modes which were directly based upon it, that we find that balance between vertical and horizontal accentuations which means perfect repose. The semicircle demands neither that ascending lines nor that retreating lines shall preponderate; and in itself it is neither passive like the lintel nor soaring like the pointed arch. It seems to have grown to its due bearing power and thus to remain, vital yet restful, making no effort either to resist downward pressure or to press upward itself.*[7]

MEIER'S DOUGLAS HOUSE

For any society that preserves its culture, venerable landmarks are not the only structures worthy of concern. Noted contemporary buildings' longevity can be jeopardized if not properly maintained. This issue is more keenly experienced in residential interiors due to the greater degree of variables in ownership. The Douglas House (1973), Harbor Springs, Michigan, by Richard Meier (1934–), falls into this category. The weekend retreat, suffering from years of absentee ownership and attempts at making the pristine structure warm and cozy, was purchased by the J. Paul Beitlers and restored by the Landahl Group (1985). The owners considered the house the most important work of residential architecture by Richard Meier, a modern classic, deserving a meticulous restoration.

Entering the house at the top level from the street side, the visitor does not perceive the grandeur of the site of the building. Magnificently sit-

EXTERIOR VIEW OF EAST FACADE, J. J. GLESSNER HOUSE, CHICAGO, ILLINOIS. H. H. RICHARDSON, 1885–1886.

The rusticated granite exterior, restored to its original color through special cleaning techniques, has reinvigorated the rich Romanesque details. Photograph by John Kurtich.

VIEW OF DOUGLAS HOUSE, HARBOR SPRINGS, MICHIGAN. RICHARD MEIER, 1973. RESTORED BY THE LANDAHL GROUP, 1985.

The careful restoration established Meier's original furniture arrangement for the living room. A new custom designed rug based on a sketch by Le Corbusier completed this scheme. Photograph by John Kurtich.

uated along a steep and isolated piece of property, Meier's five-story, 4,500 square foot promontory cascades down the eastern bluff of Lake Michigan. The house, structured in steel and clad in glass and white painted wood, creates a striking contrast against the densely wooded site. The building's interior organization is separated into public and private zones. The public space, to the west, has views of the lake on all levels through large expanses of glass, while the private space, containing bedrooms, baths, and service areas on three levels, faces east toward the bluff. Balancing the strong verticality of the structure, the multi-storied horizontal levels also provide a series of platforms for viewing the lake. Viewing becomes the essence of the house. Meier intended the original interior to be minimal, acting as a frame for the spectacular view of the lake. To ensure that his interior would not compete with the vista, Meier used neutral finishes, solid walls of white paint, transparent walls of glass, and floors of natural wood, creating a serene atmosphere. The interiors provided quiet galleries, with the lake becoming the art work.

Faced with a badly deteriorated building and an inappropriately altered interior, the current owners embarked upon the mission of returning the residence to its original condition. The structure required extensive repairs and repainting, to return it to its original Meieresque white. As a result of the house being left unheated, approximately one quarter of the glass facing the lake was damaged and had to be replaced. Additional restoration to the interior included: replacing bath-

room tile, refitting hardware, and removing the flocked wallpaper and hanging plants to diffuse the misdirected attempt to make the stark structure "homey." The terrarium adjacent to the living room and the storage area created from a guest room were returned to the original configuration. Since the house was only twelve years old when its restoration began, many of the original trades were still available to work on the residence. Their knowledge made returning the building to the original an easier task.

In the case of the original furniture, it was either replaced, restored, or recreated. The architect's plans, drawings, and original photographs were critical to this process. The furniture was a mixture of modern classic pieces such as: Le Corbusier's Grand Confort and Basculant chairs, Mies van der Rohe's MR chairs, and Meier's custom tables and built-in furniture. Meier's original living room carpet was a neutral gray rectangle. The Landahl Group replaced the rug with one based on a 1956 sketch of a stage curtain by Le Corbusier, Meier's inspiration.

This sensitive and meticulous restoration of a modern landmark exemplifies how even recent work can be vulnerable to inappropriate alterations and neglect by previous owners. The integrity of architectural interiors can easily be compromised by the whims and egos of owners, becoming inconsistent with the spirit of the building.

RENOVATION

ADLER AND SULLIVAN'S GUARANTY BUILDING

When an architecturally significant building is to be faithfully restored and renovated, not for museum purposes, but for continued commercial use, different problems arise that must be solved without compromising the historical or architectural integrity of the original building. The renovation of Adler and Sullivan's Guaranty Building (1895), Buffalo, New York, was successfully achieved by the Cannon Architects and Engineers of Buffalo, 1984.

The Guaranty Building, also known as the Prudential Building, was Adler and Sullivan's last tall office building (their fifth together). Many critics and scholars consider it their best. Sullivan, in his 1896 essay, "The Tall Office Building Artistically Considered," rhetorically itemized variations of his own philosophy of the skyscraper:

Certain critics, and very thoughtful ones, have advanced the theory that the true prototype of the tall office building is the classical column, consisting of base, shaft and capital—the moulded base of the column typical of the lower stories of our building, the plain or fluted shaft suggesting the monotonous, uninterrupted series of office-tiers, and the capital the completing power and luxuriance of the attic.

. . . Others, seeking their examples and justification in the vegetable kingdom, urge that such a design shall above all things be organic. They quote the suitable flower with its bunch of leaves at the earth, its long graceful stem, carrying the gorgeous single flower. They point to the pine-tree, its massy roots, its lithe, uninterrupted trunk, its tuft of green high in the air. Thus, they say, should be the design of the tall office building: again in three parts vertically.

. . . All of these critics and theorists agree, however, positively, unequivocally, in this, that the tall office building should not, must not, be made a field for the display of architectural knowledge in the encyclopaedic sense; that too much learning in this instance is fully as dangerous, as obnoxious, as too little learning; that miscellany is abhorrent to their sense; that the sixteen-story building must not consist of sixteen separate, distinct and unrelated buildings piled one upon the other until the top of the pile is reached.[8]

The Guaranty Building idealized Sullivan's tripartite philosophy very clearly: the street level two-story "base," designed for commercial functions, emphasizing column and corner pier structure to maximize display areas and natural light; the intermediate shaft of identical office windows, framed with slender vertical piers, terminating this section in arches; the attic, topped with a magnificent, crowning entablature, punctuated with ornate oval windows. The thirteen-story building was a classic archetype for the twentieth century skyscraper.

In 1977 there was a threat of demolishing this building, in spite of its National Historic Land-

EXTERIOR VIEW OF THE GUARANTY BUILDING, BUFFALO, NEW YORK. ADLER AND SULLIVAN, 1895. RESTORED BY CANNON, 1984.

Sullivan found the ideal tall building analogous to organic structure of plants: the root, the trunk or stem, the flower. The well-designed building was also divided into three parts: the base, the vertical center portion, and the crowning entablature. Photograph by John Kurtich.

DETAIL OF ENTRANCE DOOR, THE GUARANTY BUILDING, BUFFALO, NEW YORK. ADLER AND SULLIVAN, 1895. RESTORED BY CANNON, 1984.

Usually Sullivan decorated only non-structural elements of his buildings, but in the Guaranty Building he covered every surface which was not glazed with geometric and organic ornamentation that picked up momentum and energy as it climbed to the cornice. Photograph by John Kurtich.

mark status. The city of Buffalo, having lost the Larkin Building (Frank Lloyd Wright, 1903) about thirty years earlier to similar demands of commercial greed, came to the Guaranty Building's rescue through the auspices of the Greater Buffalo Development Foundation, who established a task force to preserve the building. Their feasibility study determined that Buffalo needed such an office building in its very location, and that filling in the original light court of the U-shaped plan would increase the flexibility and enhancement of rental space. The renovation would include replacing the mechanical systems as well as restoring the rich and copiously ornamented exterior terra cotta skin.

Although much of the original terra cotta was still in excellent condition, there were pieces missing or badly damaged due to insensitive "modernizations," cleaning attempts through incompetent sandblasting techniques, and a damaging fire in the 1970's. Boston Valley Pottery, owned by artist Andrew Krause, was commissioned to fabricate all of the terra cotta replacement pieces from molds made of existing parts as well as photographic documentation. The elaborate capitals were the most challenging. Each replacement piece of the capital was hand-pressed by mold pressers, and hand-carving was required by sculptures to reproduce the three-dimensional undercuts and deep ornamentation of the original.

The Guaranty Building is the epitomy of Sullivan's theory of the tall office building, his concern with the glorification of height grounded in his tripartite philosophy of high rise design. Students and scholars of architectural history need to be able to experience this landmark building in its three dimensional reality. "And thus the design of the tall office building takes its place with all other architectural types made when architecture, as has happened once in many years, was a living art. Witness the Greek temple, the Gothic cathedral, the medieval fortress."[9]

THE BLAIR HOUSE

The renovation of the historic Blair House, Washington, D.C., (1988), was more than a design and decorating project for designers Mark Hampton (1940–) and Mario Buatta (1935–). They were faced with the demanding job of creating elegant and inviting presidential guest quarters while establishing a positive cultural image that reflected the very best qualities of the United States. The image of America as a melting pot of equality was expressed in the interiors by achieving formality without becoming pretentious, comfort without losing elegance, and variety without destroying unity.

The house was originally built by Dr. Joseph Lovell in 1824. It was sold in 1836 to Francis Preston Blair (1791–1876) and remained in the Blair family until 1942 when it was purchased by the U.S. government under the Franklin D. Roosevelt administration. Its close proximity to the White House across Pennsylvania Avenue made it an ideal location for the presidential guest house. Under President Nixon, two Victorian era houses were added to the complex. By the early 1980s it became evident that major architectural design and security changes were required. The functional plan between the four structures was awkward. In response to this, a wing was built as a connecting link for the complex. Complicating the design task was the requirement that security elements, such as a sprinkler system, bullet proof glass, and surveillance equipment, be discreetly integrated.

The intent of the design was to maintain a personal and idiosyncratic image of a gentleman's home, avoiding the impersonal qualities found in most hotels. By taking this more personal approach, the designers were able to focus on the warm and inviting charm found in America's best interiors, qualities that act as subtle messages in our foreign policy.

The Dillon Room is a beautiful composition of color and styles, related directly to the adjacent garden court. The influence of the garden is apparent in the color scheme of gold, rose, and green silk fabric, dramatically framing the French doors leading to the court. The walls of the room continue the garden motif with eighteenth-century Chinese handpainted wallpaper depicting an exotic landscape of flowering shrubs, trees, birds, and butterflies.

The oriental theme is expanded by employ-

INTERIOR VIEW OF DILLON ROOM, BLAIR HOUSE, WASHINGTON, D.C. BENJAMIN LATROBE, 1824. RENOVATED BY MARIO BUATTA, 1988.

The eclectic mix of this salon exemplifies a gentle conversation of design and artifacts amongst various cultures which constitute America. Photograph by Ogden Robertson, Hickey-Robertson.

ing Chinese tables, porcelains, and a strategically placed Bonsai plant, near the French doors. These doors are completed by a gilded camelback valance, encrusted with Louis XIV gold tassels. This robust element visually interrupts the serene classical crown molding, symbolic of ancient Greek democracy. Below the valance, a camelback Chippendale sofa in gold brocade, repeats the form, creating a dialogue between the French window treatment and the English seating. This interior is not only beautifully coordinated, but it contains discreet messages about America's cultural diversity and equality. The eclectic quality of the room creates a sense of America's history as a melting pot of many cultures.

BURNHAM'S UNION STATION

The symbolic gateway to America was created by D. H. Burnham (1846–1912): Union Station, Washington, D.C. (1903–1907). The realized design was a product of the City Beautiful movement, which sought to bring visual order to American cities. Classical architecture of ancient Greece and Rome was the model, epitomized by the 1893 World's Columbian Exposition, Chicago. Burnham was the director of construction

for this fair; through his influence, the layout and building facades featured the classical style of l'École des Beaux Arts, Paris.

Burnham's design for Union Station epitomized the Beaux Arts dictum by employing classical Roman motifs recalling the triumphal arch of Constantine the Great wedded to the barrel vaulted hall of the Baths of Diocletian. The station was sited on axis with the Capitol within a radiating plaza. This succession of relationships reinforced the concept of "gateway." Urban planning was as important to Burnham as the design of the station itself; his building deliberately related not only to the Capitol but to the larger plan of Washington, D.C.

Union Station was built when railroads were at their zenith. Because of its location as a funnel for visitors to the capital, the terminal became the "crossroad of the world." In 1948, eighty percent of the U.S. population traveled by train. By 1968 air travel accommodated more than eighty percent of the travelers. As a result, train schedules were reduced, decreasing passengers and revenue. Union Station went into a decline. Ideas to revitalize the building included a transportation museum, an ice rink, and a bowling alley. However, the structure was converted to a visitor's center

INTERIOR DETAIL OF HEADHOUSE, UNION STATION, WASHINGTON, D.C. DANIEL BURNHAM, 1901–1907. RESTORED BY HARRY WEESE AND ASSOCIATES, UNION STATION REDEVELOPMENT CORPORATION, AND UNION STATION VENTURE LTD., 1981–1988.

The powerful barrel vault of the headhouse recalls the past glory of ancient Roman basilicae and thermae, establishing a noble and grand space that earns its title of "gateway to America."
Photograph by John Kurtich.

for the Bicentennial, opening on July 4, 1976. After the Bicentennial, the station was used by fewer and fewer visitors. By 1980, the structure had fallen into such disrepair that it was closed to the public.

In 1981, Congress approved the Union Station Redevelopment Act, initiating the renovation and restoration of the building. Work on this project began in 1984 under the auspices of the Union Station Redevelopment Corporation, comprised of a team of developers, architects, railroad company executives, and government officials. A team of architects was selected for the project with Harry Weese & Associates in charge of restoration of the exterior and all historically significant interiors and Ben Thompson & Associates Inc. providing expertise on new commercial development, which would capture Burnham's original idea for the multiuse building.

Harry Weese & Associates was primarily responsible for restoring the Roman splendor of the headhouse, one of the grand interior spaces of Washington, D.C. This main hall originally had a marble floor, which was worn down over many years of use. The management eventually replaced this floor with a terrazzo covering. Much of the terrazzo was ripped up in 1976 to create a sunken court known as "The Pit" for the National Visitor Center. In restoring the space, "The Pit" was filled in, and the floor was returned to marble, duplicating the original key pattern of 24 inch white marble tiles with 6 inch red Vermont marble square corner dots.

The barrel vault of the headhouse suffered severe water damage due to leaking over the years. Burnham had used plaster extensively to minimize the cost of creating his classical detailing. Much plaster had to be replaced, and the new coffers were cast on site. Twenty-two-carat gold leaf was then applied by hand to the coffers. The walls below had twenty-two layers of paint. Paint scrapings were studied under a microscope to determine the original 1907 color scheme. Thirty-two statues of Roman mercenaries by Augustus Saint-Gaudens (1848–1907), which stood guard over the headhouse, were cleaned and renewed.

A major departure from a precise restoration was the construction of a double-level central kiosk in the center of the hall, flanked by two fountains. This structure obstructs the visual flow of the space, diminishing the experience of the visitor. It is an oversized blemish in the interior landscape that violates the grandness of Burnham's original concept.

Union Station continues to serve as the train terminus for the nation's capital. It is also a testament to the changing attitudes of the public toward restoration. The restoration of the building has brought it back into cultural and social importance. Burnham's original idea of a large, multiuse complex has been recreated with commercial multiuse relevant to the present era. Instead of Turkish baths and gymnasiums, the restored station has nine movie theatres and many shops. The revival of Union Station has heightened the activity and vitality of the surrounding neighborhood, once again establishing it as the gateway to America.

BANKS/EAKIN'S CLARIDGE HOTEL

The renovation of the Claridge Hotel, Chicago, by Banks/Eakin (1988–1990), was intended to transform a declining transient rooming house into a first-class hotel. It was originally built in the early 1930s as a men's boardinghouse in one of the most exclusive neighborhoods in Chicago. The fourteen-story edifice was l-shaped, with a concrete frame and brick infill. The original building facade was Mediterranean Revival, combining brick and glazed terra cotta. Years of neglect had left the terra cotta in disrepair and in danger of falling. In the 1960s, an attempt to respond to this problem resulted in replacing the first two floors by an expedient, unadorned, glazed brick, incompatible with the twelve stories above.

The architects were unable to restore the building to its former state due to poor maintenance, awkward alterations, and a modest budget. Further complicating the process, portions of the facade fell while under renovation, necessitating a complete removal of all the terra cotta pieces. The unexpected loss of key elements forced a revised renovation scheme creating a

EXTERIOR VIEW OF CLARIDGE HOTEL, CHICAGO, ILLINOIS. RENOVATED BY BANKS/EAKIN, 1990.

The canopy over the main entrance lures the visitor into the reception lobby with the promise of further elegance and unparalleled service. Photograph by Garret Eakin.

INTERIOR VIEW OF TYPICAL BEDROOM, CLARIDGE HOTEL, CHICAGO, ILLINOIS. RENOVATED BY BANKS/ EAKIN, 1990.

The canopied bed dominates the room, and the headboard recalls the inviting canopy of the main entrance to the hotel. Photograph by John Kurtich.

fresh image that echoed the *moderne* sophistication of the 1930s. The model for this theme was the limestone and black granite United States post offices of that era.

To transform the austere bureaucratic model into an appropriate image of hospitality, Banks/ Eakin designed the entrance to be an alluring and memorable experience. When approaching the building, guests are welcomed by a curvilinear canvas canopy stretched over a tubular metal frame, that softens the rectilinear limestone and granite facade. To accentuate the entrance, four pairs of illuminated columns establish a visual pathway from the exterior canopy to the interior lobby. The colonnade subtly converges on the central space, a square room with mahogany paneling containing the registration desk and elevators. The centrality of this space is marked by a star-patterned terrazzo floor and a round cove light above.

The guest rooms continue the 1930s motif and the new architectural vocabulary of the entrance. King-size beds are used and emphasized as the focal point and the primary purpose of the room. A three-dimensional development of the headboard recalls the shape of the entrance canopy while providing upholstered comfort. Concealed lighting, integrated with overdrapes and sheers, introduces an unexpected sense of space beyond. A multicolored, deep-toned, chintz fabric is used for the headboard drapes, bedspread, window and wall draping throughout the room. The abundance of this fabric produces a luxurious and sensuous atmosphere. Its rich color harmonizes with the dark mahogany furniture, echoing the lobby paneling and details. Swizzle-stick chandeliers and geometric chrome-and-plastic bedside lights complete the illusion and fantasy of the 1930s.

The fabrication of this illusion formed the design concept that was sympathetic to the original era of the hotel. Renovation brought new life to this decaying property, ultimately producing a unique hotel of unified quality.

The danger of renovating is insensitivity to or misinterpretation of the historic significance or architectural quality of an older building. The rejuvenation of the past offers an element of contrast that new construction can never duplicate. This contrast can be very powerful in creating unique and exciting architectural experiences. A well-executed renovation not only updates and improves the original use of an older building but also it preserves a valuable past.

MASTRO AND SKYLAR'S RESIDENCE

The renovation of vintage homes in older urban neighborhoods is a common undertaking during an era concerned with energy conservation,

health, and environmental issues. It is vital to the health of cities to preserve the buildings that frame their streets and define the unique quality of urban life. Pedestrian streets, lined with harmonious homes of various styles, softened by mature trees, creates an engaging atmosphere. Those drawn to the turn of the century Victorian street often fall in love with the houses that represent a lifestyle past.

Claudia Skylar (1951–) and James Mastro (1946–) had dreamed of living in a grand old Victorian on a quiet tree-lined street. Their dilapidated three-story wood frame structure required complete renovation. The basic form remained with a sensitive attachment of a wrap-around porch leading to an addition in the form of a huge bay window. The original floor plan was gutted in order to open up all the small Victorian rooms into more generous light-filled spaces.

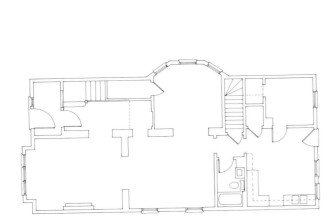

PLANS, BEFORE AND AFTER RENOVATION, MASTRO/SKYLAR KITCHEN, CHICAGO, ILLINOIS. MASTRO/SKYLAR ARCHITECTS, 1990.

A. BEFORE RENOVATION.

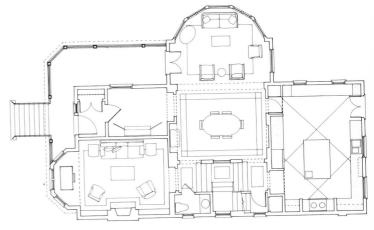

B. AFTER RENOVATION.

The new plan is a reflection of late twentieth century family needs within the original Victorian shell. Drawings by Julie Fisher.

Although the existing house had an original, but damaged, staircase adjacent to the entrance, as is common in Victorian homes, the architects built a new central stair. Not only did the skylit stair bring light into what was previously the darkest part of the plan, but it gave the large central space a focus and counterpoint to the new bay addition. Also, this plan eliminated any long corridors throughout the house.

The original three room kitchen was united by removing walls to create a simple rectangular space. The new kitchen is generous in scale, de-

VIEW OF MASTRO/SKYLAR KITCHEN AFTER RENOVATION, CHICAGO, ILLINOIS. MASTRO/SKYLAR ARCHITECTS, 1990.

The well executed kitchen takes full advantage of the Victorian proportions while integrating the latest domestic technologies. Photograph by Bill Arsenault.

signed to accommodate their monthly buffet dinners for fifty. A large granite-topped island, complete with sink and suspended lights, is perfect for the food display. The island design graciously allows uninterrupted circulation for the large parties. Two dishwashers and sinks make cleanup duty for more than two people efficient. The kitchen is focused on the idea of the hearth, where, in a large, tiled alcove, a unique English cast-iron stove, manufactured by Aga, radiates heat during the cooler seasons.

Opposite this metaphoric hearth, a built-in banquette serves as a breakfast area for the family. The granite-topped dining table is set on casters such that it may be wheeled up to the island for serving during parties.

The classic black and white checkerboard tile floors and backsplashes are given additional energy through the introduction of small strips of brightly colored tiles. The joyful tile patterns contrast the elegant two-tone maple cabinets that match the turquoise granite countertops. The color and material selection is successful functionally as well as aesthetically, producing a character that is at once quietly elegant and artfully assertive.

The sensitive renovation of older houses is an important ingredient to the refinement of urban lifestyles. The work affects families directly and offers unique possibilities of contrasting contemporary lifestyles within older structures in urban neighborhoods.

DREMMER'S KITCHEN COMPLEX FOR THE BLOCK RESIDENCE

The kitchen of a typical Victorian house in the nineteenth century was located at the rear of the dwelling; it consisted of a preparing and cooking area, with adjacent spaces for the maid's sleeping and bathing quarters, pantry, and eating area. In the kitchen renovation of the Block residence, Evanston, Illinois (1990), by Michele Dremmer (1949–   ), it was necessary to develop a spatial complex within the context of such a Victorian house that would allow a large, diverse family to be able to center their lives collectively and share their daily experiences through the ritual of dining. It was important to the family that the renovation recall and revitalize the concept of Victorian extravagance. Rich textures, opulent materials, and grand spaces were developed to express this ideal metaphorically, using late twentieth century technology to achieve this end result.

Functionally, the original separate spaces of food preparation, food storage, eating, and maid's quarters were opened up by removing some of the walls that defined these spaces. The idea was to have an openness and flow of space from the new kitchen to the adjacent dining area as well as a new family room, featuring a large, newly constructed extended bay window. The final spatial complex generates a feeling of grandness due to the original, high Victorian ceilings (eleven feet), the generous amount of natural light from the new bay, and the rich materials and textures employed in the renovation.

The Blocks did not want an authentically restored Victorian kitchen, but a contemporary one that contained state-of-the-art appliances, gadgets, conveniences, and storage innovations. Dremmer chose a black and white color scheme to reinforce the high tech drama of the room: high gloss white lacquer cabinets, countertops of speckled black and gray granite, back splashes of slate gray high gloss ceramic tile, matte textural flecked gray vinyl floor, and white walls and ceiling. The setting is accented with contemporary, stainless steel hanging light fixtures above the island and the counter top eating bar. Stainless steel trim and hardware accessories achieve a sparkling opulence to the ensemble, metaphorically connecting this kitchen to Victorian ideals of rich materials and textures for contemporary domestic interiors. The Blocks' kitchen successfully expresses their attitude about the importance of this part of the house. "What food is to the body the kitchen should be to the home. Indeed, as Brillat-Savarin has said, 'Tell me what you eat and I will tell you what you are; so one may say, 'Show me the kitchen and I can form a good idea of the home' "[10]

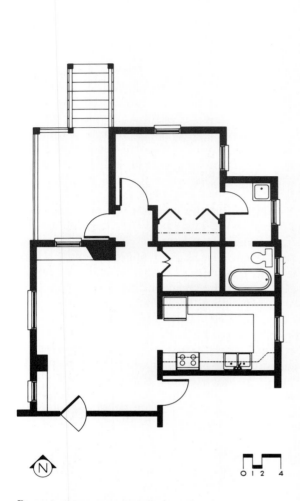

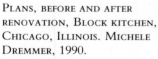

PLANS, BEFORE AND AFTER
RENOVATION, BLOCK KITCHEN,
CHICAGO, ILLINOIS. MICHELE
DREMMER, 1990.

A. BEFORE RENOVATION.

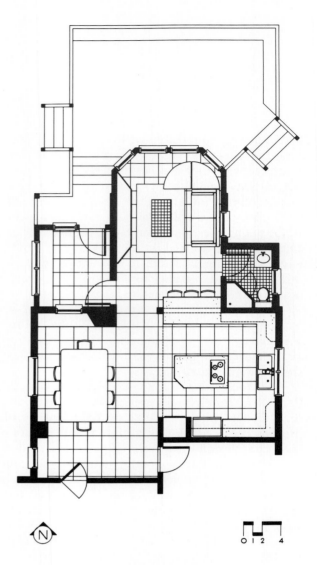

B. AFTER RENOVATION.

The original servant-oriented Victorian kitchen was renovated to accommodate centralized family activities. Drawing by Michael Sligar.

VIEW OF BLOCK KITCHEN AFTER
RENOVATION, CHICAGO, ILLINOIS.
MICHELE DREMMER, 1990.

The open integration of kitchen, dining, and family room creates an informal and cohesive atmosphere for the family. Photograph by John Kurtich.

Adaptive Reuse

BOOTH/HANSEN'S HELENE CURTIS HEADQUARTERS

Successful adaptive reuse depends on the sensitivity of the designer, coupled with the willingness of the client to integrate original elements of a building with spatial and other physical requirements of changed usage. The Helene Curtis Industries Corporate Headquarters, Chicago, Illinois (1985), exemplifies the successful adaptation of an architecturally neutral 1914 brick warehouse transformed into a high quality corporate administrative center with image-enhancing urban visibility.

The project was designed by Booth/Hansen & Associates with William Ketcham (1951–   ) as the project architect. The client chose the building it wished to transform first, then found the designer who could carry out the transformation. The client wanted to create a new image and had definite feelings about the city and urban fabric that needed to be expressed in the building. This particular building was well located in terms of proximity to the Chicago Loop and to major public transportation. It was also highly visible, situated on the north bank of the Chicago River, facing the Loop. The building was structurally sound, having originally been a warehouse, and quite neutral in appearance, ripe for transformation.

The interior design concept for a typical office floor was to create a microcosm of Chicago itself. Due to the existing 18-by-20-foot column spacing, a grid was established as an analogue of the city's grid. Boundaries of the center city downtown area of the office floor were defined by private offices and their adjacent secretarial areas, which were located at the north and south ends of the floor. Manager workstations were designed around the central columns and created the "Loop". A conference room was placed in the center of the workstations area and became the "public plaza."

The development of the workstation provided the designer with a three-dimensional visual motif that was then used throughout other parts

EXTERIOR VIEW OF HELENE CURTIS INDUSTRIES CORPORATE HEADQUARTERS, CHICAGO, ILLINOIS. FORMERLY A BRICK WAREHOUSE, 1914. RENOVATED BY BOOTH/ HANSEN & ASSOCIATES, 1985.

This is an example of taking an old, architecturally insignificant loft warehouse structure and giving it a new, Cinderella-like transformation as headquarters for a major corporation of glamour products. Photograph by John Kurtich.

of the building. The existing columns were sheathed in oversized capitals in the shape of inverted pyramids, springing from the column shaft seven feet from the floor. These capitals provided large reflective surfaces from which special lighting fixtures on the column shaft could indirectly light the entire space. The hollow interior of the capital allowed the electrical conduit to be bent from the ceiling to the floor, avoiding the necessity of junction boxes. Thus, the columns became the principal sources of light and power. Around each column, built-in furniture was then designed for the workstations themselves.

The lowered ceilings were discontinuous, allowing easy access without the necessity of removable panels. These reflective horizontal planes of acoustical tiles could be considered analogous to "clouds" over the urban landscape.

The building was crowned with a new penthouse, which focused on a central double-height boardroom surrounded by smaller conference rooms, the president's office, and executive offices. The penthouse became a green glass box, corresponding to the same tinted glass used throughout the rest of the building. The effect of this was as though a glass-skinned building within the brick shell of the original building had popped its roof and was coexisting as an interwoven presence of a new building with the old. The oval shape of the boardroom made a strong geometric statement above the existing traditional architrave of the building.

The relationship between client and architect was unusually close and trusting. The client wanted quality as well as visual expression and worked very closely with the designer. Such involvement and interest on the part of the client was not unlike that of the great patrons of art and architecture during the Renaissance in Italy. This allowed the development and refinement of the architectural solution to satisfy both the creative demands of the designer and the practical needs of the client. Because the client had bought the building prior to its occupation, the designer could present full-scale mock-ups of columnar workstations in their correct context for thorough testing and approval of the client. Various colors of tinted glass were respectively installed in test windows of the front facade which then could be viewed from across the river in a full-scale, actual environmental condition. The result of this close relationship between designer and client is a successful transformation of an ordinary older building into an elegant, urbane corporate headquarters.

INTERIOR VIEW OF TYPICAL OFFICE FLOOR, HELENE CURTIS INDUSTRIES CORPORATE HEADQUARTERS, CHICAGO, ILLINOIS. FORMERLY A BRICK WAREHOUSE, 1914. RENOVATED BY BOOTH/HANSEN & ASSOCIATES, 1985.

A view of the office floor reveals the columns as central generators of built-in workstations as well as the source of light and power. Photograph by Nick Merrick, Hedrich-Blessing.

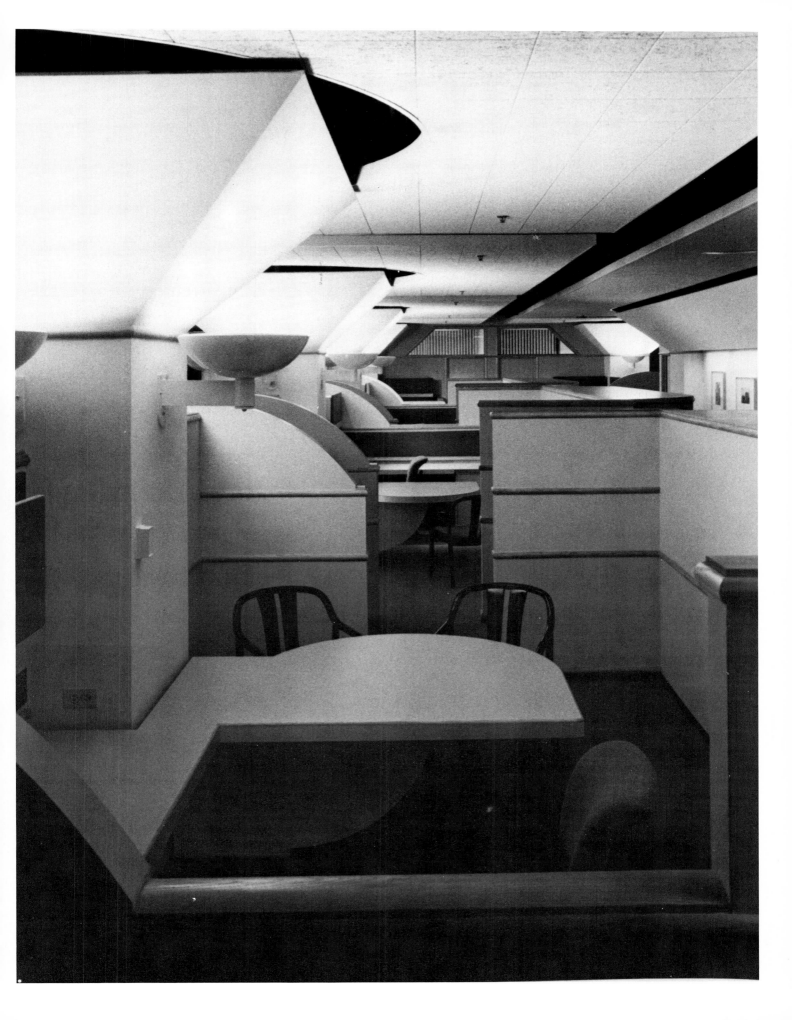

HELLMUTH, OBATA & KASSABAUM'S UNION STATION AT ST. LOUIS

The Union Station of St. Louis, Missouri, is one of the biggest rehabilitation and adaptive reuse projects to be completed in the country (1985). Not only has the main station building or headhouse been restored to its former Romanesque glory of 1894, but the transitional area known as the "midway" (between the headhouse and train shed) and the train shed itself have been transformed into an urban environment of nearly 150 retail stores and a new hotel.

The headhouse was designed by Theodore C. Link (1850–1923) in 1891. Louis Millet (1855–1923) who had previously worked for Louis Sul-

INTERIOR VIEW OF HEADHOUSE, UNION STATION, ST. LOUIS, MISSOURI. THEODORE C. LINK, WITH INTERIOR DECORATION BY LOUIS MILLET, 1891–1894. RESTORED AND RENOVATED BY HELLMUTH, OBATA & KASSABAUM, 1985.

The richly decorated barrel vault uses light and color to increase the perception of height of the vault as well as the depth of the shallow balcony spaces on the perimeter. Photograph by John Kurtich.

livan on the interior of the Chicago Auditorium Building and the interior of the Chicago Stock Exchange Trading Room, was then working for Link. Millet was responsible for the interior of the Grand Hall, the original central waiting room of the station building. This space measured 76 feet by 120 feet with a 65-foot-high barrel vault ceiling. It was richly colored, dramatizing the electrical illumination, which was new for the period.

Timothy Samuelson (1951–), a Millet scholar from the Commission on Chicago Landmarks, was the principal consultant for historic restoration. Through careful research, he learned that the original color of the Grand Hall was considered by Millet as an integrated scheme to enhance the architectural space and to complement the lighting design. Millet developed his color so that it progressed through the space in a rotational manner of changing lightness and hue. He used color to increase the appearance of height of the barrel vault by lightening the color as it approached the apex. A contrasting color (blue to contrast with the yellow and green of the main hall) was employed to visually increase the depth of very shallow balcony spaces occurring on the perimeter of the hall. The color used in the hall itself was very complicated. First, the walls had a base coat of yellow. Then a transparent glazing liquid of green was applied and wiped down at strategic places in the design to create a gradual rotation of color change through varying lightness and hue. Research for this complicated procedure was difficult because the hall had been painted over in a solid color about a decade after the building had been finished. Black and white photographs of the hall immediately after it had been completed did not accurately document the lights and darks of the color due to limitations of the film and photographic technology of the period.

In restoring the Grand Hall, not only was attention paid to the original concept of color but also how it was illuminated. It was very important to reinstall all electrical fixtures with bulbs of correct filaments of the period because of the color light they produced. Millet had chosen colors that compensated for the warm glow of early twentieth century electrical lights. The Grand Hall became the primary lobby-lounge of the headhouse hotel, located above in the renovated original terminal hotel.

There are basically three parts to this complex: the headhouse, which fronts Market Street as a monumental Romanesque building; the midway, which connects the headhouse to the train shed; and the train shed covered with its original butterfly trusses. The midway was adapted to an intense pedestrian area of kiosks for fast food, novelties, and sundries. The train shed is the dominant space in the complex, covering eleven and one half acres. The late Victorian truss roof was respected by avoiding any new construction that would detract from the floating appearance of the roof. The trusses were painted terra cotta to relate to the red roof of the Romanesque headhouse and visually couple the two together. The adaptive reuse of the area successfully mixes the new contemporary needs with existing historical fixtures, accommodating over one hundred retail shops and food services under one roof, sharing the space with a second 480-room garden hotel and a small lake.

ESHERICK, HOMSEY, DODGE & DAVIS'S MONTEREY BAY AQUARIUM

The Monterey Bay Aquarium (1985) was designed to replace most of an existing, but dilapidated, cannery on the seafront of Monterey Bay, California. The new building preserves the open, factorylike style of the original building complex, the old Hovden Cannery, the largest of any in Cannery Row.

The original concept was to convert the Hovden Cannery into a modest aquarium, but the existing building condition would not allow such simple recycling. With a $40 million gift from David and Lucile Packard, a new aquarium was possible. The architectural firm of Esherick, Homsey, Dodge & Davis of San Francisco was commissioned to design the new facility, and they preserved and restored the parts of the original cannery that were feasible, adding new construction that preserves the feeling of the cannery but

allows state-of-the-art technology to produce the largest and most innovative exhibit aquarium in the country. Ironically, the original fish processing facility was transformed into a complex that displays, protects, and preserves the unique marine life of Monterey Bay.

The 1916 pumphouse and warehouse were restored and integrated into the new design. Original boilers were refitted, preserving the flavor of the cannery operation. Industrial fittings were used throughout the new construction, and all air ducts and water pipes were exposed.

The most innovative idea about the building was that it responds directly to the cycles of nature, the Pacific Ocean. It is a four-dimensional design that celebrates the complex marine life of the central California coast (see Chapter 4). Sensitivity to preserving the original character was paramount; yet interjection of a more positive view of marine life shaped the thrust of this adaptive reuse. The giant kelp forest exhibit has a cathedral aura, with a dynamic created by a specially invented surge machine. The building complex brings the exhibition of Monterey Bay sea life to a dramatic state of art, emulating what a diver would see below water.

SCHROEDER'S COBBLER SQUARE

Cobbler Square, Chicago, is an example of creative adaptive reuse of an older, historic building complex. Kenneth A. Schroeder (1943–) adapted an interconnected group of thirty-two buildings, whose history spanned the years between 1880 and 1965, into 297 rental apartments. The original buildings were first a factory for Western Wheel Works, a bicycle manufacturer, then they became the factory complex for Dr. William Scholl, famous for shoes and foot care products. Scholl, Inc., moved out of the complex in 1981, leaving a mixed collection of buildings, which did not seem promising in their existing form.

Richard Perlman decided that there might be an interesting opportunity to develop this complex for an urban residential facility. He commissioned Schroeder to adapt the buildings into rental apartments. Because the building complex occupied such a deep site, Schroeder developed a design concept based on the "deep plan." This resulted in long, narrow units cleverly arranged about several "courtyard cases," another design concept that permitted natural light and air to

penetrate into the middle of the complex. The original building complex had no courtyards but did have an alley system. Schroeder created courtyards by demolishing noncontributing buildings.

Cobbler Square has a primary entrance on Wells Street, which gives it a single identity. A three-story commercial facade is split in the middle with a symmetrical atrium surrounded by a bold, steel-framed skylight. This purposefully overstated entrance is the strongest example of Schroeder's architectural "weaving" technique where he combines some original building elements with new ones. The observer can still pick out each distinctive piece, but the total effect is integrated.

As one moves through the entrance and into the atrium spine, there begins in the appearance of the building a gradual surrender to the context of existing reality. Instead of weaving the old and the new, Schroeder creates a collage effect, where elements of the existing factory are in more startling juxtaposition with new elements. The first major piece of "archaeology" is expressed just off this atrium walkway, where one finds the pre-served ruin of the oldest boiler house of the factory.

A second boiler house is partially preserved in the large southwest courtyard toward the rear of the complex. This represents a modified ruin, a piece of the past that has been integrated into a fountain complex for the courtyard's focus.

Another type of archaeological fragment, the ruin as void, is found in a tight auxiliary courtyard off the smaller northwest courtyard. This was created by removing an existing elevator and stair from the factory building and opening up that part of the complex to accommodate the "deep plan" concept.

Exterior steel walkways were added to the entire complex. They were painted bright red-orange to deliberately contrast with the original brick walls of the factory. The decision to use the steel walkways was to make more square footage available for rental apartments. The walkways were not merely dreamed up to achieve extra interior space but were derived from existing bridges built to span the original alley system of the complex.

The concept of collage is also used in the apartments. The frame of the building can be read distinctly. The ceilings are original and are exposed to display their structural integrity and simplicity. In smaller apartments a strip kitchen unit is installed to maximize the living space. Altogether there are fifty plan types in the nearly three hundred available apartments of the complex. This is an extraordinary amount of variety when compared to a contemporary high rise of a similar total number of apartments providing only three or four plan types.

BOOTH/HANSEN'S NORTH PIER

Unlike the complex of various buildings that comprise Cobbler Square, North Pier, Chicago, Illinois (1988), is a single, simple building form that has been transformed into retail and office space. It was built in 1906 as an exhibition center and warehouse for furniture and other products. The seven story masonry and heavy timber structure was situated on the Ogden Slip overlooking the Chicago River. For the first time, the city had

capitalized on the latent potential of its riverfront. It was originally 120 feet wide by 1,663 feet long until construction of Lake Shore Drive in the 1930s reduced the length to 630 feet. The architect, Christian Albert Eckstrom, designed the utilitarian building employing heavy mill construction with solid masonry exterior walls. North Pier was modulated by traverse brick walls defining fire compartments, complete with elevators and fire stairs. The south side, facing Ogden Slip, accommodated large cargo vessels. The north side, facing Illinois Street, provided truck loading docks. Adjacent railroad tracks provided additional freight handling. The site was a hub of commercial activity.

The building's interior was composed of heavy timber columns in a twelve foot grid, crowned by cast-iron capitals, supporting solid wooden beams, running north-south. The beautiful wood ceiling that spans between these beams was constructed of 3 inch by 6 inch joists, continuously nailed together. This unique feature not only made the structure very strong but imbued the building with a sturdy, rugged character. The

Exterior view of North Pier, Chicago, Illinois. Formerly a warehouse by Christian Albert Eckstorm, 1906. Renovated by Booth/Hansen and Associates, 1989.

The rehabilitation of this large commercial warehouse has revitalized this part of Chicago, bringing a variety of retail, entertainment, and institutional activities. Photograph by John Kurtich.

solid quality of the structure and its unique location along the river were of primary interest to the adaptive reuse developer and architect.

The developer, Robert Meers of Broadacre Management Company, envisioned the project to be a meeting place for the city at the river's edge. He met the challenge of preserving this historic structure by maintaining its architectural integrity while making the necessary modernizations. The lower three floors contained 180,000 square feet of retail, cultural, and restaurant space. On the remaining levels, 260,000 square feet of loft office was realized. A high-rise apartment tower was built along the east perimeter of the building.

By adding glassy galleria structures, crowning the elevator towers with pyramidal copper roofs, clipping on steel entrance canopies, and embellishing the ground floor fenestration, the architects transformed the austere exterior into an engaging people-oriented building. The detailing of these clipped-on steel and glass elements created a vocabulary that was sympathetic with the original warehouse aesthetic. Fabricated steel plate and exposed fasteners with a painted finish provided a rich layer of ornamentation contrasting the brick exterior.

This language of ornamentation established on the exterior was the basis for the detailing of the interior architecture. Every effort was made to create a consistency from inside to out and to avoid the predictability of detailing found in most shopping centers. Nowhere to be found were extruded aluminum storefronts, quarry tile floors, acoustic tile ceilings, ubiquitous rental planting, backlit plastic signage, and banal chain stores. However, it is not unlike the typical shopping center in its overall plan with double-loaded stores facing the linear mall, a central atrium with circulation, and major magnets at either end. Therefore, the proven, successful formula has been employed, yet the overall experience has been transformed.

This transformation was made possible by the sensitive and consistent use of materials to augment the existing heavy timber construction. The stamped metal tile floors embedded in concrete achieve the feeling of a nineteenth century industrial walking surface while providing a non-slip, cleanable finish. At random locations, a cookie-cutter stamp of the North Pier logo is inserted, providing a tertiary detail and a modest surprise of identification.

Vertical surfaces were developed with precision, expressing the joinery. Handrails were a combination of lacquered brushed steel, cast-iron connectors, flat plate stanchions, stainless steel cables, bolts, and polished ball bearings. The union of these components established a nautical reference to the river commerce of the nineteenth century. This theme was further elaborated by the flat steel plate stair stringers with their wavelike forms. Perforated metal was employed in the stair risers to visually lighten and further accentuate the parts.

INTERIOR DETAIL OF STAIR, NORTH PIER, CHICAGO, ILLINOIS. FORMERLY A WAREHOUSE BY CHRISTIAN ALBERT ECKSTORM, 1906. RENOVATED BY BOOTH/HANSEN AND ASSOCIATES, 1989.

The details were carefully planned to maintain consistency with the original materials and construction techniques. Photograph by John Kurtich.

Perforated metal, butt-glazed plate glass, and Herculite doors comprised the minimalist storefronts. Carefully controlled suspended signage at each store entrance became the counterpoint to the uniformity created by the interior corridor. The pedestrian scaled signs, each unique yet designed by the same firm, add personality to one's experience of the mall. The language of the signage is composed of a collage of various materials designed to distinctly express the character of the shops.

At the center, relieving the long, narrow shopping mall, a huge circular three-story space was literally carved out of the rectilinear column and beam structure. This space was conceived as the hub of activities, a gathering place creating a grand transition from Illinois Street to the Ogden Slip. Curvilinear stairs connected the three levels, visually creating movement with these dynamic forms. The lower level was designed for dining and entertainment surrounded by food vendors. Crowning the grand space was a colossal illuminated clock, which further animated the interior, defining its centrality. On the hour, the clock sets

off a series of mechanical events. Bells ring, balls roll down a chute to trip a hammer, chimes resonate, flags spin, and lights flash, all to the surprise and delight of the people. The holistic approach to developing the interior architecture has created a dynamic, urbane example of successful adaptive reuse.

NATIONAL BUILDING MUSEUM, WASHINGTON, D.C.

The National Building Museum, Washington, D.C., was established by Congress in 1980 to honor and celebrate architecture and building in the United States and provide a means of presenting and educating the public about the human-built environment. The museum is situated in the Pension Building, a historic structure that dominates Judiciary Square in central Washington, D.C.

Designed in 1881 by Montgomery C. Meigs (1816–1892), the Pension Building was originally built to house the Pension Bureau in an office complex where each bureaucrat would be able to

GREAT HALL, NATIONAL BUILDING
MUSEUM, WASHINGTON D.C.
FORMERLY THE PENSION BUILDING
DESIGNED BY MONTGOMERY C.
MEIGS, 1881–1887. RENOVATED BY
COOPER-LECKY, ARCHITECTS, 1981–
1983, AND KEYES CONDON FLORANCE
WITH GIORGIO CAVAGLIERI,
ARCHITECTS, 1984–1988.

*This magnificent space was inspired by
the Italian Renaissance palace plan
where surrounding rooms, each
connected with a continuous arcaded
loggia, would open out into a central
area. The Corinthian columns
supporting the central arches are thought
to be the world's tallest. Photograph by
John Kurtich.*

work in a space filled with natural light and ventilation. This was accomplished by designing the offices around a central, covered court, called the Great Hall, measuring 316 feet by 116 feet, 159 feet high at the peak of the pitched roof. Adapting the Italian Renaissance palazzo as the model, the Great Hall featured a large fountain centered between two colonnades of colossal Corinthian columns, constructed out of brick and painted to resemble Siena marble.

The exterior of the building features a terra cotta frieze that wraps around its entire perimeter. Reminiscent of the Parthenon frieze, this band of sculpture, created by Caspar Buberl (1834–1889), presents a procession of Civil War military units: infantry, cavalry, artillery, quartermaster corps, medical corps, and the navy. The strong *bas relief* captures a life-like animation, influenced by Eadweard Muybridge's motion-study photographs of animals which Meigs sent to Burberl in order that the sculptor achieve accurate motion representation in his frieze.

The Pension Bureau occupied the building between 1885–1926. The building was then occupied by several government agencies from 1926 until 1980, when Congress named it to become the location of the newly established National Building Museum. Cooper-Lecky, architects, were hired to do preliminary planning of the Pension Building's adaptive reuse and design the rehabilitation of the roof, from 1981–1983. The Washington architectural firm of Keyes Condon Florance and associate architect Giorgio Cavaglieri of New York continued and completed the renovation between 1984–1988.

The roof was the most immediate problem facing the restorers. After leaks had been stopped, a new roof of lightweight concrete panels replaced the old, using the original purlins. The exterior surface was covered with a layer of stainless steel, coated to resemble weathered copper.

The renovation remained faithful to Meigs's original interior design by keeping the Great Hall open. Various rooms peripheral to the Great Hall were converted into galleries. The original casement windows had to be reconstructed. The mechanical and electrical systems were replaced.

Appropriate color for the interior was very important to the renovation. The Corinthian columns had originally been marbleized to represent continuous shafts of Siena marble; their capitals were bronzed in such a way as to achieve a lighter cast on the edges of the acanthus leaves, giving more life and depth to this ornate order. The color

of the columns of the lower arcade were more problematic to restore. Physical analysis revealed that the first layer of paint was a dark red. Photographic records suggested a metallic reflectivity in the columns, such as bronze. The final choice was made on the basis of late twentieth century taste: bronze won over the dark red, which was considered "ugly" by the aesthetic standards of the restorers.

The mandate of the National Building Museum "is to encourage the public to take part in the on-going debate over what relationship our society should establish between the built and natural environments."[11]

THE ROOKERY, CHICAGO, ILLINOIS

The Rookery, Chicago, Illinois, by Burnham and Root (1888), was considered the largest and most costly office structure completed to date, at one-and-a-half million dollars. The eleven story structure employed masonry exterior bearing walls

EXTERIOR DETAIL OF FRIEZE, NATIONAL BUILDING MUSEUM, WASHINGTON D. C. FORMERLY THE PENSION BUILDING DESIGNED BY MONTGOMERY C. MEIGS, 1881–1887. RENOVATED BY COOPER-LECKY, ARCHITECTS, 1981–1983, AND KEYES CONDON FLORANCE WITH GIORGIO CAVAGLIERI, ARCHITECTS, 1984–1988.

The procession of Civil War military units featured in this long, white terra cotta frieze stands out vividly against the red brick of the building proper. Photograph by John Kurtich.

INTERIOR VIEW OF RESTORED TWO-STORY ENTRANCE LOBBY, THE ROOKERY, CHICAGO, ILLINOIS. BURNHAM AND ROOT, 1885–1888. REMODELED BY FRANK LLOYD WRIGHT, 1905. RESTORED AND RENOVATED BY THOMAS M. HARBOE OF McCLIER, 1991–1992.

This space had been totally destroyed in the intervening years of the early-to-mid twentieth century, where incompetent remodelings disintegrated the original spatial sequence from the street to the central light court. Photograph by John Kurtich.

with a modern cast iron interior frame. The heavy
masonry exterior belies the bright and elegant interior. A central court was carved into the cubicle
building form, flooding the interior with light and
air. This simple act of contrasting a dark, rugged
exterior with a light, delicate interior resulted in a
compelling sense of arrival.

In 1905, Frank Lloyd Wright (1867–1959) remodeled the first floor spaces. Wright clad the
original cast iron structure with white marble and
replaced some of the ornamental iron with a simpler geometric design. Root's electroliers were replaced by planters. Suspended pendant light
fixtures were integrated to brighten the central
space.

In 1930, William E. Drummond (1876–1946)
updated the public spaces, adversely affecting
Burnham & Root's original concept. The two-
story entry vestibule was eliminated to gain leas-
able space. The elevators were "modernized,"
eliminating the open grills. A restrained Art Deco
style, ignoring the sensibility of the original concept, was employed. Finally, in the 1940's, the
building management covered over the glass sky-

Interior view of court lobby
after renovation, The Rookery,
Chicago, Illinois. Burnham and
Root, 1885–1888. Remodeled by
Frank Lloyd Wright, 1905.
Restored and renovated by
Thomas M. Harboe of McClier,
1991–1992.

*With the skylight restored to its 1905
glory, fully uncovered but made
waterproof, the light court is truly the
interior focal point of the building again.
Photograph by John Kurtich.*

light of the central court with tar paper and paint to curtail the constant leakage problems.

Burnham & Root's original concept was a spatial journey in which one experienced a series of contrasting urban and architectural spaces. The monolithic building, built of dark red rusticated granite and brick, was entered via the shaded canyon of La Salle Street. Frank Lloyd Wright continued this concept with the building's elegantly scaled white and gold-incised marble-cladded two-story vestibule. This space led directly to the compressed elevator lobby with its coffered mar-

ble ceiling. The sequence terminated upon entering the grandly scaled central court. The delicate gold detail patterns in the column and beam cladding harmonized with the intricate iron roof structure and glazing grills. A dramatic central stair announced the vertical axis of the building leading to a mezzanine surrounded by shops. Opposing the stair at the mezzanine level was the symmetrical wings of the oriel stair which accessed all the typical office floors.

The restoration architect, Thomas M. Harboe (1955–   ) of McClier, working for the

INTERIOR DETAIL OF COURT LOBBY,
THE ROOKERY, CHICAGO, ILLINOIS.
BURNHAM AND ROOT, 1885–1888.
REMODELED BY FRANK LLOYD
WRIGHT, 1905. RESTORED AND
RENOVATED BY THOMAS M. HARBOE
OF McCLIER, 1991–1992.

*This detail has been preserved to record
and display the original Burnham and
Root materials in contrast to the
subsequent Frank Lloyd Wright
remodeling in 1905. Photograph by
John Kurtich.*

tion was fixed at 1910, which would embrace
Wright's renovation but exclude Drummond's alterations. The architects used Burnham & Root's
original construction drawings, Wright's marble
shop drawings, and period photographs as primary sources for the reconstruction work. Even
with this information at hand, the preservationist
faced a multitude of complex decisions regarding
the work of three separate architects.

Traversing Drummond's entrance into
Wright's lobby into Drummond's elevator lobby
into Wright's and Burnham & Root's light court
was a disjointed spatial experience. The architects
were well aware of this complex problem and
through mixing and matching of details created a
balanced composition. Burnham & Root's original marble mosaic floor pattern was to be rebuilt.
A portion of the original floor remains adjacent to
a column below the oriel stair. A section of
Wright's marble column cladding was removed,
exposing Burnham & Root's cast iron structure,
left as an "interpretative corner." The two entrance vestibules were returned to Wright's original design by heavily relying on the marble shop
drawings. The La Salle Street vestibule and the
Adams Street lobby were opened up to two stories, new stairs installed and clad with the patterned white marble. The symmetrical La Salle
vestibule contained twin stairs with a decidedly
horizontal expression. The elevator bank in the
Adams lobby was removed in order to improve
the floor plan. To retain the original design, only
the wall and the door grills were replicated.
Frosted glass was set behind the grill to give an
illusion of depth. Thereby, the original entry sequence was reestablished.

To alleviate the leakage problems inherent in
the hundreds of small glazing panels in the skylight of the central court, a new, additional skylight was installed on the eleventh floor. This
solved the original technical problem while maintaining the spirit of the space. In addition, the
original heavy sashes on the typical office floors
were maintained by routing deeper reveals to accept new double glazing. The store fronts had
been replaced at least three times. Working from
old photographs and a surviving original bay,
new store fronts were cast in aluminum. With

owner, the Baldwin Development Company,
was faced with a challenge. He wanted to return
the building to a "Class A" office status while
restoring the structure. The date for this restora-

these subtle alterations to the exterior, the building was "modernized" without changing the original architectural character or details.

Summary

Preserving older buildings is one of the most direct links to the sense of the past. The most effective way for society to connect its present generation with the past is by exposure to the rich collage of history represented through art, literature, science, and architecture. Architecture is the least abstract of these accomplishments, making it the most immediate and accessible. Part of Interior Architecture is stimulating the imagination with the intimate display of how past generations lived. Imagining former times encourages humans to have confidence in the future.

Cities need old buildings so badly it is probably impossible for vigorous streets and districts to grow without them. By old buildings I mean not museum-piece old buildings, not old buildings in an excellent and expensive state of rehabilitation—although these make fine ingredients—but also a good lot of plain, ordinary, low-value old buildings, including some rundown old buildings.[12]

Returning older buildings to their original dignity requires a sensitivity to careful historical research and the discipline to carry it through. Buildings are built to provide shelter for the human activities. The resultant interior spaces contain a visual record of architectural styles, providing some of the most important educational lessons for the practitioners of Interior Architect.

Painstaking concentration is required to sensitively restore historic architecture. The preservationist often times works behind the scenes, receiving little credit. These custodians of historical style and culture must suppress their egos in order to objectively research and realize a true picture of the past. All restoration or renovation projects have problem areas to be solved: lost records, drawings or photographs; conflicting documentation; multiple historic remodelings of the same space; destruction of original components through insensitive remodeling; essential modernization. These problems create difficult choices which must be researched, debated, and tested for viability. They must be weighed for historic appropriateness.

Some of these problems have to be solved through new design. Designers facing the responsibility of replacing missing components in historic structures must avoid the temptation to transform themselves into the reincarnation of the original architects or designers. New design calls for a disciplined, educated, and appropriate creativity.

NOTES

1. When Paul Revere's house, Boston, was restored in 1900, no records were kept concerning existing conditions prior to the restoration as well as information concerning restoration decisions.

2. David A. Hanks, *The Decorative Designs of Frank Lloyd Wright* (New York: E. P. Dutton, 1979), p. 77.

3. Brendan Gill, *Many Masks: A Life of Frank Lloyd Wright* (New York: Ballantine Books, 1987), p. 138.

4. Thomas W. Sweeney, "Frank Lloyd Wright's Dana-Thomas House Restored," *Historic Preservation News*, September, 1990, pp. 1–2.

5. Frederick D. Nichols and James A. Bear, Jr., *Monticello: A Guidebook* (Monticello: Thomas Jefferson Memorial Foundation, 1982), p. 14.

6. The front door on Prairie Avenue was original; its wood, glass, wrought iron, and lock were the very same that were originally installed in 1886. Edwin Johnson of Chicago, Illinois, was contracted to restore the woodwork of the house, including the doors. Because the Prairie Avenue door was fifty-six inches wide, it required three men to remove it in order to restore it. The process consisted of stripping the wood, cleaning it thoroughly, re-staining, sanding, wiping down, and finishing with a good quality polyurethane.

7. Mariana Griswold VanRensselaer, *Henry Hobson Richardson and His Works* (New York: Dover Publications, 1969), p. 114.

8. Louis H. Sullivan, *Kindergarten Chats and Other Writings* (New York: Dover Publications, 1979), pp. 206–207.

9. Ibid., p. 208.

10. Earl Lifshey, *The Housewares Story* (Chicago: National Housewares Manufacturers Association, 1973), p. 128.

11. National Building Museum brochure (Washington, D.C.: National Building Museum).

12. Jane Jacobs, *The Death and Life of Great American Cities* (New York: Random House, 1961), p. 187.

ESCALATOR ROTUNDA, CRATE AND
BARREL, CHICAGO, ILLINOIS.
SOLOMON, CORDWELL AND BUENZ,
1990.

Photograph by John Kurtich.

CHAPTER 9

STYLE: EXPRESSION OF CULTURE

Interior Architecture practitioners are trained to imagine in three dimensions how their design decisions will perform and how the style will fare in the future. They look into their drawings and models, imagining movement of people, the quality of light, or a detail of a room. They consider how the materials will wear and how difficult they will be to clean. Their love of good design tells them one thing while their practical side counters. Interior Architecture demands a balance between the often opposing elements of aesthetics and function. Overly designed elements can become trendy and short-lived whereas highly functional solutions can be boring and inhuman. So those practicing Interior Architecture struggle in their imaginations with the future, trying to see the truth. The test of time will certainly be passed, yet they must wait.

Through direct experience and knowledge of history, Interior Architecture practitioners slowly improve at predicting the future. Their judgements become more educated as they gain experience. They build and store various experiences all their lives to achieve credibility. Credible individuals have tremendous value to society because through their creative work they reveal the future. The success of many organizations and institutions is based on being first or ahead of the competition. These successful artists, designers, and architects are looked to for leadership.

Filmmakers have always been interested in the stylistic imagery of the future as subject matter. The subject is intriguing, filled with fantasy and fear. Films such as *A Clockwork Orange, 2001: A Space Odyssey,* and *Brazil* are intriguing examples of peering into the unknown future. These multimillion dollar motion pictures with the best cinematography, special effects artists, and creative directors have become the standard format for science fiction. Film is the best medium available to transform humanity through time and space.

In the 1985 film, *Brazil,* directed by Terry Gilliam, the viewer experiences a spectacular dramatization of a future society. The setting is within a technologically advanced urban environment that in many ways is an extension of the current era. Although it is highly theatrical, it is thought provoking because the scenes are based on present reality. For example, the sound volume is purposely raised to give the audience a sense of what the noise level will be like in the future. The sounds generated from airplanes, automobiles, mechanical equipment, and computer printers have been the sources of concern and the impetus for laws to limit the rising decibel level. It seems that high speed technology continues to push the acceptable sound level up in the name of progress. Only recently has the need for "white sound" or background music to mask the noise levels in offices and restaurants become evident. Objectional sound will continue to be a design and technical problem until the effects are quantifiable in terms of health, happiness, and economics.

The frightening level of noise amplifies the general depiction of high stress in *Brazil.* Communications via satellite have made information and news around the world available to everyone. Much of this news is stressful, such as the threat of nuclear holocaust, terrorism, war, or child snatching. It has become very real because of the media's technical advances, such as live broadcasts, improved clarity of sound and picture, and cable television. We are bombarded with the most up-to-date events around the world. Communication of these events is very important for forming public opinion and ultimately taking action. Being so aware of what is happening in the world not only makes one fantasize about the future but reconsider the past.

People generally remember the positive aspects of history, which make it nostalgic and more desirable than the present era. The slower, simpler life with a higher sense of security is very appealing to most people. History provides a birdseye view of what causes design ideas or styles to change—changes caused by economic, political, technological, educational, religious, or cultural reasons. The styles emerge as an expression of the times, persisting until there are major changes. When styles change, there is either a period of overlapping major concepts, short-lived exploratory movements, or a time of confusion and searching. These transition periods create a time for free thought and investigation. Many instances in history have shown that in these times of conversion, the fashion of design becomes trendy without substance. It generally breaks the rules of the previous period in defiance of the established dogma. Often the new style is just that; a reaction to the past. Unless it matures into an expression of the present culture, it usually is abandoned for a style more responsive to that time. In studying the history of Interior Architecture, one must consider the culture of the times to understand its resultant style.

Culture and Style

FRENCH GOTHIC

Gothic architecture began to develop in France around 1130 and continued to flourish for three hundred years. The medieval church was concerned with educating illiterate people through biblical iconography from the Creation to the life of Christ. This era is sometimes referred to as the age of faith. Humanity was thought of as a fragment of the total creation. To find or understand the total, the human being had to first have faith and accept God. Therefore, faith had to precede reason in an atmosphere of humility or humbleness.

To create this theater of education and religious awe, the medieval architects developed soaring vertical cathedrals articulated by abstract ribs of stone. By carefully infusing light into the vertical rhythm of mass and void, a breathtaking and unearthly experience was achieved. The immense scale of the interior architecture reinforced the concept of humanity's insignificance and humility, thereby demonstrating the need to have faith in God.

ITALIAN RENAISSANCE

Renaissance architecture started in Florence in 1420, developing for a period of 350 years. In contrast to the Gothic style's intent to overpower and diminish the human being's presence, the Renaissance represented a new confidence and respect for humanity. This humanitarian view was the result of a more stable, relatively secure society compared to the centuries of religious and feudal wars during the medieval period. Kings and princes took over feudal lands and organized strong national governments. There were dynamic movements from feudal farmland to cities due to increased trade and commerce. Education was no longer confined to the church and monastery but was available to all of society because of the invention of the Gutenberg moveable type about 1440. Education was further developed through the establishment of libraries by the rulers and popes. Universities were created to translate ancient literature and to study humanistic subjects. Writers and artists changed their interest from religious to human subject matter. Society in general had a renewed confidence and sense of self-esteem.

This new concern for humanity manifested itself in antiquity. After all, Roman architecture was based on human scale relationships, which make a perfect model for architecture. The opportunity to study and borrow from monuments and ruins was available throughout Italy. Classical elements symbolized a past democratic civilization that represented well this new human renaissance. An original style of architecture evolved using the human scale and details of classicism with strong geometric relationships and emphasis on centralized space to clarify the human being's new position in the world.

In viewing Interior Architecture as an expression of its culture, the shift from the Gothic to Renaissance represents a change in humanity's

EXTERIOR DETAIL OF SOUTH PORTAL, CENTRAL BAY, CATHEDRAL OF NOTRE DAME, CHARTRES, FRANCE, 1194–1260.

The sculptural iconography of the cathedral expressed the congruity of history and concordance of divinity. The central bay presents the Last Judgment presided over by Christ the Judge, flanked by the Virgin Mary and St. John. The activity below the seated Christ illustrates the weighing of the souls and assigning them to either Heaven (on the left) or Hell (on the right). Photograph by John Kurtich.

INTERIOR VIEW OF NAVE, CATHEDRAL OF NOTRE DAME, CHARTRES, FRANCE, 1194–1260.

The soaring verticality of the nave was further accentuated from the capitals of the clustered columns upward through the splaying outward of the rib vaulting. Photograph by John Kurtich.

INTERIOR VIEW OF PAZZI CHAPEL, FLORENCE, ITALY. FILIPPO BRUNELLESCHI, 1429–1446.

The modestly-scaled chapel represents one of the earliest Italian Renaissance architectural expressions of the new concerns of human-scaled space utilizing classical elements, geometrically arranged. Photograph by John Kurtich.

self-image. Illiterate medieval peasants were humbled by God's powerful presence, symbolized by the soaring Gothic cathedral, whereas educated scholars of the sixteenth century considered themselves as powerful and creative people at the center of the universe. Their interior space was created for humanity and was symbolized by classical domed architecture. The imtimidating Gothic cathedral, with gargoyles and saints peering down at humble, ignorant peasants, no longer represented the new age. Renaissance spaces based on symmetrical, axial plans capped by domes emphasized the presence of this new humanity. The scholars and the artists of the Renaissance had reacted to the low self-image of the medieval thinking with fresh new spaces to express humanity's development.

EUROPEAN BAROQUE

In Europe, the Baroque period continued and expanded the ideals of the Renaissance, shifting the azza was the grandest of all urban theatres. The space expressed the duality of openness and closeness. Its dominant oval shape created a cross-axis emphasis away from the individual. This was an architecture of synthesis, focusing on the importance of a complete architectural experience. Baroque space emphasized the idea of the center. This notion of center was epitomized by the building of the Piazza San Pietro in Rome (1675–1677) by Gian Lorenzo Bernini (1598–1680). The world became a giant theatre, with every human member a player on this stage, and Bernini's pi-

AERIAL VIEW OF PIAZZA
SAN PIETRO, THE VATICAN, ITALY.
GIOVANNI LORENZO BERNINI,
1655–1667.

*The scope and grandeur of Bernini's
piazza is best realized from above.
Photograph by John Kurtich.*

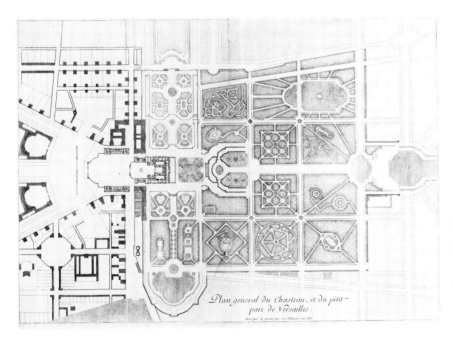

PLAN OF THE ROYAL CHÂTEAU AT
VERSAILLES, FRANCE, 1672–1689.
DRAWN BY SILVESTRE, 1680.

*Versailles established spatial and
material goals for ambitious European
royalty for the next two hundred years.
Courtesy of The Art Institute of
Chicago.*

GARDEN ELEVATION OF THE ROYAL
CHÂTEAU AT VERSAILLES, FRANCE,
1672–1689.

*The proportions of the Royal Chateau
were so long and broad as compared to
its height that it literally functioned as a
garden wall. Courtesy of The Art
Institute of Chicago.*

to the primary path leading to St. Peter's basilica. The central obelisk became the focal point to lead humanity from all directions into the embracing arms of the mother church.

The French, through the building of Versailles (1661–1765), further expanded the notion of Baroque space with the concept of the axis of infinity, symbolizing the power of absolute monarchy. The major axis of Versailles was built along the east-west path of the rising and setting sun, an appropriate expression of the Sun King. Versailles became the model of spatial development throughout Europe during the eighteenth century, encouraging powerful popes and monarchs as patrons of immense building programs, transforming the built environment.

THE INDUSTRIAL REVOLUTION

After the Baroque, the nineteenth century is regarded as a period of confusion and exploration. This was the beginning of the Industrial Revolution. The new age was not only based on agrarian production but on manufacturing and commerce. The buildings required to shelter industry had no precedent and therefore no historic model. These large halls for manufacturing, exhibition, and distribution embraced the new open space ideals of the age and employed the new technology of structural iron and glass construction.

In the beginning the structures were clothed with classical facades that were arbitrarily applied. Architects generally chose a style that best suited the building type. Often the style or motifs were borrowed and used without understanding of detail or use of materials, creating confused meaning and little substance to the essence of the industrial age.

The Crystal Palace of 1851, designed by Joseph Paxton (1803–1865), created a significant change in the emerging aesthetic. The Crystal Palace was the first major industrial age building to contain no reference to historical styles. It represented society's optimism in the future and rejection of the past. Interior space, as represented by the Crystal Palace, was conceived as large,

open, light, and flexible as opposed to contained, dark, and permanent. The traditional room was replaced by free-flowing spaces that were progressively abstracted to the essential components. These components were extended to the outdoors through the architectural use of glass. The plans were no longer ordered by axial symmetry but by logic and consistency.

THE MODERN MOVEMENT

The Modern Movement evolved as an expression of the Industrial Revolution. The concept of Modernist buildings and interiors was reinforced by the economics gained through the use of mass production. Standardization, modulation, and repetition became key ideas in creating the expression. The handmade expression of artists and craftsmen was replaced with the abstraction of the machine. By the 1890s electric lighting was in general use, reinforcing modern spaces with vastly improved illumination. Concurrently, central heating and ventilating were conceived and developed, making possible larger areas of glass while improving the comfort zones. The new systems were much more efficient for heating and lighting than past open flame methods.

As the technology evolved, the twentieth century passed through many transitions in style as a result of the search for the appropriate expression. Before the Industrial Revolution started, the tallest and therefore most dominant interior spaces were the cathedrals. Religious architecture was the most important in the towns and cities. The great halls for commercialism and transportation of the nineteenth century dominated the cathedrals in size and visual importance. The development of steel construction in the twentieth century produced tall office buildings for commerce that further overshadowed religious architecture. The F. W. Woolworth tower in New York (by Cass Gilbert, 1911–1913), described as the "cathedral of commerce," symbolized this new importance of commerce over religion.

The twentieth century started with the use of classical and medieval revival styles while pro-

INTERIOR VIEW OF THE CRYSTAL
PALACE, LONDON, ENGLAND. JOSEPH
PAXTON, 1851.

*The Crystal Palace was the first major
building to seek its own aesthetic based
on the new materials and techniques of
the Industrial Revolution. Courtesy of
The Art Institute of Chicago.*

EXTERIOR VIEW OF WOOLWORTH
BUILDING, NEW YORK, NEW YORK.
CASS GILBERT, 1913.

*The "cathedral of commerce" dominated
the early twentieth century New York
skyline as the Cathedral of Notre Dame
dominates the city of Chartres.
Photograph by John Kurtich.*

gressing through several brief experimental styles, such as Art Nouveau and Art Deco before maturing into the International Style. This modern style was the first to create unity and direction for contemporary design.

THE INTERNATIONAL STYLE

The International Style started at the Bauhaus in 1919 provided the guiding principles for many designers today. Its machine aesthetic, composed of steel and glass, is noncontextual and is intended for universal siting, making it best suited for freestanding monument type buildings. The International Style is a beautiful representation of the Industrial Revolution as it is an expression of mass production. Its construction advantages of speed, economy, and flexibility related well to the demands of a profit-oriented commercial economy. The somewhat dogmatic principles of the style were set forth by Henry-Russell Hitchcock (1903–) and Philip Johnson (1906–) in their 1932 book, *The International Style: Architecture since 1922:*

> *There is, first, a new conception of architecture as volume rather than as mass. Secondly, regularity rather than axial symmetry serves as the chief means of ordering design. These two principles, with a third proscribing arbitrary applied decoration, mark the productions of the international style. This new style is not international in the sense that the production of one country is just like that of another. Nor is it so rigid that the work of various leaders is not clearly distinguishable. The international style has become evident and definable only gradually as different innovators throughout the world have successfully carried out parallel experiments.[1]*

Generations of designers learned well the rules of mass production, which were economy through repetition, standardization, and modulation. Functionalism was the most important aspect of the plan because design must deal with the most practical aspects in the complex modern world. If the space solved the functional problem thoroughly, it was generally considered beautiful regardless of the aesthetic. Ornamentation was omitted because it had no functional purpose and

EXTERIOR VIEW OF DOUBLE HOUSE ON
STEEL STANCHIONS,
WEISSENHOFSIEDLUNG, STUTTGART,
GERMANY. LE CORBUSIER AND PIERRE
JEANNERET, 1925.

*The double house follows the dictum of
Le Corbusier's "Five Points," which
includes a raised structure on pilotis, a
roof garden on top, free plan within, free
facade without, and ribbon windows to
energize natural illumination.
Photograph by John Kurtich.*

EXTERIOR VIEW OF HIGHRISE
OFFICE BUILDINGS, AVENUE OF THE
AMERICAS, NEW YORK, NEW YORK,
1960s.

*The built environment of this avenue in
mid-town Manhattan could be
characterized as the Modern Movement
gone mad. Photograph by John Kurtich.*

it added expense. Often there was more concern
with maintaining the planning module than solving human problems. To break the grid and result
in a nonstandard detail was considered bad design. It was as though designers were no longer
able to resolve problems creatively with human
caring.

CONTEXTUALISM

The International Style was followed by a modern
style of architecture based on context in the late
1960s. This work was a reaction to the anonymity
of the International Style. The widespread environmental and social consciousness developed
during this era fueled the reaction and thereby
eroded the dogmatism of the International purists. The development of the architecture was
based on the relationship with the site. This idea
produced modern buildings that were less monumental related to their environment. Creating a

sense of place as opposed to the International Style's desire to make universal space was the intent of the contextualists. The desire to produce unique spaces resulted in more variety and less repetition and monotony. The buildings fit better in their contexts and in turn the interior designers and architects learned to make their designs appropriate for those buildings. Yet the spaces generally remained an expression of the machine—abstract and anonymous.

The Modern Movement broke from history and abstracted design to the point that there was no symbolic meaning or relationship with the past. It was generally perceived as cold, clean, and impersonal. The minimal details failed to produce human scale or personality in the interior spaces. The concepts were geared to the repetition of mass production as opposed to mass satisfaction. In general, Modern Movement building was economical to produce, more efficient to operate, and easier to design than previous styles. Its major failing was the style's inability to engage the occupant by providing human comfort in an increasingly technological world.

POST-MODERNISM

The Post-Modern Movement was clearly a reaction to the Modern Movement's shortcomings. Its leaders believe that by interjecting historical forms and ideas into modern architecture, the new environment would be less abstract and more representational. This representational work would have meaning and therefore could be understood by the occupant as well as the casual observer. Establishing a dialogue between the public and the place was intended to enrich the human experience, thereby resolving the most critical Modernist shortcoming.

As in the nineteenth century, the Post-Modernists turned full circle, clothing the interior spaces and exterior frames with any style appropriate. Chippendale, Gothic, Classical, and Art Deco were popular expressions ripe for rebirth in this period of experiment. Overnight, axial symmetry was "in" as the organizational principle, while the grid was twisted, turned, and pulled into compliance.

The Post-Modern Movement is a transitional style serving as a period of free thought and experiment. Its leaders realized lively new forms through breaking the rules of the Modern Movement. Mies van der Rohe's "less is more" was replaced by Robert Venturi's parody, "less is a bore."

In the beginning, tongue-in-cheek expressions of modern spaces with historical clothes were the vogue. The modernist-trained designers reopened their dusty history books and searched for appropriate forms and details. Not knowing the language or method of construction of the past, they improvised by translating stone details into drywall and plastic laminate. Often the translation resulted in cartoonlike images with little longevity of practical wearing or aesthetic substance.

The radical contrast of Post-Modernism's historicism to Modernism's abstraction created great debates and public attention. The Modern Movement was never totally embraced by the public, especially in residential design. When the fresh new spaces, full of memorable forms and color, began to be constructed, the public's attention was attracted. The new movement gained prominence when two major building commissions were awarded to Post-Modern architects, Philip Johnson (1906–) for the AT&T Building in New York and Michael Graves (1934–) for the Oregon State Office Building in Portland. Prior to these commissions, Post-Modernism had its roots in interiors and minor buildings. With more major commissions and competitions being secured by Post-Modern design firms, the movement gained followers. Established Modernist firms like Skidmore, Owings & Merrill (SOM) and Murphy/Jahn shifted completely in the mideighties. They saw the advantage of identity gained through the freed use of historic models as an aesthetic concept. The more complex the tops and elaborately decorated they could make the lobbies for high-rise buildings, the better.

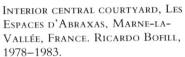

INTERIOR CENTRAL COURTYARD, LES ESPACES D'ABRAXAS, MARNE-LA-VALLÉE, FRANCE. RICARDO BOFILL, 1978–1983.

Ricardo Bofill built his reputation on large-scaled Post Modern projects, borrowing classical details, altering their scale and arrangement, and creating monumental, theatrical housing developments and commercial centers. Photograph by John Kurtich.

EXTERIOR VIEW OF THE PORTLAND BUILDING, PORTLAND, OREGON. MICHAEL GRAVES, 1980.

Central to the concept of the Portland Building was the public nature of its context to the rest of the city and also its internal function. Its main facade is a metaphoric gate which is established by the paired "columns" upon which rests a four-story "lintel," and which allows one a sense of passage through an interior street of city services. Photograph by Paschall/Taylor.

POST-INDUSTRIALISM

The U.S. economy in the 1980s entered an age where it shifted from an industrial base to one based on service and communications. This historic transformation, started in 1957 with the launching of the Sputnik and Columbia satellites, was precipitated by several factors. First, the space programs developed computer, communication, and robotics that were directly applicable to use on Earth.

Second, American industries pacified with years of dominance, became outdated and obsolete when compared to more aggressive and sophisticated competing countries. Many new U.S. products have been reduced to mediocrity through the desire of big business to appeal to larger consumer markets. The conservative practice of utilizing focus groups to evaluate new products has seriously eroded creativity in product design. In the meantime, products from Europe and the Orient have flooded the market with no relief in sight. Third World countries have attracted industry with their low labor costs and lack of unions, further reducing American companies' ability to compete.

Third, the industrial age produced a society disciplined by repetition and uniformity. Culture of the mass society was oriented to the whole as opposed to the individual. As Alvin Toffler has said, "These are societies based on mass production, mass distribution, mass education, mass media, mass entertainment, and mass political movements—not to mention weapons of mass destruction."[2] He elaborates, explaining, "This much-criticized homogenization of life was often attributed to technology: It was the machine that was depriving us of individualism."[3] This idea of repetition and uniformity is rapidly eroding with great increases of diversity and choice, driven mainly by the harnessing of industry by the computer.

In terms of designing appropriately for the future as well as the current era, the hybrid nature of Interior Architecture gives it the means to continually integrate new ideas with old, fresh technologies with timeworn techniques, recently developed materials with traditional, and en-lightened standards of human comfort, convenience, and safety. An instructive way to glimpse into possible future architectural evolution is to examine contemporary building types, from their historical beginnings to what they might become. What were the forces that shape architectural space and what was the resultant space? Typologies such as retail (shops and stores), commercial (offices), residential (habitat), and hospitality (hotels) are explored.

RETAIL SPACE

ANCIENT ROME

Space for marketing and shopping go back to the earliest beginnings of the urbanization of humanity, when people set up temporary structures and booths to trade food and wares at convenient crossroads of trade routes. In Western culture, the ancient Romans were among the first to institu-

INTERIOR STREET OF THE MARKET OF TRAJAN, ROME, ITALY. A.D. 98–113.

The covered portion of this ancient market complex is a precursor to the contemporary interior shopping mall. Photograph by John Kurtich.

tionalize shopping within large, permanent structures, such as the marketing hemicycles of the Forum of Trajan, Rome (A.D. 98–113). These structures were multilevel architectural containers for a series of permanent, uniform shops, conceptually similar to contemporary shopping malls.

The typical individual Roman shop employed a counter that separated the interior of the shop from the street and formed a barlike surface upon which transactions took place. Well-preserved remains of such shops found at both Ostia and Pompeii bear out the fact that the Romans developed a uniform building type for this activity.

EUROPEAN AND MIDDLE EASTERN MEDIEVAL SHOPS

The individual shop did not change essentially for centuries. Glazing of the facade is first documented in Holland in the seventeenth century. In cities, shops tended to be clustered in the same area. In order to encourage shopping, particularly during inclement weather, architectural features, such as arcaded streets, were developed in places

INTERIOR STREET OF THE GRAND BAZAAR, ISTANBUL, TURKEY, 1461, 1651, 1701, 1898.

The Grand Bazaar is totally internalized, with self-contained shopping protected by multiple vaulting. Photograph by John Kurtich.

TYPICAL ARCADE STREET, BOLOGNA, ITALY.

The arcaded pedestrian ways in central Bologna have remained since medieval times. Photograph by John Kurtich.

such as medieval Bologna. In the Middle East, to provide shade, the covering of entire streets became the standard architectural feature of the bazaar. The Grand Bazaar of Istanbul, originally built over the ruins of an old Byzantine market in 1461 and subsequently rebuilt and added to for the next four hundred years, covers an area of about two million square feet.

ARCADE SHOPPING

The idea of the covered shopping street became popular in Europe during the sixteenth century; London originated the *arcade* with the Royal Exchange in 1566. The arcade became popular throughout Europe in the nineteenth century due to the availability of iron and glass as structural material.[4] But arcades and their oriental cousins, bazaars, were still no more than a collection of separate shops under a common roof. The major

INTERIOR VIEW OF GALERIE VIVIENNE,
PARIS, FRANCE, 1824.

*Building techniques and processes
allowed the rapid growth of iron and
glass arcades and covered streets in
nineteenth-century Europe. Photograph
by John Kurtich.*

innovative change in shopping since the ancient Romans was the creation of the department store.

THE DEPARTMENT STORE

The department store had its origins in the grand shopping palaces of nineteenth century Europe. Starting in 1777 in England, the Industrial Revolution created vast sociological and political changes in western European countries and the United States. The reality of manufactured goods and mechanized transportation made possible a style of mass consumption never before witnessed in Western civilization. The great international expositions of the nineteenth century, starting with London's Crystal Palace of 1851 and climaxing with the 1900 Universal Exposition of Paris, exposed the masses to scientific and technical innovation that was revolutionizing daily life. Consumer merchandise began to be displayed at these fairs until it outnumbered productive tools or scientific presentations.

The Crystal Palace heralded a new building technology of iron and glass that made it possible to shelter vast numbers of acres under one roof with abundant natural light. The Paris expositions continued this building trend for the rest of the century (1855, 1867, 1878, 1889, 1900).

The department store first emerged in Paris based on the same growth of Industrial Revolution prosperity and transformation for merchandising techniques as the world fairs. Bon Marche opened in 1852 and, in 1876, moved into larger quarters designed by Louis-Charles Boileau (1837–1896) and Gustave Eiffel (1832–1923). The new building was a fantasy of glass-covered courts with aerial iron bridges, slender iron columns, grand staircases, and elaborate ornamental shapes.

The department store introduced an entirely new set of social interactions to shopping . . . Active verbal interchange between customer and retailer was replaced by the passive, mute response of consumer to things—a striking example

INTERIOR VIEW OF THE CROSSING,
CRYSTAL PALACE, LONDON,
ENGLAND. JOSEPH PAXTON, 1851.

*The realization of such a large building
as the Crystal Palace led to the concept
of a single large building housing retail
merchandising. Courtesy of The Art
Institute of Chicago.*

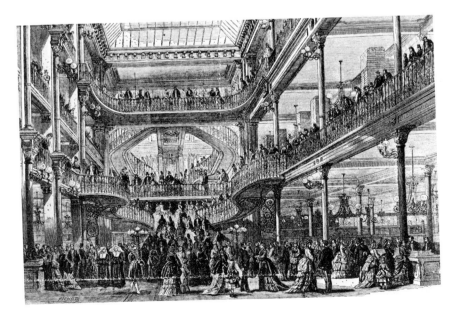

INTERIOR VIEW OF GRAND STAIRCASE,
MAGAZIN AU BON MARCHE, PARIS,
FRANCE. GUSTAVE EIFFEL AND L. A.
BOILEAU, 1876.

*The new concept of the department
store, such as Bon Marché, produced an
atmosphere of fantasy and desire which
encouraged shopping as never before
experienced. Courtesy of The Art
Institute of Chicago.*

EXTERIOR VIEW OF OAKBROOK
SHOPPING MALL, OAKBROOK,
ILLINOIS, 1990.

*The shopping mall is the antithesis of
the department store, conceptually
returning to medieval bazaars, but
minus the exotic mix of merchandise.
Photograph by John Kurtich.*

of how "the civilizing process" tames aggressions
and feelings toward people while encouraging desires and feelings directed toward things. Department stores were organized to inflame these
material desires and feelings. Even if the consumer was free not to buy at that time, techniques
of merchandising pushed him to want to buy
something. As environments of mass consumption, department stores were, and still are, places
where consumers are an audience to be entertained by commodities, where selling is mingled
with amusement, where arousal of free-floating
desire is as important as immediate purchase of
particular items.[5]

THE SHOPPING MALL

The department store served Western society very
effectively until the universality of the automobile
created the suburbs as the desired place to live.
This brought about suburban branches of downtown stores that eventually became the nucleus of
the collective known as the shopping mall, giant
covered areas, conceptually reminiscent of the
Oriental bazaar, but bland and conservative, spatially and commercially. Although the shopping
mall today contains a variety of specialty and
branch department stores, the individuality of
such stores inhibits the ease of browsing, which
in turn discourages the fantasy and desire in shop-

pers, so prevalent in the nineteenth century department store palaces.

MAIL-ORDER SHOPPING

In the latter part of the nineteenth century, another type of retail marketing became popular in
the United States—the mail order catalogue. The
development of the postal system (begun in 1847)
along with the rapid expansion and settlement of
the American West, made this innovation possible. The pioneering farmers and settlers were
somewhat at the mercy of local supply sources for
a limited selection of overpriced goods. Their
growing dissatisfaction with this means of shopping assured the success of the alternative, mail
order marketing. E. C. Allen of Augusta, Maine,
is given credit for starting the mail order concept
in 1870. At approximately the same time, Montgomery Ward, who understood the midwestern
farmers' tastes and needs from his traveling sales-
man days, established Montgomery Ward &
Company in Chicago. Sears, Roebuck & Company followed as a fully fledged competitor in
1893. Such was the success of this kind of marketing that Sears became one of the biggest and most
successful retailers by the late twentieth century,
with many retail outlet stores throughout the
country and corporate headquarters in the world's
tallest building, the Sears Tower, Chicago (1974).

INTERIOR VIEW OF ARCADIA, CARSON PIRIE SCOTT CO., CHICAGO, ILLINOIS. NIEDERMAIER DESIGNS WITH FERGUSON-HUSTON DESIGNS, 1986.

An attempt to lure shoppers back to the central business district, Arcadia was an experiment in total immersion of fantasy shopping, an attempt to revive the dream world idea of the first department stores. Photograph by John Kurtich.

ELECTRONIC SHOPPING

Interactive electronic home shopping, made possible with the combined technology of the computer, video, and telephone, became the late twentieth century competitor to mail order retailing. Now it was possible for the shopper, without leaving home, to view on a color video screen all or any objects of a given store as though traveling through the store. The telephone touch-tone buttons would allow the shopper to control what appears on the screen, from selecting the shopping place to browsing through the store aisles and choosing specific items. More button pushing would give the shopper sizes, prices, and allow the chosen item to be placed in an electronic "shopping cart." Payment was totally electronic, using a preregistered credit card. Delivery could be specified at a particular time, later on the same day, the next day, or three or four days in the future.

THE COLLECTIVE SPIRIT OF SHOPPING Electronic shopping won't make the physical store obsolete any more than mail order marketing replaced late nineteenth and early twentieth century urban department stores and specialty shops. In fact, Sears added an extensive chain of retail outlets after the mail order business took off. Why? When people shop, they need a clear sense of what they want to buy, which can come best from a physical encounter and inspection. People also like to be with people. Collective experience is a powerful and, in some ways intangible ingredient to intensify a personal activity. The format of the department store best provides the collective experience of shopping. Freedom to move from one department to the next is its essence. The individual specialty shops can inhibit the customer with intimidations to buy. Interactive electronic home shopping, although potentially offering the ultimate in freedom of choice, lacks physical immediacy and tactility. It is linear in its format. The department store's freedom is a strength that no other retailing concept has matched.

THEATER IN SHOPPING—CARSON PIRIE SCOTT The element of theater intensifies the sense of freedom. By manipulating the environment, the experience is altered to create an atmosphere in which the particular retail goods stimulate desire. In Chicago, Illinois, Carson Pirie Scott, originally designed by Louis Sullivan (1899–1904), installed in 1986 a merchandising experiment in trendy items, called "Arcadia." A small building section on Wabash Avenue was transformed inside and out through bright colors, disco music, video walls, and labyrinthine merchandise displays, which completely immersed the shopper in the fantasy of the environment. By combining related elements such as a cookie factory, an ice cream store, videos with images of rock stars, and upbeat music, a lively party experience set the tempo for buying nonessential items. The designers revived the dream world of the nineteenth century mass consumption and made it contemporary.

CRATE AND BARREL

The Michigan Avenue Crate and Barrel Store, Chicago, Illinois (1990), designed by Solomon, Cordwell, and Buenz, epitomizes the retailer's treatment of shopping-as-theater. The six-story glass and aluminum structure is designed as a unified enclosure to display home furnishings. At night the store glows, exposing its colorful contents; during the shopping day, buyers can examine the merchandise under natural light. Vertical circulation is achieved by ascending a series of escalators through a round, glassy cylinder

at the corner of the building. This exciting event exposes the shopper to all levels while enjoying a spectacular view of Michigan Avenue.

Crate and Barrel sells specialized and imported house and kitchen goods. Their spaces are carefully designed as backdrops for the colorful and ever-changing products. Materials are chosen to metaphorically represent the different kinds of home furnishings, for example, the kitchen area has a continuous quarry tile floor; the furniture area has hardwood and carpeted floor. The engaging displays are created and illuminated throughout the store by in-house, professional designers, not by stock or sales personnel. Flexibility is provided by track lighting that can be changed with each new display, similar to the way a theater's lights can be altered for a new performance. Large and well-designed checkout stations that include wrapping and packaging in reusable Crate and

INTERIOR COURT, CRATE AND BARREL, CHICAGO, ILLINOIS. SOLOMON, CORDWELL AND BUENZ, 1990.

The appeal of Crate and Barrel's merchandise is due largely to well designed and colorful displays throughout the store, which exhibit a high level of creativity and energy. Photograph by John Kurtich.

INTERIOR DETAIL, CRATE AND BARREL, CHICAGO, ILLINOIS. SOLOMON, CORDWELL AND BUENZ, 1990.

The merchandise is intimate and approachable, encouraging customers to touch or test for comfort. Photograph by John Kurtich.

Barrel shopping bags create an image of efficient service. Everything about the concept reinforces its image as a store selling items of good taste and design.

COMMERCIAL SPACE

ANCIENT EGYPT

Space for commercial transactions, primarily the office, developed from several sources. In ancient Egypt, specific space was set aside for scribes to keep written accounts of such essential items as grain as it was being stored. Proof of such "offices" can be found in small clay funerary models such as the one of a granary and adjacent "office"

for scribes from the tomb of Meketre, XI dynasty, 2130 B.C.

ROMAN COMMERCE: OSTIA

Ostia, the port city of ancient Rome, has remains of an office complex known as "the Square of the Corporations" (before 12 B.C.). Ostia was the center of a large organization, the *annona,* which was charged with supplying Rome with food. The Square of the Corporations was a large complex of seventy offices that housed the commercial associations of this organization, a sort of stock exchange or chamber of commerce of the ancient Roman world. The offices were a series of identical single interior spaces linked together to form three sides of the square. A double arcade of

MODEL OF ANCIENT EGYPTIAN
SCRIBES FROM THE TOMB OF MEKETRE,
XI DYNASTY, 2130 B.C.

The scribe was a prestigious profession in ancient Egypt, and his talents were in high demand to carry on the everyday business of that civilized society. Photograph by John Kurtich.

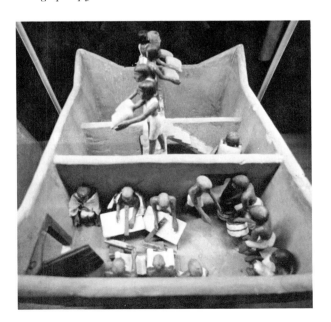

SQUARE OF THE CORPORATIONS,
OSTIA, ITALY, CA. 12 B.C.

This was the bureaucratic hub of management for food and supplies for Rome. This "mercantile exchange" was supported by many large warehouses and storage facilities, also located in Ostia. Photograph by John Kurtich.

brick columns formed a continuous porch in front of the offices, and the mosaic floor of the porch identified each office at its entry as to the provenance of each merchant and in what kind of commerce was being engaged.

DEVELOPMENT OF THE "OFFICE" BUILDING

Ostia had a large commercial section, which consisted of warehouses that were controlled and maintained by these associations. The relationship between warehouses and offices continued throughout the commercial history of western Europe, becoming architecturally evident in the sixteenth and seventeenth centuries in the Netherlands, as the Dutch at that time were the leading merchants of Europe. Government offices, on the other hand, developed as a singular building type in the late twelfth century in Italy as towns acquired independent status. A prominent example of such a specialized building was the Uffizi, Florence (1560–1571) designed by Giorgio Vasari (1511–1574) for Cosimo de Medici (1519–1574). It originally housed administrative offices for the "nine Conservatori, with their Scriptori, their Audienza and their Chancellery."[6]

NINETEENTH CENTURY BRITISH OFFICES

Commercial office space continued to be linked to the warehouse until the nineteenth century, when architectural independence first occurred in London. In 1819, Robert Abraham (1774–1850) designed the County Fire Office as part of John Nash's (1752–1835) classical Regent Street development. Following that, insurance offices such as the Westminster, Life and British Fire Office, London (1831–1832), the Sun Fire Office, London (1841–1842), and the Liverpool and London Office, Liverpool (1855–1857) were designed by C. R. Cockerell (1788–1863). All of these buildings used neoclassic elements such as elaborate cornices and classical orders for the columns on their exteriors. The warehouses that paralleled these early offices were also externally decorated

EXTERIOR VIEW OF UFFIZI GALLERY, FLORENCE, ITALY. GIORGIO VASARI, 1560–1571.

As Italy began to develop independent city-states, the need for their administration was met by a new type of building, consisting of a series of offices. The Uffizi was blessed with many windows overlooking a narrow court. Photograph by John Kurtich.

EXTERIOR VIEW OF COUNTY FIRE OFFICE, LONDON, ENGLAND. ROBERT ABRAHAM, 1819.

The nineteenth century began a real upsurge of office buildings with the widespread growth of insurance and banking industries. Photograph by RCHM England.

EXTERIOR VIEW OF ORIEL CHAMBERS, LIVERPOOL, ENGLAND. PETER ELLIS, 1864.

Oriel Chambers was a very advanced design, featuring very large bay windows for every office. Photograph by John Kurtich.

with similar ornamentation, making them similar in appearance to palaces. Windows were relatively small, so the interiors were dark.

THE FIRST SKYSCRAPER

As new materials such as iron and glass became more available, improvements in office buildings occurred. In his Oriel Chambers, Liverpool (1864), Peter Ellis (1835–1884) enlarged the window openings by using metal framework between slender stone columns. The interiors now were becoming more generous in size and natural lighting. The next structural breakthrough that affected offices was the development of the iron skeleton frame, first featured in the Home Insurance Building, Chicago (1884, now demolished), by William Le Baron Jenney. This ten-story office building is the first skyscraper actually built, and it began the movement known as the Chicago School of Architecture, which spawned the greatest designers of early twentieth century commercial architecture: Louis H. Sullivan (1856–1924), Dankmar Adler (1844–1900), Daniel H. Burnham (1846–1912), John Wellborn Root (1850–1891), John A. Holabird (1886–1945), and Martin Roche (1855–1927). A symbol of the Chicago School was an ideal window designed for the office. The

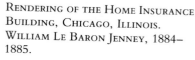

RENDERING OF THE HOME INSURANCE
BUILDING, CHICAGO, ILLINOIS.
WILLIAM LE BARON JENNEY, 1884–
1885.

*The "first" skyscraper depended upon
the development of the iron skeleton
frame and the invention of the elevator.
Deutsches Architektur Museum
Bibliothek.*

EXTERIOR DETAIL OF TYPICAL
CHICAGO WINDOW, CARSON PIRIE
SCOTT CO., CHICAGO, ILLINOIS.
LOUIS SULLIVAN, D. H. BURNHAM
AND COMPANY, 1899, 1903–1904,
1906.

*The "Chicago Window" evolved for the
practical reasons of light and ventilation,
which were from natural sources.
Photograph by John Kurtich.*

"Chicago Window" was composed of a large, fixed-view window, flanked by double-hung windows for ventilation. This design maximized both view and ventilation for the individual office, lending a unique overall character to Chicago commercial buildings.

THE ELEVATOR

Commercial office buildings could never have been possible without the invention of the elevator. An early example of this technology was a "moving apartment . . . raised by machinery"[7] which would take several people from the ground to a viewing platform at the Colosseum, Regent's Park, London (1832). Elisha Otis (1811–1861) de-veloped the world's first safe elevator, initially installed at his factory (which produced bed frames) in 1853. He invented a double rail system that guided the passenger platform, preventing it from crashing if the rope broke. The widespread use of the elevator created high densities of commercial districts, which reinforced communications. Also, a sense of prestige in high-rise office buildings was established by the ascension to lofty views, accessed via the elevator.

THE LARKIN BUILDING

Although these new office buildings were structurally innovative and their exteriors designed with flair and imagination, the interiors remained

INTERIOR PERSPECTIVE OF THE LIGHT
COURT, LARKIN COMPANY
ADMINISTRATION BUILDING,
BUFFALO, NEW YORK. FRANK LLOYD
WRIGHT, 1903.

*In addition to the generous amount of
natural light which flooded the interior,
the Larkin Building had an
extraordinary heating and ventilation
system which Wright claimed was one of
the first air-conditioned buildings in the
country. Courtesy of The Art Institute
of Chicago.*

PLAN OF THE LARKIN COMPANY
ADMINISTRATION BUILDING,
BUFFALO, NEW YORK. FRANK LLOYD
WRIGHT, 1903.

*This plan shows two floors at the same
time: on the left side of the middle
dividing line is the restaurant level (fifth
floor) and on the right side a typical
office floor. Courtesy of The Art
Institute of Chicago.*

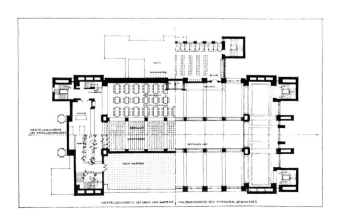

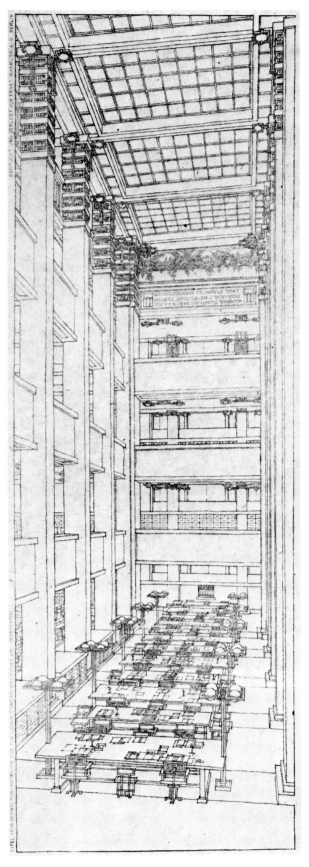

dull and standardized, particularly the actual workspaces. Frank Lloyd Wright (1867–1959) had specific ideas about office interiors for human activity, which he demonstrated in his Larkin Company Administration Building, Buffalo (1903, demolished). The interior of the five-story office building centered around a light court, which went the full height of the five levels, allowing natural light to reach all parts of the interior through double-glazed skylights at the top. The ends of the light court had a sixth level conservatory, filled with vegetation that was visible to the workers from their various office levels. Heating and ventilation, including air-purifying and cooling, guaranteed a consistent, comfortable environment, regardless of external weather conditions. Wright designed furniture, using metal for the pieces in the main block, to ensure fireproofing. His freestanding desks had folding chairs permanently attached to the desk and cantilevered with a certain amount of arc of movement, all to make cleaning the floors easier.

PHILADELPHIA SAVING FUND SOCIETY

In 1930, George Howe (1886–1955) and William Lescaze (1896–1969) designed a high-rise office building for the Philadelphia Saving Fund Society. Their design was a departure from the tradi-

tional approach of using historical styles to clothe a contemporary commercial building. Influenced by structural rhythms, ribbon windows, and absence of applied ornament of European modernism, they produced the most advanced office building for its time. The building was completed in 1932 and appeared in the Museum of Modern Art's seminal exhibition, "The International Style." The main banking floor was located on the second floor with access by a moving stair framed in highly polished granite. The interior remains one of Philadelphia's best commercial interiors, resplendent with highly polished marble, chrome, glass, and the original furnishings and fittings of 1932.

SEAGRAM BUILDING

Mies van der Rohe (1886–1969) had visions of glass and steel office buildings in his curvilinear model of a glass skyscraper for Berlin of 1922. A development of these ideas was realized after World War II. The Seagram Building (New York, 1958) is his most famous example of an office building employing a structural and service core enclosed by a glass curtain wall. Because the principles of the concept were highly efficient and economical, this building became the standard for office buildings during the fifties and sixties in

INTERIOR VIEW OF BANKING FLOOR, PHILADELPHIA SAVING FUND SOCIETY BUILDING, PHILADELPHIA, PENNSYLVANIA. HOWE AND LESCAZE, 1929–1932.

The highly polished interior of the main banking floor reflects the many lighting fixtures and extends them spatially, partially dissolving conventional structural logic and blurring boundaries. Photograph by John Kurtich.

urban America. The resulting interiors of this building form tended to be monotonous and predictable. Uniform floor to ceiling heights and continuous window walls stifled creative interior architecture. The ubiquitous fluorescent light, combined with dropped ceilings integrated with air-conditioning systems, ensured the monotony.

FORD FOUNDATION HEADQUARTERS

In a reaction to the desensitized office environment of uniformity and efficiency of the 1950s and 1960s, Roche, Dinkeloo and Associates designed a garden atrium office building for the Ford Foundation (New York, 1966–1967). The

Cor-Ten steel and glass square structure contains offices along the north and west sides, which overlook a ten-story-high atrium. This lush interior space contrasts with the hard urban quality of midtown Manhattan, and it unifies the foundation physically and spiritually. The multilayered garden is landscaped with mature trees, shrubs, and flowers, creating the essential link between humanity and nature. Sliding glass doors permit the offices to physically connect to this oasis, allowing the staff to moderate their personal environment. The Ford Foundation Building was a turning point in humanizing the office environment by unifying the entire staff through a common space, which metaphorically represented the philanthropic goal of the foundation itself.

UNION CARBIDE HEADQUARTERS

The Ford Foundation's humanization of its building was expensive, however. Corporations in general were not yet ready to invest this kind of capital for the comfort and convenience of their employees. The quest for efficiency in large office complexes led to a coordinated systems approach. An example of total integration of lighting, air handling, furniture, partitions, and surface materials was Skidmore, Owings & Merrill's Union Carbide Headquarters, New York (1959). Basing the design layout on a module system compatible with the building architecture, the spatial size and arrangement of offices could reflect current corporate hierarchies and be easily altered to express changes in those hierarchies.

THE OPEN OFFICE: WEYERHAEUSER TECHNOLOGY CENTER

A different approach to large office planning developed in Europe. Instead of developing partitioned modules that coordinated with the building architecture, the building and its geometry were ignored. Called the "open office" or the "office landscape," this concept was first developed by Eberhard and Wolfgang Schnelle from Quickborner, Germany. As principals of a management consulting group called the Quickborner

Team, they thought that office arrangement should delineate work process and traffic flow. Fixed partition walls and heavy office furniture were abandoned in favor of an open floor and lightweight furniture that accommodated everyone, including the chief executive office. Skidmore, Owings & Merrill used this concept for the Weyerhaeuser Technology Center, Tacoma, Washington (1971).

This center was one of the first buildings to be totally designed for an open office landscaped interior. The San Francisco office of SOM designed the building and its interiors. Breaking away from the traditional hierarchical organization of contained offices, SOM was able to free the glass curtain wall of any visual interruptions, preserving the spectacular view of the 230-acre wooded site for all of the employees. To maintain the continuous open interior, the architects designed an open workstation produced by Knoll that provided a flexible and efficient environment. Current lighting technology no longer applied to the floating offices. Individual task-oriented lighting in each workstation with ambient lighting at the tops of each station became the primary source of interior lighting. The Technology Center was a major installation that established a credible new design idea. That idea was manifested in the numerous manufactured systems that offered open landscape: flexibility in unlimited quantities. This new approach and its new technology related well to the demands of the everchanging corporate structure.

John Naisbitt, the author of *Megatrends,* said: "We're at the beginning of a renaissance in the arts and literature. All this high tech that we have to put up with, particularly the computer, is obliging us to reexamine our humanity, which we do in the arts and literature."[8] Naisbitt continues, describing his famous phrase "high tech/high touch,"

When you put high tech into a society, the technology that displaces humans always seems antihuman. So we human beings try to create a compensatory 'high touch' to restore the balance between our technology and our humanity or humanness. High tech dissonance results when you put your computer in an environment of minimalist furniture. The more computers in our

Interior view of typical office
floor, Weyerhaeuser Technology
Center, Tacoma, Washington.
Skidmore, Owings and Merrill,
1971.

*The "open office" was a new concept
which altered and transformed
subsequent office and office furniture
design. Photograph by Ezra Stoller.*

houses, the more likely the other aspects of the environment, the furniture—say, the sofa, the curtains—will get softer, plumper, cuddlier, or whatever in contrast. Remember when companies moved to the open space office separated by white sound instead of physical partitions? Very high tech—you don't hear anyone nearby because of the white sound. Then you got the high touch—the phenomenon of the many forests of plants that sprang up in the offices.[9]

RESIDENTIAL SPACE

INDIGENOUS MATERIALS

The home, necessary for survival, was humanity's first architecture. Indigenous and readily available materials dictated the character of the dwelling, providing a working palette that led to many different and regional developments in the history of architecture. Trees and branches were used in neolithic Mediterranean regions. Animal bones and skins dominated construction in northern Europe and Asia. The building material of the ancient Near East was mud. Marble and other stone were common building materials in ancient Greece, as the natural supply of wood became exhausted. The Romans invented concrete from the volcanic composition of sand that was common throughout Italy. The Japanese house evolved from the use of paper as a primary material. The Industrial Revolution made iron and glass technology widely available for the first time. The mid-twentieth century created plastic as a building material. The late twentieth century space age brought highly developed ceramics.

TERRA AMATA DWELLING

The oldest "designed" freestanding shelter to date was recently discovered at Terra Amata near Nice, France, dating at ca. 300,000 B.C. This oval-shape structure was formed from a series of bent tree stakes that served as the walls and roof simultaneously. The palisadelike walls were set in sand and propped by a circle of large stones on the outside. Hefty wood posts provided structural

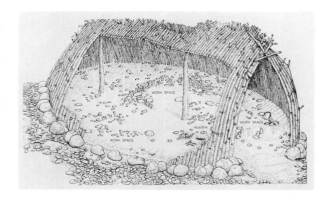

PERSPECTIVE RENDERING OF OVAL HUT AT TERRA AMATA (NICE), FRANCE, CA. 30,000 B.C.

This is a reconstruction of the earliest known "built from scratch" human habitat yet identified. From: "A Paleolithic Camp at Nice" by Henry de Lumley. Illustration by Eric Mose.

support along the long axis of the shelter, and the center of the space featured a hearth.

CRO-MAGNON SHELTER

During the late Ice Age, ca. 35,000 B.C., Cro-Magnon humanity dominated Europe and developed housing made of mammoth bones and skins. They installed cobblestone floors, which were ingeniously placed by first heating the stones, then arranging them into the frozen mud ground. The stones melted into the mud, forming durable, dry, insulated floors. The interior featured a hearth, which was the center of warmth, sustenance, and social activity.

Model of a Cro-Magnon shelter, ca. 35,000 b.c.

This full scale reconstruction shows how the late Ice Age humans could recycle natural materials such as animal bones and skins to create a dwelling. Courtesy Department of Library Services, American Museum of Natural History.

Reconstruction of a courtyard house, Ur, Iraq, ca. 1900 b.c.

This urban dwelling looked inward to a private courtyard, for both security reasons and climate control. Besides everyday domestic activities, the courtyard was used for such special events as weddings and funerals. Drawing by John Kurtich.

SUMERIAN HOUSE

The typical houses of the ancient Sumerian city of Ur (1900 b.c.) were constructed of sun-dried mud bricks. Mud was the major building material of this arid region due to the lack of timber and stone. The houses were clustered together, defining narrow, irregular streets. The two-story houses were internally oriented to an open court for light and ventilation, with little or no openings to the street.

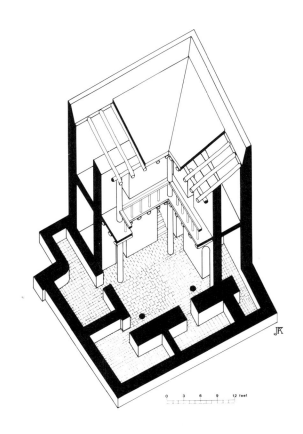

GREEK HOUSING

Although houses of ancient Greece were originally made of wood and clay, the Greeks eventually depleted their forests and built their shelters of brick, stone, and tiles, reserving timber for roof framing and beams. Their urban house form was that of the atrium, with rooms developed around this central, open, airy space. The house was thus internally oriented as those of Ur, presenting blank walls to the outside street. The internal design was based on the organization of the family and movement of everyday life. There were areas for day activities and zones for night functions. The house also had separate quarters for men and women. The Greek house reached its zenith on Delos during the second century B.C. where marble was used extensively for door and

HOUSE COURTYARD WITH MOSAIC TILE, DELOS, GREECE, CA. 2ND CENTURY B.C.

This luxurious house was built around a large, airy courtyard, which served as the main activity space and focus for the family, for daily life as well as entertaining. Photograph by John Kurtich.

window frames, atrium and courtyard colonnades, and veneer over the stone rubble walls. Floors featured elaborate tile mosaics.

ROMAN ATRIUM HOUSE

The Roman single-family dwelling borrowed the idea of the peristyle from the Hellenistic Greeks and combined it with the rainwater-collecting atrium of the Etruscan house. This hybrid house, best exemplified by those preserved in Pompeii and Herculaneum, were inward-looking brick structures, roofed with wooden beams and terra cotta tiles. Usually the walls were plastered and painted with elaborate frescoes, featuring mythological themes, architectural fantasies, or nature scenes, all of which helped to enhance and brighten the otherwise small and dimly lit interior spaces. These single-story houses incorporated elaborate mosaics on the floors.

INTERIOR VIEW OF AN ATRIUM HOUSE ATRIUM, POMPEII, ITALY, BEFORE A.D. 79.

The basic atrium consisted of the fauces *or "throat" of the house which led from the street to the atrium proper, the atrium with its* compluvium-impluvium *complex, and the* tablinum *which was on the main axis of the front door and* fauces *and was considered the most important space of the house. Photograph by John Kurtich.*

Inset plan: a. fauces   b. atrium
c. tablinum   d. dining   e. bedroom
f. shop. Drawing by Garret Eakin.

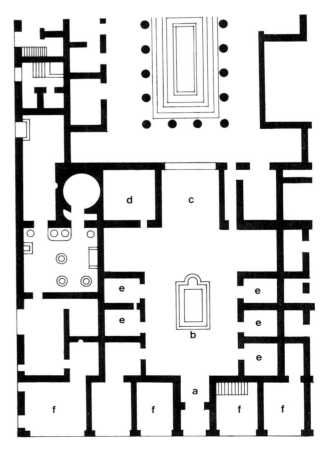

ROMAN APARTMENT BUILDINGS: OSTIA

As Roman cities became more populated during the Imperial period, urban housing included extensive multistoried apartment buildings. The remains of such buildings in Ostia represent the typical vertical development necessitated by crowded conditions. The average apartment building was four stories high surrounding an internal courtyard. Unlike the single-story atrium house, windows opened to both the street and courtyard. Brick, again, was the dominant building material, but usually the exterior walls were not plastered. The major room in each flat was placed on the exterior with smaller flanking rooms. These rooms were considered to be flexible and used as each tenant wished. These flats were prototypes for the modern, multistoried apartments found in every Western city.

JAPANESE HOUSE

Over the course of fifteen hundred years the Japanese developed and refined paper as a major building material for their houses. The ephemeral qualities of houses constructed of paper united the Japanese with nature and with one another. Privacy was internalized affecting the total design of the dwelling and how the spaces were used. The rooms were multifunctional with appropriate storage to make them flexible. Portable furnishings were used in the center of the spaces allowing the screens to be unobstructed. In Japanese culture it is considered rude to put a guest against the wall as the construction is delicate and cannot be leaned against. Shoji screens are movable partitions constructed of a single layer of rice paper pasted to wood frames to allow diffused light penetration. Fusuma panels made of multiple layers of paper

INTERIOR COURTYARD, HOUSE OF DIANA, OSTIA, ITALY, A.D. 2ND CENTURY.

This four-story insula *or apartment block featured a large central courtyard that provided natural light and ventilation to the inner rooms and centered on a fountain that supplied the apartments with domestic water needs such as cooking, hygiene, and laundry. Photograph by John Kurtich.*

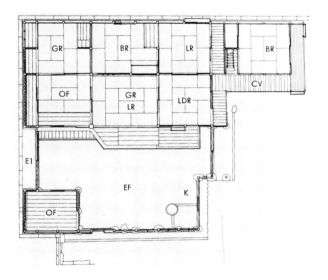

PLAN OF A TRADITIONAL JAPANESE HOUSE, THE IMANISHI HOUSE, NARA PREFECTURE.

The major determinant of sizing individual spaces within a traditional Japanese house was through the configuration of the tatami, *a standard sized (three feet by six feet) mat of rice straw packed within a woven rush cover. Copyright A.D.A. Edita Tokyou Co. Ltd. 1991.*

forming an air pocket provide insulation and increased privacy. These panels are interchangeable, allowing the owner to easily alter the interior to respond to seasonal conditions and changing functions. Modular wood and paper panels allowed a flexibility unprecedented in the West.

TASSEL HOUSE, BRUSSELS

Victor Horta's (1861–1947) house for Mr. Tassel in Brussels (1898) utilized the new technologies of glass and iron construction. This residential structure was revolutionary, crystalizing the ideas of the Art Nouveau movement. The highly personal and artistic use of these materials resulted in a free and flexible ground floor plan and a light-filled interior. Iron columns eliminated bearing walls while iron and glass skylights allowed sunlight to fill the interior. The once classical and geometric elements of structure were transformed into flowing organic compositions where structure and decoration could not be separated. The stair of the Tassel house exemplifies this synthesis. The iron column supporting the stair is like a tree with three-dimensional ribbon branches that merge with sinuous two-dimensional tendrils on the ceiling. The tile pattern of the floor continues the swirling motif of the ceiling. In fact, all the surfaces are a riot of organic growth. This overall effect transformed the period's limitations of urban dwellings into a new sense of freedom.

GEODESIC DOME

Plastic was employed by R. Buckminster Fuller (1895–1983) as the skin on his geodesic dome (1948 onward) enclosing his autonomous house. The concept for this house was to manufacture a standardized enclosure for habitation. Fuller rationalized that "we have building materials which are admirably suited to the erection of structures without any limitation as to their form. This affords us the opportunity of building more efficiently and to greater functional advantage."[10] Fuller pointed out the advantage of speed of erection due to the simplicity and lightweight quality

of the prefabricated components. Traditional construction has always been handicapped by inclement weather conditions; the premanufactured dome greatly reduced this problem. Mass production was Fuller's key ingredient in the development of a new efficient, technically advanced, and economical house of the future. Destroying conventional images of the house, he sought to redefine the functions and construction within a flexible enclosure. This was critical to freeing one's conditioned perceptions of what a house should or could be. The masses had difficulty accepting the idea of living in plastic domes, lacking in human traditions. As a result, Fuller's innovative and practical ideas were not fully appreciated.

URBAN LOFT LIVING

Once considered experimental or even trendy, loft living has evolved over the last thirty years of the twentieth century into a major direction in residential design. The conversion of nineteenth century warehouses and factories into residences (see Chapter 8, Schroeder's Cobbler Square project, for further discussion of the adaptive reuse of a factory complex into condominiums) has promoted a change in attitude toward city living. Reclaiming these urban structures as housing has established new neighborhoods in the "heart of town," creating a revival of city centers. Residents no longer face time consuming commutes from suburbs but live close to city restaurants, theaters, shopping, offices, and are willing recipients of urban conveniences.

Raw loft space, usually open and expansive, punctuated by structural columns, requires a unique approach to the delineation of interiors. While residential design traditionally has dealt with dwelling as a series of rooms, lofts were initially defined as a series of more open and communicative spaces, spilling into each other. Over the years, loft design has evolved to meet the re-

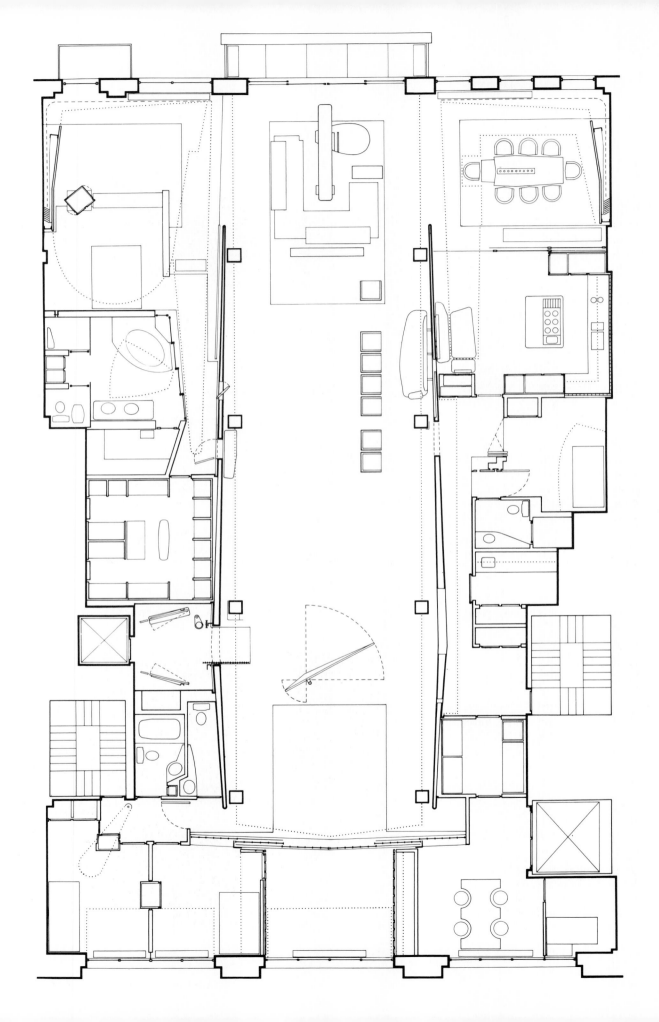

quirements of a broader range of occupants, providing a balance between public and private living zones. Lofts are a celebration of space, the greatest luxury experience in an otherwise crowded urban environment.

The firm of Tod Williams and Billie Tsien and Associates, Architects, transformed a 5,000 square foot Greenwich Village loft, New York, New York (1991), into a serene retreat from New York's hectic pace. The architects achieve a rare harmony by harnessing the opposing forces of serenity and activity. The interior becomes the subtle realization that serenity requires a degree of activity, and activity demands a level of quietness in order to establish a true balance.

To accomplish this spatially, the designers developed a highly symmetrical plan with the central volume accommodating a generous living room, with the kitchen, dining room, and bedrooms along the perimeter. Counteracting the static configuration, the living room interior is invigorated in several ways. The long walls of the living space bow outwardly, giving the interior a subtle, ever-expanding quality. Black plywood bookcases march down the western side of the living room, providing strong visual activity. The asymmetrical seating arrangement demonstrates a highly charged balancing act. The living room floor softly reflects the tranquil interior but springs to activity as footsteps fall on the terrazzo.

A series of partitions are employed to delineate space. Sliding panels of pigmented plaster, separate the dining room and the master bedroom from the large living space. When the partitions are opened, the serene living area is energized with increased natural light flooding the expanded vistas. At the opposite end of the living room, near the loft's entrance, is a rotating partition. The plywood screen revolves around a metal pole. Copper-leafed on one side and painted gray and white on the other, the faceted partition divides the living room into spacious and intimate areas.

Williams and Tsien were able to bring into balance the best features of private and public space within the residential confines of the loft. Separate bedrooms and baths provide a peaceful private zone while the expansive living room, dining room, and kitchen create public zones, re-

PLAN OF A LOFT, NEW YORK, NEW YORK. TOD WILLIAMS, BILLIE TSIEN AND ASSOCIATES, ARCHITECTS, 1992.

The 5000 square foot loft design employs a central space that unifies and floods the interior with light. Drawing by Billie Tsien.

VIEW OF LIVING AREA OF LOFT, NEW YORK, NEW YORK. TOD WILLIAMS, BILLIE TSIEN AND ASSOCIATES, ARCHITECTS, 1992.

The spacious symmetrical living room takes full advantage of the view while the black plywood bookcases float in contrast, forming an intimate library. Photograph by Peter Paige.

ceptive to activity. The architects' appreciation for the spatial opportunities in loft design made it possible to bring the power of luxuriant expanses of space into the urban residential realm.

SMART HOUSE

In the late twentieth century plastics and other manufactured synthetic materials became standard for many of the components of home construction. The list, such as PVC plumbing piping, molded foam decorative trim, vinyl-covered window frames, and fiberglass shower stalls, was virtually endless and reduced the building cost. At the same time, electronic and computer technology was developed to integrate and automate such basic functions as security, safety, energy control, and entertainment, making the house more convenient. The "Smart House," was a project first built in 1987 by the National Association of Home Builders who directed thirty manufacturers to design a new home wiring system, organizing all functions of power and telecommunications into a centrally controlled computer. Semiconductors were integrated into the appliances, giving them the ability to communicate through an advanced wiring system (containing electrical, telephone, audio, visual, and security) which was controlled by the house computer. These systems allowed the house to catch up with current technologies but they initially did not affect the architectural expression of the new age.[11]

MASS HOUSING

Housing of the twenty-first century will rely on more and more manufactured components in order to control cost and maximize availability. Unfortunately today, house construction is an archaic industry that relies on a labor-intensive individual craft that is no longer abundant. On-site house construction is vulnerable to weather conditions and it is difficult to coordinate all the various trades necessary to complete the building. This traditional process has not kept pace with contemporary needs, thus making such housing unavailable for much of the population.

SWEDISH HOUSING INDUSTRY

The Swedish housing industry has not only created flexibility in its houses but, through industrialization, has given the public an affordable, energy efficient, and technically advanced product. As a reaction to the oil embargo of the 1970s, Sweden developed three systems for industrialized housing: a volume-element system similar to a "mobile home"; a large panel system; and a small panel system. Of the three, the small panel system is an architect's dream. It is essentially a kit of flexible parts that allows a minimum crew to assemble a weather tight enclosure in less than two days after the foundation work has been completed. Because the system is modular, great variety can be achieved in the floor plans and details, satisfying the owners' specific needs. Possibly due to their severe climate, the Swedes focus on their interiors and care less about the external

SWEDISH INDUSTRIALIZED PREFAB HOUSING, 1947.

The pre-cut panels and accompanying construction kit made possible a breakthrough in the time it took to assemble a prefabricated house. Courtesy of Arkitektur Forlag AB Copyright 1991.

appearance. With their proven advantages, these systems have not addressed the issues of individuality in a democratic society. A further disadvantage is that the construction is limited to wood, which does not offer enough selection in style or quality.

The components systems relate well to computerized design, selection, budgeting, and construction sequencing. The computer promises speed, efficiency, accuracy, variety, and synthesis of a wide spectrum of information at the designer's fingertips. Unfortunately, none of these advantages guarantees an aesthetic and functional house. This could be the downfall of the hope of affordable, well-designed housing.[12] Since most housing is not currently designed by architects and designers, the computer-generated house would likely be embraced by developers and builders who dominate the market. The computer does not design.

HOSPITALITY

Early travel was predominantly stimulated by commerce, religion, and politics. The earliest accommodations for travelers were based on residential forms that were modified to provide basic security, shelter, and sustenance. These shelters were comprised of two types, transient and destination. Transient lodging was geographically determined by the distance one could travel by foot or animal in a day. These remote facilities tended to emphasize the basic needs of security and shelter. Destination lodging was generally located in urban or religious centers. These facilities, designed for longer visits, related to their surrounding environments, such as markets and shrines. The basic functions of transient and destination hostelries have not changed throughout the history of Western civilization.

STOA, SAMOTHRACE, GREECE

An example of an ancient Greek Hellenistic building built for transient overnight shelter in a religious sanctuary is the Stoa of the Sanctuary of the Great Gods, Samothrace, Greece (first half of the third century B.C.). The Greek stoa originated as a colonnaded shed, open to sunlight on one of its long walls and enclosed on its remaining three sides. Generally the stoa was a principal building in the *agora* (market place) of the city, providing shelter for shops, public discussions and debate, or simple loitering. The Stoa at Samothrace, however, was used for lodging by the initiates who traveled great distances to participate in the rituals of the Mysteries. Such travelers would bring their own bedrolls and claim sleeping space in the Stoa's expansive porch, dormitory style.

EXTANT REMAINS OF THE STOA, SANCTUARY OF THE GREAT GODS, SAMOTHRACE, GREECE, 300–250 B.C.

Although the stoa was normally a building reserved for commercial purposes in the Greek agora or marketplace, here it provided overnight shelter for the initiates who had traveled from afar to take part in rituals of the Mysteries. Photograph by John Kurtich.

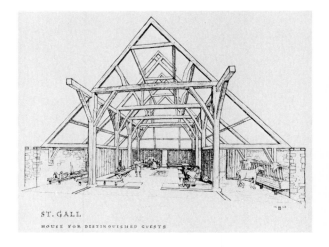

ST. GALL
HOUSE FOR DISTINGUISHED GUESTS

PERSPECTIVE SECTION OF THE HOUSE FOR DISTINGUISHED GUESTS, ST. GALL, SWITZERLAND, A.D. 820–830. RECONSTRUCTED AND DRAWN BY WALTER HORN AND ERNEST BORN.

The generous facilities for distinguished guests use a simple triangular roof frame supported on a central column and beam system. Copyright, University of California Press.

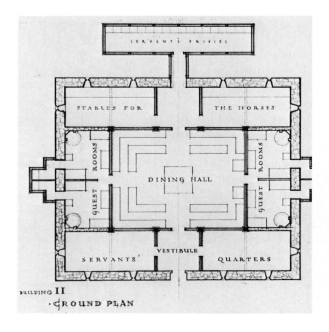

SERVANTS PRIVIES

STABLES FOR   THE HORSES

GUEST ROOMS   DINING HALL   GUEST ROOMS

SERVANTS'   VESTIBULE   QUARTERS

BUILDING II
·GROUND PLAN

PLAN OF THE HOUSE FOR DISTINGUISHED GUESTS, ST. GALL, SWITZERLAND, A.D. 820–830. RECONSTRUCTED AND DRAWN BY WALTER HORN AND ERNEST BORN.

This reconstruction demonstrates a hierarchy of spaces from public to private as well as from nobleman to servant. Copyright, University of California Press.

THE MONASTERY OF ST. GALL

After the fall of the western Roman Empire, travel in western Europe was precarious, if not dangerous. The safest and most comfortable lodging developed in the many monasteries that sprang up throughout the continent. These walled complexes were self-sufficient, allowing them to survive in isolated locations. The monastery at St. Gall, meticulously reconstructed by Walter Horn and Ernest Born in their 1979 study, *The Plan of St. Gall* (University of California Press, Berkeley), featured separate guest houses for distinguished visi-

tors and for pilgrims and paupers. The plan of each centered on a large hearth, surrounded by generous space for dining. This grand central space was framed by heavy timbers and illuminated by a lantern structure on the roof ridge and dominated by the large quadrangular stone fireplace. Peripheral to this space were sleeping quarters, stables, servants' quarters, and storage. Each guest house had an annex that contained a kitchen, bake room, and brewing facilities. In the House for Distinguished Guests, the luxury of privacy was extended by individual sleeping rooms complete with corner fireplaces and attached privies.

DIONYSOS MONASTERY, MOUNT ATHOS

Although the eastern Roman Empire lasted about one thousand years longer than the western, the needs of both monasteries were similar: security, shelter, and sustenance. Some of the best-preserved eastern monasteries are located on the peninsula of Mt. Athos in northern Greece. Although it is not known when monasticism first appeared in this area, the earliest surviving monastery, the Great Lavra, was founded in A.D. 963. Two major types of monastic orders existed on the peninsula: the *cenobites* (who lived as a community and abstained from meat) and the *idiorrhythmes* (who lived as individuals and were allowed to eat meat).

The generic architectural plan developed by these monastic groups consisted of a central church in a court defined by monks' cells, guests' quarters, refectory, and library. These perimeter elements formed a wall that provided security for the autonomous community within the complex. Each monastery had access to the sea. The monasteries were linked by overland trails. Visitors were common and welcome. Today it is still possible to visit the surviving monasteries and experience their medieval hospitality if one is male and previously approved by the Greek Orthodox Church.

The cenobite monastery of Dionysos, located on the western side of the peninsula near Mount

EXTERIOR VIEW OF THE MONASTERY OF DIONYSOS, MT. ATHOS, GREECE, A.D. 1375.

The forbidding, fortress-like monasteries of Mt. Athos had security and defense as a high priority. Dionysos seems to grow organically out of the rocky cliffs which support it. Photograph by John Kurtich.

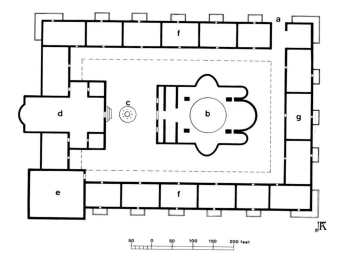

TYPICAL PLAN OF A MT. ATHOS MONASTERY.

a. entry   b. cathelicon (church) c. phiale (shelter for Holy Water) d. trapeza (refectory)   e. bell tower and library   f. monks' cells   g. archontaria (guest rooms). Drawing by John Kurtich.

Athos, was built on a steep cliff overlooking the sea in A.D. 1375. It takes a visitor about thirty minutes to climb the steep trail from the pier to the entry gate. Visitors are received by a monk who is responsible for their stay at the monastery. He leads them to their "cells," which are actually bright and airy rooms built into the peripheral wall. Each room has its own heating system, a corner ceramic stove that becomes the dominant architectural feature of the space. The spectacular views from these proto-hotel rooms more than compensate for their austerity.

Prior to taking meals, guests must participate in prayer at the monastery chapel. Then they are led to the refectory, a surprising interior space full of color and detail. The simple, symmetrical, apsidal hall is made complex by its wall paintings, depicting Greek Orthodox iconography. Because

the Dionysos monastery is cenobite, the monks and guests eat together in silence while one monk reads incessantly from the Scriptures. The long wooden tables, flanked by benches, feature a continuous perimeter cloth napkin, shared by all. When the reading stops and the Book closes, the meal ends.

PERSIAN CARAVANSERAI(S): MADIR-I-SHAH, ISFAHAN

The medieval Persian world produced spectacular structures committed to hospitality along the trade routes connecting the cities. These structures were indispensable to commercial and economic prosperity because of the hostile climate created by numerous civil wars, organized banditry, and opportunistic marauders. Located roughly one day's travel apart, caravanserais were designed to provide security, shelter, and sustenance for the caravans. The generic plan was concentric, featuring a central court surrounded by arcades containing the guest quarters and service facilities. The animals were isolated on the perimeter of the guest quarters, immediately within the external wall. This separation ensured security for the indispensable pack animals while providing a more hospitable environment for the travelers.

Security was guaranteed by massive exterior walls penetrated by one portal only, making defense controllable. These portals were often embellished and decorated with enameled tiles rivaling the entrances to the great mosques. Inside, service amenities usually included baths and kitchens. In the bigger caravanserais, luxury quarters, often located on the roof, were provided for distinguished guests. Such interiors usually consisted of fired brick, occasionally combined with stone or embellished with painted murals.

The caravanserais in urban areas were generally located near bazaars, bridges, and madrassas. The Persian madrassa was a theology school associated with a mosque. The Madrassa Madir-i-Shah, Isfahan, built between 1706 and 1714, had an attached caravanserai, which was built to produce income for the students and faculty of the madrassa. The plan of this caravanserai was typical, with a central courtyard surrounded by ar-

caded guest rooms. In the mid-twentieth century, this caravanserai became the most luxurious hospitality complex in Isfahan, the Shah Abbas Hotel. The appropriateness of the medieval caravanserai plan lent itself to conversion into a contemporary hotel. The conversion ensured the longevity and historic continuity of this unique building form.

CALIFORNIA MISSIONS: SAN JUAN BAUTISTA

The California mission system was established to bring Spanish order and religion to the native population. A string of twenty-one missions was built between 1769 and 1823, linked by the El Camino Real and spaced approximately a day's journey apart by horseback. Since the founding padres came from Mexico, the influence of Spanish architecture was predominant. The purpose of these settlements was to provide protection, education, religion, sustenance, and social order to the region.

The form of these building complexes was similar to the European monasteries, with a patio (quadrangular court) surrounded by arcaded chambers connected to the mission church, guest rooms, and other service buildings. Due to the scarcity of wood, the construction was solid and massive adobe and stone walls, ranging in thickness from three to six feet. This wall mass produced an internal thermal stability, keeping the buildings cooler in the summer and warmer in the winter. The molded quality of these adobe walls created a distinctive, sensuous aura. Decoration in special areas, such as portals, windows, and wainscoting, was achieved by the colorful and exuber-

ant use of paint. The combination of free-hand painting on these imperfect walls evoked a naive spirit, giving warmth to the spaces.

Mission San Juan Bautista (1797) was built in one of the most fertile valleys of California, making it one of the richest of missions. The picturesque composition of the gabled facade, bell tower, and arcaded porch epitomized the "mission style" in this area. The unpretentious image of security and shelter created the symbol of hospitality. The bell tower itself was used to beckon travelers and local inhabitants for spiritual and physical sustenance.

THE EUROPEAN PALACE AS A MODEL

The industrialization of the West brought about a new building type during the first half of the nineteenth century: the urban hotel, using the European palace as a model. The palace was designed to be an elegant place of hospitality, accommodating many guests. "The very formality and anonymity of the plan gave the palace a certain flexibility of accommodation, all the more because it was designed to house large numbers of servants and courtiers."[13] The word "hotel" meant in French an urban palace or public building. During the French Revolution, America's sympathy resulted in a Francophile movement, influencing manners, dress, vocabulary, and cuisine. "Hotel" was adopted to describe a new building type, a palatial hospitality center for guests to act out their latent fantasies in elite luxury.

The hotel was invented in New York. New York was expanding at this time, with a population of 30,000 when the seventy-three-room City Hotel was built (1794–1796). The City Hotel was not an inn but a structure designed to afford comfortable lodgings and the best in food and drink. The Tremont House, Boston (1829), marked the beginning of America's grand hotels. It occupied an entire city block and was considered the largest in the world with 170 rooms. It featured single and double rooms with individual, separate locks. The hotel employed gas lights throughout all public areas and provided eight water closets and

EXTERIOR VIEW OF MISSION SAN JUAN BAUTISTA, CALIFORNIA, 1797.

Constructed of thick, brick walls and surrounded by heavy arcades, the mission is naturally insulated to conserve heat in the winter and maintain coolness in the summer. Photograph by John Kurtich.

EXTERIOR VIEW OF THE MIDLAND
GRAND HOTEL AND ST. PANCRAS
STATION, LONDON, ENGLAND. SIR
GEORGE GILBERT SCOTT, W.H.
BARLOW, AND R.M. ORDISH,
1863–1876.

*The incongruity of forms between the
hotel and train station reveal the
Victorian lack of concern about the
integration of architecture and
technology. Photograph by John
Kurtich.*

English Gothic Revival, Scott created a fantasy of
medieval spires, pinnacles, towers, and pointed
arches of brick and stone. The lavish 400-room
hotel was outfitted with the latest modern conveniences of the period, such as gas chandeliers,
electric bells, rubbish chutes, and hydraulic lifts.
The architect described his hotel as "possibly too
good for its purpose." The train station it was
attached to was the engineering marvel of its day
in terms of the unsupported span of its roof shed
—230 feet—making it the largest iron structure in
the world.

Ironically, the technology developed in the
train shed was contrasted by the lack of originality
in the hotel itself. In fact, the collision of the horizontality of the shed and the verticality of the
hotel were very poorly resolved. Although the
critics of the day praised the building complex for
its harmony and style, its real lack of architectural
integration is apparent to the modern eye.

RESORT HOTELS: THE GREENBRIER, WHITE SULPHUR SPRINGS

The grand resort hotels were fully developed in
the nineteenth century. Location was everything:
a spectacular mountain view, a choice seaside setting, a unique healing spring, a shimmering lake.
These establishments catered to the rich and priv-
ileged. The resulting architecture was palatial,
designed to accommodate the demanding expec-
tations of the elite guests. Generally, the design of
these hotels reflected local traditions in a style
sympathetic with their sites. The interiors were
spacious to provide an elegant setting for the
many cotillions, galas, banquets, receptions, teas,
and other indulgent amusements.

The Greenbrier was established in White Sulphur Springs, West Virginia, in 1778 initially as a
retreat featuring the curative powers of sulphur
springs. During the nineteenth century, the
Greenbrier complex's first hotel, the Old White,
was built as a gathering place for the wealthy and
prominent. By the early twentieth century, a
larger hotel called The Greenbrier replaced the
Old White as a resort with every amenity, where
the visitor never had to leave the grounds to find
all desired outdoor sporting activities and enter-

bathing facilities in the basement. The hotel
swiftly became the pride of Boston and the center
of political and social life.

Another type of palatial hotel was developed
in England in the 1840s. This was the "terminus"
hotel, an essential attachment to the new railway
stations that were located in major cities due to
the rapid development of the railroad. One of the
most lavish and largest of these Victorian hotels
was the Midland Grand Hotel (1866–1876) at St.
Pancras Station, designed by Sir George Gilbert
Scott (1811–1878). Designing in his favorite style,

tainments. It was a sumptuous adult camp where every imaginable sporting activity was engaged in during the day, with grand parties being de rigueur in the evening.

This glamorous setting was conceived by interior designer Dorothy Draper (1889–1969), who had a complete understanding for what a wealthy audience would require from its surroundings. This knowledge resulted from being reared in a well-connected family. Capitalizing on this background, she opened her own interior design firm, Dorothy Draper and Company, in 1925. She was the first American woman decorator to concentrate on nonresidential design, specializing in hotels, restaurants, shops, and hospitals.

By the time Draper was commissioned in 1946 to redecorate The Greenbrier, she had fine-tuned her neo-Baroque style, a style emblazoned with strong and boldly scaled elements, vivid colors, and rich pattern. Overscaling decorative elements gave her work a surrealistic quality. With an $11 million budget and a great amount of design freedom, Draper used her vibrant technique to transform The Greenbrier into a world of romance.

Sympathetic to the period and style of the Greenbrier's architecture, Draper used Georgian antiques throughout the interiors. She had an innate talent for mixing old and new styles, giving her clients the comfort of the familiar while introducing fresh new ideas that gave her interiors a sense of delight. Quality of detailing was paramount in her design scheme. The public spaces exuded a serene elegance while the private guest rooms displayed Draper's sense of originality. No two rooms were alike, giving each guest a subtle message that he/she was special and would receive such care while staying at The Greenbrier. Upon entering a guest room, one might find kelly green walls, vivid cabbage rose chintz draperies and bedspreads, and whimsically painted four-poster Georgian beds in pristine white. Dorothy Draper created an elegant resort filled with panache while resonating its rich heritage. She celebrated the South's formality and elegance without reducing its serenity to a level of stuffiness often created when interiors are highly designed.

MIXED USE:
THE AUDITORIUM BUILDING, CHICAGO

The Auditorium Building, Chicago (1889) by Adler and Sullivan, pioneered the idea of mixed use development. It was comprised of a 400-room hotel, an office block of 136 units, and a 4,237 seat theater. The concept behind this massive development, the largest in the world at the time, was two-fold: (1) to create a complex that generated energy from its mixture of activities; and (2) to decrease the development risk by building three profit centers.

This optimistic program provided a stimulating challenge for one of the great creative architects of the time, Louis Sullivan. Integration of these three distinct functional elements on a tight urban site resulted in a compact ten-story granite and limestone monolith. The hotel faced Michigan Avenue and the lake beyond and was entered through a bold Roman arch. The lobby contrasted the monochromatic stone exterior with a polychromed marble mosaic floor, a Mexican onyx wainscot, and a riot of gilded plaster foliate reliefs. A dramatic stair, framed by another Roman arch, spilled into the lobby, inviting guests to ascend to the second floor reception room. Here they found a spectacular view of Lake Michigan through an open loggia that projected over the hotel entrance.

The reception room was rich with Sullivan's patterns in gold and green, claret draperies, and Wilton carpeting. Three sources of illumination

Interior view of the Victorian Writing Room, The Greenbrier, White Sulphur Springs, West Virginia. Dorothy Draper, 1946–1948.

The overscaled and heavily-framed mirror works well as a prime focus point for the fireplace wall. Photograph by Hans van Nes.

EXTERIOR VIEW OF THE AUDITORIUM BUILDING, CHICAGO, ILLINOIS. ADLER AND SULLIVAN, 1889.

The three-fold mixed-use building maintains a strong visual unity with its continuous two-story granite base and a facade of arched colonnades wrapping around four stories of its mid-section. Photograph by John Kurtich.

INTERIOR OF HOTEL LOBBY, AUDITORIUM BUILDING, CHICAGO, ILLINOIS AS THE LOBBY OF ROOSEVELT UNIVERSITY IN 1992. ADLER AND SULLIVAN, 1889.

The openness and luxuriously decorated grand staircase of the original lobby invited guests to ascend to the second floor reception room overlooking Lake Michigan. Photograph by John Kurtich.

enhanced this visual opulence: a large fireplace with its flattering flame; electric lights spraying out of ornate ceiling medallions; and natural light transformed through stained-glass windows on the north wall.

Adler and Sullivan's brilliant design for this unprecedented building type marked a turning point in the history of hospitality. The powerful sequence of spaces, from the austere exterior to the opulent interior, created an overwhelming sense of arrival. Grand spaces were formed by constructing gigantic girders that transfer the small-bay columns of the guest room floors into large bays in the public spaces. The monumental scale of these spaces is articulated and unified through Sullivan's boundless ornamentation.

INTERIOR OF HOTEL DINING ROOM,
AUDITORIUM BUILDING, CHICAGO,
ILLINOIS. ADLER AND SULLIVAN,
1889.

*The arched vault of the dining room
ceiling continued the theme of the
Roman arch as a major design element,
both for wall openings and volumetric
massing. Courtesy of The Art Institute
of Chicago.*

INTERIOR OF LIBRARY, ROOSEVELT
UNIVERSITY (HOUSED IN THE ADLER
AND SULLIVAN AUDITORIUM
BUILDING), CHICAGO, ILLINOIS, 1992.

*The dining room was transformed into
the central library for Roosevelt
University after they purchased the
Auditorium Building in 1946.
Photograph by John Kurtich.*

THE ATRIUM HOTEL:
HYATT REGENCY, ATLANTA

In 1966–1967, 1969, John Portman (1924–   ) designed and developed the large-scale atrium hotel, the Hyatt Regency, Atlanta, which became the prototype for a series of centralized convention hotels. An early predecessor for this type of hotel was the Brown Palace Hotel, Denver, 1892. The Brown Palace Hotel was centered around an eight-story skylighted court that functioned as the lobby. Each level contained open galleries surrounding and overlooking the lobby. These galleries replaced conventional hallways and provided a direct transition between lobby and guest room.

Portman magnified the idea of the galleried, centralized lobby by building an interior space of seventeen galleries and three stories of suites in the Hyatt Regency, Atlanta. This prototype established a formula that was to influence a generation of hospitality, commercial, and retail design. The formula consisted of a spectacular skylighted atrium, multistoried galleries with hanging plants, crystalline capsule elevators, gigantic suspended mobiles, aediculated coffee shops, and a "town square" scheme of shops and activities.

THE MOTEL: THE MADONNA INN,
SAN LUIS OBISPO

The motel, a contraction of "motor hotel," was an all-American invention. In the early twentieth century, the automobile became a popular means of travel, creating a demand for convenient lodgings along the highways. One of the earliest motels was built in Douglas, Arizona in 1913. In the 1920s, a chain of motels was developed in California with the prototype built in San Luis Obispo. Motels proliferated during the depression years, providing an economical alternative to the more expensive hotels.

The motel provided travelers with convenience, informality, efficiency, accessibility, and economy. The general architectural form was low and spread out. The earliest motels tended to be separate cabins with adjacent parking. As motel

INTERIOR OF LOBBY, HYATT REGENCY, ATLANTA, GEORGIA. JOHN PORTMAN, 1966–1967, 1969.

The Hyatt Regency spawned a new generation of hotels with "super-space" lobbies, which spatially connected every guest room to the central lobby. Photograph by John Kurtich.

INTERIOR VIEW OF THE "CARIN
ROOM," THE MADONNA INN, SAN
LUIS OBISPO, CALIFORNIA, 1958.

*The "Carin Room" features a king-size
bed with an over-scaled headboard,
illuminated with candelabra-carrying
"putti" (naked baby-angels) flying in
the cathedral-ceiling space. Courtesy of
the Madonna Inn.*

INTERIOR VIEW OF THE "CAVEMAN
ROOM," THE MADONNA INN, SAN
LUIS OBISPO, CALIFORNIA, 1958.

*The "Caveman Room" reproduces the
space of a primordal cave, incongruously
furnished with late-twentieth-century
hotel furniture and theatrical grotto
lighting. Courtesy of the Madonna Inn.*

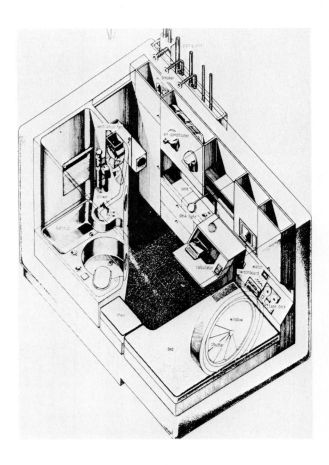

chains developed, they became architecturally anonymous and visually bland. To break this trend, some motels used visual gimmicks to attract visitors, such as disguising the cabins as Native American teepees. Eventually motels added other amenities, such as restaurants and swimming pools.

An unusual motel, the Madonna Inn, was built in San Luis Obispo, California, in 1958. It featured elaborate interiors for the guest rooms, reflective of Alpine chalet kitsch, with no two alike. The Swiss imagery was reinforced by employing Native rock extensively to create rock "rooms," rock waterfall showers, and rock fireplaces. The motel grew from twelve rooms to 109 rooms over the next twenty years, an outgrowth of its popularity and convenient location.

A fantasy world is created with an overwhelming sense of naive grandeur. The variety of outrageous public spaces encourages guests to explore the Silver Bar, the Gold Rush Dining Room, the Early American Horseshoe coffee bar, and the men's restroom with its electronically-controlled rock waterfall urinal. The guest rooms are a mastery of kitsch, featuring mixed metaphor with wild abandon. Each room has a theme with its own name, such as Old World, Just Heaven, Love Nest, and Rock Bottom. Old World is a stone cavern that frames a king-size bed in shocking reds. Stone is extensively employed in the fireplace, floors, shower, and wash basins with cascading waterfalls. The bed's huge stone headboard is sharply contrasted by golden chandeliers, illuminating cupid's gymnasium.

CAPSULE HOTELS: THE ARCHITECTURE OF KISHO KUROKAWA

In response to urban density and economics, the capsule hotel emerged in the 1970s in Japan. The

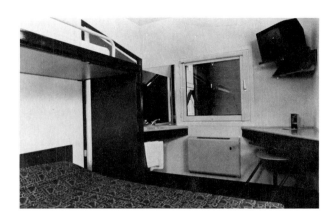

INTERIOR VIEW OF TYPICAL ROOM,
FORMULA 1 HOTEL, FRANCE, 1990–
1991.

*Each room can sleep three people in
comfort, but the space does not include a
built-in bathroom. Courtesy of
HOTEC, Hotel Formule 1.*

EXTERIOR VIEW OF FORMULE 1
HOTEL, FRANCE, 1990–1991.

*By the end of 1991, 213 hotels of
this design were built throughout
France. Courtesy of HOTEC, Hotel
Formule 1.*

building that engendered this idea was the Naka-gin Capsule Building, designed by Kisho Kuro-kawa (1934–) in 1972. The hotel form is composed of two elements: (1) an on-site structural system containing the vertical communications and mechanical services; (2) an off-site, mass-produced module containing the guest rooms. Limited services and size of prefabricated capsules were intended to compete with the more traditional hotel design. Kurokawa designed the capsule as simple as possible as an all-welded, lightweight, steel-truss box.

The Nakagin capsule was a complete living system in an eight foot by twelve foot space. The ergonomically designed space accommodated all of one's living needs, including built-in bathroom, double bed, kitchen, desk, chair, storage, electronic entertainment, and heating, ventilation, and air-conditioning (HVAC). The advantage of this compact and highly organized living module was the ease of maintenance and accessibility to all functions. The disadvantages were that such a tight space created a sense of claustrophobia and limited flexibility.

A variation of this hotel type was developed in France in the early 1990s, creating the state-of-the-art transient hostelry of the late twentieth century. Called "Formule 1," the hotel was built from prefabricated modules assembled on the site. The idea was to provide inexpensive lodgings for up to three people (in 1991, a room for three was the equivalent of $24.00). Each 90 square foot air-conditioned, soundproofed room included a double bed, single bed, sink, desk, chair, closet, and television set. One bathroom was allotted to every three rooms, the shower of which was cleaned automatically after each use. The Formule 1 hotels were built near airports and major highways, capitalizing on the volume of travel.

Summary

Style has always been a subject of great debate. History has given humanity overviews of stylistic periods complete with their rise and fall related to the culture of the times. Through careful analysis, it is found that persisting styles are the ones that clearly express the spirit of the era. Whether the era was driven by economic, social, technological, political, or religious developments, the resultant style was a direct expression of that unique period.

Historic case studies have been emphasized in this chapter to illustrate history's importance as a wellspring of ideas. Past generations have created a wealth of solutions to generic design problems. These historic layers of ideas are like a great catalog from which the designer may draw upon. It is important that these solutions be understood in relationship to the culture and technology of the time. Emulation of ideas without this historic knowledge can result in inappropriate designs, not fully steeped in today's needs.

The development of four generic building types (retail, commercial, residential, and hospitality) have been explored to demonstrate how these forms evolved from their infancy to contemporary times. By having a broader historic view, designers have a sense of their place in time. This perspective can be essential to the creation of mature and appropriate Interior Architecture.

The creation of space that supports the purpose of retailing must not only be functional but trigger the emotional response of the consumer. The primary purpose of retail marketing is to attract customers and sell them goods. The architectural interior of a store can give the merchant a competitive edge. This was a concern of the nineteenth century merchant who understood the psychology of creating dreams that motivated. Creating dreams will be just as important in the future. Architecture is a natural vehicle for starting a dream on the street by attracting potential customers. Interior Architecture is the embodiment of the dream by creating an experience that stimulates desire. The realization of the dream occurs when customers purchase their goods.

Ancient Egypt has provided one of the earliest examples of architectural space devoted to commercial transactions. The evolution of this building type involved both warehouse storage and administrative facilities. The ancient Roman port of Ostia built numerous permanent masonry warehouses, controlled by a separate complex of administrative offices known as the Square of the Corporations. Commercial space is decidedly urban, and therefore is an essential part of the fabric of cities. The Industrial Revolution brought about a rapid expansion of business facilities due to mass production of goods and their distribution. The design of commercial office space has become very sophisticated, addressing the pressures of competition, cost, and flexibility. With the phenomenal expansion of communications and computers in the business world, the concern of Interior Architecture is to create the balance between technology and humanity.

The home, necessary for survival, was humanity's first architecture. Indigenous and readily available materials dictated the character of the dwelling, providing a working palette that led to many different and regional developments in the history of architecture. Trees and branches were used in neolithic Mediterranean regions. Animal bones and skins dominated construction in northern Europe and Asia. The building material of the ancient Near East was mud. Marble and other stone were common building materials in ancient Greece, as the natural supply of wood became exhausted. The Romans invented concrete from the volcanic composition of sand that was common throughout Italy. The Japanese house evolved from the use of paper as a primary material. The Industrial Revolution made iron and glass technology widely available for the first time. The mid-twentieth century created plastic as a building material. The late twentieth century space age brought highly developed ceramics.

The designer is not only influenced by the materials available, but also the variety of human needs. The ubiquitous nuclear family is no longer the norm in this country. The nonnuclear alternatives include double-income households, unmarried heterosexual couples, single-parent families, gay and lesbian couples, single adults, handicapped adults, retired adults, and shared households, to name a few. Such social complexity requires new forms to accommodate specific needs.

Since the beginning of civilized travel, lodging providing shelter, sustenance, and security has not changed significantly. The two basic types, transient and destination hostelries, continue to be patterned functionally after residential models. It is unfortunate that the majority of hospitality design continues to rely on a manufactured residential image, which usually rings as a false comfort. Used by transients, who have a variety of tastes and accommodation needs, these spaces result in predictable and inoffensive designs. The lack of conviction in developing a specific personality brings about "safe" spaces, void of memorable identity.

Furthermore, the contemporary hospitality industry in general is uninterested in geographical variety and is focused on the economy of homogenization. Why should a hotel room in Peoria, Illinois, be indistinguishable from one in Seattle, Washington? For a business traveler, such a standardized accommodation may provide a comforting degree of familiarity, reducing the stress of traveling. On the other hand, such interiors lack the variety that makes traveling stimulating by emphasizing a sense of style and place.

The two extremes of contemporary hospitality design, the predictable chain model and the idiosyncratic one-of-a-kind accommodation, mirror the plurism of culture. All too often, designers limit their solutions to pragmatic and superficial aesthetic issues. Interior Architecture practitioners are committed to a vision beyond the immediate programmatic requirements, requiring a simultaneous juggling of pragmatic and idealistic ideas in completing work of potent identity.

Epilogue

The world today is one of specialists versus generalists, partly because of the vast increases in knowledge in the world. The desire to be efficient with the use of this knowledge has led people in many fields to concentrate on limited areas of expertise. Interior Architecture demands a holistic outlook from its practitioners. Students pursuing this field must first be made sensitive to a total design attitude. Truly functional spaces perform as a whole, not as isolated parts. Therefore the space must be developed as an integrated total. Traditional academic institutions have separated the responsibility in the name of specialization and efficiency, resulting in problematic solutions that solve only parts of the puzzle. Interior Architecture requires an educational approach somewhat different than the typical education for either the architect or the interior designer.

The architect is usually trained at one of the many accredited schools of architecture found in both private and public universities and colleges throughout the nation. Accreditation is connected to the state licensing procedures, which determines certain aspects of the curriculum. This is well and good because licensed architects are legally responsible for the public welfare and safety of their executed buildings. Most architectural curricula, however, avoid or ignore any serious attention to the design of interior space. The prevalent attitude is that architecture is the ultimate art and interior design is a secondary, less important aspect. Thus architecture students receive virtually no formal schooling in creative lighting, color theory, furniture design, fabric selection, interior materials and finishes, comprehension of interior product design, and planning of interior spaces. They generally learn to plan buildings well, but they are not taught to study and develop the use of the space within the structure. It is evident in their drawings, void of any suggestions of furniture or finishes, that they lack an awareness of Interior Architecture. Architecture is created to define interior space, yet for generations architecture students have been taught to ignore the heart of buildings. They also lack the understanding of human quality in their designs, a much different attribute than technical quality (a technically "perfect" building might very well have no bearing whatsoever on human participation or interaction). Yet, in the real world, the completion of interior spaces of newly constructed buildings and the development of interior space of recycled older buildings constitute a growing majority of commissions for practicing architects.

On the other hand, the interior designer has traditionally been trained in programs that, for a large part, are outgrowths of college home economics departments. With recent title licensing in place the curricula has expanded becoming more professional. Yet the course of study originated as home decorating classes for family-oriented women and was looked down upon by the architects as frivolous and shallow. These interior design students lack schooling in building structure, not only the basic way a building is constructed, but also building systems and how parts go together, which consequently affect how details go together. Without the understanding of detailing, they lack a powerful means of developing the unity of space; a whole language of details must be understood. Often mechanical systems and services are not taught, so the students do not know how to take advantage of them as part of the palette of manipulable materials for reinforcing their schemes, whether it is a simple HVAC register cover or a comprehensive ceiling system that coordinates with the plan. Moreover, there also is not enough emphasis on three-dimensional development of spaces. Whereas architecture students are trained to work in three dimensions with scale models, interior design students generally concentrate on the plan, elevation, and selection of materials and furniture. Although these students learn how to do perspective renderings, they usually do not use them as a tool to develop and visualize space in the design process. Architects are better trained at custom designing things out of raw materials; interior designers tend to be more dependent on selecting manufactured products out of catalogs. Teamwork experience is sometime lacking in many interior design programs; instead the individual ego is encouraged and fostered, which makes the transition from school to the professional world difficult for many. Many interior designers do not think in the context of how space should respond to existing conditions, such as views, natural light, building materials, and so forth; on the other hand, architects generally learn how to create a sense of place responding to context.

There is a tendency for interior designers to put budgetary emphasis on fine finishes and furniture rather than manipulating the space in a significant way. The interiors profession has a stigma of being concerned with the cosmetics of interior space and are looked down upon as "decorators" by the architects. But interior designers are trained to be sensitive to the tactile qualities of materials and furniture, which results in the humanizing of interior space. On the other hand, many architects are guilty of being slaves to the systemization of space, such as column spacing, dominance of grid, or detailing as an end in itself. The interior designer feels that the architect lacks the ability to create interior space centered on human quality, which triggers positive reactions to human perceptual senses. The space that the architect leaves for the designer to complete is very often poorly considered for furniture arrangement or appropriate proportions for the intended use. Clients usually do not consider such architects for the completion of the interiors because of their lack of sensitivity.

Neither the architect nor the interior designer is taught enough about real world situations such as designer-client relationships. Working with the client, communicating with the client, and understanding what it means to be a client are issues not generally addressed in the academic setting. Yet the school can be an effective place for students to learn to be professionally responsive, assertive, and sensitive to client needs. The academic setting can provide the opportunity to develop the skill of listening. Such experiences are learned (sometimes the hard way) in the real world, but the school offers a "safe" environment to practice these experiences.

Many clients are becoming more sophisticated in their desire for properly completed interior space that has meaning and significance for their functional and aesthetic needs. These clients interview prospective architects and designers much more carefully, trying to avoid both architects who cannot complete interior space and interior designers who are ignorant of architectural and structural aspects of interior space. Design cannot be taught by formula, nor should it respond primarily to any current or fashionable trend. The student should not be trained only for a particular job upon graduation, but must be trained for life, to be able to adjust to the inevitable social, political, technological, and aesthetic changes that continually occur. For that reason, the design process should be the basic method or approach for creating anything—a house, an automobile, a city, a suit of clothes, a chair, a gourmet meal.

The reintegration of art within the physical environment will play an important role in making architectural space more humane. Environmental art, or what some call "space art," are those optimistic experiences in Interior Architecture where art is at one with architecture (see Chapter 4 for the four-dimensional aspect of art infused with architecture). Fully integrated art in architecture will produce complete purposeful spaces that provide humanity with experiences related to the high tech world. The artist Marc Di Suvero reinforced this ideal of integration, saying

The artist needs to be into the architecture at a much earlier stage, at the building design stage. At that moment the relation between sculpture and architecture would become real; and the possibility of that great moment of the unity of a great building in dialogue with a great piece of sculpture could be real.[14]

The architect Stanton Eckstut recalls his experience of working with artist Mary Miss in a revealing quotation:

In many ways working with Mary reminded me of what architecture is all about, that it's an artistic endeavor. It's not just building. It's not just financial. It's not just working with context and trying to respond to a place. It's much more about emotional experience and memory.[15]

All great interior spaces have possessed this intangible and unquantifiable sense of emotion. The medium of space has been manipulated in such a way as to engage the perceiver in a memorable experience. These experiences will become more common in the future as aesthetic advances strive to keep pace with the explosion of technology.

The practitioners of Interior Architect, as the generalist and coordinator of interior space, will find it desirable to again include the artist as a natural part of the team. The desire of contemporary artists to have greater impact in interior space, as evident in the high tech, environmental, and performance arts, will make it easier for the designer to find and integrate appropriate artists. This rediscovery of art in architecture will have a profound effect on the practice and will redefine the current aesthetic limits.

The vocabulary of the third dimension is the primary method of dramatizing the spirit of space. This aspect of Interior Architecture is critical to the quality of everyday life in an increasingly complex world. The exploitation of the third dimension can create variety, relief, unity, and drama while reinforcing the purpose of space. Mediocrity in a commercially biased world has seriously undermined the importance of three-dimensional spatial development. The future will prove that exploitation of space will not only be necessary for humanity's well-being but also will be demanded commercially for economic success.

History has provided the world with a legacy of interior spaces that destroy the constraints of normalcy and transform them into experiences that ignite the senses. This is the fourth dimension, and it will become part of the common vocabulary of all who practice Interior Architecture. Although such spaces as the Pantheon or Unity Temple have consistently been studied, the essence of their fourth dimension is not entirely understood. This abstract element of Interior Architecture can only be realized by comprehending the whole, not by focusing on the parts. Interior Architecture is the holistic integration of the arts that form profound space.

Light and color are the elements that the designer uses to reinforce three- and four-dimensional space and can become the magic that reinforces humanity's well-being. Light is the essential definer of space. Color not only reinforces space, but it establishes physical and psychological atmosphere. Sensitivity to how these elements affect people in space is the raison d'être for the study of behavioral response to color and light, spatial perception, cultural awareness, aesthetic potential, and latent creative promise. Technology has produced an overwhelming array of sophisticated lighting devices from which the designer can select. Unfortunately, technology does not ensure better illumination; but hands-on understanding of lighting applied from a conceptual point of view can draw a veritable relationship with the architecture.

Interior Architecture depends on the designer's ability to relate the contents to the enclosure. Furnishings are the links that establish the intimate connection between the architecture and its human occupants. The personality or character of a space is revealed through the expressive qualities of its furniture. Its direct contact with the human body demands the designer be sensitive to the inherent sensuality of furnishings. The comfort factor of furniture is strategic in combating the everyday stress generated by the postindustrial world. Perhaps design professionals need to reexamine the value of intimate objects in interior space. These are the elements that most directly shape, organize, nurture, and reflect one's humanity. The mandate of Interior Architecture is to reveal and implement the latent complexion of society's many levels of existence. This transcends the mere functional and decorative aspects of design and allows one to realize individual freedom of expression.

The maturity to restrain the freedom of expression is vital to the success of achieving authenticity in historic preservation and restoration. Architecture representing a past era is indispensable to a society's continuity and stability. The historically sensitive practitioners who devote their careers to such preservation and restoration are unfortunately invisible in this future-oriented world. These unspoken heroes are painstakingly preserving the connection to the best the past has to offer to the future.

The key to preserving the future is rooted in a commitment to education. The fruits of this task are not immediately evident to the students or the teachers. Education is a lifelong process; it does not end with the completion of formal schooling. One of the goals of education is the development of a passion for Interior Architecture. Such love for the profession is essential to sustain the drive necessary to handle the day-to-day mundane de-

tails of the work. Another goal of education is to prepare students for their social responsibility to the public. This charge can best be examined in a secure academic environment. Finally, the students' education should weave self-discipline, creativity, resourcefulness, and vision into the fabric of their lives, providing perpetual inspiration.

Interior Architecture is inspired humanism. Space is generated by human needs and aspirations. The intimate connection between people and their shelter is a primary concern for the sensitive designer to determine. Historically, great designers have always understood and capitalized on this connection, while most practitioners have been isolated by the polarization of their respective professions. Design education should not perpetuate this unhealthy philosophy of dissociation. Architecture cannot be separated from its interiors. It is those practitioners who have risen above this split who have been recognized by society as masters of holistically designed space. The time has come for such unification to be the norm rather than the exception. The emergence of Interior Architecture establishes the link between architecture and interior design. Interior Architecture postulates an equality of interest between interiors and exteriors that advocates a new direction in design education as well as the professions. The philosophical challenge of Interior Architecture will demand qualified and motivated professionals cleansed of the dogma and -isms of the past. For the future of Interior Architecture is bright and expanding.

NOTES

1. Henry-Russell Hitchcock and Philip Johnson, *The International Style* (New York, W. W. Norton & Co., Inc., 1932), p. 20.

2. Alvin Toffler, "The Data Deluge—Artificial Intelligence," (*Omni,* Oct. 1984), p. 42.

3. Ibid.

4. The earliest glass-covered arcades seem to appear in Paris in the late eighteenth century: arcades in the Palais Royale (1786–1788) and the Passage du Caire (1798–1799).

5. Rosalind H. Williams, *Dream Worlds* (Berkeley: University of California Press, 1982), p. 67.

6. Nikolaus Pevsner, *A History of Building Types* (Princeton: Princeton University Press, 1976), p. 32.

7. Ibid, p. 221.

8. Anthony Liversidge, "Interview: John Naisbitt," (*Omni,* Oct. 1984), p. 114.

9. Ibid, pp. 164–165.

10. Donald W. Robertson, *The Mind's Eye of Richard Buckminster Fuller* (New York: St. Martin's Press, 1974), p. 33.

11. See the "artist's" rendering of the first Smart House on page 10, *Smart House* by Ralph Lee Smith, (Columbia, SC: GP Publishing, 1988). It is unfortunate that the technological advances of this structure were not expressed in the architecture.

12. Well-designed, in this case, means functional excellence, structural integrity, and aesthetic distinction—the three components of Vitruvius' definition of architecture.

13. Lewis Mumford, *The City in History* (New York: Harcourt, Brace, and World, Inc., 1961), p. 378.

14. Jeanue Parkin, *Art in Architecture* (Ontario, Canada: Visual Arts Ontario, 1982), p. 102.

15. Victoria Geibel, "The Act of Engagement," *Metropolis,* July/August 1986, p. 30.

INDEX

Numbers in bold type indicate pages on which illustrations are to be found.

Picasso, Pablo (cont.)
 Le Corbusier, architecture, relationship to,
  138–140, **139**
 "Les Demoiselles d'Avignon", 138, **138**
 "Still Life", Lichtenstein interpretation, 43, **43**
 "Wineglass", 138, **139**
Pinturicchio (1454–1513):
 cathedral floor, Siena, Italy, 266–269, **267, 268**
Plano, IL:
 Farnsworth House, 150–151, **151**
Poe, Edgar Allen (1809–1849):
 The Pit and the Pendulum, quote from, 156
Poissy-sur-Seine, France:
 Villa Savoye:
  color, 288, **289**
  cubist paintings, comparison to, 144
  description, 7–8, **8,** 143–144, **143**
  Eiffel Tower, comparison to, 144
  interpenetration of space, 7–8, 144
  light, natural, 144
  space-time, 144
Pollock, Jackson (1912–1956):
 creative process, 38
 process of painting, 38, **38**
Pompadour, Madame de (1721–1764):
 royal chateau, Versailles, use of color, 275
Pompeii, Italy:
 atrium house:
  light, natural, 183, **184**
  color, 261–262
 House of the Vettii, linear perspective, 86, **86,**
   light **184**
 markets, 419
Porter, Edwin S. (1869–1941):
 cinema, intercutting, 135
 "The Ex-Convict", 135
Portland, OR:
 Oregon State Office Building, 416, **417**
Portman, John (1924–   ):
 Hyatt Regency Hotel, Atlanta, GA, 456, **456**
Post-Industrialism:
 definition, 418
Post-Modernism:
 definition, 416
 effect on preservation, restoration, renovation,
   and adaptive re-use, 28
 les Espaces d'Abraxas, Marne-la Vallée,
   France, **417**
 Oregon State Office Building, Portland, OR,
   417
Potsdam, Germany:
 Schloss Charlottenhof, tent room, 321, **320**
Powolnay, Michael (1871–1954):
 sculpture, Palais Stoclet, Brussels, Belgium,
   327
Pozzo, Andrea (1642–1709):
 nave ceiling painting, Saint 'Ignazio, Rome,
   Italy, 270, **272**
Prairie house:
 development, Frank Lloyd Wright, 4–6, **5**
 interlocking form and space, 76–78, **77**
preservation:
 categories, 16, 357–358
 defining Interior Architecture, 4
 definition, 16, 357, 358

in situ example:
 Johnson Wax Administration Building,
   Racine, WI, 359, **359**
 Notre Dame, Paris, France, 16
Modern Movement effect, 28
museum preservation examples:
 Art Institute of Chicago, Chicago, IL:
  Chicago Stock Exchange Entrance Arch,
    366, **366**
  Chicago Stock Exchange Trading Room,
    364–365, **365**
 Metropolitan Museum of Art, New York,
   NY:
  F.W. Little living room, 363–364, **363**
 Staatliche Museum, Berlin, Germany:
  Babylon, Gate of Ishtar, 358, **358**
  Miletus, Agora, 358
  Pergamon, Altar of Zeus, 358, **358**
Post-Modernism effect, 28
research procedures, 363
Ruskin, John, theories and practice, 17
United States philosophy, 27–28
Viollet-le-Duc, theories and practice, 16–17

Q

Quickborner, Germany:
 Eberhard & Wolfgang Schnelle, 432
 Quickborner Team, 432

R

Racine, WI:
 Johnson Wax Administration Building:
  Home and Studio, Oak Park, IL, influenced
    by, 237
  light, 237, 242, **243**
  preservation, in situ, 359, **359**
Rasmussen, Steen Eiler (1898–   ):
 working class housing, Pessac, France, color,
   287–288, **288**
Ravenna, Italy:
 Mausoleum of Galla Placidia, 262–263, **262, 263**
Renaissance, Italian:
 cassone, 312, **312**
 cassapanca, 312, **312**
 culture and style, 408–410
 education, 408
 furniture, general, 312
 Gutenberg, 408
 humanitarian view, 408
 Pazzi Chapel, Florence, Italy, **410**
 space, 410
renovation:
 defining Interior Architecture, 4
 definition, 16, 359, 376
 historic examples:
  England:
   Middlesex: Osterley Park House, 21, **21**
  Italy:
   Rome:
    Capitoline Hill, 19–21, **21, 21**
    Pantheon, 18–19, **19**

Turkey:
 Ephesus: Temple of Artemis, 18, **18**
United States:
 Buffalo, NY: Guaranty Building, 376–
   378, **377**
 Chicago, IL:
  Block residence, 385–386, **386**
  Carrigan residence, 359–360, **361**
  Claridge Hotel, 381–383, 382
  Mastro and Skylar residence, 383–385,
    383, 384
  Rookery, 22–23, **22,** 399–403, **399, 400,
    401, 402**
 Washington D.C.:
  Blair House, 378–380, **379**
  Union Station, 380–381, **380**
Modern Movement effect, 28
Post-Modernism effect, 28
restoration:
 defining Interior Architecture, 4
 definition, 16, 359
 historic examples:
  United States:
   Charlottesville, VA:
    Monticello, 370–373, **371, 372**
    Rotunda, University of Virginia, 359–
      360, **360**
   Chicago, IL: Glessner House, 373–374,
     373, 374
   Harbor Springs, MI: Douglas House,
     374–376, **375**
   Oak Park, IL: Frank Lloyd Wright Home
     and Studio, 366–368, **367**
   Springfield, IL: Dana House, 368–370,
     369, 370
   Williamsburg, VA, 17–18, **17**
Modern Movement effect, 28
Post-Modernism effect, 28
retail space:
 Allen, E. C., mail-order concept, 422
 collective experience of shopping, 420–422,
   423
 electronic shopping, 423
 historic examples:
  England:
   London:
    Crystal Palace, influence, 420, **421**
    Royal Exchange Arcade, 419–420
  France:
   Paris:
    Bon Marché, 420, **421**
    Galerie Vivienne, **420**
  Italy:
   Bologna: arcaded streets, 419, **419**
   Ostia, 419
   Pompeii, 419
   Rome: Forum of Trajan, 418–419, **418**
  Netherlands:
   glazing of shops, seventeenth century,
     419
  Turkey:
   Istanbul: Grand Bazaar, 419, **419**
  United States:
   Chicago:
    Carson Pirie Scott, 423, **423**

DATE DUE